Peterson's Guide to
College Admissions

Getting into the College of Your Choice

Second Edition

by **R. Fred Zuker** and **Karen Collier Hegener**

Peterson's Guides

Peterson's Guide to College Admissions: Getting into the College of Your Choice. Book orders should be sent prepaid to: Book Order Department, Peterson's Guides, P.O. Box 978, Edison, New Jersey 08817. $8.95 plus $1.25 postage/handling charges. New Jersey residents must add 5% sales tax.

Copyright © 1976, 1977, 1980 by R. Fred Zuker and Karen Collier Hegener

All rights reserved

Printed in the United States of America

ISBN: 0-87866-122-0

Library of Congress Catalog Card Number: 80-81122

The sample SAT questions in this book are reprinted by permission of Educational Testing Service, the copyright owner. The sample ACT questions are reprinted by permission of American College Testing, the copyright owner.

Other Peterson's Guides publications of interest to readers of *Peterson's Guide to College Admissions:*

Peterson's Annual Guide to Undergraduate Study
Peterson's Annual Guides to Graduate Study (5 vols.)
National College Databank
Peterson's Travel Guide to Colleges: Northeastern States
Peterson's Travel Guide to Colleges: Middle Atlantic States
Your Own Financial Aid Factory: The Guide to Locating College Money
How to Pay for College: A Guide to Financial Planning for Applicants to Selective
   Colleges *(pamphlet)*
The Admissions Process at Selective Colleges *(pamphlet)*

Contents

Contents

Contents

Photographs

Preface

How Can This Book Help You?

For many high school students and their families, college admissions seems as mysterious as a tribal ritual and as uncertain as a roulette game. The reason, of course, is that the college application and selection process is not clearly understood. This book was written to explain the process to students and help the applicant see the point of view of admissions officers.

Because college admissions generally involves some selectivity—and inevitably some degree of personal bias—it cannot be a "certain" process. It can, however, be stripped of its mystery, for admissions counselors are, by and large, a very communicative bunch of people who, contrary to legend, are not out to trick or foil college applicants.

Be a Good Consumer

Understanding the admissions process is not a virtue in itself. But by learning how admissions offices operate, how applications are processed, what qualifications are considered important, and why decisions are made the way they are, you can carry out your end of the application process to give yourself your optimum chance of success. Your success as a candidate at the college you choose might well depend on knowing what is expected of you and being able to respond effectively to these expectations.

Be an Active Applicant

Our experience in the admissions field has convinced us that the most successful college applicants are the ones who take an active role in their own selection and application process. They are the ones who choose with thought, apply only to institutions that they feel are right for them and at which they believe they have a realistic chance of acceptance, and take care to do all that is required of them by each college.

Admissions officers try to find the best possible candidates for their colleges by traveling across the country to talk with students, encouraging graduates to recruit for their alma mater, and producing a good deal of literature. For your part, a comparable amount of energy and research activity should be spent, since you play the determining role in your own application process.

A Book of Basics

Peterson's *Guide to College Admissions* provides the tools you need to become the kind of effective college applicant we are talking about. It offers a thorough explanation of the admissions process; it suggests many helpful guidelines for approaching the selection of a college; and it gives profile information on more than 1,600 four-year U.S. institutions to help you get started in your search. We intend this to be a reference tool that you'll continue to turn to throughout the application process—there are checklists provided just for that purpose. But, more important, we hope this book will make you confident and relaxed about the admissions process.

The number and variety of institutions of higher education operating today are reflected in differing admissions philosophies, procedures, and selection criteria. Obviously, large universities recruit larger classes than small colleges, although size is not necessarily an indication of an institution's selectivity: Many large universities have much more strenuous admissions criteria than some small colleges. On the other hand, a number of state-controlled universities are obliged to accept virtually all applicants who are state residents, provided they meet minimal admissions requirements. Many community colleges, junior colleges, and technical institutes operate on still other standards and procedures.

In this book our discussion deals generally with four-year institutions—both public and private—that select their students from a pool of applicants. These institutions generally employ the kinds of admissions procedures that most need explanation and are most appropriate to illustrate the points we want to make. Much of our discussion, however, will be useful for anyone who is thinking about applying to any type of college.

A Note to Parents

Many factors have combined to produce more stress and wider options in the choice of college today. Parents can help reduce their teenagers' anxiety and at the same time contribute to a felicitous array of choices if they will bear in mind that ultimately it is their son or daughter who must make the decision and live with the final choice. This is a time for support, encouragement and wise counsel, but parents' own preferences—whether based on family history, hearsay, or personal experience—should be kept out of the picture while their youngster works out his own ideas about what will be best and possible.

A Word About Our Survey of Admissions Officers

To give our readers a cross section of admissions approaches, we have been in touch with directors of admission at four-year public and private colleges and universities around the country. Their responses to our questions required time and thought, and we are grateful to them for their help and encouragement.

About the Authors

R. Fred Zuker is Director of Admissions at Tulane University in New Orleans, Louisiana. A ten-year veteran of college admissions work, Mr. Zuker discovered the need for this book in the course of interviewing and counseling students. He holds an M.Ed. in Guidance and Counseling from Duke University and is currently pursuing part-time doctoral studies in the same field.

Karen Collier Hegener is the founding editor of Peterson's Annual Guides to Graduate and Undergraduate Study. An alumna of Bennington College and executive vice-president of Peterson's Guides in Princeton, she has been involved in education and publishing for nineteen years.

R.F.Z.
New Orleans

K.C.H.
Princeton

The Admissions Office

Your parents or teachers may remember the days when it was possible for college applicants to visit the college of their choice, speak with the director of admissions, and learn on the spot whether they would be admitted. This, of course, was well before the number of college applications sky-rocketed to the point that a well-known university can expect to have 11,000 applications for the 2,000 places in its freshman class.

Sheer volume combined with an interest in finding the best-qualified students—whether from across the nation or from a particular region—has led colleges and universities to develop larger and increasingly more sophisticated admissions staffs and selection procedures.

The complexity of the admissions office operation has also increased in response to the projected drop in the number of high school students who will be going to college in the 1980s and '90s. The decline in numbers of high school students will place great pressure on some institutions to maintain a specific level of enrollment. This may make acceptance at some colleges easier—but don't count on it!

Admissions Officers: Who Are They?

The men and women who make up the admissions staff of any institution have generally chosen this line of work because they have a strong interest in higher education and in people. Many have had teaching experience at the college or secondary level. And many are graduates of the institution for which they are recruiting. In our survey, at least one member of the admissions staff was a recent alumnus (or alumna) at 86 percent of the colleges represented.

Most admissions offices are headed by a director or dean of admissions and staffed by associate directors, assistant directors, and counselors. At smaller schools, recent graduates are often able to rise to assistant and associate positions quite rapidly, whereas larger schools with larger staffs generally reserve these positions for their more experienced people. You may deal with the director of admissions at one college and a counselor at another. Applications are given to staff members on a random basis, and your acceptance has nothing to do with the office rank of the person who interviews you.

Sometimes an admissions officer has a regional responsibility, an area of the country for which he or she is responsible. The officer with a regional assignment usually travels in that area and presents to the admissions committee all candidates who apply from the area. (This is a basic reason why it is important for you to speak with college representatives when they visit your school or city.)

Every admissions office tries to have a group of people whose combined interests will permit a good assessment of any student's qualifications in terms of the offerings and needs of the college. Thus, one staff member may be particularly knowledgeable about athletics, another about the creative arts, and still another about science, for example. Their varied abilities and opinions can go a long way toward ensuring a fair review of each applicant's credentials. Perhaps even more important, a variety of personalities can help guarantee a fair reading of each applicant's folder.

Variety Is the Spice...

Russell Shunk, former admissions director at Wilson College, Chambersburg, Pennsylvania, confesses to a certain love for the idiosyncracies of the admissions process—a feeling no doubt shared by the vast majority of his colleagues. "Somehow I think *that if 200 young women with 600 verbal and 600 math test scores and upper-tenth-of-class ranking walked into our office, unsolicited, with Wilson as their first choice (and no financial need), I wouldn't be happy."*

Faculty Involvement

Faculty members often contribute to the admissions process in several ways. At the University of Southern California, the College of Wooster, Bucknell, and many other colleges of all sizes, admissions policy committees include faculty members (and sometimes students) who suggest guidelines for the admissions office to use in selecting the incoming class. At other colleges, faculty members work as part-time or substitute admissions interviewers, serve on committees that read applications, and travel on behalf of the admissions offices to speak at high school gatherings.

Honesty Is the Best Policy

Honesty—both on your part and on the part of the admissions staff—is probably the most necessary element in your arriving at a successful and satisfactory college choice. As the applicant, you are the one who first has the "need to know." You must carefully choose the institutions to which you may eventually apply, and, to do so, you must be candid about your reasons for wanting to apply. You need basic facts about each institution, and you should have other people's impressions of how you would fare there.

But once you have evaluated your college choices and submitted your applications, the evaluating hat shifts to the admissions officers who, in turn, will weigh your credentials as a candidate in approximately the same terms: why you want to go to their college, what they know about you, and how they think you will do if they admit you.

Utopia!

Knox College Director of Admissions William McIlrath projects that in an ideal admissions system a college would honestly and fully disseminate information that each applicant would thoroughly read and digest.

Then all applicants would know exactly where to apply, how to apply, each factor needed for an acceptance, and why a college is a "right choice." Interestingly, that bit of advice boils down to the acronym WHEW.

The accuracy of this two-way evaluation is threatened if either party misrepresents itself. If you have any doubts about something you've heard or read about a college—let's say the catalog presents the student union as the center of campus life, but all you can find when you visit are a few empty vending machines—check things out with several sources to make sure you're operating on correct assumptions. You can be sure that if there is something inconsistent in *your* record—for instance, a high school transcript of C's in chemistry while you list president of the Chemistry Club as one of your most meaningful activities—the admissions office will check with your high school to straighten out the facts. Being honest in the first place saves time and trouble for both you and the colleges you apply to.

The Admissions Process on Campus

The size and philosophy of a school will usually determine the complexity of its admissions operation. Institutions with open admissions policies (where virtually all applicants with high school credentials are accepted) do very little screening at the admissions level and spend more time placing students in the proper course level after admission. Selective schools place far greater emphasis on the admissions screening process, devoting a great deal of time and energy to locating, recruiting, and evaluating candidates. In most cases, however, the basic goal of admissions officers is the same: to ensure as harmonious a match of applicant and institution as possible.

E Pluribus Unum?

When asked whether "creating a diverse class" or "selecting students who will fit your institution" held a higher priority in their admissions decision-making process, the majority of the responding admissions directors judged a suitable fit to be more important.

Committee Screening

The large number of applications received by selective institutions has necessitated the formation of admissions committees to help with decisions that were once made solely by the director of admissions. Whereas an admissions *policy* committee helps in wide-ranging ways as explained in Chapter 1, admissions *screening* committees exist specifically to read and evaluate applications for the purposes of recommending acceptance or rejection of applicants. Screening committee members consist of admissions officers, faculty members, administrators, and even occasionally students.

At such colleges as Haverford, Hobart, Skidmore, and Lake Forest, admissions committees read and vote on every complete application received. At some, like Loyola University and Union College, committees read only the folders of the middle group of applicants who are not clear-cut cases of admission or rejection.

Figuring the Numbers

Before most admissions committees meet, they have a good idea of how many applicants they will be able to accept. The admissions policy committee, the board of trustees, or another administrative body will have indicated the number of students they feel should be in the next freshman class. Admissions officers then project the larger number of students they will need to accept in order to have the correct number of freshmen on campus in the fall. This projection of the percentage of accepted students who will enroll is called the "yield rate." It is extremely important for colleges to make accurate predictions of this figure, which varies from one institution to another and depends on several factors. A college that happens to be many students' second or third choice will have a low yield rate if those students' first-choice schools accept them. Conversely, colleges that are the first choice for many or most of their applicants will have high yield rates—that is, a high number of students who are offered acceptance will enroll. The five U.S. service academies—West Point, Annapolis, and the Air Force, Coast Guard, and Merchant Marine academies—have among the highest yield rates of all colleges. Obviously, students are not likely to seek the necessary congressional nominations and undertake the extensive application procedures unless they are seriously interested in attending the academy they've applied to.

Selection Criteria

Determining the strength of one applicant in relation to the rest of the applicant pool requires a standard criterion for evaluation. Standardized test scores (SAT or ACT) provide one index, but admissions officers need additional indications of how your high school work and outside interests compare with those of other applicants.

Large universities often turn to a computer at this point, feeding in test scores and school grades for each applicant, and relying on it to predict each student's anticipated freshman grade point average. This predicted average alone does not determine a student's acceptance or rejection, but it is an important factor at such colleges in considering each application.

Other schools, such as Hamilton College, use a point system to evaluate the academic and extracurricular strengths of each student. The Hamilton admissions staff assigns a separate numerical level to the academic and extracurricular records of each candidate; the academic score is doubled and added to the extracurricular score. At Johns Hopkins, two admissions counselors or faculty members read each application and rank it on a 1 to 5 scale (with 5 at the top), after which it is reviewed by a committee.

Tulane University combines both computer and point system approaches. Each applicant is assigned a scholastic index based on the high school grade point average and SAT or ACT scores. The computer then determines what chance out of 100 the student will have of achieving at least a 2.5 grade point average during the first year at Tulane. Each application is then evaluated by individual staff members and assigned a rating of 1 to 7 for academic criteria and nonacademic criteria, after which a total evaluation is assigned. These figures are used as a starting point for discussion by the admissions committee when each applicant is reviewed. No decisions are made by the computer alone. All candidates are reviewed individually.

Most students who have total evaluations of 6 or 7 will be admitted; students below that will be looked at very carefully by the committee to determine final admissions status.

The Good Word

Keuka College in Keuka Park, New York, uses a memorable acronym in its admissions work: ADMIT. When asked by parents, prospective students, and counselors what criteria Keuka uses to evaluate an applicant, the admissions office cites:

A̲chievement (quality and consistency of secondary school grades)

D̲ependability (evidence of assuming responsibility)

M̲otivation (that special drive which overcomes past mistakes and unfavorable conditions)

I̲nterest (after investigation of Keuka by reading its literature and visiting the campus)

T̲ests (scores from the SATs and ACTs)

Keuka's admissions staff considers an applicant's grades the most important predictor of a student's success—the more recent, the more significant. Test scores, on the other hand, are measures of an applicant's potential but are ranked last in order of importance.

What the Admissions Office Expects of You

No matter what kind of admissions process is used at the colleges you are applying to, it will be your responsibility to shepherd your application through each admissions office—making sure you have submitted all required forms and test scores and reminding your guidance counselor and other recommenders to submit their statements promptly. The earlier you complete these tasks, the more it will be to your advantage.

You may send in your application forms any time they are complete. You do not have to wait for your high school record to be sent in or the results of standardized tests to arrive at the admissions office. Receipt of your application opens your file in the admissions office, and everything that arrives relative to your candidacy will be filed with your application.

Most schools will notify you when the deadline nears and a required item is missing from your application folder. Some even notify you when your application folder is complete. But if you hear nothing from a school after your full application has been in their hands for two months, you should certainly write them a note or call to inquire if anything is lacking. Only complete folders are read and evaluated by admissions officers.

How To:

1. Make a Self-Appraisal
2. Compile a Fact Sheet
3. Narrow Your College Choices
4. Work Well with Your Guidance Counselor

1. Make a Self-Appraisal. Perhaps the most important part of the initial phase of the college admissions process is making a critical appraisal of yourself. Before you can begin to know which college or university is right for you, you must have a clear picture from your grades, your interests, and your achievements, of what your strengths are.

This is the time to look at what you have done with your high school career. You can evaluate very easily whether you have done well academically in high school, if you have challenged yourself with a demanding academic program, or if you have done less well in a more modest curriculum. This will help you decide at which colleges and universities you will be able to compete from an academic viewpoint. You can also evaluate your extracurricular activities. Have they been significant enough to make you a stronger college admissions candidate? Have you worked and saved money? Been involved in local politics? Given a consistent amount of time to a service organization? These will be among the things the admissions committees will notice. Have you considered the goal of your college education? If you want to be a physician, attorney, or engineer, you may need to think about attending different types of institutions in order to reach such a goal. If you want engineering, architecture, nursing, or some other specific field, you will consider only those colleges that offer such programs. On the other hand, if you are undecided, you will want a school strong in the liberal arts to offer you as many options as possible.

2. Compile a Fact Sheet.   Before you begin to narrow your college choices, you should pause for a few minutes and compile a fact sheet about yourself. Your fact sheet should include your Social Security number, the complete address and phone number of your high school, the ETS code number of your school, and your date and place of birth. Then you should list your academic goals for college. After that, list any special features or honors of an academic nature; then add a list of extracurricular activities and honors. List them in order of their importance. List any work experiences you have had, both in the summer and during the academic year. List any special activities, hobbies, interests, summer travel, Boys or Girls State, summer camps, etc., that you have participated in. Finally, list the names of three people you could ask for references. You will find that assembling all these facts early in the process will save you enormous amounts of time later on when you are filling out application forms.

The fact sheet can be used solely for your own reference. If, in addition, it is typed in some organized fashion, it will also be handy to give to people when you ask them to write recommendations for you (see page 70).

3. Narrow Your College Choices.   Don't begin your college search in a whirlwind. Take time to sit back and carefully assess the kind of characteristics you seek in a college. Think clearly and be honest with yourself.

Think About Basics

First, consider all the most basic questions you should ask yourself about the college experience you want. Give full thought to each item, even if you're tempted to skip one or two.

Location
—Do you want to stay near your home or travel several times a year?
—Do you want the fast-paced life of a metropolitan campus or the easygoing serenity of a small college town?
—Does your constitution require nearby mountains for skiing or oceans for swimming?
—What kind of weather do you really like?

Student Body
—Is a single-sex or a coed school more to your liking?
—Are you looking for a student body drawn from across the nation or from a smaller geographic area?
—Do you want to be surrounded by thousands of classmates or only a few hundred?

Academic Requirements
—How do you realistically view yourself as a student?
—Do you have the academic record to be seriously considered by a highly competitive institution?
—Do you want an academically demanding college program, or would you prefer a school where you can make respectable grades without knocking yourself out?
—Do you expect you'll be aiming for graduate school?
—How have you fared on the PSAT, SAT or ACT?

Academic Structure

—Do you feel attracted to a larger university encompassing many schools and colleges or to a small single-purpose institution?

—Does a liberal arts or a professional curriculum seem more in line with your career interests?

—Do your interests require specialized facilities?

—Are you looking for a specific major?

—Do you need a highly structured academic framework in order to work effectively, or can you work with a curriculum that allows for independent projects or has no requirements at all?

—Do you need the incentive of grades, or would you work equally well under a pass/fail or comment grading system?

Campus Life

—Do you want to live in a dormitory or off campus?

—Do you care whether the majority of students live on campus or commute?

—Is it important to you that there be something happening on campus every minute, or would you be happiest in a more leisurely setting?

—Are you interested in fraternity or sorority life?

—Are you an inveterate joiner who is looking for a school with a wide assortment of extracurricular activities?

—Can you live with restrictions and regulations?

—Do you want an extensive athletic program?

Cost

—Is your family able to pay the generally higher tuition of a private college (or can you get a scholarship), or does a public college seem more feasible?

—If you are sure you won't qualify for scholarship assistance, would you be

willing to work part-time and/or take loans to pay for your education?
—Are you interested in co-op programs, in which the college allows you to alternate periods of employment with periods of study?

While a hundred institutions may at first seem to meet your criteria, you should limit your working choices to a manageable number—about 20 at the maximum—then decide on a final four or five. To determine initially which schools have the basic characteristics you desire, consult the college profiles that begin on page 147 of this book or one of the college guides listed on pages 38-39. At least one computer-assisted system is under development that will produce descriptions of the colleges that have the characteristics a student specifies. The book *National College Databank* (see page 38) was created using the same principles.

Try a Personal Ranking

Next try ranking your selections on two bases. First, rank them according to your initial reaction to their descriptions—your favorite at the top, then on down the line. Second, rank the same colleges on the basis of their selectivity. Identify (through test score ranges of accepted students, percent of applicants admitted, and similar data) which of your choices are (1) most selective, (2) selective, and (3) less selective. You will want to talk to your guidance counselor during this process, as we discuss below.

There are without a doubt many colleges at which you would be happy and do well. There is little point in your applying to any college you really don't want to attend or one that demands entirely different credentials than the ones you can present. Spend your time, money, and energy instead in applying carefully to the colleges that excite you and at which you have a reasonable chance of being accepted.

4. Work Well with Your Guidance Counselor. One person you can't afford to bypass in your college search is your school's guidance counselor. Whether you attend a small private school where counselors seek you out or a large metropolitan public school where counselors are only occasionally heard from, it is important for you to develop the kind of student-counselor relationship that will help you discover colleges that are suitable for you and that will enable your counselor to write a knowledgeable letter of recommendation for you.

There is no "right" time to start investigating colleges. Many counselors encourage students to send for catalogs and skim through college guides as early as their sophomore year. Certainly, if you are a junior and you still don't know where your guidance counselor's office is, it's time to get acquainted. Make an appointment and arrive prepared to talk about your past academic record, the subjects you are most interested in pursuing, your career plans (or your lack of them), your interest in further study (how many more years are you really committed to?), and the kinds of college characteristics you value most.

Sophomores and juniors should also be thinking of their remaining high school academic program. Aspiring physicians and engineers should take as much mathematics and science as possible. The admissions office will evaluate the quality of your course selection as well as your academic performance. Avoid the "senior slump" syndrome. Students who elect to take easy courses and avoid academically challenging ones do themselves a double disservice. First, the admissions office will be unimpressed with a long list of nonacademic electives; second, the preparation for a demanding college curriculum will be lacking in such courses.

Your counselor may have some immediate suggestions about careers and specific institutions you should investigate, and will also have on hand many of the reference sources you'll require to start your search. If you have never taken any vocational interest or aptitude tests, your counselor can arrange for them to be administered. The guidance office is also the place for information on the Scholastic Aptitude Test (SAT) and American College Testing (ACT) program, one of which is required for admission to most colleges.

Once your name, face, and interests are well ingrained in your counselor's head, don't stop there. Without becoming a nuisance, drop by his or her office whenever you have news to report or questions to ask. You may be surprised to find that keeping your name out front has added dividends. Admissions recruiters, after visiting a guidance counselor, will often ask to spend a moment with a few interested students. If the college seems within your interest and ability range, your counselor will think of you—if you've made yourself known around the office.

Independent or Private College Admissions Counselors
In many parts of the country, usually near large metropolitan areas, college-bound students may be able to consult with private counselors. Some of these are completely independent and some are associated with a secondary school but are willing to meet privately with students from other schools. If you are considering private counseling, you should first ask yourself if you have exhausted all the counseling assistance available at your own school. If so, and you feel there is still a need to get more information about the college admissions process, a private counselor may offer what you need. Private counselors can be located in the telephone book or be recommended by friends

who have used them in the past. Before selecting a private counselor you should check the following factors:

1. What is the educational background of the counselor?

2. What are the counseling credentials of the counselor?

3. How long has the counselor been in this field?

4. How much do the services cost, and what is included in the cost? Are you required to pay for phone calls and postage in addition to the fee that goes directly to the counselor? How many visits are allowed?

5. Does the counselor offer a testing program to help you define academic and career interests? Are courses offered to help you prepare for standardized tests? Contact other families the counselor has worked with, and find out how they felt about the services rendered.

Students should be extremely wary of any counselor who "guarantees" admission to a particular college. A counselor may have a very good idea, based on experience and knowledge of a certain college and its admissions criteria, of how a student will fare in admissions, but no one at all can make a guarantee of admission to any college.

Students who seek private counseling should also realize that private counselors cannot make a student a better college candidate. They can provide more personalized information and guidance and perhaps suggest some alternatives the student had not considered, but they cannot change the facts or the effects of your grades, test scores, and high school achievements.

Admissions Officers on the Road

Because the number of college applications outweighs the number of available freshman openings, you might wonder why colleges find it necessary to seek out applicants. There are still, to be sure, a few colleges—either because of established reputation and drawing power or lack of travel funds—that don't engage in recruiting campaigns, but they are true exceptions. In general, colleges do all they can to locate what they consider the "right" students for their program and to persuade them to apply. (Even 600-student Nathaniel Hawthorne College in Antrim, New Hampshire, visits more than 1,200 secondary schools each year.)

A Saintly Profession

For Lorna Blake, Director of Admissions at Smith College, admissions work takes on an occasionally divine perspective. "Sometimes," she notes, "when I'm talking with a ner- *vous young applicant I'm tempted to say, 'Relax, I'm not St. Peter.' As a matter of fact, as I look at my travel schedule, I feel more like St. Paul!"*

The process of attracting students would be far less complex for colleges if there were fewer institutions competing for each student's attention. But with more than twenty-five hundred two-year and four-year colleges and universities in the United States, each institution must attempt to stand out in the crowd.

The Recruiting Circuit

Probably the most effective way for a school to make itself known to students is through personal contact. The autumn months are traditionally the time when admissions officers take to the road to make calls at secondary schools in their specified recruiting areas. (A good number of admissions officers don't like the connotations of "recruiting," but the word is now used by almost everyone.) When possible, guidance counselors set aside a half hour or more for admissions representatives to speak with interested students about their institutions. If time prohibits such a session, the admissions representative talks about his or her institution to the guidance counselor, headmaster, or principal and leaves college literature behind in the hope that it will be passed on to interested students.

Naturally it is impossible for admissions staffers to visit all secondary schools in their recruiting area, and for this reason "college nights" and "college fairs" are a particular help. College nights are evenings set aside by high schools or groups of high schools as college information sessions for upperclassmen. Representatives from a wide selection of colleges—often as many as 100—are provided with a room or meeting area, and students and their parents have the opportunity to meet with as many admissions representatives as time allows.

College fairs are similar but larger events that may run for several days. Usually held in public auditoriums, hotels, or shopping centers, the fairs provide college representatives with booths from which they can distribute catalogs and other literature, show films or slide shows, and chat informally with students. The National Association of College Admissions Counselors annually sponsors seventeen such fairs across the country. Others are organized by regional school boards, fraternal organizations, and similar groups interested in higher education.

Many colleges are now inviting students and parents to what they call "admissions forums" or "information sessions." These sessions are usually held in hotel or club meeting rooms and can include presentations by admissions staffers, faculty members, current students, and alumni. Many sessions will feature slide or film presentations. If you are known to a particular college because you have written to them or are on a student mailing list, you will probably receive an invitation to attend its session. These forums are good opportunities for you and your parents to learn the answers to many of your basic questions about a specific institution.

In a version of the information session, many colleges and universities send consortia or federation representatives out to a metropolitan area to talk about all the colleges in their group at one session. Students can learn about a number of colleges at one visit this way.

Although it might seem to be a waste of time to go to a meeting that will describe any colleges you think you won't be interested in, many students have been surprised to find that they learned a great deal at such sessions, both about themselves and about colleges they had never considered.

Alumni Volunteers

Another valuable recruiting arm of any college—although not usually on the institutional payroll—is its alumni group. Schools like Amherst, Vassar, Princeton, and Smith regularly work with alumni volunteers in each recruiting area to personalize their admissions approach. Many schools supply alumni representatives with the names of applicants from their area and encourage them to meet with these students. Others ask alumni representatives to visit guidance counselors or to represent their alma mater at college nights.

Admissions Officers Are Human Too.

Let all students who approach their admissions experience (in general) and their interview (in particular) with fear and trembling review the following anecdote. Never again will these students quake before the sternest admissions officer. Indeed, we may expect to find a secret smile in their hearts!

It is Friday afternoon. You are an admissions officer with a week of exceptionally successful school visits behind you.

You have stayed with dear friends who are also alumni of your college, and this aura of friendship blends with your professional success. You are packing your bag and preparing to leave for the last school visit of the day. From there you will leave for the airport.

Downstairs, the housekeeper, who speaks no English, is vacuuming. The three-year-old daughter hums to her dolls, and you intelligently decide on a visit to the W.C. before leaving.

Ah-ha! The daughter, seeking and questing (no doubt, a future Knox student), insists on joining you. Politely you demur, reinforcing the denial by turning the lock on the inside of the door.

When you are ready to exit, you turn the lock handle. There is a metallic snap, only slightly louder than the clanging of the gates of hell, and your eyes confirm the message sent by your fingertips. The lock handle twirls freely, and nothing else happens!

How does one describe the deafening jetlike roar of the vacuum cleaner, the futility of call for aid, the palpable shrinking of the walls and ceiling, the minute size of the one window in the room?

Consider, gentle applicant, the sight of the admissions officer squeezing like a pretzel through that tiny second-floor window. Envision him hanging, appalled, from the edge of the roof. Picture him shinnying down a tall, white column, leaving a neat row of black hand prints down each side. Imagine him reappearing in the house to claim his luggage.

Suffice it to say that no resourceful admissions officer will miss an appointment.

—William S. McIlrath
Director of Admissions
Knox College

HOW TO:

1. Maintain Your Objectivity with College Recruiters
2. Get the Most out of College Nights and Fairs
3. Use Alumni in Your Area for Prime Information

1. Maintain Your Objectivity with College Recruiters. Admissions recruiters realize the profound influence a college experience will have on a student's future and are sensitive to the importance of encouraging only those students who they think will be happy at—and stay four years at—their institution. However, they also naturally present a viewpoint that is biased in favor of the college they represent. Furthermore, they make an impression on you personally that you must try to distinguish from the impact of the information you are learning about the college itself. A recruiter's looks, facility with words, or amiability have no bearing on the quality of the curriculum his or her college offers, the tenor of campus life, or—most important—the way you would get along at that college.

2. Get the Most out of College Nights and Fairs.

College Nights

The usual format for high school college nights divides the evening into half-hour time blocks. Activities may get under way with a general assembly addressed by your principal or guidance counselor. You're then on your own to go to the rooms assigned to the recruiters from the colleges that interest you. Every half hour or so, a bell rings and you move on to another college's room. In the course of the evening you will probably meet with five or six college representatives.

As in most aspects of college admissions, advance planning can be a huge asset when approaching college nights and fairs. Rather than waiting until you arrive to select the recruiters you'll visit, make your choices ahead of time. Ask your guidance counselor a few days in advance of a college night for a list of the colleges that will be represented. Consult your counselor's collection of college guides for brief factual descriptions of each institution, match your interests with their offerings, and narrow your list of colleges down to a workable number for the evening, considering especially those colleges that you might not be able to afford to visit later on. Do some basic research on your top choices by reading their catalogs in your counselor's office or school library. Doing your homework in this way should enable you to question the representative about meaningful topics that otherwise would never have occurred to you, and at the very least should prevent you from wasting your time on some colleges that are definitely not for you.

You can double or triple the amount of information gathered at these college nights by asking your parents to help. They will no doubt be interested in joining you, and college representatives will welcome them. But rather than having all of you move from one recruiter to another, you might ask your mother to talk to people from certain colleges and your father to see representatives from other colleges, while you visit still others that interest you. If there are one or two colleges that you already consider to be strong possibilities for yourself, you may want your parents to meet the admissions people from these colleges with you, but the rest of the evening would be well spent with each member visiting different representatives.

College Fairs

You can probably also benefit from bringing your parents to college fairs. At these, there is no structured time limit on your sessions with each college representative, so you can move freely from booth to booth as your interest warrants. Even if you are able to visit each booth yourself, you may gain some important information by having your parents make the rounds independently. Representatives often stress certain aspects of their college to parents (traditions, career guidance, distinguished faculty) and other aspects to students (opportunities for independent study, active social life, access to major cities), and you may be able to draw a more complete picture of an institution by pooling your family's impressions.

3. Use Alumni in Your Area for Prime Information.   Your interest in a particular college may have been generated by someone who went there. Friends,

neighbors, relatives, and business associates of your parents will probably all be glad to discuss their colleges as you begin your search. You might also seek out people you know in professions that interest you and ask whether they recommend their alma maters for a good preparation in their field.

Many college catalogs and viewbooks list the names, addresses, and phone numbers of their area alumni representatives and encourage applicants to call or write to them for information. These representatives also often conduct interviews for the admissions office when applicants are unable to visit a campus because of distance.

Spreading the Word

Dartmouth College's Hanover, New Hampshire, location qualifies it for "far off the beaten track" status, but with a corps of enthusiastic alumni spread across the nation, no one is about to call the college inaccessible for information purposes. Alumni admissions representatives annually meet with 90 percent of all Dartmouth applicants in their home communities. Many students follow their alumni visit with a trip to Hanover, but for others, the alumni visit is enough to persuade them to enroll.

Alumni—especially recent graduates—are valuable firsthand sources of information about a college. They have experienced the campus atmosphere, taken the courses, and worked with the faculty at their college and are free to share their impressions with you. If they don't volunteer specific information you want, ask your questions directly: What is it like to live in a huge dorm? How manageable is the work load that everyone is expected to carry? Is it true that the men (or the women) always get the top student positions? Use these grads to learn of personal reactions rather than the factual material that is already available in the college catalog. Of course, you will have to take into consideration how long these people have been away from their campuses and weigh the information they give you accordingly.

Colleges in Print

Because few if any colleges can guarantee that an admissions representative will personally meet with every potential applicant, they have come to rely heavily on the printed word. Until recently, the catalog served as a college's basic information piece. Full of facts, figures, rules, and course listings—and originally intended for enrolled students only—catalogs present the administration's official and legal viewpoints.

Viewbooks and Brochures

In recent years, colleges have turned to producing informal "viewbooks" or "prospectuses," as they are sometimes called—often written by students— to interest applicants. Largely pictorial, viewbooks usually outline the academic offerings of a college but devote most of their space to campus atmosphere, student activities and concerns, faculty/student rapport, the location of the institution, and careers its graduates have chosen. Readers should remember that a viewbook is probably an institution's most subjective portrait of itself and is not intended to be used as a sole reference source.

Colleges with liberal publication budgets are able to supplement their basic viewbook and catalog with additional literature on specific items, such as departmental offerings, dual-degree programs, foreign study plans, consortium arrangements, financial aid, and minority group activities. These can be very helpful if you have specific interests, which you should be sure to specify when you first write for information.

College Mailing Lists

The easiest way for you to learn about a college is to write and ask for appropriate literature. For their part, colleges want to ensure that their recruiting literature receives a wide and strategically selected reading audience. Many admissions offices distribute their publications to high school students by using selected mailing lists.

For example, when you register to take the standardized admissions tests administered by the College Entrance Examination Board, you will be asked if you want your name made available to colleges and scholarship agencies in their Student Search mailings. If you check "yes," you will probably receive literature from colleges interested in attracting students like you to their campuses. Students taking the American College Testing Program's Student Assessment will similarly receive college literature if they participate in ACT's Educational Opportunity Service.

Admissions officers specify to these organizations the characteristics they seek in prospective students and then purchase the names and addresses of students who have registered for participation and meet the stated qual-

ifications. These qualifications are broad and the process is strictly computerized, but you may be helped by receiving information about colleges you hadn't considered before. (Incidentally, those lists are not made available for noneducational use.)

Such college mailings can provide some pleasant discoveries, but the literature can just as often be from colleges that are completely off target for you. Furthermore, you must keep in mind that colleges are looking for students just as actively as you are looking for a college. If you are particularly attracted to a college because of something you read in a mailing piece, be sure that in your follow-up research you look closely at whatever intrigues you and acquire a complete picture of the institution.

College Reference Guides

Colleges are described with varying amounts of detail in a number of college guides. Available in bookstores, public and high school libraries, and guidance counselors' offices, such books offer summary descriptions and basic information about most colleges and universities. Because they contain most of the facts you want to know for your initial research, reputable college guides are handy references for comparing institutions. Among the best known are:

Peterson's Annual Guide to Undergraduate Study (in the U.S. and Canada).
National College Databank. Both revised annually.
> Order from: Peterson's Guides Inc., P.O. Box 978, Edison, New Jersey 08817

The College Handbook. Revised annually.
> Order from: College Board Publication Orders, Box 2815, Princeton, New Jersey 08541

A Comparative Guide to American Colleges. Revised every two years.
> Order from: Harper & Row, 10 East 53d Street, New York, New York 10022

Barron's Profiles of American Colleges. Revised every 1½ years.
> Order from: Barron's Educational Series, Inc., 113 Crossways Park Drive, Woodbury, New York 11797

Lovejoy's College Guide. Revised periodically.
> Order from: Simon & Schuster, 1230 Avenue of the Americas, New York, New York 10020

HOW TO:

1. Gather the Information You Really Need
2. Read a College Catalog
3. Chart Your Options

1. Gather the Information You Really Need. Once you have determined which colleges you are seriously interested in, as well as which ones are within your academic ability range, it's time to gather further background information from these institutions. Your guidance counselor, school library, or public library should have an up-to-date collection of catalogs and viewbooks for you to begin your in-depth research. If you want your own copy of one or more of these publications to pore over late at night at home, you should write directly to the admissions office at each college you are considering.

> ## The Number in New Jersey
>
> *Drew University's admissions office believes in keeping all lines of communication open to their prospective students. Since they installed toll-free telephone lines to handle admissions questions from students in the New England and Mid-Atlantic region in the fall of 1973, over twice as many phone inquiries have been handled annually. The school also encourages admissions-related collect calls from students outside the toll-free area.*

Requests for catalogs and application forms are routinely handled by admissions office secretaries, and there is no need to labor over composing an eloquent letter. A postcard is easiest for both of you. Simply state the publications you would like to receive and give your name, address, and the date you would expect to enroll. If you want information on a specific program or department, be sure to indicate this. Such information may not exist in printed form, but in that case you might receive a personal letter in answer to your request. If you will need financial aid to attend college, ask for a financial aid application, unless you have read that all requests for aid applications should be directed to the financial aid office. Be sure to be alert to all such specific instructions throughout your application process, for your attention to instructions and details will be looked on with favor.

Including your Social Security number on your card or letter will help the admissions office put your name quickly into their system. If you do not have a Social Security number, you should contact your local Social Security office and apply for one. Most colleges and universities use it as the student identification number.

2. Read a College Catalog. A catalog is a legal document that sets forth the offerings of an institution. Most catalogs aim for comprehensiveness rather than literary style and consequently can be tedious reading. But the information contained in them is valuable, and you should take the time to read the catalog of every college you are considering.

Academic Stance. First, read the introductory material that gives you an overview of the college. What degrees are offered at all levels of the institution? What professional schools does it encompass? What academic role does it seem to give itself: traditional, progressive, deeply scholarly, career-oriented? Learn what the viewpoint is, and keep it in mind as you read each section of the catalog.

Calendar System. It may just look like a list of dates—but they are dates that could become very meaningful to you if you were to enroll at that school. Does the school operate on a semester, trimester, quarter, or modular schedule? If you want to accelerate your program, is year-round study possible? If you will need to earn money, are there substantial vacation periods between terms?

Statement of Purpose. Most colleges feel obliged to present their catalog readers with a formal proclamation of being. Almost all fail to say anything distinctive in this section, but the exceptions are worth seeking out. When a school does summarize its operating philosophy well, see if the ideas are in line with the kind of educational experience you seek.

History. The thought of a decade-by-decade synopsis of a 150-year-old institution may sound deadly, but many college histories are rather colorful. Also, by reading this section you may uncover details that influence the college's current attitudes and goals.

Physical Plant. Many colleges use their catalogs to name all the buildings on their campus. It's a section worth a quick skim to give yourself an idea of the size of the college and an indication of its activities. Check to see how many facilities are devoted to your areas of interest. If the catalog doesn't say that the college has a gym, it's safe to assume there isn't one. Often exclusions can be more important than the facilities mentioned, so look for gaping holes in any area that is important to you.

Housing. Between building descriptions and housing regulations you should be able to piece together a fairly accurate picture of the campus living situation. Do the majority of students live in large dormitories or small houses? Are there suites (several bedrooms grouped around a central living room), or are most accommodations traditional doubles (two students sharing one room)? Do members of all four classes live in each dorm, or is there housing specifically for freshmen? Is there coed housing? If not, what are the visiting hours in the dorms? Are underclassmen and upperclassmen able to live off campus? Are room and board available as separate packages if you prefer to live on campus and cook your own meals, or to live in town but eat on campus? In this era of financial squeeze, is housing available for four years? How is it allocated? Is there a lottery system? Priority by class? Is off-campus housing available if you cannot live on campus, and is public transportation adequate if you must live some distance from school?

Student Activities. One of the quickest ways to decipher the flavor of student life at a particular college is by studying the formal student activities offered. Usually such activities are student-initiated, so they serve as a barometer of the interests prevalent on campus. Are the featured activities and clubs relatively traditional (yearbook, newspaper, band, homecoming), exotic or issue-oriented (flying, mountain climbing, political lobbying, consumer research), or artistic (poetry, dance troupe, chamber ensemble)? Does the selection seem to indicate that there are people like you on campus? Do descriptions of athletic events outweigh the descriptions of other extracurricular activities? How many levels and what types of athletic competition are offered—club, intramural, intercollegiate? Are religious organizations active on campus?

Rules and Regulations. Some schools reserve printing the specific rules and regulations of college life for a student handbook distributed to students after they are admitted. Others include this section in their catalog. Again, it's not a section to spend hours pondering, but even the simplest statement could have a significant bearing on your happiness at that institution. Regulations about dress, curfews, cars, smoking, etc., can seem unimportant now, but try to imagine honestly if you would be uncomfortable with any particular restriction later.

Course Descriptions. This should be the meatiest section of the catalog. Course descriptions give several clues to the academic excellence of an institution. Do the contents of the courses sound substantive? Are the unusual courses simply faddish, or would they really contribute to your education? Note how many courses would actually be open to you in your particular four years by checking for footnotes that indicate "Offered every other year" or "Not offered this year." Turn to the academic department that most interests you. Do the same few professors seem to teach most of the classes even though there are several other faculty members listed for the department? How many offerings appear to be large lecture courses? How many seminars are there for majors and nonmajors? Is there logic to the progression and assortment of courses offered? Do students receive credit for independent research projects? How many departmental requirements are there? Finally, is it clear what degrees are actually awarded?

Academic Requirements. Some colleges will send prospective students a prospectus or bulletin which is not the official "catalog." The official catalog will be so designated and will include a very important section on academic regulations and continuation requirements. In this era of evaluation of requirements it is important for students to know what they must do to graduate. Many colleges, most notably Harvard and Stanford, are reviving, or have already revived, what is often called a core curriculum. There is an indication that many colleges will require more foreign language and "basic skills" courses in the curriculum. Other colleges will continue with a system that utilizes "distribution requirements," which means that students must take a certain number of courses from subjects grouped into humanities (art, music, languages, philosophy, religious studies, English, etc.), social sciences (history, political science, sociology, anthropology, education, psychology, etc.), or science and mathematics (biology, chemistry, physics, earth sciences, mathematics, etc.). Most colleges have an English composition requirement of some sort, and many are expected to upgrade that requirement to include some measure of writing competence. Other colleges, of course, will continue to offer students a largely elective program. Be sure you know what will be asked of you.

Faculty. The academic credentials of faculty members are traditionally material for a catalog listing. While the caliber of a curriculum can hardly be said to rest on the number of degrees the faculty members hold or the institutions that awarded their degrees, these are valid indicators of an institution's ability to attract qualified teachers and scholars. (A notable exception is in the creative arts, where real talent is more important than schooling.) What appears to be the average age of the faculty? Have most joined the staff recently, or have they taught there for some time? How many have earned advanced degrees? (You should realize that earned doctorates are prevalent in research-oriented universities and are much less meaningful at four-year colleges that concentrate on teaching.)

Student Roster. When space and budget permit, many colleges list the names, home addresses, and class year of all students; some list only the graduating class. These are handy references for determining which geographic areas are most heavily represented in the student body. If there are current students who live in your area, you can make a point of contacting them when they are home on vacation.

Admissions and Financial Aid. Probably the most well-thumbed area in any catalog is the admissions and financial aid section. Here is where a college gives the details about the high school background it seeks in its applicants. The supporting documents that must accompany the admissions application and the deadlines for each step of the admissions process are given. Fee information generally includes the cost of attending the institution as well as the methods and schedule of payment. Some colleges require full payment once a year, others at the beginning of each term, others once a month; still others have deferred payment programs.

You will also usually find a statement concerning the percentage of students who receive financial aid and the college's commitment to meeting each student's need. The procedure for applying for aid will be outlined, and you should note this together with the admission application deadline on the Applications Flowchart on page 65. Many colleges also list the named scholarships they offer with a brief description of the requirements for each. Skim the awards available to freshmen to see if you qualify for any. Often the stipulations may sound farfetched—a lineal descendant of John Alden, an engineer's daughter studying for the ministry, a native of Peoria—but if you are lucky enough to meet the requirements for any named grants, be sure to point this out on your financial aid application.

3. **Chart Your Options.** You're bound to reach a point in your research on colleges when the facts and figures seem to blur and it becomes difficult to distinguish one college from the next. For this reason it's often wise to take notes as you read—and, for maximum utility, these notes should be organized so that you can easily compare the offerings of one institution with those of another. The College Comparison Worksheet that follows will help you outline and later weigh whatever college facts and figures are important to you.

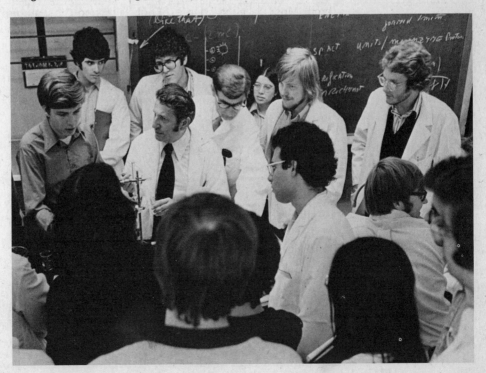

College Comparison Worksheet	College A	College B
Admissions		
Items to be submitted with application		
Percent of applicants accepted		
Tests required		
Average test scores of applicants		
Average high school GPA or class rank of applicants		
Special admissions plans—rolling, early decision, advanced placement		
Academic Life		
Academic or career orientation		
Majors of interest		
Special programs—study abroad, fieldwork, unusual degree programs		
Individual or dual majors		
Grading systems		
Academic calendar		
Student-faculty ratio		
Faculty advising programs		
Percent of faculty holding Ph.D.'s		
Graduate schools/programs (relevant to your area of interest)		
Student Body		
Total enrollment		
Undergraduate enrollment		
Freshman enrollment		
Area most students come from		
Male-female ratio		

College C	College D	College E	College F

(continued on pages 46-47)

College Comparison Worksheet (continued)	College A	College B
Student Body (continued)		
Percent of commuters vs. campus residents		
Percent of matriculants who graduate		
Percent who go on to graduate study		
Campus Life		
Distance from your home		
Nearest major city		
College setting		
Facilities of interest to you		
Athletics		
Extracurricular groups		
On/off campus housing; board plans available		
Regulations worth noting		
Costs/Financial Aid		
Application fee		
Enrollment deposit		
Tuition		
Room and board		
Traveling costs		
Off-campus living, dorms, etc.		
Forms required for aid		
Typical aid package		
Sample on-campus jobs		
Work-study programs available		
College's estimated total budget		
Percent of students receiving aid		

College C	College D	College E	College F

Your Campus Visit and Interview

Because admissions officers are charged with finding students who will enjoy and benefit from their institution sufficiently to stay for four years, it is only logical that most of them encourage applicants to visit their campus early in the application process. Neither photographs nor the most vivid description an alumnus or admissions representative can give will fully capture a college's spirit and life-style for you. These qualities need to be experienced to be understood.

A Slice of Campus Life

A campus visit—the longer the better—will give you the most accurate indication of your suitability for an institution and its suitability for you. If you have been raised in the city, you may be intrigued by the idea of an idyllic rural campus. However, a visit may reveal that the life-style is too low-keyed for you after eighteen years of urban bustle. Or the reputation of a history department may make a certain university your first choice until a campus visit shows you that the department's formal lecture approach is not to your liking. Campus visits provide a basic way to prevent mismatching—which benefits a college every bit as much as it does a student.

The Fine Art of Browsing

Sizing up a college during a campus interview requires an alertness to numerous details ranging from architecture to student attire. Most visitors cut a quick path through the college bookstore, but Gary Knight, former Director of Admissions at Colorado Women's College, suggests that this is a place worthy of a longer stop. It's his opinion that studying not only the general contents of the bookstore, but particularly the used-book section—noting which books and which chapters are the most dog-eared—is one of the most accurate ways of deciphering the true campus temper.

Many colleges offer overnight accommodations to potential applicants who would like to visit their campus. If you know someone at a particular campus, you may prefer to make independent plans to stay with your friend. Otherwise, by all means work through the admissions office.

Campus Visits

Try to arrange your visits at least two weeks in advance. Inform the admissions office of your travel plans as soon as they are finalized. If you want to stay on campus, give the office as much lead time as you can. Also, special requests, such as interviews with coaches or professors in specific disciplines, should be made in advance. Most offices will have some means of arranging for you to sit in on classes.

In planning your visits, request a campus map if one has not been sent, and find out where there is a convenient place to stay if you are not staying on campus. If you are driving and plan to park on campus, request a parking permit to be sent to you in the mail. This will allow you to avoid ticketing and possible towing on campuses where parking is limited.

Don't Skip a Personal Meeting

Try to arrange for an interview with an admissions officer when you visit a campus. Personal interviews are one of the best ways for you to find out about a college—if you take advantage of the opportunity. The key is in the fact that these are indeed "personal" meetings—one interviewer, talking with you and you alone, and you should not hesitate to discuss anything that interests you about the college.

If you have already submitted an application to a college before you have your interview, the interviewer may be familiar with your background. If you have not yet applied, you may be asked to complete a brief biographical card before the interview. You, for your part, should have read all the college's literature that was available to you and, if possible, have spent some time on campus before your interview. In this way, both you and your interviewer will be informed enough about each other not to waste time on superficial matters.

The Bon Mot

There are ways of stating even the worst of news in a positive light—a proposition proven by an interviewee at Eisenhower College in Seneca Falls, New York. When the student was asked whether he ranked in the top one half of his high school class, his reply was a candid, "No sir, I am one of those who make the top half possible."

At some large universities, you may encounter a phenomenon known as group information sessions. Instead of granting personal interviews, these colleges schedule group question-and-answer gatherings. You and perhaps 5 to 12 other applicants will meet with an admissions interviewer. Obviously, because of the size of the group, the interviewer can't be expected to remember specifics about you for your file. The time is offered simply, as the name implies, for applicants to gather information.

Besides the many institutions that no longer give interviews, there are many colleges that "strongly recommend" but no longer "require" them. For your own benefit, however, if time and finances don't present serious problems to you, it would be wise to ask for interviews at every institution you are considering. Think of interviews and campus visits as important fact-finding missions and not as experiences to be feared or avoided.

The Colleges' Point of View

Admissions officers at colleges that do grant interviews vary greatly in the significance they attach to them. Some colleges hold them only for the applicants' sake and do not even record facts or impressions brought out during the talk. Others such as Wagner and Beloit, which do not require interviews, nevertheless rely heavily in the final evaluation on the interviewer's impressions of a candidate who has been interviewed—especially if some extra factor is needed to swing the balance in a difficult decision. Completing the spectrum are colleges like Bennington and Wells, which still require interviews and treat them as one of the most important items in the applications procedure.

Usually interviews can only help your case—not hurt it. First, they are information exchanges, not inquisitions. Admissions interviewers do not maintain a handy bag of tricks guaranteed to fluster even the calmest applicant. While many admissions staffers tend to develop a distinct style of interviewing and to have favorite questions, most of them are flexible enough to follow the general direction of the conversation—and that direction should be set by *you*. Furthermore, interviewers are looking for positive factors. It is their job to perceive your strengths.

After an interview you may feel that you have ruined your chances for admission because you didn't have enough to say about your science fair project or because you knocked a pile of papers off your interviewer's desk. But fears about such matters are needless, for nervousness is expected. In all probability—unless you totally lacked enthusiasm or interest in the school—your interviewer will record only positive comments. And when decisions are made, if you fall in the group of "maybe" applicants, your interview is likely to be reviewed only if it strengthens your case for admission.

Peer Judgment

Some colleges feel strongly that another student's impression of an applicant is helpful in judging his or her future well-being on their campus. For this reason Bennington, for instance, requires an applicant to talk to a student as well as an admissions officer. Other colleges receive similar student input by encouraging their student guides (those that conduct campus tours for the admissions office) to add their comments to an applicant's file.

How To:

1. Plan a Good Campus Visit
2. Approach an Interview with Confidence
3. Dress for an Interview

1. Plan a Good Campus Visit. There is no best time to visit a campus, but there *are* some notable worst times. Vacation periods, exam periods, and "big" weekends all give a very unnatural perspective to life on campus. Check ahead before you schedule your visit to avoid these occasions. Most high school students begin college visits in the spring of their junior year and continue them through the fall of their senior year.

As you tentatively map out your visits, keep in mind that you'll gain interviewing confidence as well as a keener eye for observing a campus with each successive interview. Therefore, for your sake, arrange to visit your first-choice college last if possible, so that you will be a bit "seasoned."

If you want to spend a night in a campus dormitory, request this of the admissions office when you arrange for your interview. If they can accommodate visitors, they will probably assign you to the care of a student who will show you the campus, escort you to meals, and generally keep you entertained. Staying on campus rather than in a motel allows you to meet students in natural situations and get a fuller view of campus life, so make the most of your time there by keeping your eyes and ears open and asking all the questions that come to mind.

If you have a strong interest in a particular academic department, mention this when you first write or call the admissions office to arrange your interview. It may then be possible for you to meet with a faculty member in that department and sit in on a class or two. If the admissions office can't make these arrangements for you, introduce yourself to a student and ask to join him or her for a class.

If you have interests in certain activities—athletics, drama, publications, student government—ask to speak with people who can answer your questions about the availability of such opportunities at the colleges you visit.

Whether spending the night or only an hour on campus, you should be alert for any signs of interesting happenings. Bulletin boards, message boards, and posters on trees all give an indication of typical campus activities.

Because campus visits will be most productive if you do a good deal of independent scouting, it is probably best if your parents do not accompany you on overnight visits or sit in on interviews. Admissions officers usually can't provide accommodations for families and are not concerned about questioning them: They need to focus their attention on *you*. However, if your college visits are part of a special family trip or vacation, just be sure to make some time available at each campus to go off and talk to students on your own. Chances are great that they'll be more candid with you alone than they would be in the presence of your parents.

2. Approach an Interview with Confidence. If thinking of an admissions interview as an information exchange—a casual question-and-answer period—is not enough to banish all the preinterview butterflies from your stomach, perhaps knowing what will happen during the interview will give you extra confidence.

While admissions counselors all have their own approach to interviewing, there are some questions that you are almost sure to encounter in all your interviews. This sample should get you thinking about what your honest responses would be at the colleges you are now considering.

—Why are you interested in our college?
—What do you expect to gain from a college education?
—How have you prepared yourself for college?
—What academic areas are you most interested in?
—What are your most important extracurricular activities and why?
—How would you describe yourself to someone who didn't know you?
—How have you spent your summers and free time during the school year?

Some of these questions may appear rather simple, but effective and interesting answers are less common than you may think. The first question is a good example. Every admissions officer likes to hear favorable words about his or her college, and you should certainly have good and specific reasons for your interest in applying. Therefore, be sure you mention enough of these pluses—the curriculum, the new science building, the urban location—to support your interests. But don't go overboard: Don't say you're impressed with the performing arts facilities if you clearly have no past, present, or future interest in the performing arts. Most important, be honest with your interviewer about your current college choices. If you have just become interested in this college and are at the exploratory stage, say so. It is not fair to the interviewer or yourself if you claim a college is your first choice when it holds no such place in your mind.

Throughout the interview, try to keep a perspective on the significance of various questions. If you are asked how many brothers and sisters you have, undoubtedly the interviewer is looking for a simple numerical answer, not a treatise on family life. The opposite is true for a deliberately open-ended question such as "How have you liked your high school courses so far?" Here a simple "Fine, thanks" will be rather unimpressive and can waste a perfect opportunity for you to turn the conversation toward your special areas of

interest or expertise. Similarly, claiming a deep interest in Latin American politics may make your interviewer sit up and take notice, but if you can't carry through with an intelligent discussion of the subject, your distinction is lost and your credibility is damaged.

Unless the interviewer takes an unusual tack, you will probably be given several opportunities during the conversation to take the initiative and shift roles, i.e., to become the interviewer. Many admissions interviewers prefer the conversation to turn this way so that they can see what really interests a prospective student.

Before each interview, jot down specific questions you would like answered, and, if you find them fading fast from your mind, refer to your notes during the interview. It is perfectly all right for the interviewer to see that you have real concerns and that you thought about them ahead of time. On the other hand, don't ask questions just for the sake of asking them. The interviewer is no doubt more familiar with the college catalog than you are and knows very well if your questions are completely answered there. If you ask, for instance, when the college was founded, it only shows that you either came to the interview unprepared or have no substantive areas of inquiry about the institution.

3. **Dress for an Interview.** College students today dress in a wide variety of styles. Therefore, the type of clothes you choose for your interview will probably be all right as long as you avoid extremes of fashion. The current style is a conservative one, with a return to the tailored look of suits, sport coats, and dresses. If you are comfortable both with how you feel physically and with the appropriateness of your clothes, then you have probably made the right selection. The admissions officer will not judge you by the cut of your suit, but it will help you if you feel confident and relaxed about the way you look.

Natural Style

Goddard College in Plainfield, Vermont, has something of a reputation for informality, and this theme is reflected in its admissions philosophy.

Its advice to applicants is to relax and avoid trying to make a big impression.

A Small Tale

This is Wendy. What is Wendy doing? She is filling out a college application form. Why is Wendy doing that? She wants to go to college. She likes the college whose application form she is filling out. She hopes that it will like her. Good luck, Wendy.

"Now let me see," says Wendy. "What is the first question? Oh, that is easy." But she can't remember her Social Security number. Where can she find it? Oh, it is on her driver's license. Where is her driver's license? It is in her wallet. Where is her wallet? It is in her purse. Where is her purse? God knows.

See Wendy look. Look, Wendy, look. Oh, there it is. My, you are dusty, Wendy. You had better wash up, or Mother will be unhappy. "No," says Wendy, "I will finish this thing first." All right, Wendy, do not get excited.

"Oh dear," says Wendy, "there is no room for the CEEB code except on the next line. Is that all right? Will the college still like me? Oh dear, oh dear, I hope I am not doing a bad thing. Mother! Mother!" But Mother is not sure either. Instead, she asks Wendy why she is so dusty. See Wendy look at the form again. Why is she holding her head in her hand? Maybe her head hurts. Poor Wendy.

See Wendy decide which teachers to have write things about her. That is not an easy thing to do. She likes her teachers, but do they like her? You know how teachers are. See Wendy sweat. Sweat, Wendy, sweat.

Now Wendy must remember everything she has ever done in high school. Why is she frowning? If she does not put down enough interesting things, the college will not like her. It will say, "This is a dull uninteresting person. We do not want that kind of person here." See

Wendy scowl and gnash her teeth. Scowl, scowl, scowl. Gnash, gnash, gnash. Wendy is a little dramatic, isn't she?

Why is Wendy smiling now? She is almost done, that's why. All she has to do is write a little one-page essay. She can even pick the topic herself. See Wendy think about a topic. Four days later, what is Wendy doing? She is still thinking. Maybe the range of topics was a little too wide.

"What can I write about?" Wendy asks her family. "You could write about how exciting it will be to go to college," suggests Father. "That is a wonderful idea," says Wendy. "I will say how bored I am in high school and how different and interesting college will be." "No, no, no, Wendy," says Mother. "You must not say that you are bored. Intelligent people are never bored, and the college will think that you are not intelligent. That will never do. Why don't you write about your Christmas diet?" "Oh, Mother," says Wendy, "diets are not interesting. I will write about the gerbil. He makes messes all over and smells and is ugly." "He is cuter than you," says Big Brother. See Wendy kick Big Brother. "Now, children," says Mother.

What is Wendy doing now? She is wringing her hands. "I still cannot think of a topic," says Wendy. Wring, wring, wring. See Wendy tear her hair. "I am going bats," says Wendy. Tear, tear, tear.

Now what is happening? Three nice men have come. They are wearing white coats. Wendy is going on a long trip to a place where she will never have to fill out a college application form again. Nice going, Wendy.

— Submitted with an application
to Lawrence University

Application Forms and Essays

Admissions applications are as varied as the institutions that devise them. Highly selective institutions usually have applications that number several pages in length and require sizable essay responses. Some public colleges, on the other hand, use one-page computer-keyed applications that require little more than your name, place and date of birth, high school, graduation date, and course of proposed study. These are the two extremes, and between them fall an incredible array of application formats. Whatever kinds of applications you encounter, approach each one with care and consideration. Remember that every question has some point; if you don't understand it, ask your guidance counselor.

A Reflection of You

Of all the materials required in the admissions process, the application offers you the best opportunity to advance your case. Even the most routine sort of application form can be turned into a forceful, interesting profile of you if you are willing to make the effort.

Admissions officers are able to detect many facets of you from an application, but it is wise to remember that prime among them is illiteracy. While no one expects prose of Pulitzer Prize caliber, admissions counselors are far from impressed by poor syntax, ignorance of basic grammar rules, and colloquialisms that have no place in formal writing. They also quickly note the spelling errors and other mistakes that indicate a hastily completed application. Even the most outstanding academic or extracurricular record can be tarnished by a poorly written or carelessly handled application.

Basic Information on Most Forms

Applications usually involve three types of responses: (1) biographical facts, (2) brief lists or mini-essays, and (3) a lengthy, detailed piece of writing. As previously noted, public and less selective institutions may not include the last item.

Do You Pay Taxes?

Because of their mandate to provide a college education to their own state residents, public institutions must verify an applicant's resident status through questions on their admissions applications. Don't be surprised, therefore, if you encounter questions like these found on the University of Arizona's application: "Does your father or mother own a car?" "When did your father and mother last vote?" "Where?"

First the Facts

Biographical facts—name, address, parents' names and occupations, number of brothers and sisters, Social Security number, schools attended, health record, etc.—are useful to the admissions office simply for identification purposes. Questions that require lists or paragraphs in response, however, begin to give a fuller picture of you as an individual. Academic interests, extracurricular activities, and part-time employment information all say something about how you have invested your time. Leadership roles, of course, are of particular interest. Sheer volume, however, is not. A list of twenty high school activities tells an admissions officer nothing more than that you have showed up at enough organizational meetings to get your name on the membership roster of each one. They would much rather see a briefer version of your activities—one that accurately reflects your key interests and the ones to which you devote the most time and energy.

Make sure your facts are correct. Check your numbers, names, and dates. Include a mailing address if you need to, in addition to your permanent address. If any of your information is incorrect, it may slow or halt the processing of your application.

Mini-essays: When Less Is More

Brief essay questions asked by selective institutions require a more creative response. Some current examples include:

—What is the most difficult experience you have ever had, and how did you cope with it? (Antioch)
—What high school courses have you liked most? What academic accomplishments have been most rewarding to you? (Haverford)

While questions such as these may seem to merit longer answers than the inch or so of space provided for you on the form, remember that the application designers would have allotted more space if they had wanted a lengthier response. Instead, they are testing your ability to organize your thoughts and present them concisely. Don't start out on a note of seeming incompetence by writing at great length when you have not been asked to do so.

Take Your Choice.

Smith College believes that adding variety to its application will make essay writing all the more enjoyable for applicants and make essay reading all the more enjoyable for the admissions staff. So they offer a choice of essay topics: (1) In a recent speech at Smith College, alumna Anne Morrow Lindbergh spoke on a theme of Montaigne, "The Journey, Not the Arrival, Matters." How would you respond to this idea? (2) If you were the governor of your state, what priorities would you set in formulating your budget? (3) Present a summary of your address to the American Academy of Arts and Sciences on a moral issue raised by technological change.

The Major Creative Essay

The longer personal essay required by many selective colleges probably gives you the most leeway—both in length and subject matter—to express yourself in your application. Originally used by admissions offices primarily as a measure of writing ability, the personal essay has come to be valued also as an indicator of personality, interests, and general outlook on life. Therefore you'll probably encounter fewer and fewer applications that ask you to discuss the "three people you admire most" or "your five favorite books" and an increasing number that pose questions like:

—You are shipwrecked and alone on a desert island. Serendipity enables you to select the companionship of a work of art or intellect (a book, painting, piece of music, film, et cetera). What do you choose? (Bennington)
—Write a letter of recommendation for yourself, detailing your personal attributes and weaknesses. (Notre Dame)
—Tell us about yourself—specifically, what challenges, interests, or concerns you. (Wells)
—Explain how you relate USC to your educational and occupational goals. (University of Southern California)
—Describe in detail some special interest, experience, or achievement or anything else you would like us to know about you. Essays on a personal, local, or national issue that is of particular concern to you are also welcome. (Common Application form)

These substantial questions are obviously not meant to be answered casually in fifteen or twenty minutes. Indeed, they were intended to be

difficult—not only so that admissions officers can weed out the lazy from the serious but also to help them gain a fairly definitive idea of how an applicant thinks.

A Way with Words

Bucknell Admissions Director Richard Skelton recalls that the most memorable student application essay he has encountered closed along the following lines: "If my application is being read by a bunch of old fogeys, sitting around an oak table, puffing on their pipes, feigning intellectual pomposity, who cannot see the intended humor of the remarks I have made on this application, I have much pity for your University. You will undoubtedly elect not to offer me admission and will penalize my candidacy because of the fun I have poked at you on this application. On the other hand, if the committee reviewing my credentials have been able to interpret my exceptional talent for humorous writing and can respond in some way to that writing, I will be most happy to consider attending your University!" The student was sent a two-word telegram the next day: "You're in."

Support Your Application Without Hesitation

You will find that some colleges encourage you to submit additional materials in support of your application—exceptional term papers, handcrafted items, anything that illustrates a special interest or ability. While such materials take additional time for evaluation (and hence are requested mainly by highly selective colleges), they often unveil truly unusual talents that may be completely buried in the ordinary application process.

If you are given the option of presenting additional material of your own choosing, consider seriously what item will strengthen your application. Weaving, pottery, home-baked goods, and cassettes of musical performances have been submitted to various admissions offices. But imagination has no bounds. Williams College once received silk-screened T-shirts; Colgate, a budding architect's blueprint for the city of tomorrow; Union, a burglar alarm; Hobart, original cartoons; and Duke, cassettes containing impersonations of Groucho Marx and W. C. Fields. And the Smith admissions staff still cherishes the memory of the applicant who asked her interviewer to step out to the parking lot to view the huge sculpture she had toted to campus in a van.

If you wish to send additional material to update your application file, do not hesitate to do so. If you have been named to an academic honors group or have won some other kind of distinction, the admissions office should be informed right away. If you hesitate to send new information, you may miss the chance to tip an admissions decision in your favor.

Two poems submitted as part of an application to Lawrence University.

BROKEN
The
law
of
fantasy
has
been
defied
Jack
who
was
not
supposed
to
died.

THE SMILE
When I'm very lonely,
I close my eyes
envisioning your smile,
like imagining the sun
in the early morning darkness.
The gold-orange warmth
that always surrounds you
pervades, fills, eases.
The light of your smile
illuminates the darkest corners.

Group Application Forms

The thought of completing applications to a dozen, six, or even three colleges may appear awesome to you, but in some cases there are shortcuts available. Several states, for instance, have a standard application which all of the state's public institutions use. Thus, when you have completed one application, you can simply make duplicate copies for any other of the state's colleges to which you plan to apply.

The Common Application

A great many colleges now accept the Common Application. This form has the advantage of allowing a student to write one essay and compile one set of recommendations that can be duplicated and sent to a number of colleges and universities. If you do not have a separate application form from a particular college, you should check with your counselor whether that college subscribes to the Common Application program. If so, you can use the single form, which will be available from your counselor.

Many applicants feel their chances will be less if they use the Common Application. This is not true; they will receive the same consideration. Conversely, some college admissions officers feel the Common Application encourages students to apply to colleges in which they are not really interested. If you intend to use the Common Application, you should treat it as seriously as you would an individual application, and you should judge all colleges by the same standards regardless of whether they use the Common Application or not.

Preliminary Applications

A few of the more selective schools have adopted a system of preliminary applications which are then followed by the full application once the preliminary form has been submitted with the application processing fee. This system allows students to begin the application process earlier but requires careful attention to deadlines for the final forms. In some cases, students are required to have their secondary school report, recommendations, and test scores submitted in one envelope along with the full application. Pay close attention to the deadlines, and follow the instructions carefully to avoid delays in processing this type of application.

Application Fees and Waivers

Most application fees are anywhere from $10 to $30—a major investment if multiplied by a large number of applications. While application fees are intended to discourage less-than-serious applicants (besides covering the administrative costs of processing your application), they should not force you to restrict your applications if you are honestly interested in applying to a wide selection of colleges. Most institutions will waive their application fee in cases where low parental income makes it impossible to manage even the most minimal amount. If you feel you would qualify for such a waiver, ask your guidance counselor to write a note of explanation and attach it to your application.

How To:

1. Approach Each Application Individually
2. Make an Applications Flowchart

1. Approach Each Application Individually. It is tempting to tackle the completion of college applications with an assembly-line mentality, first completing all the biographical sections on each, then the lists and short essays, and finally—after a sufficient breather for gathering strength—the personal essay on each form. Much as this piecemeal approach may appear to be timesaving, ultimately it detracts from your application. Each college should have a well-rounded picture of you, and it is easiest to achieve this if you approach your applications one at a time and follow these guidelines.

Organize. Keep all materials for each college in a separate place or folder. Thus if you need to refer to a catalog or viewbook while completing an application, you can do so quickly.

Start early. Don't wait until the last minute to complete and mail your applications. If you know in the fall of your senior year which institutions you are interested in attending, complete your applications and mail them without delay (whether or not you are interested in an early decision). You are likely to do your best, especially on the essays, if you write when you are not under pressure—and you certainly gain peace of mind by applying early. Also, if any of the colleges you apply to operate on a rolling admissions plan (where applications are evaluated as they are received and decisions are made continuously until the class is full), your chances for admission are actually increased.

Review each application thoroughly before beginning. Once you are familiar with the information requested, answer all list and essay questions on scrap paper. Review them for consistency in presentation. For example, if you begin an activities list by naming the club, the office you held, and the years you participated, use this order of facts throughout your answer—don't switch the order and emphasis in midstream. Look also for incomplete answers and ambiguities. You may know perfectly well that the "Newtowners" you belong to are a volunteer emergency rescue squad, but, to an admissions counselor unfamiliar with your town, the term could refer to anything from a cheerleading team to a cub reporters' group. In fact, unidentified proper names are among the most common problems on applications. (Is "The Log" a yearbook, sailing magazine, or poetry booklet?) Question each proper name you use in your application, and see if it needs further explanation for someone who does not know your school or town.

Seek an objective opinion. If, after reading through your essay responses, you aren't satisfied that you have stated your case adequately, ask a parent, an older brother or sister, or your English teacher to review your answers and offer suggestions. The final product should by all means be your own work, but it is certainly acceptable to ask for advice along the way.

Aim for neatness. It is good if you can type the final version of your application, simply to make it easy to read. However, don't go to such extremes as having a professional typist handle your application for you. Admissions committees are not looking for error-free copy at the expense of seeing your own efforts. Some schools require essays to be handwritten. If you apply to such a school, be sure your handwriting is legible, neat, and well spaced for easy reading.

Save copies of all pieces. Before mailing an application, make a duplicate copy of all portions of it. If you do not have access to a copying machine, at least save the final drafts of your responses. This way, if your application is lost in the mail—and it *can* happen—you'll be ready to complete another with minimal panic. Also, you might want to refer to your application responses before an interview in case you feel a need to amplify or explain anything you wrote.

Mail immediately. Once an application is completed and copied, rush it (with the correct fee enclosed) to a mailbox. Don't let finished applications lie on your desk to be chewed by the family dog or buried under old term papers and magazines.

2. **Make an Applications Flowchart.** If you apply to several colleges, keeping track of where you stand in the admissions process at each one can be a mind-boggling chore. To help yourself, set up an Applications Flowchart like the one on the next page, and record all significant dates in your dealings with each institution. Even though most colleges will notify applicants who have items missing from their file, meeting deadlines and submitting the proper forms to the right offices are ultimately your responsibilities.

Applications Flowchart	**College A**	**College B**	**College C**	**College D**

Official Deadlines

	College A	College B	College C	College D
Application deadline				
Financial aid application deadline				
FAF or FFS application deadline				
Candidate notification date				

Personal Timetable

	College A	College B	College C	College D
Application completed and mailed				
High School record form and counselor recommendation form delivered to Guidance Counselor Forms mailed				
First recommendation form delivered to _____ (name) Form mailed				
Second recommendation form delivered to _____ (name) Form mailed				
SAT/CEEB Achievement/ACT scores requested to be sent to college				
FAF or FFS completed and mailed				
Institutional financial aid form completed and mailed				
Interview appointment	Date _____ Time _____	Date _____ Time _____	Date _____ Time _____	Date _____ Time _____

Recommendations

Gathering and evaluating several viewpoints on a subject is a tried and true method of reaching a decision. What one person fails to mention, another person may emphasize. Different perspectives help create an accurate analysis. This is why many selective colleges still rely on personal recommendations to round out an applicant's formal application. They feel they can determine a good deal about an applicant by learning how others—teachers, employers, and also occasionally peers—view the individual and his or her ability to handle college work.

Colleges' Varying Attitudes

The weight placed on recommendations has decreased slightly because of the Family Educational Rights and Privacy Act, commonly known as the Buckley Amendment, which gives students access to their admissions files once they have been accepted and have enrolled at an institution. Knowing that their recommendations may be read by the students they are writing about, many recommenders now hesitate to be as candid as they might once have been. As one observer said, "The Buckley Amendment has turned most recommendations into Hallmark greeting cards. Now everyone cares enough to send only the very best."

Colleges have countered this problem in several ways. Some, like Colgate and Rollins, are careful to explain to recommenders that students can see their files only if and when they enroll—never during the application process. Many further assure recommenders that once the admissions office has acted upon an application, the recommendations will be returned to the writers or even disposed of.

Some colleges accept recommendations but consider them (and did so before the Buckley Amendment) fairly weak admissions tools. In their view, many recommenders have failed to be balanced, presenting only positive comments. This is a natural tendency, of course, because (a) applicants select recommenders whom they expect to speak well of them and (b) most recommenders are courteous enough to tell applicants in advance if they would find it difficult to write a good recommendation for them, realizing that faint praise is damning.

Except for its College of Performing Arts, Butler University has completely eliminated recommendations from its admissions process. Butler's staff agrees that there is frequently too much of an incongruity between recommendations and an applicant's academic record and test data. When a college begins receiving recommendations from an applicant's mother, minister, congressman, mayor, and local bank president—long before the academic credentials arrive—it can be assumed that the academic record will be weak. A good record does not require recommendations to bolster it; it speaks loudly and clearly for itself. Be sure your recommendations clearly supplement your record rather than try to substitute for it.

The Seldom Heard Discouraging Word

While glowing recommendations are everyday fare in most admissions offices and may or may not be treated importantly, the occasional deadly ones are noticed. An opening refrain like "Given sufficient tutoring and a program of minimal difficulty, this student may survive" is guaranteed to knock a student out of the running.

Characteristics That Are Evaluated

Most recommendation forms provided by colleges allow recommenders to respond in an informal essay style, often to specific questions. Others are more structured and ask recommenders to evaluate specific traits on a scale. If a college sends you recommendation forms to distribute, take a moment to read the traits mentioned. If, for example, you see that most of the questions deal with academic abilities, it would be wise to direct the form to a faculty member. However, if the questions lean more heavily toward personality traits that you feel couldn't be judged by someone who has known you only in a classroom context, send the recommendation to a family friend, counselor, or employer who has known you on a more personal basis.

Some colleges send recommendation forms directly to the recommenders you list on your application form. In this case, you'll have no idea of what questions are being asked, and it is therefore wise to select a group of recommenders who have known you in different capacities and can offer a wide range of comments.

A recent look at a wide variety of forms reveals that recommenders—guidance counselors in particular—are most often asked to comment on the following abilities or qualities:

(1) participation in discussion
(2) pursuit of independent study
(3) critical questioning attitude
(4) personal responsibility
(5) involvement in classroom activities
(6) evenness of performance
(7) depth of understanding
(8) consideration for others
(9) motivation for college work
(10) maturity
(11) promise as a scholar
(12) promise as a productive person
(13) leadership abilities
(14) humor
(15) energy
(16) reaction to setbacks
(17) self-confidence
(18) relation of ability to achievement
(19) written/oral expression
(20) originality and imagination

Checking the Facts

Whenever there is a discrepancy in an applicant's record, or when the admissions committee would like more information about a student than what is provided in existing recommendations, colleges like Duke often call the high school guidance counselor for further comment. Over a period of years, counselors can develop a "credibility record" with college admissions offices, and, if you are fortunate enough to have a counselor who has a close working relationship with the colleges you are interested in, his or her verbal recommendation can be one of the most significant factors in your acceptance or rejection.

How To:

1. Choose the Right People to Recommend You
2. Brief Your Recommenders

1. Choose the Right People to Recommend You. Colleges that specify the people they wish to receive recommendations from—perhaps an employer, a teacher, and a peer—obviously simplify your job considerably. When the selection is in your hands, however, it requires more effort and thought.

Keep in mind that your selection should represent a balance of your interests. Even if you plan to major in mathematics, three recommendations from math teachers would give admissions officers a one-dimensional picture of you. A group consisting of, for instance, your coach, a math teacher, and a guidance counselor would present a more balanced picture.

It is probably best to choose a different group of people to complete the forms for each institution. Busy people have been known to write one statement about a prospective student and send a copy to each institution—even though each college may not have asked for quite the same information. Spreading out your choice of recommenders increases your chances of getting original—and meaningful—statements.

When you set out to ask people to write your recommendations, you will probably head first to your favorite teachers. It is worth stopping to consider, however, whether your favorite teacher will necessarily be the one who can offer the strongest recommendation for you and whether the same teacher is everybody else's favorite, too, and will be swamped with recommendation requests.

Even the most conscientious teacher eventually succumbs to the pressure of having to write too many recommendations in a short space of time, and the recommendations can begin to develop a sameness. Applying early can help you avoid being part of the recommendation crunch. But also be ready to go elsewhere if the backlog of requests looks too large.

A cautionary note should be sounded about trying to dazzle an admissions committee with recommendations from politicians and other prominent people. If you are lucky enough to know such people *very* well and can be sure that their recommendations will discuss you personally, by all means contact them. However, if they do not really know you as an individual, don't even approach them. Admissions committees are impressed by content, not by names.

Similarly, admissions committees do not make their decisions according to the weight of an admissions folder. If a college requests three recommendations, they do not mean four, five, or six. Your attributes can be covered just as well by three well-chosen people as by six. As in most phases of the admissions process, succinctness and compliance with directions are virtues.

2. Brief Your Recommenders.   Once you have decided which people are the best recommenders for each college, give some thought about how you will approach them. Consider in advance what points in your academic record, your life-style, and your personality you would like each person to emphasize. A past employer might write about your industry, conscientiousness, and quickness to learn; a friend might speak of your amiability, your thoughtfulness, your interests; a teacher might describe your classroom abilities and your promise as a college student. Also let recommenders know why you are attracted to the different institutions on your list so that their comments can be tailored as much as possible to each college. Give your recommenders a copy of your fact sheet. It will help them remember key facts when they write your recommendation.

Make sure you have added your name, address, and any other required information to your recommendation forms before you distribute them. When you approach each person who has agreed to write you a recommendation, mention the deadlines he or she needs to know. If your recommenders don't contact you within a few weeks to let you know that they have mailed their recommendations, check back with them. Each time you learn that a form has been mailed, record the date on your applications flowchart.

Meaningful Words

Dear Sirs:

Those very high verbal scores on the SAT and AT probably reflect Susy's voracious reading. Readers score well on College-Board-type verbal tests, no getting around that fact, and—as a harried headmaster whose job it is to place his seniors in college—I wish I could pass that habit to all the giggly little ninth-grade girls who tumble in the door each fall. But it is so much easier to turn on the "boob tube." E. F. W. Alexanderson, you have much to answer for! (He invented the home TV set, as I just learned from consulting an encyclopedia!)

 Voracious readers, as it happens, are often "loners" and homebodies (reading being a solitary activity and home being a comfortable place to do it), and, of course, the chicken-first-or-egg question arises. I read Susy as a shy, basically introverted person who probably finds herself elbowed out of the center of things by more aggressive peers. Rather than festering, Susy went the healthy route, cultivating her good mind through reading, learning to sew, helping around the house—a familiar pattern. In school Susy's activities have been the "group kind"—Glee Club, Library Club, French Club—again, a familiar pattern.

 Also marking Susy off from your run-of-the-mill "college preppie" type of girl (ours is an old, traditional, college-preparatory school for girls) are her family and background. She has been raised by her elderly father and considerably older sister. They are "working class" people who have sacrificed—really have—to provide Susy with this sort of education. Susy's sister, whom I mistook for her mother the first time that I met her, I believe functions as a mother in most respects. They live in a blue-collar neighborhood nearby.

 Now, then, to my thesis! (You must have wondered whether I had one or whether I suffer from verbal diarrhea, a disease of English teachers.) Dropping into the relatively sophisticated, affluent environment of [this school] must have meant a wrenching adjustment for Susy. But she took it completely in her stride, settled in, achieved, and made a real place for herself in the school and the class. There is, then, a strain of mental toughness in Susy that will serve her well wherever she goes. I must say that I admire what she has accomplished here.

 In writing this summary, I have worked on the assumption that the reader needs little help in interpreting a transcript. Susy has a commendable record in difficult subjects. On the chance, however, that I may be addressing a "statistics-prone" school, may I point out that class rank in a completely college bound class of under fifty girls is virtually meaningless. If I had the courage of [another school], I would also refuse to rank, but when it comes to possibly jeopardizing a girl's college chances, I am a rank coward (pun intentional). At any rate, if Susy had received a "C+" rather than a "C" in Chemistry, she would have moved up a quintile. That's how stupid the process can be.

 I am delighted to recommend Susy for college.

—Recommendation from a headmaster

Standardized Tests

The variety of academic programs and standards in secondary schools throughout the nation makes comparisons of students' high school achievements extremely difficult. An A earned at a less-than-rigorous high school may be equivalent to a B or even a C at another.

Colleges that draw applicants from particular schools year after year can make fairly accurate assessments of these schools' caliber—and thus the meaning of their grades. But for most admissions offices, another means of placing student achievement in a national perspective is considered necessary, and that means is usually standardized tests.

The nationwide tests generally used are the Scholastic Aptitude Test (SAT) of the College Board Admissions Testing Program administered through Educational Testing Service of Princeton, New Jersey, and the ACT Student Assessment administered by the American College Testing Program of Iowa City, Iowa. Each test is given at least five times a year at numerous testing sites across the country (and abroad). Many students—particularly those interested in applying under early decision plans—take the tests in the spring of their junior year of high school, while others take them in the fall, winter, and even spring of their senior year. As you pursue your college selection, be sure to note when and which tests are required or recommended by each institution that interests you.

Testing probably reached its peak in importance in the mid-1960s, when many admissions committees simply established cutoff scores for entrance into their institution: Students scoring below the stated figure were not even considered for admission. Today, admissions officers recognize that such arbitrary decisions have many drawbacks, especially for candidates who do not test well. Consequently, your test scores will be one, but by no means the only, factor considered in your application.

Recently a public controversy has been stirred by Ralph Nader's claim that the SAT does not accurately predict success in college and constitutes a barrier to many students' opportunity for higher education. While the answer to this question remains to be found, students can be reassured that test scores alone don't make or break their admissions chances. A survey by the College Board has shown that only 1.8 percent of the selective colleges consider the SAT the most important factor in admissions decisions.

Preliminary Scholastic Aptitude Test (PSAT)

No doubt you will have encountered several standardized tests before you reach your upperclass years in high school. One test specifically administered to give high school sophomores and juniors an idea of how they will probably score on their college entrance exams (and hence a better idea of the kind of college they should begin to consider) is the Preliminary Scholastic Aptitude Test.

PSAT Contents

There are two sections to the PSAT—one verbal, one math—and you receive a separate score for each.

Can We Break the Test Habit?

As long ago as January, 1970, Bowdoin College in Brunswick, Maine, became the first selective college in the nation to announce it would no longer require applicants to submit SAT and achievement test scores as criteria for admission. In spite of this, 72 percent of the 3,250 applicants for the Class of 1983 submitted SAT scores!

The verbal section contains four types of questions: antonyms, sentence completions, analogies, and reading comprehension. These are the same categories found on the SAT verbal section. For a look at typical questions, see the SAT samples in this chapter (page 78). A strong working vocabulary and a good comprehension of grammar rules are essential to scoring well on this section.

The mathematical section similarly tests you on your ability to reason and use given information rather than on your recall of specific facts. Basic formulas are provided, and you are required to apply graphic, spatial, numerical, symbolic, and logical techniques to familiar material, and, conversely, to study new situations and solve problems through original thinking. Samples of the type of questions found in the mathematical section are found on page 80.

PSAT Scoring

PSAT scores range from 20 to 80, and your score can be considered high or low only in comparison with the scores of other groups of students who have taken the test—i.e., all those in your class, all those in your state, all those in the nation. The tests are devised so that a score earned one year is comparable to one earned in another year.

While not a precise measuring device, the PSAT does have a valid correlation to the score range you can expect to achieve on your SAT: A PSAT score of 50 would equal a 500 SAT score; a 64 PSAT, a 640 SAT. (The PSAT, produced by the same testing group that provides the SAT, cannot be numerically correlated to a predicted score on the ACT.)

PSAT as National Merit Qualifier

The PSAT is also used as the qualifying exam for the National Merit Scholarship Program. Students who score sufficiently high win letters of commendation or achieve semifinalist or finalist status. Finalists—some 4,000–5,000 students each year—receive National Merit Scholarships (or National Achievement Scholarships for Outstanding Negro Students) of up to $1,500 or more per year for four years, based on demonstrated need, or a $1,000 one-time award. National Merit winners with no demonstrated need receive a $250 honorarium per year for four years. The names of semifinalists and letter-of-commendation winners are distributed to colleges, so that these students also stand a good chance of winning scholarships from the colleges to which they apply.

Scholastic Aptitude Test (SAT)

The Scholastic Aptitude Test is the standardized admissions test required by most Eastern colleges as well as many other private institutions throughout the nation. As the name implies, and like the PSAT, it is intended to measure your aptitude for academic work, not your actual knowledge of a specific subject area.

SAT Contents

The SAT is a multiple-choice test in two parts—verbal and mathematical. Each test contains five sections, and you are given 30 minutes to work on each. The distribution of math and verbal parts on any SAT test is random. All contain two verbal and two math sections, but the fifth section can be either. Your test may have three verbal sections, while the person sitting next to you in the testing room may have three math sections.

A separate half-hour test has been added to the regular two-and-a-half-hour SAT. This Test of Standard Written English (TSWE) is used primarily to help place students in an appropriate freshman English course after they have been accepted and enrolled at a particular college. The test consists of 50 multiple-choice questions that are similar to, but easier than, those on the SAT verbal section. The score is reported on a 20 to 60+ scale and does not affect your regular SAT verbal score.

SAT Scoring

Each part of the SAT rates your aptitude within a percentile range, using a 200–800 scale. Each score should be interpreted within a fairly wide range. For example, the College Board states that a verbal score of 450 means that there is a 66 percent chance that your true score falls in the range of 420 to 480. The national average SAT verbal score for college-bound seniors in the high school class of 1979 was 427, and the average SAT mathematical score was 467. Selective and highly selective institutions generally look for scores in the high 500s and above.

It is not necessary for you to complete every question on the exam in order to score well. Whenever the test is administered, a sizable number of students find that they are unable to complete one or more sections. But you should work as quickly as you are competently able to, for your raw score will be determined by a simple formula of subtracting a percentage of the number of wrong answers from the number of right answers. You receive one point for every correct answer and lose 1/4 of a point for each wrong answer on a question with a five-choice response, or 1/3 of a point on a question with a four-choice response. Raw scores are converted to scaled scores of 200 to 800 so that they can be compared with the scores of other students who have taken the tests.

SAT Score Report

When you receive your score report, you will find not only your own scores in the verbal and math sections but also some percentile rankings to show you how your scores compare with those of other students who took the test. One percentile shows you how you rank in comparison with all high school students in the nation; another shows where you placed in terms of all college-bound high school students in the nation; and another shows how your scores compare with those of the freshmen at your three top-choice institutions. While you should not consider this rating an absolute predictor of your chances of admission to these colleges, it is nonetheless useful to show whether your scores at least measure up to the average score earned.

Taking the SAT; Guessing

Even though the SAT is scored on a right-minus-percentage-of-wrong basis to discourage random guessing, enlightened guessing can help your score. For example, if you are not sure of an answer, but are able to rule out one or possibly two of the choices offered, the chances are above average that you will select the correct answer. The 1/4 point or 1/3 point that you could possibly lose by answering a question you feel moderately sure about is a good risk considering the 1 point you could gain if you're right. However, if you cannot eliminate any of the choices with certainty, a guess is not worth the risk, and you would do better to leave the question unanswered.

Sample SAT Questions

A complete sample SAT is now available to all students and provides an excellent opportunity to familiarize yourself with the question formats and the pace necessary to complete as much of each section as possible with accuracy. This sample is contained in the pamphlet *Taking the SAT*, which should be available from your guidance office.

You can get a briefer idea of the types of questions you will encounter on the exam on pages 78 to 82. Try your hand at answering each of them.

Registering for the SAT

To register for the SAT, ask your guidance counselor for a copy of the official registration brochure and other informational materials, or write directly to the College Board Admissions Testing Program, Box 592, Princeton, New Jersey 08541, for these materials, which are provided free of charge. When registering, you will be required to supply some brief biographical information and to indicate when and where you would like to take the exam. (The test will usually be administered at your own high school or at another institution within easy commuting distance of your home.) The registration fee (under $10) covers the cost of administering the program and sending score reports to you and your guidance counselor and to three colleges or scholarship agencies of your choice.

About two weeks before the test date, you will be sent an admission packet, which will contain your admission ticket. Put this in a handy place until the test date, and then bring it with you to the testing site.

Take a Number.

Registration forms for both SAT and ACT exams ask you to supply your Social Security number. Several college applications are also processed by this number. If you haven't joined the nation's work force by the time you begin to apply to college, a trip to your local Social Security office to register for a number is in order.

SAT Student Search Option

When you register, you will be given the option of completing the Student Descriptive Questionnaire on the form. If you choose to complete this section, some of the information you supply will be sent along with your test scores to the institutions that you have indicated. The first question asks if you wish to participate in the Student Search Service—a free arrangement that makes your name, address, sex, and high school available to colleges and scholarship agencies seeking students with your background or academic interests. If you check "yes," many of these groups will no doubt contact you through mailings. Some students, who are sure of their college choices and do not want to receive any additional literature, check "no." Others feel that the institutions that will contact them through Student Search mailings can provide new or helpful ideas about their educational plans and consequently check "yes."

Sample SAT Questions

SAT—VERBAL

For each question in this section, choose the best answer and blacken the corresponding space on the answer sheet.

Antonyms

Each question below consists of a word in capital letters, followed by five lettered words or phrases. Choose the word or phrase that is most nearly opposite in meaning to the word in capital letters. Since some of the questions require you to distinguish fine shades of meaning, consider all the choices before deciding which is best.

1. FEROCITY: (A) mildness (B) inaccuracy (C) originality (D) awkwardness (E) uselessness

2. UNDULATING: (A) level (B) profuse (C) fragmentary (D) pompous (E) buoyant

Sentence completion

Each sentence below has one or two blanks, each blank indicating that something has been omitted. Beneath the sentence are five lettered words or sets of words. Choose the word or set pair that best expresses a relationship similar to that expressed in the original pair.

3. The castles of the feudal lords were primarily forts and therefore were constructed more for ---------- than for ----------.
   (A) privacy . . seclusion
   (B) protection . . comfort
   (C) convenience . . security
   (D) permanence . . preservation
   (E) retaliation . . defense

4. Hinckle tried to explain the differences between those controversies that demand an absolutist, moralistic approach and those that call for a pragmatic, ---------- solution.
   (A) conciliatory (B) permanent
   (C) immoderate (D) categorical
   (E) inexpedient

Analogies

Each question below consists of a related pair of words or phrases, followed by five lettered pairs of words or phrases. Select the lettered pair that best expresses a relationship similar to that expressed in the original pair.

5. MOTH:CLOTHING:: (A) woodpecker:hole (B) bear:trap (C) lamb:wool (D) puncture: tire (E) termite:house

6. HOMOGENEOUS:KIND:: (A) contemporary:age (B) enigmatic:force (C) precipitous:length (D) superficial:surface (E) suitable:form

Reading passages

Each passage below is followed by questions based on its content. Answer all questions following a passage on the basis of what is stated or implied in that passage.

(The passages for this test have been adapted from published material. The ideas contained in them do not necessarily represent the opinions of the College Board or Educational Testing Service.)

In past days Captain Bailey had handled many thousands of pounds of his employers' money and of his own; he had attended faithfully, as by law a shipmaster is expected
(5) to do, to the conflicting interests of owners, charterers, and underwriters. He had never lost a ship or consented to a shady transaction. He had buried his wife, had married off his daughter to a man of her unlucky
(10) choice, and had lost much in the crash of the notorious Travanacore and Deccan Banking Corporation, whose downfall had shaken the East like an earthquake. And he was sixty-seven years old.
(15) His age sat lightly on him, and of his ruin he was not ashamed. He had not been alone in believing in the stability of the Banking Corporation. Men whose judgment in matters of finance was as expert as his seamanship
(20) had commended the prudence of his investments, and had themselves lost much money in the great failure. The only difference between him and them was that he had lost his all and yet not his all. There remained
(25) to him from his lost fortune a very pretty little barque, Fair Maid, which he had bought to occupy his leisure as a retired sailor.
He had formally declared himself tired
(30) of the sea the year preceding his daughter's marriage. But after the young couple had

gone to settle in Melbourne, he found that
he could not make himself happy on shore.
He was too much of a merchant sea-captain
(35) for mere yachting to satisfy him. He wanted
the illusion of affairs, and his acquisition
of Fair Maid preserved continuity in his life.
He introduced her to his acquaintances in
various ports as "my last command." When
(40) he grew too old to be trusted with a ship, he
would lay her up and go ashore and be
buried, leaving directions in his will to have
the barque towed out and scuttled on the
day of the funeral. His daughter would not
(45) begrudge him the satisfaction of knowing
that no stranger would handle his last command after him. All this would be said with
a jocular twinkle in his eye: the vigorous
old man had too much vitality for the
(50) sentimentalism of regret; and yet a little
wistfully because he was at home in life,
taking genuine pleasure in its feelings and
possessions, in the dignity of his reputation,
in his love for his daughter, and in his satis-
(55) faction with the ship—the plaything of his
lonely leisure.

7. The passage primarily concerns

   (A) Captain Bailey's memories of his career
       at sea
   (B) the events that contributed to Captain
       Bailey's success as a shipmaster
   (C) Captain Bailey's actions and attitudes
       after retirement

   (D) the conditions that caused the loss of
       Captain Bailey's fortune
   (E) the experiences shared by Captain
       Bailey and Fair Maid

8. The expression "his ruin" (line 15) refers to
   Captain Bailey's

   (A) physical condition
   (B) discredited reputation
   (C) loss of his fortune
   (D) isolation from his former friends
   (E) departure from his job as shipmaster

9. It can be inferred that Captain Bailey's
   employers believed that, as a shipmaster, he
   was

   (A) loyal but unambitious
   (B) competent and ethical
   (C) talented but undependable
   (D) eccentric and unpopular
   (E) restless and erratic

10. Captain Bailey wished to have Fair Maid
    sunk on the day of his funeral because he

    (A) knew that no one else could handle the
        boat
    (B) resented the boat's seductive power
        over him
    (C) realized that maintaining the boat
        would be a burden for his daughter
    (D) did not want the boat to be under any
        command but his own
    (E) feared that the boat would fall into the
        hands of his creditors

SAT—MATHEMATICAL

Quantitative comparison questions

<u>Questions 11-13</u> each consist of two quantities, one in Column A and one in Column B. You are to compare the two quantities and on the answer sheet blacken space

- A if the quantity in Column A is greater;
- B if the quantity in Column B is greater;
- C if the two quantities are equal;
- D if the relationship cannot be determined from the information given.

Notes:
1. In certain questions, information concerning one or both of the quantities to be compared is centered above the two columns.
2. A symbol that appears in both columns represents the same thing in Column A as it does in Column B.
3. Letters such as x, n, and k stand for real numbers.
4. Since there are only four choices <u>NEVER MARK (E)</u>.

Column A	Column B

11. $e(f + e)$ $(e + f)e$

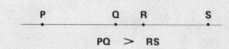

$PQ > RS$

12. PR   QS

Let n* be defined by the equation
$n* = (n - 1) (n) (n + 1)$ where n
is an integer.

13. $\dfrac{6*}{3*}$ $2*$

Standard multiple-choice mathematics questions

In this section solve each problem, using any available space on the page for scratchwork. Then indicate the <u>one</u> correct answer in the appropriate space on the answer sheet.

The following information is for your reference in solving some of the problems.

Circle of radius r: Area = πr^2; Circumference = $2\pi r$

The number of degrees of arc in a circle is 360.

The measure in degrees of a straight angle is 180.

Definitions of symbols:
$=$ is equal to
$\neq$ is unequal to
$<$ is less than
$>$ is greater than
$\leq$ is less than or equal to
$\geq$ is greater than or equal to
$\parallel$ is parallel to
$\perp$ is perpendicular to

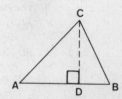

Triangle: The sum of the measures in degrees of the angles of a triangle is 180

If   CDA is a right angle, then

(1) area of   ABC = $\dfrac{AB \times CD}{2}$

(2) $AC^2 = AD^2 + DC^2$

Note: Figures which accompany problems in this test are intended to provide information useful in solving the problems. They are drawn as accurately as possible EXCEPT when it is stated in a specific problem that its figure is not drawn to scale. All figures lie in a plane unless otherwise indicated. All numbers used are real numbers.

14. If $11 + xy = 12 + 11$, then the pair x, y could be any of the following EXCEPT

(A) 12, 1
(B) 6, 6
(C) 4, 3
(D) 3, 4
(E) 2, 6

15. The formula for the power P of an electric appliance is P = EI where E is the number of volts and I the number of amperes of current. What is I when P = 1,620 and E = 120?

  (A)   13.5
  (B)   19.4
  (C)   135
  (D)   19,440
  (E) 194,400

16. What is half of the perimeter of a square of area 36?

  (A) 3 (B) 6 (C) 12 (D) 18 (E) 24

17. If abe = 0, bcd = 1, and bce = 0, which of the following must equal 0?

  (A) a (B) b (C) c (D) d (E) e

18. Container R is full of water and has twice the volume of container S, which is empty. If 1/4 of the water in R is poured into S, what fraction of the volume of S is occupied by water?

  (A) 1 (B) 1/2 (C) 1/4 (D) 1/8
  (E) None of the above

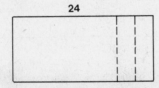

24

19. In the figure above, a rectangular piece of paper with length 24 is cut into strips of equal width as indicated by the dotted lines. If the area of two of these strips is 25 per cent of the area of the rectangle, how wide is each strip?

  (A) 8 (B) 6 (C) 4 (D) 3 (E) 2

20. What is the difference between the greatest and least of all three-digit positive integers, each of whose digits is a different nonzero multiple of 3?

  (A) 324 (B) 540 (C) 567 (D) 594 (E) 604

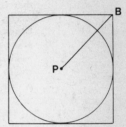

21. In the square above, Q is the intersection of segment PB and the circle with center P. What is the ratio of the length of QB to the length of PQ?

  (A) $\sqrt{2} - 1$

  (B) $\dfrac{\sqrt{2}}{2}$

  (C) $\sqrt{2}$

  (D) $\sqrt{2} + 1$

  (E) $2\sqrt{2}$

THE TEST OF STANDARD WRITTEN ENGLISH

Usage questions

The following sentences contain problems in grammar, usage, diction (choice of words), and idiom. Some sentences are correct. No sentence contains more than one error.

You will find that the error, if there is one, is underlined and lettered. Assume that all other elements of the sentence are correct and cannot be changed. In choosing answers, follow the requirements of standard written English.

If there is an error, select the one underlined part that must be changed in order to make the sentence correct, and blacken the corresponding space on the answer sheet. If there is no error, mark answer space E.

22. Most people will <u>find it easier</u> to adjust to
                          A
    the metric system <u>if you become</u>
                           B
    familiar <u>with</u> it before the changeover
              C
    occurs. <u>No error</u>
      D   E

23. Many travelers claim <u>having seen</u> the
                            A
    Abominable Snowman, <u>but</u> no one has
                          B
    proved that <u>such</u> a creature <u>actually</u>
                  C   D
    exists. <u>No error</u>
      E

Sentence correction questions

In each of the following sentences, some part of the sentence or the entire sentence is underlined. Beneath each sentence you will find five ways of phrasing the underlined part. The first of these repeats the original; the other four are different. If you think the original is better than any of the alternatives, choose answer A; otherwise choose one of the others. Select the best version and blacken the corresponding space on your answer sheet.

This is a test of correctness and effectiveness of expression. In choosing answers, follow the requirements of standard written English; that is, pay attention to grammar, choice of words, sentence construction, and punctuation. Choose the answer that produces the most effective sentence—clear and exact, without awkwardness or ambiguity. Do not make a choice that changes the meaning of the original sentence.

24. The shorter bearpaw snowshoes are the best choice if you are looking for <u>an easy to lift and maneuver model.</u>

    (A) an easy to lift and maneuver model
    (B) a model that is easy to lift and maneuver
    (C) an easy model as far as lifting and maneuvering goes
    (D) a model with ease of lifting and also maneuver
    (E) an easily lifted and also maneuvered model

25. <u>Althea Gibson was the first black American to win major tennis championships and played in the 1950s.</u>

    (A) Althea Gibson was the first black American to win major tennis championships and played in the 1950s.
    (B) Althea Gibson, being the first black American to win major tennis championships, and playing in the 1950s.
    (C) Althea Gibson, playing in the 1950s, being the first black American to win major tennis championships.
    (D) Althea Gibson, who played in the 1950s, was the first black American to win major tennis championships.
    (E) Althea Gibson played in the 1950s, she was the first black American to win major tennis championships.

SAT ANSWER KEY

THE TEST OF STANDARD WRITTEN ENGLISH 22. B 23. A 24. B 25. D

20. D 21. A

SAT—MATHEMATICAL 11. C 12. A 13. A 14. B 15. A 16. C 17. E 18. B 19. D

SAT—VERBAL 1. A 2. A 3. B 4. A 5. E 6. A 7. C 8. C 9. B 10. D

College Board Achievement Tests

Achievement Test Contents

The College Board Admissions Testing Program also offers a selection of Achievement Tests designed, in contrast to the SAT, to measure how much you have learned in particular subject areas. Achievement Tests are administered in English composition, literature, mathematics (two test levels), American history and social studies, European history and world cultures, biology, chemistry, physics, French, German, Hebrew, Latin, Russian, and Spanish. Each test is multiple-choice in format and one hour long.

There is now an English Composition Achievement Test with Essay. This test is being offered on only one test date each year at the present time, but students should try to schedule it as it provides a chance for them to demonstrate their writing ability in essay form. It also contains a section of multiple-choice questions.

Although the College Board estimates that "about one third of the colleges that require the SAT also require two or three Achievement Tests," fewer than one quarter of such institutions in our survey indicated that they require Achievements. The Achievement Test most frequently required is the English Composition test.

Achievement Test Scoring

Achievement Tests are scored on the same scale and by the same right-minus-percentage-of-wrong formula as is used on the SATs. Again, enlightened guessing may help your score, while totally random guessing will probably only hurt it.

Achievement Test Score Report

A specific score for each of your Achievement Tests will be recorded on your score report, as will a composite (average) score for all your Achievement Tests. As with your SAT scores, you will receive an indication of what percentile these scores place you in compared with (1) all high school students in the United States, (2) all college-bound high school students in the United States, and (3) the freshman class at the first three institutions that you have named to receive your score report.

Preparing for the Achievement Tests

Because Achievement Tests measure factual knowledge rather than academic aptitude, it is possible to study for them. Reviewing textbooks in the appropriate subjects is one of the best ways to refresh your knowledge. The College Board will also send you a booklet containing sample questions when you register for the tests. If you feel you would benefit from even further exposure to test questions, there are several commercial handbooks devoted to preparation for the Achievements available in bookstores and libraries. They contain several sample tests in each subject, and, while the probability of encountering a question that will actually be asked on the test you receive is slim, knowing the range of questions asked provides a good form of review.

Plan Your Test Dates Carefully

Of the institutions that require Achievement Test scores, some indicate the subjects in which they must be taken, while others leave the choice to you. Once you have determined which colleges you plan to apply to, make a list of which Achievement Tests are required by each college. If you must take more than three different tests, you will have to take them on two separate testing dates, as you may not register for more than three tests on each testing date. The registration fee, however, remains the same whether you take one, two, or three exams. Registration materials should be available in your guidance counselor's office, or you can write directly to: College Board Admissions Testing Program, Box 592, Princeton, New Jersey 08541.

While Achievement Tests are usually administered on the same test days as the SAT, you may not take both on the same day. Thus it requires planning on your part to be sure that you have taken all the necessary tests early enough for the scores to be reported to your chosen colleges before each of their application deadlines. It takes approximately six weeks for tests to be scored and reported.

American College Testing Program Test (ACT)

Several private colleges in the Midwest, far West, and Southeast, as well as most public institutions across the nation, require the American College Testing Program exam rather than the College Board exam for admission or placement. The ACT is administered throughout the nation and abroad at least five times a year.

ACT Contents
The ACT Assessment Program consists of four academic tests—each 35 to 50 minutes long—designed to measure your background in English usage, mathematics usage, social studies reading, and natural sciences reading. While much of the test concerns reasoning and solving problems with given information, some questions do require recall of specific facts. All questions are multiple-choice, with four or five optional responses provided.

ACT Scoring
Your raw scores on the four sections of the ACT Student Assessment are determined simply by the total number of correct answers you supply. In this scoring method there is no penalty for guessing, so even if you are unable to make more than a wild guess at an answer, go ahead—it can only work to your advantage. Raw scores are converted to scaled scores (on a 1–36 scale), which enables you to compare your scores with those of others who have taken the exam and slightly lowers the scores of those taking it late in their senior year so that all scores are equalized.

ACT Score Report
Your ACT score report will record a score for each of the tests as well as your composite (average) score on the four. The current average composite score for all college-bound high school students is 18.6. Of course, the more selective institutions look for higher-than-average scores. Your copy of the report will also give you a brief profile of each college that you have designated to receive your scores.

Preparing for the ACT
Since some factual knowledge is required, it is useful to review books and notes in each of the subject areas before taking the ACT test. However, familiarity with the test format is probably an even more valuable form of preparation. If you want to try your hand at some exercises, begin with the samples that follow or the others contained in the ACT registration brochure. These brochures are available in your guidance counselor's office, or from ACT Registration, P.O. Box 414, Iowa City, Iowa 52243.

Sample ACT Questions
For preliminary practice on the ACT, review the sample questions on pages 85 to 94.

Sample ACT Questions

TEST 1: English Usage

Directions:

Questions on the English Usage Test are based on passages which contain expressions that are inappropriate in standard written English; you are to decide how these expressions can be made appropriate and effective. The passages are presented in a spread-out format in which various words, phrases, and punctuation have been underlined and numbered. In the right-hand column, opposite each underlined portion, you will find a set of responses numbered to correspond to that of the underlined portion. Each set of responses contains a "NO CHANGE" option and three alternatives to the underlined version. Since your judgment about the appropriateness and effectiveness of a response will depend on your perceptions of the passage as a whole, the author's purpose, and the type of audience, first read through the entire passage quickly. Then reread the passage slowly and carefully. As you come to each underlined portion during your second reading, look at the alternatives in the right-hand column and decide which of the four words or phrasings is best for the given context. Since your response will often depend on your reading several of the sentences surrounding the underlined portion, make sure you have read ahead far enough to make the best choice. If you think that the original version (the one in the passage) is best, blacken the oval marked A or F in the corresponding row on the test answer folder. If you think that an alternative version is best, blacken the oval whose letter corresponds to the alternative that you have chosen as best. In every case, consider only the underlined words, phrases, and punctuation marks; you can assume that the rest of the passage is correct as written.

Thor Heyerdahl became famous for a unique sailing expedition, which he later described in *Kon-Tiki*. Having developed a theory that the original Polynesians had sailed or drifted to the South Sea Islands from South America, it then had to be tested.
_____
1

After careful study he built a raft that was as authentic as possible. Using only primitive equipment, he and five other men sailed into the South Seas from Peru, which he judged to be in
_____
2

the same general area as the land of the original Polynesians. As a result, his group and him will long be
_____
3

remembered not only as thorough scientists but also as courageous men.

Heyerdahl's courage was first tested in Ecuador. His search for trees that was large enough for the
_____
4

expeditionary raft sent him to Quito, a city high in the Andes. There, he and his companions were warned about headhunters and bandits on the trail. Feeling undaunted, they hired a
_____
5

1. A. NO CHANGE
   B. he set out to test it.
   C. it was decided that it must be tested.
   D. the theory was then to be tested.

2. F. NO CHANGE
   G. Peru, being judged as
   H. Peru, which had been
   J. Peru judged as being

3. A. NO CHANGE
   B. him and his group
   C. his group and himself
   D. he and his group

4. F. NO CHANGE
   G. which would be of sufficient size
   H. of adequate size
   J. of certainly sufficient size

5. A. NO CHANGE
   B. trail. Undaunted, they
   C. trail, but they were undaunted, and
   D. trail; undaunted they

driver and jeep from the U.S.
<u>Embassy, going on with their</u>
  6

dangerous task.

  <u>After the raft was done, Heyerdahl</u>
        7
made final preparations for the
expedition. Even before his crew came
aboard,

<u>the courage which Heyerdahl possessed</u>
                    8
was tested again. As the raft was being
towed out of the harbor, it drifted
under the stern of a tug. Heyerdahl
had to struggle to save it.
<u>Dangers at sea were present, but</u>
      9

Heyerdahl and his men did not show
fear. Instead they developed games
that were actually tests of courage.
Although man-eating fish were
nearby, the men swam to relieve their

<u>tension, maintaining that the fish were</u>
          10

not dangerous unless a man had
already been cut or scratched.
One game consisted of luring
sharks within reach, catching
<u>them, and then they would yank it</u>
                    11
onto the raft.

<u>Being on the raft, the sharks thrashed</u>
          12

about and snapped viciously at the
men. Another game was even more
dangerous: two men would paddle
away on a rubber dinghy until they
<u>could catch only an occasional</u>
                13
glimpse of the raft; then they would
have to paddle violently to return.

  The final portion of the voyage was
the most thrilling. As the raft neared
Raoia, it was carried rapidly toward the
reef, where the waves beat it <u>very bad.</u>
                              14

6. F. NO CHANGE
   G. Embassy; and went on with
   H. Embassy and proceeded with
   J. Embassy, and kept on

7. A. NO CHANGE
   B. When the raft was ready,
   C. The raft was speedily completed
      and
   D. The raft having been constructed,

8. F. NO CHANGE
   G. Heyerdahls' manly courage
   H. Heyerdahl's courage
   J. the courage of this man

9. A. NO CHANGE
   B. (Do not begin new paragraph)
      At sea, dangers
   C. (Begin new paragraph) Dangers,
      at sea
   D. (Begin new paragraph) At sea,
      dangers

10. F. NO CHANGE
    G. tension. Maintaining
    H. tension. He maintained
    J. tension, because it was maintained

11. A. NO CHANGE
    B. then to yank it
    C. and then to yank them up
    D. and yanking them

12. F. NO CHANGE
    G. At that point,
    H. Once there,
    J. At that time,

13. A. NO CHANGE
    B. (Place after *until*)
    C. (Place after *they*)
    D. OMIT

14. F. NO CHANGE
    G. mercilessly.
    H. very violent.
    J. without any mercy.

Almost miraculously the men survived, only to find theirselves
_____
15

on a deserted island. At last their struggle with the sea had ended. They radioed Rarotonga and set up camp to await rescue.

Thor Heyerdahl's expedition on the Kon-Tiki did not necessarily prove his migration theory, but it did prove that hardy pioneers with courage, determination, and luck
could make the same trip, even with
_____
16

very primitive equipment.

15. **A.** NO CHANGE
    B. and only found themselves
    C. only to find themselves
    D. but only found themselves to be

16. **F.** NO CHANGE
    G. could now do the same trip,
    H. could do the same,
    J. could have accomplished this the same,

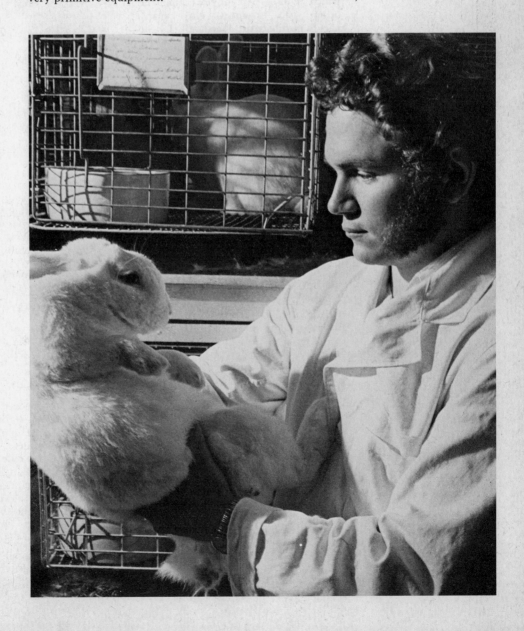

TEST 2: Mathematics Usage

Directions:

In the Mathematics Usage Test you are to solve each problem and then choose the correct answer. In some of the problems the fifth alternative, E or K, is "None of the above." In those problems, if your answer is not among the first four alternatives, blacken oval E or K.

1. Two wells pump oil continuously. One produces 4000 barrels of oil per day, which is $33\frac{1}{3}$ percent more than the other well produces. How many barrels of oil are produced daily by the 2 wells?

    A. $5333\frac{1}{3}$ D. $8333\frac{1}{3}$
    B. $6666\frac{2}{3}$ E. 9000
    C. 7000

2. If a car travels a miles in b minutes, how many minutes will it take to travel c miles?

    F. c/a J. ab/c
    G. c/b K. cb/a
    H. c/ab

3. In the figure below, what is the sum of the measures of the angles labeled x and y?

    A. $90°$
    B. $100°$
    C. $130°$
    D. $140°$
    E. None of the above

    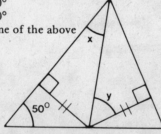

4. A man purchased 100 shares of stock at $5 a share. If each share rose 10 cents the first month, decreased 8 cents the second month, and gained 3 cents the third month, what was the value of the man's investment at the end of the third month?

    F. $505   J. $1545
    G. $520   K. None of the above
    H. $525

5. The following multiplication scheme uses symbols other than the usual numerals. $\triangle$ corresponds to which base-10 numeral?

    $$\triangle \times \theta = \theta$$
    $$\theta \times \triangle = \theta$$
    $$\triangle \times \triangle = \triangle$$

    A. 0   D. 5
    B. 1   E. 10
    C. 2

6. What is the length, in inches, of a 144-degree arc in a circle whose circumference is 60 inches?

    F. 24   J. 36
    G. $12/\pi$ K. $36/\pi$
    H. 12π

7. What does x equal in the equation

    $$\frac{1}{x} = \frac{1}{5} - \frac{1}{x} ?$$

    A. $\frac{1}{10}$ C. 5
                 D. 10
    B. $\frac{1}{5}$ E. None of the above

8. In the universe of all people, let circle M represent all Mary's friends, circle B all Bill's friends, and circle P all Pete's friends. What is represented by the shaded portion of the figure?

    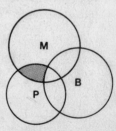

    F. All the people who are friends of Mary, Bill, and Pete
    G. All the people who are friends of Mary and Pete
    H. All the people who are friends of Mary and Pete but not of Bill
    J. All the people who are friends of Pete but not of Bill
    K. All the people who are not friends of Bill

9. A ship sailing due north past an island travels a course that is 12 miles from the island at its closest point. If a gun

on shore has a firing range of 13 miles, for how many miles will the ship remain within range of the gun?

A. 1   D. 10
B. 5   E. None of the above
C. 9

10. What is the area of the unshaded sector of circle O shown below?

F. $\frac{\pi r}{8}$

G. $\frac{\pi r^2}{2}$

H. $\frac{\pi r^2}{4}$

J. $\frac{\pi r^2}{8}$

K. $\frac{\pi r^2}{45}$

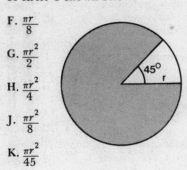

11. What set of values for x and y (x, y) satisfies the equations below?

$$3y = x + 4$$
$$6x + 2y = 16$$

A. $(-2, 2)$ D. $(2, 2)$
B. $(2, -2)$ E. None of the above
C. $(-2, -2)$

12. What is the value of the expression below?

$$\frac{A^{4p+3} \cdot A^{3p+4}}{A^{2p+2}}$$

F. A^{9p+9} J. A^{-3p-3}

G. A^{6p+6} K. A^{5p+5}

H. A^{3p+3}

TEST 3: Social Studies Reading

Directions:

The Social Studies Reading Test measures your ability to comprehend, analyze, and evaluate reading materials in such social studies fields as history, political science, economics, sociology, anthropology, and psychology. To answer these questions, you will have to draw on your background in social studies as well as on your ability to understand new material. In addition to the questions based on reading passages, there are some questions that test your general background knowledge in social studies.

Read the passage through once. Then return to it as often as necessary to answer the questions.

Over the past several decades the growth of the United States economy has been marked by expansion of metropolitan areas and by "regionalization" of production—that is, a more even geographical distribution of industries over the United States. Such rapid growth causes drastic changes in the geographical structure of metropolitan areas. Manufacturing industries, which were initially attracted to the core of the city by the proximity of the railroads, a steady labor supply, and the economic advantages of mass production, are now moving toward peripheral locations.

No single explanation can be given for this trend toward suburbanization, but as cities have grown, the supply of undeveloped land has decreased. The advantages of the central metropolis continue to attract economic activity, but congestion in the central city and the development of production techniques which demand more space have tended to push industry into the suburbs. The net result has been a pattern of geographical specialization within metropolitan regions. The central city increasingly becomes geared to white-collar and service activities, and the periphery attracts manufacturing, transportation, and other blue-collar job activities.

The development of residential areas has followed industrial movement to some extent, but suburban living (undoubtedly desired for its amenities) is still largely reserved for those who can afford it. Consequently, the central city has been losing middle- and upper-income families to the suburbs. Now people can live in dispersed residential locations; rising incomes and the proliferation of automobiles have made this both economically and technically feasible. However, this "urban sprawl" creates serious financial problems. Since tax-paying industry has fled to the suburbs, the central city has had to bear the cost of public assistance payments and other welfare service for low-income groups.

When housing developers began building on a large scale, many suburbs rapidly doubled and tripled in size. This new population required more schools and teachers, more fire and police protection, and sizable expenditures for water and sewer lines and roads. Frequently, these towns were entirely dependent on property taxes for their revenues.

To meet ever-increasing expenses and broaden their tax base, some communities have tried to attract new industry. However, when town officials found themselves competing intensely for these industries, they often conceded partial exemption from property taxes to new industry in order to bargain more favorably. As a result, an area often found its tax base weakened rather than strengthened by winning new industry. As a consequence of all these changes, both the suburbs and the central city are entangled in thorny financial problems.

1. According to the author, a rise in wages earned by employees of service industries will principally tend to:

   A. increase the physical separation between zones of residence and zones of work.
   B. decrease the tax revenues of the suburbs.
   C. decrease the tax revenues of the metropolitan areas.
   D. increase the work force in the periphery.

2. The most efficient way to solve the financial problems of a metropolitan area would be to:

   F. cut personal taxes in central cities.
   G. cut personal taxes in the suburbs.
   H. decrease public expenditures in central cities.
   J. place the entire area under one fiscal authority.

3. Which of the following problems should be given first consideration on the basis of the changing urban structure outlined in the passage?

   A. Commuter traffic between areas of residence and areas of work
   B. Highway passenger traffic between two metropolitan areas

   C. Congestion due to heavy truck traffic in downtown areas
   D. The centralization of railroad freight stations in downtown areas

4. The author would consider the giant modern city essentially a by-product of the:

   F. invention of the internal-combustion engine.
   G. development of monopolistic industries.
   H. Industrial Revolution.
   J. capitalist system.

5. If the trend outlined in paragraph three continues, the centers of large American cities are more likely than the suburbs to have a high percentage of:

   A. small-scale manufacturing firms.
   B. large-scale factories.
   C. railroad stations.
   D. banks and insurance companies.

In 1845, Congressional leaders debated the annexation of Texas. The issues considered were many and complex, as the following excerpts from the debate illustrate.

Speaker 1

In annexing Texas, we do not adopt its war with Mexico, if any such exists. In annexation, we will not abide by Texas law; Texas will abide by ours. The United States are not to be merged in Texas, but Texas in them. When we purchased Louisiana from France, France was at war; we did not assume the French war. Mexico, however, may regard annexation as an act of extreme unfriendliness and make it the pretext for declaring war on the United States.

Speaker 2

Since the landing of the Pilgrims, our people have moved forward, acquiring territory, unfurling the banner of liberty and equality, creating a power (more potent than that of armies) before which the nations of this continent will continue to give way. No nation can withstand the impact of this principle of enlightened liberty. Under this principle—though I regret to say, sometimes backed by the sword—we have been a progressive, but peaceful people.

Speaker 3

The Anglo-Saxon race, like a mighty flood, has swept over the continent. Some say the flood ought to stop at the Del Norte. I can tell them that it will not. In fifty years it will cover Mexico; in a hundred, Argentina.

Speaker 4

The question of admitting Texas seems to make many apprehensive about the balance of political power. Let them look at the complexion of the House. Let them look also at the map, and see the broad expanse of land in the north and northwest which is yet to be made into states where slavery can never exist. In addition, by rejecting Texas we ensure the spread of slavery. Admit Texas, and the Río Bravo constitutes the limits of this institution. Reject her, and slavery will not stop until its standard waves in triumph over Mexico.

Speaker 5

Those who advocate annexation contend that the federal government is one of limited powers. Yet they ask that Congress assume the important power of adding a foreign nation to our own. We are referred to the provision in the Constitution that authorizes Congress to admit new states. History shows that this clause was intended only to confer on Congress the power of admitting new states created from territory already belonging to the United States.

Speaker 6

This is the true cause of most of the opposition: fear that an influence opposed to the interests of the manufacturers would be added to the national councils.

6. Which speaker's argument seems to stem directly from a belief in the inevitability of historical events?

   F. 5   H. 3
   G. 4   J. 1

7. Which of the following is true of Speaker 2's description of the United States method of acquiring new territory as "peaceful"?

   A. It is contradicted by other parts of his statement.
   B. It is supported by U.S. success in acquiring territories.

C. It supports a Marxist interpretation of history.
D. It is an accurate but unsupported statement.

8. What earlier action of Congress was based on the principle of "balance of power" to which Speaker 4 refers?

   F. The Northwest Ordinance
   G. The Judiciary Act
   H. The Missouri Compromise
   J. The Great Compromise

9. The argument of which speaker implies that United States territory should be limited to that acquired by an agreement?

   A. 5   C. 2
   B. 3   D. 1

The following questions are not based on a reading passage. You are to answer these questions on the basis of your background in social studies.

---

10. Andrew Jackson's term as president is noteworthy largely because during that period:

    F. peaceful relations were established with the Plains Indians.
    G. the common man came to have more of a say in government.
    H. a national bank was established, resulting in this country's first stable currency.
    J. women received the right to vote for the first time.

11. The 80-day injunction provision of the Taft-Hartley Act was included for what purpose?

    A. To provide a cooling-off period allowing labor and management additional time to resolve disputes
    B. To permit the unions to arrange for a survey of membership opinion regarding a strike
    C. To permit management to update the profit-loss picture for the forthcoming quarter
    D. To give government negotiators the time to make a decision about whether a strike would be advisable

12. Which of the following might anthropologists find similar in purpose to the rain dance of the Pueblo Indians?

   F. The playing of the national anthem before sporting events
   G. Traditional country folk dancing
   H. Studies carried out by a college of agriculture to improve the yield of wheat
   J. A prayer meeting in an American church

13. The most significant advance of the Charter of the United Nations over the Covenant of the League of Nations is the:

   A. article providing for an international police force to prevent aggression.
   B. provision granting veto power to the five permanent members of the Security Council.
   C. belief in the maintenance of world peace by international cooperation.
   D. establishment of a council with authority to formulate plans for the reduction of armaments.

14. The main purpose of the Bill of Rights is to:

   F. prevent presidents from telling states what to do.
   G. enlarge the scope of the powers of the federal government.
   H. reduce the power of the Supreme Court to declare acts of Congress unconstitutional.
   J. limit the power of the federal government to abuse individual freedom.

15. When Western Europe was cut off from some of its Middle Eastern oil by the Suez crisis in 1956, most of the petroleum deficit was made up by the United States and:

   A. Canada.
   B. Eastern Europe.
   C. Indonesia.
   D. Venezuela.

TEST 4: Natural Sciences Reading

Directions:

The Natural Sciences Reading Test measures your ability to understand, analyze, and evaluate passages on scientific topics and descriptions of experiments in such fields as biology, chemistry, physics, and physical science. To answer these questions you will have to draw on your scientific background as well as on your ability to understand new material. In addition to the questions based on reading passages, there are some questions that test your general background knowledge in the sciences.

Read the passage through once. Then return to it as often as necessary to answer the questions.

As the cells that make up different tissues and organs differ in structure and function, so also do they differ in their response to radiation. The law of Bergonie and Tribondeau states that the radiosensitivity of a tissue is directly proportional to its reproductive capacity and inversely proportional to its degree of specialization. In other words, immature, rapidly dividing cells will be most harmed by radiation. In addition, three other factors are important: undernourished cells are less sensitive than normal ones; the higher the metabolic rate in a cell, the lower its resistance to radiation; and cells are more sensitive to radiation at specific stages of division.

Radiation alters the electrical charges of the atoms in the irradiated material, breaking the valence bonds holding the molecules together. For example, radiation passing through a cell is most likely to strike water molecules. The breakdown products from these molecules may combine with oxygen to form bleaches, which in turn can break down protein molecules in the cell. One class of these proteins comprises the enzymes that not only play a role in nearly all biochemical reactions but also control cell division. Such inhibition of cell division may permit cells to grow to an abnormal size; when such a cell dies there is no replacement to fill the void in the tissue. If the cell has been altered so that its daughter cells are genetically different from the parent cell, the daughter cells may die before they reproduce themselves; they may continue to grow without dividing; or they may divide at a higher or lower rate than the parent cell.

Because of these possible effects, doctors and scientists have been concerned about the exposure of humans to radiation. A study of the effects of radiation on the human body indicates that the following organ and tissue groups are most affected by radioactivity: (1) blood and bone marrow, (2) lymphatic system, (3) skin and hair follicles, (4) alimentary canal, (5) adrenal glands, (6) thyroid gland, (7) lungs, (8) urinary tract, (9) liver and gallbladder, (10) bone, (11) eyes, and (12) reproductive organs. Although no permissible level for exposure of humans to radiation has been established, data reported in 1957 indicate that 25 roentgens cause no observable reaction, 50 roentgens produce nausea and vomiting, 400 to 500 roentgens give the individual a fifty-fifty chance of survival without medical care, and 650 roentgens are lethal.

1. In the first paragraph, the "metabolic rate" of a cell refers to the cell's:

   A. chemical activities.
   B. degree of specialization.
   C. stage of division.
   D. maturity.

2. Why is muscle tissue relatively unaffected by radiation?

   F. Its cells contain no water.
   G. It is highly specialized.
   H. It is protected by the bony skeleton.
   J. Its cells have a unique method of reproduction.

3. If radiation can *cause* cancer, as implied in the second paragraph, then which of the following best justifies the use of radiation in treating cancer?

   A. Cancer tissue is highly specialized, hence very sensitive to radiation.
   B. Only the cancer cells receive the radiation.
   C. Cancer cells divide relatively rapidly.
   D. The patient may die anyway, and desperate measures are appropriate in such instances.

4. Which of the following would the author probably consider the most serious long-range effect of exposure to radiation on human populations?

   F. Possible destruction of natural resources essential to survival
   G. Hereditary changes that might occur in the population

   H. The world's population increasing at a higher rate than the world's food supply
   J. The daughters of people exposed to radiation dying before they can have children

5. Why would a man in outer space be in greater danger from radiation than a man on earth?

   A. He would not be shielded from cosmic rays by the earth's atmosphere.
   B. The reduced pressure in a space vehicle inhibits cell division.
   C. Biochemical reactions essential to life cannot occur in outer space.
   D. In a weightless condition, cells are more vulnerable to radiation.

A series of experiments was designed to determine how bats are able to fly at night without colliding with obstacles. Bats were released in a closed room across which were strung fine wires adapted to register every time they were touched by one of the bats. The bats were released in the room under the following conditions:

Experiment 1

The room was well illuminated.

Experiment 2

The room was completely darkened.

Experiment 3

The room was darkened and the bats' eyes were sealed with soft black wax.

Experiment 4

The room was darkened, the bats' eyes were waxed closed, and numerous small radar transmitters were set in operation throughout the room.

Experiment 5

The radar transmitters were replaced with loudspeakers which emitted high-frequency sound waves. The room was dark and the bats' eyes were waxed closed.

Experiment 6

The lights were turned on and the bats, without wax on their eyes, were released while the loudspeakers were still producing high-frequency sounds.

On the basis of these experiments, the following observations were made:

In Experiments 1 through 4, the bats did not collide with the wires.

In Experiment 5 the bats seemed confused and frequently collided with the wires.

In Experiment 6 the bats were initially confused and collided with the wires; however, the number of collisions soon decreased.

6. Which conclusion, if any, can be drawn from Experiment 1?

F. Bats need light to see where they are going.
G. Bats need sound waves in order to avoid obstacles.
H. Bats can see in the dark.
J. None of the above

7. Which conclusion, if any, can be drawn from Experiment 4?

A. Bats evidently use some sort of radar to guide themselves.
B. The presence of radar waves has no apparent effect on the bats.
C. The presence of radar waves confuses the bats by obstructing their natural means of locating obstacles.
D. None of the above

8. Which experiment or group of experiments listed below shows that bats can ordinarily fly safely without using their eyes?

F. 3 only   H. 1 and 3
G. 1 and 2   J. 1, 2, and 3

9. Which of the following is true about the statement: *bats are nocturnal animals because daylight interferes with their ability to avoid obstacles?*

A. The statement agrees with the data.
B. The statement is contradicted by the data.

C. The statement cannot be judged without more data.
D. The statement is an experimental assumption.

The following questions are not based on a reading passage. You are to answer these questions on the basis of your background in the natural sciences.

---

10. The emergence of new strains of houseflies capable of withstanding the poisonous effects of the chemical DDT is an example of:

F. adaptation.
G. the Mendelian law.
H. implementation.
J. regeneration.

11. What is the main difference between a gas and a liquid?

A. Molecular weight
B. Shape of the particles
C. Geometric arrangement of the molecules
D. Average distance between the molecules

12. How were the coral reefs of tropical seas formed?

F. By the accumulation of the remains of small marine animals
G. By the erosion of islands by wind and sea
H. By the accumulation of salts and minerals precipitated by the sea
J. By undersea earthquakes

13. A warm breeze may seem cool to a bather who has just come from the water because:

A. water is a good conductor of heat.
B. moisture from the air condenses on the skin and cools it.
C. the evaporation of water from the wet skin absorbs heat.
D. water is denser than air.

ACT ANSWER KEY

Registering for the ACT
When registering for the ACT test, you will be asked to answer a Student Profile Section and an Interest Inventory. While it is not mandatory to complete these sections, it is to your advantage to do so. Working with your responses, ACT projects your strongest areas of interest and suggests several career areas that would complement them.

The Student Profile Section asks you to provide admission and enrollment data, biographical facts, and information about your academic and extracurricular achievements and aspirations, your high school curriculum, and grades.

The Interest Inventory is designed to measure the strength of your interest in six areas—social service, business contact, business detail, technical, science and creative arts—against the profiles of college seniors in a variety of majors. This kind of information can help when you plan your college program. Your Inventory report will also contain information that, when used in conjunction with a supplied handbook, shows what kinds of careers utilize the interests you have indicated.

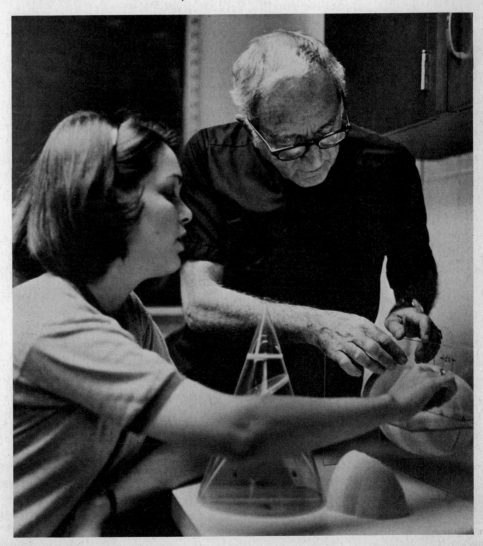

The ACT registration fee (under $10) covers the cost of sending one score report to you, one to your guidance counselor, and three to the institutions or scholarship agencies you name on your registration form. Additional and subsequent copies involve a small cost per copy.

ACT Educational Opportunity Service
When registering for the ACT you will be asked if you wish to participate in the Educational Opportunity Service. Under this arrangement, an institution with a particular educational or financial aid program can ask ACT to search (by computer) its files of registered students. Students who qualify for the program and who have the desired characteristics will receive a letter from ACT describing thc program and a card that they can send to the college for further information if the program interests them. This differs from the College Board system mentioned earlier, in which students are contacted directly by the colleges and organizations that receive their names.

Coaching for the SAT and ACT

Many studies have been conducted recently to determine whether coaching improves a student's performance on the SAT. One study, sponsored by the Federal Trade Commission, has determined that coaching does improve a student's performance on the test; other studies, particularly those conducted by the Educational Testing Service, minimize the effect that coaching has on the outcome of the SAT. Students who have the opportunity to receive coaching should keep in mind that coaching is usually expensive and will often cover many things that they could do on their own. On the other hand, students who receive coaching often feel more confident of themselves and, therefore, improve their chances of doing their best work on the test.

Truth in Testing Legislation

The controversy surrounding the use of testing in the college admissions process has centered around several legislative actions taken in the state of New York and pending in a number of other state legislatures as well as Congress. In essence, this legislation calls for the public release of test questions and answers on the SAT and other standardized tests. The testing agencies are resisting this legislation because they say it will have an effect on their ability to construct the tests. They contend that if each test and set of answers can be seen by the public, the test services will have to continually create, evaluate, and redesign test questions which they say will be prohibitively expensive and will reduce the number of times the tests can be offered.

College admissions officers and secondary school guidance counselors are divided on the issue of test disclosure; however, all agree that the tests are simply one aspect of a student's total performance in high school and should be taken as well as evaluated in that context.

How To:

1. Study for Admissions Tests
2. Prepare for the Test Day
3. Take the Exam
4. Use Your Scores as an Acceptance Yardstick

1. Study for Admissions Tests. There are firms and individuals that offer "review" courses for standardized tests—particularly the SAT—claiming that their course will substantially raise your test scores. Admissions directors and testing officials are not in favor of such plans, except to introduce you to the test materials, which you also can do yourself (at a substantially lower cost). Similarly, there is little that "cramming" for the tests can do to increase your basic skills. A good working vocabulary, a good grasp of grammar and sentence structure, and the ability to examine and solve problems logically are what you need most to take these tests.

The College Board Achievements are an exception to this don't-study rule. Because they test factual knowledge, it is possible (even preferable) to study for them. However, skimming madly through old textbooks and notes 24 hours before the exam is hardly studying. Start at least two weeks before the test date, and set aside a certain number of review days for each subject. You are much more likely to retain information if you review in this relaxed and thoughtful manner.

One of the biggest problems that students have been known to encounter is a sudden mental "freeze" when they are handed their exam.

Suddenly even the simplest directions become mind-boggling, questions blur, and valuable test-taking time is wasted. The best way to handle this problem is to counteract it in advance—by getting to know the kinds of questions asked, the format in which they will be stated, and the correct method for marking the answer sheet. Then when you are actually handed the exam on testing day, at least the territory will look familiar.

2. Prepare for the Test Day.   The night before a college admissions test is not the time for frantic activity, late-hour partying, or last-minute cramming. You'll need a clear head in the morning, so it is best to spend a quiet evening (far removed from any books or study guides) and go to bed early.

Set an alarm clock to wake you at an early enough hour to allow you time to have a sizable breakfast and get to the test site ten to fifteen minutes early. Before leaving home, remember to take your test admission ticket and two or three sharpened No. 2 pencils. (The computer that scores your test sheet will pick up only lead-pencil-marked responses.)

By arriving early, you will probably have your choice of seats in the testing room. For some people, this provides a psychological advantage.

3. Take the Exam.   Once you receive the signal to begin the first section of the exam, read the directions carefully. Even if you have studied sample test formats until they are permanently inscribed on your brain, don't take the directions for granted and skip over them. Ignoring a key phrase like "different from" or "most closely describing" could result in your answering the entire section in the wrong way. It is far better to take the time to make sure you understand the directions than to lose time erasing half your answers, or, worse yet, marking a whole set of answers in the wrong way.

Periodically—perhaps after every ten questions—check your answer sheet to make sure that your answers correspond to the questions. It is easy to forget to leave the appropriate number of blank spaces on the answer sheet if you have skipped a question or two. Frequent checking prevents the possibility of a serious error.

Pace yourself throughout each exam. Note how many questions are asked in the section you are working on and how much time you are given to complete them. Check when a quarter of the allotted time has passed to see if you have answered about 25 percent of the questions. If you have not, push on at a faster pace. As you work through each section, mark questions that you feel you can work on later but are too difficult to attack on your first pass. When you have gone through the section once, return to these questions and answer as many as possible. You will not be allowed to return to this section once the stated time has passed, so it is important to work as quickly as possible. Remember to check your place on the answer sheet carefully each time you fill in an answer block.

4. Use Your Scores as an Acceptance Yardstick.   Once you have received your SAT, Achievement, or ACT scores, you will have one further tool for measuring your chances of admission at the colleges that most interest you. Remember that scores are just one—and not the primary—factor in an admissions committee's decision. But also don't be unrealistic in your pursuits. If your SAT scores fall in the low 500s or your ACT is in the 20–22 range and your high school record consists primarily of Cs, it would not be wise to apply only to the most highly selective colleges where you would be competing with many students who have straight A averages and very high test scores.

Score ranges of freshmen at many of the nation's colleges and universities are available for you to study and use for comparison. (See the latest edition of *Peterson's Annual Guide to Undergraduate Study.*) Most colleges provide these figures to help you make application decisions—you may be surprised to see that a college you thought would be "safe" in fact has far higher average scores than yours, or you may be equally surprised to see that a university you didn't dream of applying to has 20 percent of its current freshmen precisely in your score range. You can be quite certain that a college with at least half of its freshmen in your test range will be interested in you as a candidate (provided that your high school record does not dramatically contradict your scores). Do not, however, restrict all your college choices to schools that have the largest percentage of students in your test range. Particularly if you are a bad tester and have an academic record that attests to higher academic abilities, aim higher, but also keep some realistic (and more certain) options open.

Financial Aid

Although cost may ultimately be an important factor in your ability to attend college, it should not be the pivotal point in your first round of selections. Rather, it is wiser to decide which colleges truly attract you for academic and personal reasons and then investigate possible ways of dealing with their costs.

For instance, it is true that attending a college 1,000 miles away from your home adds a sizable transportation cost to your basic expenses for tuition, room, and board—a cost you would not incur if you attended school closer to home. It is also true, however, that financial aid offices take transportation expenses into account when determining your need, and usually compute the price of two trips home each year into their aid packages. Thus, a California college might offer a scholarship package to a New York student that equaled or even more than compensated for the additional costs of travel.

Similarly, the relatively lower tuition at most public institutions frequently leads students with financial need to ignore private institutions. Yet, private institutions often award aid packages that make up for any differences in tuition.

Quite possibly, no expense will be the same for any two of the institutions you are considering. Some colleges do not charge for special lessons, for example, and those with larger libraries may require that you purchase fewer books. Even clothes will vary with the climate, and personal expenses will depend on the campus life-style in ways that range from the necessity of joining a fraternity to restrictions against smoking to the popularity of a relatively expensive sport like skiing. The total cost may well span a surprising range from college to college.

Once you have come up with fairly accurate projected costs, talk with your parents to see how much they feel they can realistically contribute to your education. Their estimate (which should reflect a level of support at least comparable to the amount they have been providing for you to date), plus your own expected earnings and savings, may cover the full cost at any of the colleges in your list. Most families, however, don't find this to be the case. Instead, the estimated cost usually exceeds the estimated contribution—a sign that it's time to begin investigating sources of financial aid.

Knowing your approximate need early in the application process gives you the time you'll need to explore various ways of closing the gap between costs and available funds. You may want to consider the lowered costs of living at home and commuting to a nearby school. You might accelerate your academic program or attend school year round. You could become a campus entrepreneur who sells a product or service to other students—usually through an established student agency. Finding colleges that allow you to pursue any of these plans takes time. Finding colleges or groups that grant outright aid takes more time. But ingenuity and industry can put even the highest-priced colleges within the financial reach of most qualified students.

The Ivy Bargain

A New Jersey student who needed full financial support reports: "For my first year at a public community college my financial need was $2250. The college provided me with a $500 work-study award and I needed a $1750 student loan. When I transferred to a private four-year college, *my financial need jumped to $5750. However, this private college awarded me a $1500 tuition-aid grant, a $2750 university scholarship, and a $500 work-study award, so that the loan I needed was actually reduced to $1100."*

Need Counts Most

While some scholarships are awarded for athletic prowess or academic merit alone, the vast majority are based on a qualified student's demonstrated financial need.

Need, of course, is a relative term and subject to interpretation. Just as college admissions officers rely on standardized tests to provide them with a nationwide standard for interpreting a student's academic promise, so do financial aid officers rely on nationwide financial need analysis services to determine equitably the financial need of each applicant. The two services used by most institutions are the College Scholarship Service (CSS) of Princeton, New Jersey, and the American College Testing Program Need Analysis Service of Iowa City, Iowa.

Standard Forms

Each of these services has devised a questionnaire to be completed by students and their parents. The responses are used according to a set formula to compute the amount a family can contribute to college costs and the amount they will need to make up the balance. These "need projections," which are sent only to the institutions and scholarship agencies you name when you fill out the form, are simply dollar amounts that are the results of numerical calculations. No recommendations are made about who should receive financial aid or why.

Some colleges routinely meet the need estimates computed by the analysis services, although they are under no obligation to do so. Most carefully evaluate each estimate, sometimes agreeing with, sometimes lowering, the amount that the service's formula has produced. All colleges agree that it is the responsibility of every family to contribute as much to their children's education as they possibly can, and all expect students to apply their own savings toward their college expenses.

Admissions offices go to great lengths to avoid letting the financial aid status of applicants interfere with the decision on admission, and financial aid offices at most colleges are kept separate from their admissions counterparts. This conscious separation of functions is intended to ensure that financial need has no bearing on an applicant's acceptance or rejection. Most colleges aim for the ideal of unbiased admissions followed by the granting of financial aid to all qualified accepted students. However, as the cost of higher education continues to rise, the ability to pay may conceivably become a factor in the decision to admit a student. All those who work in admissions try very hard to see that sufficient financial aid resources are available to avoid being influenced by financial aid factors. But students should be aware of the potential weight that may soon be given to this situation.

College catalogs usually give the deadlines for submitting required forms to a specified need analysis service. Note these dates for each of your selected colleges, record them on the applications flowchart on page 65, and be sure that your forms are completed and mailed on time. You and your parents may also have to complete additional financial aid forms prepared by the colleges for their own estimates.

College Scholarship Service

Institutions that require admissions test scores from the College Board Admissions Testing Program generally also require the College Scholarship Service's Financial Aid Form (FAF) for determining financial aid.

On the FAF (obtainable from your guidance counselor, through college financial aid offices, or by writing to: College Scholarship Service, Box 2700, Princeton, New Jersey 08541) your parents will be asked to itemize income, assets, and debts in accordance with their latest federal income tax form. You will also need to itemize your own savings and earnings. Working with this information—and taking into account such factors as family size, number of children in college, and parents' ages—CSS estimates the amount your parents should be able to contribute to your first year of college. That figure, plus the amount CSS determines that you should be able to contribute from your own earnings and savings, is your "family contribution" estimate. To arrive at this estimate, CSS uses what is known as "uniform methodology," which means that all Financial Aid Forms and information are evaluated in the same way with the same weight given to such factors as number of children, number of children in college, age of parents, etc. This ensures fairness in evaluating your need. The family contribution estimate is embodied in what is known as the Financial Aid Form Needs Analysis Report, which, along with the FAF, is forwarded to the institutions and scholarship agencies that you indicate should receive it. The initial FAF charge covers the cost of sending one need report to one institution. Additional reports are available at a small additional charge, as is a parents' copy of the report of the CSS estimated contribution. (Many colleges will require you to complete the Financial Aid Form Supplement, which is part of the basic FAF. Read the FAF instructions carefully to determine if you are applying to a college that requires the Supplement. If there is a question, call the financial aid office of the college to which you are applying and ask them.)

Upon receiving your Needs Analysis Report, financial aid officers subtract the CSS family contribution estimate from the figure they have determined to be the full cost of your attending their school for one year. Their cost estimate takes into account tuition, room and board, special fees, books, personal and medical expenses, and transportation costs. *If the anticipated cost is greater than your projected family contribution, you qualify for financial aid.* When budget permits, institutions generally try to meet this estimated need (or slightly exceed it) for each of their accepted students. However, each institution to which you apply for financial aid has final responsibility for determining your contribution. This figure may differ from the CSS estimated contribution.

Self-supporting students—those living independently of their parents' income—fill out a special section of the FAF outlining their own assets and debts. Some parental income data are required, however, if during the past year the student has (1) lived with his or her parents for more than six consecutive weeks, (2) received $750 or more in financial assistance from them, *or* (3) been claimed as a deduction on their last federal income tax form. CSS then computes a student—rather than a family—contribution figure, which it supplies to institutions in the Financial Aid Form Needs Analysis Report.

FAFs are not available to students until November 1 and cannot be filed until *after* January 1. Students who are applying for Early Decision may file what is known as the "Early Version" of the FAF but will be required to file the regular version later. In some cases parents or the student will be required to authorize CSS to obtain an official copy of their income tax return from the Internal Revenue Service. But you and your parents should not send copies of your income tax forms with the FAF to CSS. Income tax information will be kept confidential and may not be released to other colleges or agencies. Some colleges will request a copy of the income tax return from your parents. It should be sent directly to the college. Failure to do so may result in a denial of financial aid.

The College Board also offers an Early Financial Aid Planning Service (EFAPS), which is a kind of dress rehearsal for the real financial aid application process. EFAPS will give you and your family an idea of approximately how much financial aid you might expect if you attend colleges with different costs, and how much those colleges might ask you to pay. To use the service, the family completes a simple application called the Family Financial Reporting Form that asks 18 questions about the family's income, assets, and size. A small fee for processing is sent to CSS with the completed form. In return, the family receives a report of probable eligibility for aid from different sources plus a 21-page planning guide. Because this service gives an *early* reading, things may change by the time the student enters college. However, many people feel that an early estimate—even a rough one—helps avoid a rude financial awakening later.

The FAF is also the form by which students apply for the Basic Educational Opportunity Grant. Most financial aid offices will require financial aid recipients to apply also for the BEOG. With the FAF this is not difficult. Also, many state scholarship and loan programs use the FAF for students who may be eligible.

American College Testing Program Need Analysis Service
The Family Financial Statement (FFS) is the American College Testing Program's counterpart to the Financial Aid Form. Generally it is required by the same institutions that require ACT test scores in their admissions process.

The parental income, asset, and debt information required on the FFS is comparable to that required on the FAF, and, like its counterpart, the FFS computation of family contribution takes into consideration the parents' ages, family size, and number of children attending college. Students also supply details of their own finances. Self-supporting students simply complete the student portion of the FFS and leave the parental income portion blank. FFS forms are available from high school guidance counselors, participating college financial aid offices, and: ACT Student Assistance Program, 2201 North Dodge, P.O. Box 1000, Iowa City, Iowa 52243.

Once ACT has determined a family contribution figure, it reports it and other data to the institutions the student has stipulated on the Comprehensive Financial Aid Report (CFAR). Because the FFS (unlike the FAF) is not sent on to the financial aid office, if it contains references to any special circumstances surrounding parents' application for financial aid, they may want to describe these in a separate letter to the financial aid office.

Filling Out the Forms

While a first glance at any financial aid form may be alarming, there is no need to feel that only accountants' children have a chance of receiving aid. The figures and facts required on these applications are very much like those your parents report on their federal income tax form and many can simply be copied from their latest return. In fact, it is advisable to follow their federal tax figures precisely rather than rely upon estimates or rough guesses, for college financial aid offices can and do request parents to provide them with copies of IRS forms to substantiate information received from CSS and FFS, or to question the accuracy of information provided. Whether unintentional or deliberate, any serious discrepancies between figures reported on a tax form and those reported on your financial aid form may jeopardize your chances of receiving aid.

Income as an Admissions Criterion

While most colleges make a point of separating admissions applications and financial aid requests, Berea College in Kentucky specifically asks for family income information on its admissions application. Why? This Ap- *palachian college is dedicated to serving low-income students and thus reviews financial data as well as academic abilities when considering a student's application.*

Renewable Aid

Most institutions make their scholarship commitments for one year only, but they usually indicate that if you continue to have the same financial need and if your academic work continues to be satisfactory, they will do everything possible to extend your aid throughout your four college years. Usually, however, students are requested to file a new FAF or FFS each year.

Increases in tuition, room and board costs and other fees will be considered in the renewal of aid from year to year. Most colleges review financial aid recipients yearly to see if they have maintained the minimum academic average required for the renewal of particular types of awards, especially institutional scholarships or grants. Students should be aware of renewal requirements.

Students should also know that the total financial aid package they receive from a college usually includes what they are expected to receive from the Basic Educational Opportunity Grant. They cannot receive Basic Grant money in addition to their final package.

Some colleges, including Washington University in St. Louis, have begun tuition payment plans that allow students to pay all their tuition in advance, calculated at the freshman year rate and thereby guaranteeing that their tuition will not go up even if it is raised for others. Parents can borrow the money for this and repay it at a rate of interest that still makes the plan attractive. (Families interested in this should be sure of the repayment schedule and the loan obligation they incur in the event that the student does not complete his studies.) This is an interesting concept that may be more widely implemented as the cost of higher education goes up.

Helping Yourself

Some first-year students may wish to wait a year before undertaking campus employment. However, most financial aid offices do not hesitate to suggest work under the College Work-Study Program. These campus jobs usually take no more than 10 to 13 hours per week and are scheduled to allow the student maximum time for study. It is important to realize that financial aid offices, in general, subscribe to the self-help principle, meaning that they expect students to contribute as much as is reasonably possible toward the cost of their education—whether through employment during the school year, summer jobs, or loans. Because of this, even if your need continues at its original level, it is quite possible that an institution will slightly reduce your scholarship in successive years and instead offer you a campus job or loan to compensate for the difference.

Financial Aid Packages

Financial aid offices are charged with administering institutional scholarship funds, usually on the basis of considered need and merit. Most colleges itemize the qualifying criteria for these scholarships in their catalogs and supply information on how to apply for these outright grants of money. Scholarships, however, are actually only one segment of the financial aid picture. Since few, if any, institutions have the funds to meet all their students' needs with scholarship dollars, and since most believe a student should contribute as much money as possible to his or her education, most financial aid offices offer financial aid "packages."

The elements financial aid officers work with when compiling aid packages are scholarships (sometimes called "grants-in-aid"), low-interest loans, and federal work-study awards.

Either through their own institutional loan funds or through federally insured loan plans, colleges are able to offer loans to students at terms well below the usual lending rate. All students are eligible for federal interest benefits on such loans. By this arrangement, the government pays the interest on the loan as long as the student is in college or graduate school, and allows the student a nine-month grace period following graduation before repayment must begin.

FINANCIAL AID AWARDS FOR FALL 1979 FRESHMEN AT TULANE UNIVERSITY					
	Applicants		Freshmen Enrolled Fall 1979 with Scholarship		
				Amt. of Scholarship + Loan + Employment	
Family Income	% Awarded Aid	% of Awards Including Scholarship	Number of Recipients	Average	Range
$ 0- 7,999	76%	98%	15	$6,006	$4,526-6,876
8,000-11,999	80%	89%	32	$4,987	$ 650-7,126
12,000-15,999	75%	88%	36	$4,930	$ 750-6,826
16,000-19,999	86%	89%	39	$4,661	$1,900-6,326
20,000-23,999	76%	92%	28	$4,315	$2,200-7,126
24,000-27,999	85%	89%	32	$3,539	$ 700-6,050
28,000-35,999	74%	89%	43	$3,187	$ 500-5,276
36,000 +	51%	85%	23	$3,051	$1,000-4,626
Totals	73%	89%	248	$4,235	$ 500-7,126

Note: These figures do not reveal family circumstances, which are of course critical in determining the parental contribution.

Federally funded work-study opportunities annually help over half a million students meet the cost of their college education. Each year colleges identify campus jobs—receptionist, cafeteria worker, laboratory assistant, etc.—that they wish to make available to students with financial need. The federal government then supplies 80 percent of the money for the salaries for these jobs, while the college contributes 20 percent.

Students should carefully consider the components of each financial aid package they are offered, not just the "bottom line." The total amount of money received will include as many as four or five different forms of aid. Students should understand how much of this is scholarship, which does not have to be repaid, how much is loan, which it is the recipient's responsibility to repay under the stipulations of the loan agreement, and how much is in the form of a job.

Cooperative Work-Study Programs

Cooperative work-study programs are an integral part of many institutions' academic rather than financial aid plan. Hundreds of institutions across the nation offer these plans, in which students formally combine employment and study. At some colleges, such as Northeastern and Antioch, students are *required* to alternate terms of full-time study with terms of full-time employment. Other colleges integrate "parallel" cooperative plans into a weekly schedule, with study in the mornings and work in the afternoons. Not only does cooperative employment make college possible for many students who might not otherwise find it financially feasible, but also the work experience gives students a head start in locating permanent employment. If your cooperative experience is with a federal agency, you do not have to take the Civil Service exam in order to work for the Government later. Each cooperative plan works in a slightly different manner; however, most require five years for completion of the bachelor's degree. Further information on institutions that offer cooperative work-study programs can be obtained from: the National Commission for Cooperative Education, 360 Huntington Avenue, Boston, Massachusetts 02115.

Loans

Guaranteed Student Loan (GSL) Program

This program enables qualified students to borrow up to $2500 a year directly from a bank, credit union, savings and loan institution, or other lending agency. The loan is guaranteed by a state or private nonprofit agency or insured by the federal government. The federal government will pay the interest on the loan until you begin repaying the principal. Repayment begins six months after you leave college. Students are assured of a five-year minimum repayment period, which may be extended up to ten years if the lender is willing. Recipients are charged a maximum of 9% simple interest and must repay a minimum of $30 a month. Service in the Armed Forces, Peace Corps, or VISTA allows students to defer repayment for up to three years. Repayment may also be deferred during enrollment for further periods of full-time study at an eligible graduate school. For further information on state-sponsored loan programs, contact the state departments of education in the list beginning on page 113.

Federally Insured Student Loan (FISL) Program

Students living in the twenty-four states that do not operate their own guaranteed student loan program are eligible for FISL loans. In most cases, terms and conditions are comparable to those of the Guaranteed Student Loan Program. For further information contact: Office of Postsecondary Education, U.S. Department of Education, 400 Maryland Ave., S.W., Washington, D.C. 20202.

National Direct Student Loan (NDSL) Program

Financed by the federal government, NDSL loans are obtainable by application through a participating college financial aid office. Undergraduates (enrolled at least half-time in a participating institution) are eligible for up to $6000 in loan funds during their undergraduate years. No interest is charged students while they are in college, and repayment (at 4% interest) begins six months after students graduate or leave college. A deferment program for Armed Forces, Peace Corps, and VISTA participation is available. Teachers in designated overseas, low-income, or special education schools are eligible for partial concellation of their loan. For further information, contact the financial aid office of the colleges to which you are applying.

United States Aid Funds

USA Funds is a nonprofit agency that guarantees educational loans made by lending institutions. USA Funds administers state loan programs for

Alaska, Delaware, Hawaii, Maine, Maryland, Nevada, and the Virgin Islands and also endorses loans through participating institutions. Qualified undergraduates may borrow up to $2500 annually ($7500 maximum) at a 7% simple interest rate. Many recipients of these funds qualify for federal interest benefits. USA Funds also guarantees educational loans to parents up to $3000 per year at a maximum 9% simple interest. For further information contact: USA Funds Inc., Executive Office, 200 East 42nd Street, New York, New York 10017.

Federal Loans for Designated Professions

To encourage students to train for professions in need of more manpower throughout the nation, the federal government makes available special loan funds. Student nurses in full-time or half-time programs of study are eligible for up to $2500 per year ($10,000 maximum) under the Nursing Student Loan Program. Repayment begins one year after graduation or departure from college. Through active duty in the uniformed services or the Peace Corps or through further study, a recipient can defer repayment up to five years. Up to 85 percent of a nursing education loan may be canceled for employment in designated areas having a shortage of nurses. For further information contact your guidance counselor or: Bureau of Health Manpower, National Institutes of Health, 9000 Rockville Pike, Bethesda, Maryland 20014.

Students enrolled in law enforcement programs at institutions designated by the Law Enforcement Assistance Administration are eligible for Law Enforcement Education Program loans of up to $2200 per academic year. These loans plus any interest may be excused at the rate of 25 percent for each year of public law enforcement work following graduation. For further information contact: Law Enforcement Assistance Administration, U.S. Department of Justice, 633 Indiana Avenue, N.W., Washington, D.C. 20530.

Private Sources

Several companies make loan funds available to employees to cover the cost of their children's education. Among the first loan sources you should investigate are your parents' employers. It would also be advisable to check with the business, labor, civic, educational, and religious groups identified in the publications listed at the end of this chapter for other possible loan sources.

Your parents may also be members of credit unions that make educational loans. Money may be borrowed in two ways from a credit union: (1) as a partial amount each semester or quarter or (2) as a total amount at the time of college entry. In the latter case the extra funds can be deposited in an interest-bearing credit union share account.

Local banks also make low-interest educational loans to parents; however, they usually do not contain the deferred repayment provisions available in loans to students.

Probably the most expensive form of loans is offered through finance companies. However, because some families have not established bank credit ratings, they do not have any alternative source of college funding. Several finance companies like Educational Funds Inc. and Tuition Plan Inc. have been set up specifically to disburse educational loan funds and often work in conjunction with college financial aid offices to publicize and administer their loans. Simple interest on finance company loans fluctuates with the general economy and should be checked carefully.

Scholarships, Grants, Benefits

Basic Educational Opportunity Grants (BEOG)

Undergraduates with exceptional financial need who are attending school at least half-time and who are working toward an eligible degree or certificate in an eligible institution can apply for federal BEOGs of $200 to $1800 or more per year. The BEOG program is an "entitlement" program, which means that no eligible student will be denied a grant. To determine your eligibility, you must complete and file an Application for Determination of Basic Grant Eligibility. Copies of the form are available from your high school guidance counselor or from: Basic Grants, P. O. Box 84, Washington, D.C. 20044.

Supplemental Educational Opportunity Grants (SEOG)

SEOG provides grants to undergraduates attending school at least half-time who have exceptional financial need. Grants are made in amounts ranging from $200 to $2000 per year. Applications for SEOGs are available from college financial aid officers. If you are selected for an SEOG, your college must match the amount of your grant in the form of a scholarship, loan, or part-time job.

Army, Navy, and Air Force ROTC Scholarships

Two-, three-, and four-year scholarships are offered at selected institutions to encourage students to become military, naval, or air force officers upon graduation. ROTC scholarships can cover tuition, fees, books, uniforms, and other personal expenses. Each program has different stipulations; however, the grants are generally repaid through two to four years of military service after graduation. For further information contact: ROTC Scholarships, U.S. Army Training and Document Command, Fort Monroe, Virginia 23651; Chief of Naval Personnel, Washington, D.C. 20370; or Air Force ROTC, Maxwell Air Force Base, Alabama 36112.

Federal Service Academy Appointments

The nation's five service academies—the U.S. Military Academy, the U.S. Naval Academy, the U.S. Coast Guard Academy, the U.S. Air Force Academy, and the U.S. Merchant Marine Academy—provide free undergraduate educations to qualified men and women. Appointments to the Military, Naval, Air Force, and Merchant Marine academies are made through presidential, vice-presidential, or congressional nomination (based on students' academic records, physical fitness, and qualifying test scores). Coast Guard cadets are admitted on the basis of competitive examinations, and congressional nomination is not required. Graduates of the service academies receive a commission and must serve up to five years of active duty. For further information contact: Director of Admissions, U.S. Military Academy, West Point, New York 10966; Dean of Admissions, U.S. Naval Academy, Annapolis, Maryland 21402; Director of Admissions, U.S. Coast Guard Academy, New London, Connecticut 06320; Registrar, U.S. Air Force Academy, Colorado Springs, Colorado 80840; Director of Admissions, U.S. Merchant Marine Academy, Kings Point, New York 11024.

Social Security Benefits
Dependent unmarried children (aged 18-22) of eligible retired, disabled, or deceased parents are entitled to monthly cash educational benefits. Such funds can be applied toward full-time study at any four-year, two-year, or other approved institution. For further information contact your local Social Security office or: Office of Public Affairs, Social Security Administration, U.S. Department of Health and Human Services, Baltimore, Maryland 21235.

Veterans Benefits
Eligible veterans may receive monthly allowances for study at approved educational institutions at and above the secondary level. Generally, eligible veterans and servicemen on active duty with more than 181 days of active duty after January 31, 1955, may receive up to thirty-six months of assistance. In addition, the children, wives, and widows of veterans whose death or permanent disability was service-connected are eligible for up to thirty-six months of educational benefits. Wives or children of servicemen missing in action or prisoners of war are also eligible for assistance. However, there are time limits for eligibility. For further information contact any regional Veterans Administration office or: Veterans Administration, 27H, Washington, D.C. 20420.

Railroad Retirement Benefits
Children of deceased railroad employees who were insured for survivor benefits under the Railroad Retirement Act of 1966 are eligible for educational benefits if they are between 18 and 22 and engaged in full-time study. For further information contact: U.S. Railroad Retirement Board, 844 Rush Street, Chicago, Illinois 60611.

Native American Grants
The Bureau of Indian Affairs administers a grant program based on need for Native Americans who are at least one quarter American Indian, Eskimo, or Aleutian. Applications for aid are handled by college financial aid offices. For further information contact: Bureau of Indian Affairs, Indian Resource Center, P.O. Box 1788, 123 Fourth Street, S.W., Albuquerque, New Mexico 87103.

State Grants
Each state administers a variety of scholarship and grant programs. Some offer incentive grants, tuition aid grants, tuition waivers, and other cash awards. A number disburse their own Educational Opportunity Funds to economically disadvantaged students. Eligibility for state aid is usually

determined by need plus scholastic record, although some grants may also be based on competitive examinations, citizenship, specialized abilities, potential for college achievement, or other criteria. Many states also give grants for study in a particular field such as teaching, social work, environmental studies, mining, home economics, and forestry. For further information on state grants—in your home state and the state in which you plan to study—contact the appropriate office listed below.

ALABAMA
Student Assistance Program
Alabama Commission on Higher Education
One Court Square
Montgomery 36104

ALASKA
Student Financial Aid Division
Pouch F
State Office Building
Juneau 99801

ARIZONA
Commission for Postsecondary Education
Suite 115
1650 West Alameda Drive
Tempe 85028

ARKANSAS
Department of Higher Education
1301 West 7th Street
Little Rock 72201

CALIFORNIA
Student Aid Commission
1410 Fifth Street
Sacramento 94814

COLORADO
Commission on Higher Education
1550 Lincoln Street, Room 210
Denver 30203

CONNECTICUT
Student Financial Assistance Commission
P.O. Box 1320
Hartford 06101

DELAWARE
Delaware Post-Secondary Education Commission
1228 North Scott #1
Wilmington 19801

DISTRICT OF COLUMBIA
Office of Educational Assistance
1329 East Street, NW, Room 1005
Washington 20004

FLORIDA
Student Financial Assistance Commission
Knott Building
Tallahassee 32304

GEORGIA
Higher Education Assistance Authority
9 LaVista Perimeter Park, #110
2187 Northlake Parkway
Tucker 30084

HAWAII
Hawaii State Postsecondary Education Commission
Bachman Hall, Room 124F
2444 Dole Street
Honolulu 96822

IDAHO
State Board of Education
650 West State Street
Boise 83720

ILLINOIS
State Scholarship Commission
102 Wilmot Road
Deerfield 60015

INDIANA
State Student Assistance Commission
219 North Senate Avenue
Indianapolis 46202

IOWA
College Aid Commission
201 Jewett Building
9th and Grand
Des Moines 50309

KANSAS
Board of Regents, State of Kansas
Merchants National Bank Tower
Topeka 66612

KENTUCKY
Higher Education Assistance Authority
691 Teton
Frankfort 40601

LOUISIANA
Governor's Special Commission on Education
  Services
P.O. Box 44127
Capitol Station
Baton Rouge 70804

MAINE
Division of Higher Education Services
Department of Education and Cultural Services
Education Building
Augusta 04333

MARYLAND
State Scholarship Board
2100 Guilford Avenue
Baltimore 21218

MASSACHUSETTS
Board of Higher Education
31 Saint James Avenue
Boston 02116

MICHIGAN
Higher Education Assistance Authority
P.O. Box 30008
Lansing 48909

MINNESOTA
Minnesota Higher Education
Division of Financial Aid
901 Capitol Square Building
St. Paul 55101

MISSISSIPPI
Governor's Office of Job Development and Training
P.O. Box 22808
Jackson 39205

MISSOURI
Department of Higher Education
1130 East Elm
Jefferson City 66101

MONTANA
Montana Board of Regents of Higher Education
33 South Last Chance Gulch
Helena 59601

NEBRASKA
Nebraska Coordinating Commission for
    Postsecondary Education
301 Centennial Mall, South
P.O. Box 95005
Lincoln 68509

NEVADA
Board of Regents, University of Nevada System
405 Marsh Avenue
Reno 89509

NEW HAMPSHIRE
New Hampshire Postsecondary Education
    Commission
66 South Street
Concord 03301

NEW JERSEY
State Board of Higher Education
Office of Student Assistance
225 West State Street
Trenton 08625

NEW MEXICO
Board of Educational Finance
1068 Cerrillos Road
Santa Fe 87503

NEW YORK
Higher Education Services Corporation
Tower Building
Empire State Plaza
Albany 12255

NORTH CAROLINA
State Education Assistance Authority
P.O. Box 2688
Chapel Hill 37514

NORTH DAKOTA
Student Financial Assistance Agency
Tenth Floor, Capitol Building
Bismarck 58505

OHIO
Ohio Board of Regents
Student Assistance Office
30 East Broad Street
Columbus 43215

OKLAHOMA
Oklahoma State Regents for Higher Education
500 Education Building
State Capitol Complex
Oklahoma City 73105

OREGON
State Scholarship Commission
1445 Willamette Street
Eugene 97401

PENNSYLVANIA
Higher Education Assistance Authority
Towne House
Harrisburg 17102

RHODE ISLAND
Higher Education Assistance Authority
274 Weybosset Street
Providence 02903

SOUTH CAROLINA
Tuition Grants Agency
411 Kennan Building
Columbia 29201

SOUTH DAKOTA
Office of the Secretary
Department of Education
Kneip Building
Pierre 57501

TENNESSEE
Student Assistance Corp.
707 Main Street
Nashville 37206

TEXAS
Coordinating Board, Texas College and
    University System
P.O. Box 12788, Capitol Station
Austin 78711

UTAH
State Board of Regents
807 East South Temple Street
Salt Lake City 84102

VERMONT
Student Assistance Corporation
Five Burlington Square
Burlington 05401

VIRGINIA
State Council of Higher Education
700 Fidelity Building
Ninth and Main Streets
Richmond 23219

WASHINGTON
Council for Postsecondary Education
908 East Fifth Avenue
Olympia 98504

WEST VIRGINIA
Higher Education Grant Program
950 Kanawha Boulevard East
Charleston 25301

WISCONSIN
Higher Education Aids Board
150 East Kilman Street
Madison 53702

WYOMING
Community College Commission
1720 Carey Avenue
Cheyenne 82002

AMERICAN SAMOA
Department of Education
Pago Pago 96799

GUAM
Student Financial Assistance Office
University of Guam
P.O. Box EK
Agana 96910

PUERTO RICO
Council on Higher Education
Box F, U.P.R. Station
Rio Piedras 00931

TRUST TERRITORY
Student Assistance Office
Headquarters Department of Education
Saipan, Mariana Islands 96950

VIRGIN ISLANDS
Department of Education—PPS
P.O. Box 630, Charlotte Amalie
St. Thomas 00801

Scholarships in Designated Professions

Architecture. The American Institute of Architects sponsors a scholarship program for students enrolled in accredited architecture programs. For further information contact: AIA Scholarship Program, 1735 New York Avenue, N.W., Washington, D.C. 20006.

Communications. Scholarships available to students enrolling in journalism and communications programs are outlined in two publications. The Newspaper Fund, P.O. Box 300, Princeton, New Jersey 08540, publishes a "Journalism Scholarship Guide," which lists sources of more than $2-million in financial aid. "Awards, Citations, and Scholarships in Radio and Television" lists similar scholarship opportunities and is available from the National Association of Broadcasters, 1771 N Street, N.W., Washington, D.C. 20036.

Dental Health. The American Fund for Dental Health offers scholarships to students studying dental laboratory technology, dental laboratory teacher training, dental hygiene, and dental assistant teacher education. The fund also offers dental scholarships beginning with the final year of predental studies for needy members of disadvantaged minority groups. For more information contact: American Fund for Dental Health, Suite 1630, 211 East Chicago Avenue, Chicago, Illinois 60611.

Education. Students who have completed at least two years of college preparation for a teaching career may apply to the Teacher Corps. If accepted, they will be placed in part-time teaching jobs (usually in disadvantaged areas) and will receive a grant covering the cost of their university training plus a living allowance.

Undergraduates enrolled part-time or full-time in programs concerning education of the handicapped are eligible for federal traineeships or assistantships. For further information contact: Office of Special Education and Rehabilitative Services, Department of Education, 400 Maryland Avenue, S.W., Washington, D.C. 20202.

The American Association for Health, Physical Education, and Recreation sponsors scholarships for students preparing for a teaching career in health, physical education, and recreation. For further information contact: AAHPER, 1201 16th Street, N.W., Washington, D.C. 20036.

Engineering. The National Society of Professional Engineers administers twenty four-year scholarships and six $1000 grants for graduating high school seniors who are planning engineering careers. For further information contact: NSPE Educational Foundation, 2029 K Street, N.W., Washington, D.C. 20006. In addition, many state engineering societies and local chapters offer awards to outstanding undergraduates.

Home Economics. Some affiliated state associations of the American Home Economics Association award scholarships. State associations are listed annually in the October issue of the *Journal of Home Economics*, which is in most school libraries.

Nursing/Allied Health Professions. The Health Resources Division of the new Health and Human Services Department has scholarships and traineeships for students preparing for nursing and allied health careers. For further information contact: Bureau of Health Manpower, National Institutes of Health, 9000 Rockville Pike, Bethesda, Maryland 20014.

Junior and senior year students enrolled in occupational therapy and physical therapy programs are eligible for federally funded traineeships in vocational rehabilitation. For further information contact: Rehabilitation

Services Administration, Office of Special Education and Rehabilitative Services, U.S. Department of Education, 330 C Street, S.W., Washington, D.C. 20201.

Other nursing-related scholarship opportunities are listed in "Scholarships and Loans—Beginning Education in Nursing" available from the National League for Nursing, 10 Columbus Circle, New York, New York 10019.

Science. The Westinghouse Science Talent Search annually offers forty scholarship awards to students who have demonstrated exceptional abilities in the sciences through a senior year high school science project and outstanding high school record. Awards range from $250 to $10,000 (first prize). For further information contact: Westinghouse Science Talent Search, Science Service, 1719 N Street, N.W., Washington, D.C. 20036.

National Merit Scholarships
Each year the National Merit Scholarship Program (explained in more detail on page 74) provides one-time $1000 scholarships and awards ranging from $250 to $1500 or more per year for up to four years. The latter scholarships must be renewed each year. Scholarship winners are selected through a competitive examination usually administered in the junior year of high school and through personal recommendations. NMSC also conducts the National Achievement Scholarship Program for Outstanding Negro Students, a scholarship competition specifically for black students. For further information on both programs, contact: National Merit Scholarship Corporation, One American Plaza, Evanston, Illinois 60201.

National Honor Society Scholarships
Students who are members of their high school national honor societies are eligible for $1000 college scholarships. Awards are made on the basis of demonstrated leadership, scholarship, character, and service, not on need. For further information contact your high school principal or honor society adviser.

National Scholarship Service and Fund for Negro Students
The NSSFNS maintains a limited scholarship fund for students in all minority and low-income groups who are registered with the service's advisory and referral service (designed to help them locate institutions where they are likely to be admitted and obtain financial aid). Scholarship grants range from $200 to $600 per year, are available on the basis of need, and are renewable. For further information contact: NSSFNS, 1776 Broadway, New York, New York 10019.

General Motors Scholarship Program
General Motors annually offers scholarship grants to students at 123 participating colleges. Grants depend on need, and preference is given to students who wish to have careers in industry. For further information contact: GM Scholarship Program, 8-163 General Motors Building, Detroit, Michigan 48202.

Reference Sources

College Blue Book: Scholarships, Fellowships, Grants and Loans. 4th ed., 1979. Macmillan Information. Macmillan Publishing Co., 866 Third Avenue, New York, New York 10022.

Financial Aids for Higher Education 1980-81 Catalogue. 9th ed. Oreon Keeslar. Wm. C. Brown Co., 2460 Kerper Boulevard, Dubuque, Iowa 52001.

Financing College Education: A Handbook for Students and Families. 1980. Kenneth A. Kohl and Irene C. Kohl. Harper & Row, 10 East 53 Street, New York, New York 10022.

Need a Lift? 1980. American Legion, P.O. Box 1055, Indianapolis, Indiana 46206.

The Official College Entrance Examination Board Guide to Financial Aid for Students and Parents. 1979. Elizabeth W. Suchar with Phyllis Harris. Simon & Schuster, Inc., 1230 Avenue of the Americas, New York, New York 10020.

Your Own Financial Aid Factory: The Guide to Locating College Money. 1980. Robert Leider. Peterson's Guides/Octameron, P.O. Box 2123, Princeton, New Jersey 08540.

HOW TO:

1. Estimate Your Financial Need

While the dollar figure that most students and parents hunt for first in a college's admissions literature is the cost of tuition, this is only one—and in some cases not the largest—item in your education budget. Numerous other factors will affect the price you pay for your education. In order to see clearly the amount of money you will need at each institution you are considering, it is best to itemize your estimated expenses early in the application process. You can set up a comparison chart with the following costs, which should be considered basic.

Expenses	College A	College B	College C	College D
Tuition:				
Room:				
Board (if you intend to live at home but your parents expect you to contribute to your room and board, don't ignore this in your calculations):				
Miscellaneous fees (student activity, laboratory, certain courses such as music):				
Books and Supplies:				
Transportation to and from home (two round trips a year minimum, or daily commutation):				
Personal living expenses (clothes, laundry, social activities, entertainment, toiletries, snacks, records, gasoline and related car costs, etc.):				
TOTAL:				

Financial aid regulations and programs have grown in complexity every year. The methods and the standards for awarding aid also change from year to year. To be the best consumer of higher education you need to stay abreast of the latest developments in the financial aid picture. Changes in government regulations may affect your award. Changes in your college's financial aid philosophy may also have an effect on your financial aid situation. Stay informed and get the latest information from your guidance counselor and from the financial aid offices at the colleges to which you expect to apply.

Special Admissions Situations

Colleges today realize that no single admissions plan can adequately serve the needs of all applicants. Some students, for example, have definitely decided on their first-choice college as early as their junior year and do not want to wait until the following spring to learn of their acceptance or rejection there. An increasing number of high schools offer courses equivalent to those at the college level, and students from these schools feel sure they will find their freshman year of college repetitive. There are students who definitely plan to go to college but would like to take some time out—possibly for work or travel—before enrolling. And still others are adults who have been out of high school for some time and require a special admissions procedure.

The following special admissions programs—once rarities—are now found quite regularly at institutions throughout the country. If any of them appeal to you or offer solutions to a concern you have about college, check the college profiles beginning on page 147 to see which institutions offer the kinds of programs that are in line with your plans.

Early Decision

Early decision is designed for students who have evaluated their college choices at an early date and have determined their first-choice institution.

Colleges offer this admissions service to students who wish to resolve their college search relatively early in their senior year of high school. Under this plan, students submit their applications in the fall of their senior year with the understanding that they will receive a definite decision on their acceptance or rejection by early January. Some colleges will accept early decision applications only from students who apply to no other institution. Others allow students to apply to several colleges with the restriction that, if they are accepted, they must withdraw any applications they have submitted to other colleges and must send an enrollment deposit. You should use an early decision plan with care, reserving it for your top-choice college.

Early decision candidates are reviewed well before a college has received the majority of its applications, and admissions officers naturally look for students with exceptional records—students who would clearly stand out among all of that year's applicants.

When you have narrowed your college choices to a manageable, reasonably certain number by the beginning of your senior year, and your first-choice institution offers an early decision plan, consider submitting an early decision application. First, however, assess your academic and extracurricular record realistically to see if you are a strong enough candidate for such a highly competitive screening. If the answer is yes, by all means apply. If you are not accepted early, all is not lost, for students who are rejected as early decision applicants are usually reconsidered later with the rest of the applicant pool. Early Action, on the other hand, generally lets you know if you are accepted, does not require you to enroll at the college that accepts you, but does *not* consider you again later if you are rejected.

Rolling Admissions

An increasing number of institutions review admissions applications on a rolling (continuing) basis. At these colleges, a committee of admissions officers reads each candidate's application and makes a decision as soon as a group of applications has accumulated—perhaps as often as once a week.

Each student is evaluated both in relation to other students in that group and in relation to the applicants already accepted or rejected. Therefore it is to your advantage to *apply early* under a rolling admissions plan: There will be fewer applicants and less competition.

Early Admission

Students who have outstanding high school records or are attending schools with especially rigorous curricula are allowed by a number of colleges to apply for college entrance directly after their junior year. Skipping a year at this level is considered a serious move in education, and admissions officers look for signs of both academic and emotional maturity in early admission applicants as indications that they can handle the transition from high school to college.

Early admission is not a plan to be considered at the last minute. You must decide in the beginning of your sophomore year of high school if you wish to pursue this course so that you take the necessary courses as well as the required standardized tests in time.

Midyear or January Admission

A number of colleges and universities are now offering some applicants the option of accepting admission to a class that starts in January or in the second semester instead of in the fall. Often, these are applicants who are on the waiting list for regular fall admission but have no guarantee of getting in for that term. January-admission candidates may stay on the waiting list during the summer if they wish; in this way they assure themselves of a place in either case.

If you are offered such an option, you should determine what is required and learn about your option before accepting. (Particularly look into whether required fall classes will be offered again in the spring.) There are usually special orientation programs for January students, and you will probably be given on-campus housing options. It may even be possible for you to attend another college during the fall and transfer your earned credits to the college you enter in January, thus losing little if any real time.

Deferred Entrance

For decades it was routinely accepted among educators that students should move directly from high school to college without interruption. However, in recent years this traditional move has been increasingly questioned—especially by students. In response, colleges have initiated deferred entrance programs that give students breathing space between high school and college but also guarantee them a place in a college class when they are ready to begin college study.

Typically the plan works as follows: Once accepted by a college, the student is given the option of deferring admission for up to three years. If the student chooses this plan, he or she simply submits an enrollment deposit to reserve a space in a future class.

The years between high school and college can be used for work to help finance college study, for travel, independent study, or even a general sorting out of goals. Often students report that experiences encountered in this period have a significant influence on their later classroom work.

Because it usually is not necessary to indicate your intention to defer your admission when you file your college applications, you probably will not need to commit yourself to this program until after acceptance. It is important, however, to make sure that this program is offered by the colleges you have selected if there is a strong chance you will want to take advantage of it.

Advanced Standing

Many colleges permit students to receive "advanced standing" in some or all subjects as a result of superior past work or unusually high test scores. Such students can skip over certain typical general-purpose or survey freshman courses. At some colleges advanced standing enables students to accelerate work toward their degree, while other colleges offer the program only so that students will not have to take courses that repeat their high school work.

Advanced Placement Courses

Well over half of the nation's colleges give academic credit to students who have taken designated advanced placement courses in high school. "AP" courses are more demanding than the usual high school courses and are recommended only for academically superior students. Since only about 15 percent of the nation's high schools offer such courses to juniors and seniors, you may not be presented with the opportunity to take them. However, if they are offered by your high school, and if your past academic work indicates that you could handle the more challenging level, it would be advisable to enroll.

Your proficiency in the AP courses is measured by standardized Advanced Placement tests given once a year (in May). Tests are scored on a five-point scale. Most colleges accepting AP credits will automatically recognize scores of 4 or 5 as fulfilling the requirements of college-level courses, and some will also accept 3s. Thus, an acceptable score in an AP course will usually exempt you from 6 to 8 semester hours or 10 to 12 quarter hours of college classes.

College-Level Examination Program

CLEP was established in 1965 as a national system for awarding college credit for life experiences as opposed to institutional academic course work. It is designed to give formal recognition for knowledge acquired outside the usual educational channels—on the job, through travel, through independent study, or in other nontraditional ways.

Two types of CLEP tests are offered. There are five general examinations—English composition, mathematics, natural sciences, social sciences, and humanities—which test basic knowledge equivalent to what is required for entrance into many freshman or sophomore college courses. Subject examinations (in 41 areas) are roughly comparable to the final exam that would be given in undergraduate courses in those subjects. By scoring high enough on either type of test, you may be able to receive college credit and thereby gain a head start on your degree.

For further information contact: CLEP, College Entrance Examination Board, 888 Seventh Avenue, New York, New York 10019, or your state board of education.

Hope for Those with Low GPAs

Several colleges confirm that a student's high school record is not a definitive indicator of future academic success or failure, but Gonzaga University in Spokane, Washington, has done something about it. Each year the University accepts into its "New Start Program" a limited number of students whose high school records (in the 2.0 to 2.49 range) would not normally qualify them for admission. Acceptance into the program hinges largely on recommendations, standardized test scores, and evidence of achievement in the senior year.

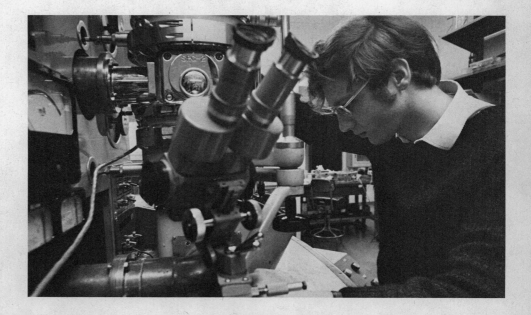

Applying from Another Country

Natives of another country and Americans living abroad face a more complex and difficult college admissions process than students who live in the continental United States. In addition to considering where to apply and what type of school to choose, students living outside the United States must deal with these additional concerns:

—Sheer distance and the problems attendant upon unreliable or delayed mail delivery.

—Differences in educational systems, calendar, curriculum, and grading, and the comparison of these different systems with the American model. Grading scales in some countries appear to indicate weak performance when they actually represent strong academic achievement.

—Language differences. Even Americans living abroad are often influenced in their performance on standardized tests and classroom work by the absence of daily exposure to colloquial English.

—Students living abroad may take external examinations that are unfamiliar to American admissions officers.

—Officials at schools outside the United States often have little understanding of the types of information American colleges need for admissions evaluations. They may provide the wrong information or inadequate information, which results in delays and misunderstandings.

—Some U.S. colleges with sagging domestic enrollments are using high-pressure tactics to persuade international students to attend their institution regardless of a suitable "match" of student and college. International students should be extremely wary of sales pitches or "guaranteed" acceptances.

Being forewarned of the problems should help students from overseas to deal with the American admissions process effectively and efficiently.

Basic Steps

1. Begin your college admissions process as early as possible. In the junior year, about 1½ years before you wish to enroll, is a good time to write for information. By writing early, you will give yourself enough time in which to complete the requirements of the colleges to which you apply. Foreign students must often provide additional information about English proficiency and financial support, or must complete special forms. This takes time.

2. Send international postal certificates to cover unexpected additional mailing costs, and be sure to stipulate that the colleges use foreign airmail in sending their material to you. Surface delivery can take months.

3. If you live in a country where your address is written in an unusual form, enclose several mailing labels filled out with your address. The admissions office will greatly appreciate your thoughtfulness.

4. *If you are an American citizen, be sure to mention that fact in your card or letter to the admissions office.* Many admissions offices send special foreign student materials to all inquiries coming from foreign addresses, no matter what the name of the inquiring student may be.

5. If there is a problem with the delivery of mail to your home, consider using your school's address or the business address of your parents. If you live near a U.S. military installation, embassy, or consular office, it may be possible to use APO addresses or diplomatic delivery. Check first, however, because there are restrictions on the use of these services.

6. Getting information is crucial. Therefore, while you wait for material to arrive by mail, do not neglect other sources. The counselor's office is a good place to start in American schools abroad. You may also use the agencies of the U.S. government, such as the International Communications Agency, embassies and consular offices that have cultural affairs officers, and international education agencies, such as IIE (Institute for International Education), AMIDEAST, and ECIS (European Council of Independent Schools).

Your School System and the American Admissions Office

Students attending American schools abroad need not be concerned whether grading and curriculum will conform to American patterns: They will. However, an academic profile of the senior class would be very helpful for admissions officers if you can arrange to have one sent. If you attend a local school in a country outside the United States, with different curriculum and grading practices, be sure the admissions offices at the colleges you are interested in have the following information:

1. Grading scale and the range for conversion. For example, if the scale is 0 to 20, admissions officers must know what ranges equal A, B, C, D, and Failing.
2. Distribution of grades. By American standards, a C average is not particularly exciting; however, in some countries only the very best students receive marks better than "average."
3. Course descriptions. "Additional math" will not mean much to an admissions officer; be sure you specify trigonometry, analytical geometry, or whatever you actually took.
4. School calendar. Be sure your school provides information about when its terms begin and end and when grade reports will be available.
5. General information about your school, e.g., a description of the student body, faculty, type of curriculum, methods of instruction. This is always helpful.
6. Explanation of externally administered examinations, such as the GCE,

Abitur, etc. This should include when they are given, how they are scored, and the categories of results, such as "first division," honors, etc.

7. English translations of transcripts. If your transcript is not in English, have it translated and have copies of the translation made and certified by a U.S. consular office or an organization such as IIE or AMIDEAST. Certification by local attorneys or solicitors will not be acceptable to some American colleges.

If your school cannot provide information on its grading scale, curriculum, and external examinations, the Ministry of Education, the examination council, or another government agency in your country may be able to do so.

Language Considerations

For non-native speakers of English, an evaluation of their ability to use the English Language will rank in importance with that of their proven academic ability. Even Americans living abroad can face language problems because of their relative lack of exposure to English-language media, such as newspapers, magazines, and television. This may lower their standardized test results. Americans who have spent many years abroad should inform the admissions office of their international background.

If English is not your native language, you will be required to submit the results of some measure of your English ability. The most popular instrument is the Test of English as a Foreign Language (TOEFL). This test is administered by Educational Testing Service for the College Entrance Examination Board, has three subparts, and is scored from 0 to 800. The three subtests include Listening Comprehension, Structure and Written Expression, and Reading Comprehension and Vocabulary. An examination to test proficiency in spoken English is in the development stage by the College Board and may be required in the future. Many schools set minimum TOEFL total scores at 500, others as high as 600. Some schools will accept a lower total score if subscores indicate strong written expression and reading comprehension. Students who have spoken English in their homes or at school but do not consider it their native language should certainly consider taking the TOEFL; it will probably be a better measure of their English-language ability than their SAT or ACT results.

In some cases, colleges will waive TOEFL requirements if the student can submit the results of another test. The most frequently administered are the Michigan Test and the American Language Institute of Georgetown University Test (ALIGU). Some colleges accept the General Certificate of Education (GCE) from Oxford, Cambridge, or the University of London, or the results of the Scholastic Aptitude Test (SAT) verbal section. The Michigan and ALIGU are not as welcome to admissions officers as the TOEFL, however, because of problems involving test security and validity.

Foreign students who have been in American high schools or colleges for two years or more are often exempt from the requirement to take the TOEFL. This is particularly true if they can present evidence of good performance in English courses taken in the United States.

ESL Programs

If you would like to attend an American institution and you are afraid your English ability is not up to acceptable standards, you may wish to consider intensive study of English. There are many English as a Second Language (ESL) programs available in the United States. Many of them are located on college and university campuses. Entrance requirements are minimal, since students are placed at the correct "level" of study through testing of their ability. These programs may last from five weeks to as long as a year. Consider the following points if you are thinking of ESL study:

1. What are the admissions requirements?
2. Can you live in a dormitory on campus? If not, what housing options are available?
3. Does the program issue form I-20? Will your country allow students to go abroad to study English only? Some countries grant exit permits only to students enrolled in full-time degree programs.
4. What facilities are available to ESL students? (Language laboratories, classrooms, library, student center, athletic facilities?)
5. How much does the program cost, and what does that include? Are all expenses listed in a comprehensive student budget? Is financial aid available?
6. How are students placed at the appropriate level of instruction? Are tests administered on campus, and are students retested at the end of the program?

7. Have other students you know attended the program? If so, what was their experience?

8. Does a large block of students from any one country attend the program? If so, this will inhibit informal conversations in English.

Students considering such intensive English study in the United States should remember that much of the benefit of this kind of study comes from total immersion in the language and culture of America. Foreign students who spend all their out-of-class hours with home-country friends are defeating the purpose of their study. Many ESL programs arrange for students to live with American families. If this is available, take advantage of the opportunity to learn about the language and the culture outside the classroom.

Getting the Information You Need

Because distance and travel costs may prevent you from visiting the colleges in which you are interested, you may well have to place greater reliance on the printed word. The first response foreign students get to their inquiry will probably be a form letter printed on an aerogram. They may be asked to complete a preliminary application form that asks about their educational background, English ability, and financial condition. This material should be read carefully, and instructions should be followed precisely.

Do not limit your mail search to the very well known American colleges you have heard a great deal about. Many of these colleges are also the most difficult to gain admission to. America has a vast array of colleges to consider, an amazing number of which have extremely strong academic programs. Several reference books are available that will help you to identify suitable colleges for yourself (see the listing on pages 38-39). At least one reference—Peterson's—shows you the percentage of foreign nationals in the student body at each reporting college.

Be sure to write early for information. Follow the instructions in the first section of this chapter so that your mail is delivered as quickly as possible. If you do not receive responses from any college within a reasonable amount of time, do not hesitate to write again.

Avoiding High Pressure and the Unscrupulous

Many American colleges and universities recruit international students in order to bridge the gap between the declining number of American college-age students and the space available in their classrooms. In many foreign countries there are also a number of so-called "educational agencies" that prey on prospective students, offering them guaranteed admission to American colleges and automatic procurement of I-20 forms and exit visas. There are also many reputable and highly responsible agencies designed to help students. The problem that you, as a student, must face is distinguishing the good from the bad.

Be careful of anyone who insists on having you sign a contract for specified services to be delivered in a certain period of time. No one can guarantee that any student will be admitted to any American institution. No one can even reasonably guess at your chances of acceptance except the admissions officers of a particular college. Any agency which represents itself as being able to "guarantee" admission (and immigration and student status) must be avoided. Reputable organizations will work with you to determine a number of colleges and universities to which you should apply, and will help you to assess your strengths and weaknesses so that you can determine the institutions that are best suited to your needs.

In the years ahead, more and more American institutions will be sending representatives abroad to speak with international students directly. If you have the chance to meet such representatives, take advantage of the occasions to ask about academic programs, support services for international students, financial aid funds, and anything else that will be important to you as an international student in a strange culture and community. If these representatives are not completely honest with you or seem to be reluctant about answering your questions, check further before making any kind of commitment.

Finances

Along with academic achievement and English proficiency, the consideration that will be most important to an international student applying to a college in the United States is his or her ability to meet the costs of an education in America. The basic cost for tuition, room, and board at many private colleges now runs as high as $8,000 or $9,000 per year. This of course does not include any personal expenses, travel, or summer school, which are important factors for international students. Unfortunately, financial aid for foreign students is not available in any great amount. Most of the funding for American financial aid programs comes from the U.S. federal government. Students who are citizens of foreign countries are not eligible for these funds; therefore, any aid they might receive would have to come from a particular college and not from the government. For extremely talented students, there is financial aid available at some institutions. However, students should begin by looking in their home countries before seeking financial assistance abroad. Many governments sponsor students who wish to study abroad in certain fields, particularly in the technological and health sciences areas. If you are a particularly able student, you should explore all these possibilities.

Complicating matters for foreign students further has been the fact that until recently it has been difficult for them to receive work permits which they need if they wish to make money during the summers. Although this situation is changing somewhat, it is still important for foreign students to appraise their financial condition realistically. If admissions officers judge that a student does not have the funding necessary to cover projected costs, that may, in itself, be sufficient cause for rejection.

Many students who apply to colleges in the United States are asked to document their financial condition by sending statements from banks or other financial institutions. Many colleges require a substantial deposit before issuing form I-20. They may require that a student pay a semester's or even a year's tuition in advance, or request a separate and substantial deposit to assure that a student will be able to return to his home country. Be sure you understand these requirements before you make a commitment, and also insist that any deposits held by an institution will pay interest. Make certain you understand the means by which this money may be withdrawn in case of an emergency that requires you to return home suddenly.

Check with your local financial institutions to determine the laws governing the exchange of currency. Even when students have substantial financial resources, it is often difficult to have money sent out of the country. This can be a problem for students trying to send an application fee, as they are not allowed to exchange any money until they are officially admitted. If this happens to you, request a waiver of the application processing fee, explain the situation, and indicate your willingness to pay it once you have been admitted and are allowed to exchange currency.

Many colleges require foreign students to subscribe to an insurance program. This should be done by all international students before they enter the United States in order to avoid finding themselves without funds in the event of a health emergency.

Immigration

The rules and regulations governing the entrance of all foreign nationals into the United States are voluminous and complicated. To add to the complexity, these rules are constantly being revised, particularly for those who wish to come to the United States specifically to study.

Students who expect to attend a college or university in the United States are granted an F-1 visa upon presentation to the American consular officer their form I-20, properly completed and signed by the American institution they have been admitted to, with a valid passport from their home country. In addition, American consular officers will seek additional information to substantiate what is on the I-20. They may request information regarding the student's academic ability, English language ability, or financial assets before granting the entrance visa. Students should report their academic credentials as accurately as possible to American consular officers, since there are substantial penalties for misrepresentation.

Once students have arrived in the United States, they are under the jurisdiction of the Immigration and Naturalization Service which requires that they report directly to the college to which they have been admitted. Students are currently admitted for "duration of status," which means that, as long as they maintain full-time student status they will not need to renew their permission to stay in the United States. This law is being reconsidered, however, and may revert to a one-year permission, which must be renewed each year. Students who desire a change in status should check with their institution's foreign student adviser and the nearest Immigration and Naturalization Service field office.

In all matters relating to immigration rules and regulations, it is always wise to consult with the foreign student adviser on your campus. This individual is specially trained and kept informed of the latest information on laws, work permits, health insurance, and other matters relating to foreign students and their dependents.

Canadian Students

Canadian students who seek postsecondary education in the United States do not face many of the problems experienced by their counterparts overseas. For example, they are not required to have a passport or visa. However, they must meet the same immigration requirements as other international students. They must submit form I-20 to the U.S. consular office. (The official name for I-20 is the Certificate of Eligibility for Nonimmigrant "F-1" Student Status.) Upon arrival in the United States, students will be issued form I-94, the Arrival-Departure Record. Thereafter, of course, they must comply with the immigration and naturalization requirements that apply to international students.

In general, English-speaking Canadian students have an easier time in fulfilling the admission requirements of American schools. They do not face the problems of English language proficiency, and they have easier access to the SAT and ACT tests than students living overseas. In addition, the thirteenth year of education in the Canadian system is often awarded college credit by colleges in the United States. Canadian students who have performed well in their thirteenth year may be admitted as students with "advanced standing" or as sophomores. This will vary from college to college and should be checked by the applicant.

Decision Time for the Colleges

The most difficult period of the application process is, in many respects, the time spent waiting to learn of a college's decision on your application. Unless you have applied under a rolling admissions or early decision plan, there is little you can do to hasten the arrival of your letters of acceptance or rejection.

Notification Dates

Many colleges subscribe to the standard notification date of April 15 and gear the mailing of their admissions letters accordingly. Other colleges complete their decision-making process as early as March and notify candidates immediately. Colleges that follow a policy of rolling admissions notify the candidate of a decision as soon as his or her file is complete.

Basic Criteria

Colleges employ a bewildering variety of methods for evaluating prospective students—or at least it may seem so to candidates. However, no matter how varied their criteria for selection, all college admissions officers operate on the same basic premise: To be accepted, a student must demonstrate the potential for becoming a successful member of that particular academic community.

To many, the discussions and deliberations of admissions committees may appear to hold the key to every student's acceptance or rejection, but there is alternatively much truth in the observation that admissions decisions are determined by the contents of each candidate's folder. While it may seem slightly objectionable to reduce the attributes of a living, breathing candidate to a 9" x 13" manila file folder, it is true that the case you make for yourself on paper—through your application, high school record, test scores, and recommendations—will ultimately have to speak for you when your application is up for consideration.

In our survey of college admissions directors, the three factors identified as most important in determining an applicant's admission were high school record (35 percent), test scores (27 percent), and recommendations (10 percent). Public institutions also frequently cited "rank in high school class" as a key factor.

Because the selective admissions process relies heavily on the personal reactions of admissions committee members to elements in a candidate's background—and because the composition of every admissions committee varies widely—it is not possible to say definitively how much weight is placed on each factor in every case. However, experience suggests that the following generalizations are valid.

Specific Qualifications

Admissions committees, when evaluating your application, are going to look at:

Your grades and rank in class. Rank is less important when the senior class is small and the competition is known to be keen.

Your overall academic record. In the evaluation of your academic record the admissions committee will not limit their examination of your transcript to your senior year grade point average and your rank in class. Your entire record of academic achievement will be reviewed. The grade trends will be noticed, and your most recent work will be of considerable importance. This means your junior year performance may be the most important year of all. If you have reversed a lackluster academic career in your junior year and are continuing to achieve at a high level as a senior, your admissions stock will rise enormously. If your performance declines dramatically, this may hurt your chances even though your overall record is strong.

If there is some factor in your personal or family life that has negatively influenced your performance, it should be noted in your application. This is an area in which your counselor can be very helpful because the counselor can talk about such matters in the recommendation, whereas it might be difficult for you to be objective about the effect of such a situation on your performance.

Your selection of high school courses. Committees look for signs that you have taken the most demanding academic program offered, and advanced placement and honors courses obviously stand out as key indicators. Don't feel, however, that your chances for admission to a competitive college are seriously jeopardized if, for example, you have attended a small public high school that does not offer a large number of honors or advanced placement classes. The committee will understand the situation and will look instead to see if you have taken advantage of whatever academic opportunities were available to you, no matter how few.

The caliber of your high school. Academic caliber is often measured by such factors as the percentage of seniors who go on to college, the curriculum offered, the academic record of past graduates who have attended the college considering your application, and, in many cases, an admissions officer's personal knowledge of your high school or guidance counselor.

Extracurricular activities. Like course offerings, opportunities for extracurricular activities vary from school to school. Some institutions have elaborate outside activities, including trips to Europe, independent research, study at nearby colleges, and other unusual programs. Most schools support only the traditional student government, service and interest clubs, and athletic offerings. Whatever the case at your school, it is the quality of your participation that counts, not the number of activities joined nor their exotic nature. Admissions counselors look to see how you have participated—as a leader or as a joiner—and if you have coordinated your activities and part-time jobs with your academic interests.

Application and essay.   The application is the only item required in the admissions process that allows you the luxury of speaking for yourself. It is no time to be modest, but neither is it an open invitation to ramble on. The applications that have the most impact on admissions committee members usually owe their success to tight organization and effective writing style. Crafting the most important information about yourself into a succinct, every-sentence-loaded application is an editorial challenge. It can also be crucial to your acceptance.

Standardized test scores.   Generally test scores are seriously counted only as long as they substantiate your past academic record. Poor test scores can be overlooked if you have a strong high school record. On the other hand, exceptionally high test scores may be questioned if your past work doesn't indicate such academic ability.

Recommendations.   Solid statements that expand upon, rather than reiterate, the record you have presented elsewhere in your application will most help your case for admission.

Special considerations.   A number of admissions offices hold special committee meetings to consider applications that fall into special categories. Tulane University, which has separate professional schools such as architecture and engineering, considers these applications independently from those of the rest of the freshman class. Minority students, athletes, and children of alumni are also discussed in separate sessions at some colleges.

Regardless of the number of factors itemized as official criteria for admission, your acceptance or rejection usually hinges on one factor—the competition. Your B+ high school record and healthy list of activities may appear lacking in comparison to the backgrounds of the applicants to one college, while at another college the same record may make you a standout. There is more than an element of chance involved in the admissions process, but a realistic selection of schools and careful preparation of your admissions folder will help put the odds in your favor.

Decision Time for You

Though more than a few admissions directors would shudder to hear the admissions process compared to a game, we began with the analogy and we can return to it because in the end there are the same three options—win, lose, or draw. A win is an acceptance; a lose, a rejection; and a draw, waiting list status. Multiply these three options by the number of institutions to which you have applied, and you'll be able to envision a number of perplexing situations.

Perhaps two colleges which you consider equally desirable have accepted you. How do you ultimately make your choice? Or perhaps you have been placed on the waiting list at your first- and second-choice colleges, would like to wait to see if you will be admitted, but are afraid that you may lose everything if you don't accept the admission offer of your third choice.

These results cast the decision-making process back into your hands. Now—when you have invested so much energy in the admissions process—is no time to panic. A rational review of your goals and needs should help you toward your decision.

Choosing That One

Those lucky enough to be accepted by several institutions may feel the only way they can arrive at a final decision is by resorting to cutting cards or flipping coins. Although this is one way to solve the problem, there are better approaches.

First, gather all the literature from the colleges involved and reread it carefully. Weigh course offerings against each other, distance from home, cost, size—any of the factors which are important to you. You may have come up with some new ideas or perceptions since you first applied. This is certainly the time to be honest with yourself if you've had deep-down changes in your choices. You might want to revisit one or two campuses with specific points in mind now that enrolling is a real possibility.

If travel is out of the question, talking to local alumni or current students from your town may add new perspectives. At this point, alumni may well take the initiative in getting in touch with you. Colleges that actively involve their alumni in the recruiting process routinely send the names of accepted students to representatives in their area and ask them to encourage these students to enroll.

Once you have collected all available insights, it is simply a question of choosing the institution that, in your eyes, offers the most pluses. If you have outlined and updated the pros and cons of each of your choices on your worksheet on page 44, seeing the facts spelled out, with one school next to another, can be of help in sorting out your impressions and coming to a decision.

While you shouldn't decide too hastily, it is courteous to notify each college of your intentions as soon as you can after you have been accepted. Once you decline an offer of admission, the college may be able to offer acceptance to someone on the waiting list. For everyone's sake, therefore, you should not prolong your response unnecessarily.

Surviving Waiting List Status

Probably the most troublesome news an admissions letter can contain is that you have been placed on the waiting list. This "not-accepted-but-not-rejected" status places you in a frustrating limbo.

Many students assume that if they wait long enough they will eventually be accepted from the waiting list. In the course of waiting, however, they may pass up the chance to say "yes" to other colleges, only to learn finally that the college they've had their eye on has a full freshman class and will not accept any more waiting list students.

Colleges maintain waiting lists as protection in case an unusually large number of accepted students decide to go elsewhere. Thus a college hoping for a freshman class of 1,500 may accept 3,000 students and put an additional 300 on a waiting list. If 50% of the accepted students agree to enroll, the college will have a full freshman class and not one student will be taken from the waiting list. However, if only 45% (1,350) of the accepted students enroll, there will be room for 150 waiting list students to be admitted.

Of the colleges we surveyed, only about a quarter used waiting lists. At those colleges, only 22% of the students placed on waiting lists were eventually accepted each year. Some colleges help students by telling them whether they are in the top quarter, second quarter, bottom half, etc., of the waiting list group. Those in the lower half of any waiting list should consider their chances of admission quite unlikely.

Better Safe than Sorry

If you have been placed on the waiting list at your first-choice college but have been accepted at your second- or third-choice college, you are faced with a major dilemma. As the deadline for submitting the enrollment deposit at the college to which you have been accepted approaches, and you still have heard nothing from your waiting list college, you should call the admissions office and explain your predicament. Ask an admissions officer for a realistic appraisal of your chances of acceptance. If you are told your prospects look dim, accept the fact and turn your attention to your other choices. If you are told your chances look good, or even very good, be encouraged—but do not be foolish. An over-the-phone remark is simply the honest judgment of someone trying to be helpful. It is not a formal notification of anything and is not meant to be interpreted as a commitment.

Although you may get a last-minute acceptance from the college you want, you would probably be wise to ensure yourself a college place by sending in the enrollment deposit to the best (for you) of the colleges that have accepted you. Enrollment deposits range from token amounts ($10 to $25) to as much as $250. Most public institutions require no deposit.

Appealing a Decision

Admissions officers like to think that their decisions reflect not only the best interests of their college but your own best interest as well. Occasionally there is valid room for discussion, and you may be one of those who—if rejected—feel that you have excellent reasons to question the admissions office's decision. It is then time to consider an appeal.

But first a word of warning. Pressure techniques never help a case. If you have good reason to appeal a decision, approach the appeal in the same orderly way you did your application. Irate phone calls, threats from alumni parents to cancel their annual contribution, and other acts of desperation only serve to erase, rather than advance, your chances for reconsideration now or transfer later.

Of the colleges in our survey, 90% indicated that they are willing to consider appeals on admissions decisions. Some schools routinely handle a large number of appeals each year and admit a significant number of them. Other schools entertain only a few appeals and rarely change their minds.

The single reason regularly cited by admissions directors for reconsidering a decision is new information. Perhaps you finished an otherwise far from superior high school career with a straight A average in your senior year. Or you may have received late notification of a national award or high standardized test score that you feel would strengthen your record.

Don't be overly optimistic about your chances of being accepted on an appeal. The admissions committee's original decision was made with care and is therefore not easily reversed. However, if you do want to restate your case, write or call the appropriate admissions officer, give any new information you wish to have considered, and wait for a new reading of your case. Your guidance counselor is a good person with whom to discuss the advisability of an appeal and may also be willing to initiate the process for you.

Preventive Medicine

David Erdmann, Acting Director of Admissions at Rensselaer Polytechnic Institute in Troy, New York, helps cut down on appeals of admissions decisions by personally rereading the cases of all rejected applicants before the notification letters are mailed. Thus each case has, in essence, already had an appeals hearing before it even reaches the applicant.

Trying Again

If you have followed our earlier advice and made your college selections by carefully matching your abilities and needs with colleges' offerings and requirements, you should have been accepted by at least one institution that is suitable for you. However, it is possible that after a term or two of college you may come to believe that you and your institution are mismatched.

While certain elements of the college experience are bound to tax any student, college life is not meant to be—nor should you allow it to become—an unpleasant experience. If, after giving yourself and your college a fair period of time (usually a year) to work out your problems with each other, you foresee no improvements, it is time to consider transferring.

It may be that you still yearn to be admitted to your original first-choice college if you weren't accepted as a freshman. Now is a good time to try again, especially if your college work has demonstrated greater academic potential than your high school record had indicated. This kind of new information could result in your admission as a transfer. The likelihood of your acceptance would also be enhanced if there were a high attrition rate in the college's current freshman class, or if you plan to major in a field for which the college is recruiting students.

You can refresh your memory by turning the page and—with your new knowledge of colleges—running through the whole gamut of possible choices. You may be surprised at your choices the second time around!

For guidelines on selecting colleges to transfer to, you could simply thumb back to page 15 and begin this book again. But by this time your requirements should be more specific, and you should have developed a more finely tuned sensitivity to the kind of environment in which you work best. Thus your trial-by-experience should greatly simplify your college selection and application process on the second time around.

Read On!

The next portion of the book gives you basic information about the colleges you will be considering. Study the facts to start forming in your mind a picture of the type of college you think you want to go to. Do not hesitate to write to— or even call—those admissions directors whose names and phone numbers appear in the nutshells. They're a pretty nice bunch of people, eager to meet you if you're interested in their college. And remember—they once applied to college, too!

Nutshell 1:
Profiles of Four-Year Colleges and Universities

In this section, colleges are presented in alphabetical order by state. Each profile contains the most basic information you need about a college to start your research. (The tuition level for each college is presented in the next section.) Abbreviations used are: C–certificate or diploma program, A–associate's degree, T–total, U–undergraduate, B–bachelor's degree, M–master's degree, D–doctorate.

ALABAMA

ALABAMA AGRICULTURAL AND MECHANICAL UNIVERSITY

Normal 35762. Public; suburban. Awards A, B, M. Enrolls 4,483 T, 3,615 U (49% women, 85% state res., 75% on fin. aid). Entrance difficulty: moderately difficult. Application deadline: rolling. Contact: Mr. A. G. Adams, Director of Admissions, (205) 859-7469.

ALABAMA CHRISTIAN COLLEGE

Montgomery 36109. Private; suburban. Awards C, A, B. Enrolls 1,119 T (31% women, 69% state res., 75% on fin. aid). Entrance difficulty: less difficult. Application deadline: rolling. Contact: Mr. Wayne Baker, Vice President–Enrollment Planning, (205) 272-5820.

ALABAMA STATE UNIVERSITY

Montgomery 36101. Public; urban. Awards A, B, M. Enrolls 4,096 T, 3,653 U (59% women, 86% state res., 80% on fin. aid). Entrance difficulty: noncompetitive. Contact: Mr. Henry E. Ford, (205) 832-6072.

AUBURN UNIVERSITY

Auburn 36849. Public; small town. Awards B, M, D. Enrolls 18,329 T, 16,336 U (42% women, 68% state res., 50% on fin. aid). Entrance difficulty: moderately difficult. Application deadline: 9/1. Contact: Mr. Herbert N. Hawkins, (205) 826-4080.

AUBURN UNIVERSITY AT MONTGOMERY

Montgomery 36109. Public; urban. Awards B, M. Enrolls 4,847 T, 3,627 U (52% women, 100% state res., 10% on fin. aid). Entrance difficulty: moderately difficult. Application deadline: 9/1. Contact: Mr. Lee Davis, (205) 279-9110 Ext. 211.

BIRMINGHAM-SOUTHERN COLLEGE

Birmingham 35204. Private; urban. Awards B. Enrolls 1,402 T (49% women, 75% state res., 68% on fin. aid). Entrance difficulty: moderately difficult. Application deadline: 8/15. Contact: Mr. Robert D. Dortch, Vice President for Admission Services, (205) 328-5250.

DANIEL PAYNE COLLEGE

Birmingham 35214. Contact: Mr. Ronald E. Truss, Director of Admissions.

HUNTINGDON COLLEGE

Montgomery 36106. Private; suburban. Awards B. Enrolls 693 T (55% women, 70% state res., 83% on fin. aid). Entrance difficulty: less difficult. Application deadline: rolling. Contact: Mr. Bruce Triftshauser, (205) 834-3300.

JACKSONVILLE STATE UNIVERSITY

Jacksonville 36265. Public; small town. Awards B, M. Enrolls 7,018 T, 6,208 U (51% women, 80% state res., 27% on fin. aid). Entrance difficulty: noncompetitive. Application deadline: rolling. Contact: Mr. Jerry D. Smith, Registrar, (205) 435-5514.

JUDSON COLLEGE

Marion 36756. Private; rural. Awards B. Enrolls 355 T (100% women, 85% state res., 25% on fin. aid). Entrance difficulty: less difficult. Application deadline: 8/25. Contact: Mr. Mike Forehand, Admissions Director, (205) 683-6161.

LIVINGSTON UNIVERSITY

Livingston 35470. Public; small town. Awards A, B, M. Enrolls 1,194 T, 1,055 U (51% women, 86% state res., 55% on fin. aid). Entrance difficulty: less difficult. Application deadline: rolling. Contact: Mr. Clarence W. Egbert, (205) 652-9661.

MILES COLLEGE

Birmingham 35208. Private; rural. Awards B. Enrolls 1,152 T (60% women, 85% on fin. aid). Application deadline: rolling. Contact: Rev. Nelson Gooden, (205) 923-2771.

MOBILE COLLEGE

Mobile 36613. Private; suburban. Awards A, B. Enrolls 1,074 T (33% women, 91% state res., 65% on fin. aid). Entrance difficulty: less difficult. Application deadline: rolling. Contact: Dr. Eugene M. Keebler, Academic Vice President and Dean, (205) 675-5990.

OAKWOOD COLLEGE

Huntsville 35806. Private; rural. Awards A, B. Enrolls 1,266 T (52% women, 16% state res., 90% on fin. aid). Entrance difficulty: less difficult. Application deadline: 9/15. Contact: Dr. R. Malcolm, Director of Admissions, (205) 837-1630.

SAMFORD UNIVERSITY

Birmingham 35209. Private; suburban. Awards A, B, M. Enrolls 4,094 T, 2,860 U (58% women, 67% state res., 75% on fin. aid). Entrance difficulty: less difficult. Application deadline: 8/10. Contact: Mr. E. T. Cleveland, (205) 870-2793.

SOUTHEASTERN BIBLE COLLEGE

Birmingham 35205. Private; urban. Awards C, A, B, M. Enrolls 251 T, 243 U (45% women, 50% state res., 40% on fin. aid). Entrance difficulty: less difficult. Application deadline: rolling. Contact: Mr. Leon Gillaspie, Academic Vice President, (205) 251-2311.

SPRING HILL COLLEGE

Mobile 36608. Private; suburban. Awards C, B. Enrolls 904 T (46% women, 32% state res., 49% on fin. aid). Entrance difficulty: moderately difficult. Application deadline: 8/15. Contact: Ms. Carey Creagan, (205) 460-2130.

STILLMAN COLLEGE

Tuscaloosa 35401. Contact: Mrs. Evelyn E. Nall, Director of Admissions.

TALLADEGA COLLEGE

Talladega 35160. Contact: Mr. John H. McCray, Director of Admissions.

TROY STATE UNIVERSITY

Troy 36081. Public; small town. Awards A, B, M. Enrolls 6,489 T, 5,394 U (37% women, 95% state res., 48% on fin. aid). Entrance difficulty: moderately difficult. Application deadline: rolling. Contact: Mr. Ervin L. Wood, (205) 566-3000.

TROY STATE UNIVERSITY AT FORT RUCKER/DOTHAN

Dothan 36301. Public; urban. Awards A, B, M. Enrolls 1,584 T, 926 U (48% women, 100% state res., 10% on fin. aid). Entrance difficulty: noncompetitive. Application deadline: rolling. Contact: Mr. Gordon Carpenter.

TROY STATE UNIVERSITY AT MONTGOMERY

Montgomery 36104. Public; urban. Awards C, A, B, M. Enrolls 2,496 T, 1,700 U (22% women, 100% state res., 10% on fin. aid). Entrance difficulty: noncompetitive. Application deadline: rolling. Contact: Ms. Monica Kolaya, Director of Admissions.

TUSKEGEE INSTITUTE

Tuskegee 36088. Private; small town. Awards B, M. Enrolls 3,435 T, 2,978 U (52% women, 36% state res., 92% on fin. aid). Entrance difficulty: moderately difficult. Application deadline: 7/15. Contact: Mr. Herbert E. Carter, Assistant Dean for Student Services, (205) 727-8500.

UNIVERSITY OF ALABAMA

University 35486. Public; small town. Awards C, B, M, D. Enrolls 16,807 T, 13,776 U (49% women, 82% state res.,

35% on fin. aid). Entrance difficulty: moderately difficult. Application deadline: 8/1. Contact: Dr. Lawrence B. Durham, (205) 348-5666.

UNIVERSITY OF ALABAMA IN BIRMINGHAM

Birmingham 35294. Public; urban. Awards C, B, M, D. Enrolls 14,214 T, 9,794 U (53% women, 94% state res., 27% on fin. aid). Entrance difficulty: less difficult. Application deadline: rolling. Contact: Dr. Don Belcher, Assistant Dean for Admissions, (205) 934-5268.

UNIVERSITY OF ALABAMA IN HUNTSVILLE

Huntsville 35899. Public; suburban. Awards B, M, D. Enrolls 4,702 T, 4,114 U (52% women, 95% state res., 25% on fin. aid). Entrance difficulty: moderately difficult. Application deadline: 8/14. Contact: Mrs. Nan G. Hall, (205) 895-6210.

UNIVERSITY OF MONTEVALLO

Montevallo 35115. Public; small town. Awards B, M. Enrolls 2,994 T, 2,526 U (59% women, 90% state res., 57% on fin. aid). Entrance difficulty: less difficult. Application deadline: rolling. Contact: Mr. Larry A. Peevy, Director of Admissions and Records, (205) 665-2521 Ext. 457.

UNIVERSITY OF NORTH ALABAMA

Florence 35630. Public; urban. Awards B, M. Enrolls 5,189 T, 4,592 U (53% women, 88% state res., 35% on fin. aid). Entrance difficulty: noncompetitive. Application deadline: 8/12. Contact: Mr. J. Hollie Allen, (205) 766-4100 Ext. 318.

UNIVERSITY OF SOUTH ALABAMA

Mobile 36688. Public; suburban. Awards C, B, M, D. Enrolls 7,331 T, 5,996 U (50% women, 75% state res., 45% on fin. aid). Entrance difficulty: moderately difficult. Application deadline: 9/10. Contact: Mr. J. David Stearns, (205) 460-6141.

ALASKA

ALASKA PACIFIC UNIVERSITY

Anchorage 99504. Private; urban. Awards A, B, M. Enrolls 120 T, 106 U (72% women, 95% state res.). Application deadline: rolling. Contact: Mr. Robert Costigan, Director of Admissions, (907) 276-8181.

INUPIAT UNIVERSITY OF THE ARCTIC

Barrow 99723. Contact: Dr. R. C. Harcharek, Director, Postsecondary Education.

SHELDON JACKSON COLLEGE

Sitka 99835. Private; small town. Awards C, A, B. Enrolls 170 T (50% women, 85% state res., 97% on fin. aid). Entrance difficulty: noncompetitive. Application deadline: rolling. Contact: B. B. Bigelow, Manager, Advancement Office, (907) 747-5224.

UNIVERSITY OF ALASKA, ANCHORAGE

Anchorage 99504. Public; urban. Awards C, B, M. Enrolls 3,625 T, 2,935 U (63% women, 93% state res., 20% on fin. aid). Entrance difficulty: moderately difficult. Application deadline: rolling. Contact: Miss Kay Wilson, (907) 263-1480.

UNIVERSITY OF ALASKA, FAIRBANKS

Fairbanks 99701. Public; small town. Awards A, B, M, D. Enrolls 3,489 T, 3,153 U (50% women, 80% state res., 21% on fin. aid). Entrance difficulty: less difficult. Application deadline: 8/1. Contact: Mrs. Ann Tremarello, (907) 479-7521.

UNIVERSITY OF ALASKA, JUNEAU

Juneau 99803. Public; small town. Awards C, A, B, M. Enrolls 2,200 T, 1,700 U (60% women, 98% state res., 2% on fin. aid). Entrance difficulty: noncompetitive. Application deadline: rolling. Contact: Mr. Gene Hickey, (907) 789-2101.

ARIZONA

ARIZONA STATE UNIVERSITY

Tempe 85281. Public; suburban. Awards B, M, D. Enrolls 37,755 T, 27,570 U (45% women, 66% state res., 34% on fin. aid). Entrance difficulty: moderately difficult. Application deadline: rolling. Contact: Dr. Christine K. Wilkinson, Director of Admissions and High School/College Relations, (602) 965-3255.

DEVRY INSTITUTE OF TECHNOLOGY

Phoenix 85016. Private; urban. Awards A, B. Enrolls 2,562 T (5% women, 22% state res., 77% on fin. aid). Entrance difficulty: noncompetitive. Application deadline: 10/1. Contact: Mr. Art Geiger, (602) 957-0140.

GRAND CANYON COLLEGE

Phoenix 85017. Private; suburban. Awards B. Enrolls 1,143 T (52% women, 82% state res., 56% on fin. aid). Entrance difficulty: moderately difficult. Application deadline: rolling. Contact: Mr. Barry L. Thompson, Registrar, (602) 249-3300.

NORTHERN ARIZONA UNIVERSITY

Flagstaff 86011. Public; small town. Awards A, B, M, D. Enrolls 12,750 T (49% women, 75% state res., 40% on fin. aid). Entrance difficulty: moderately difficult. Application deadline: 7/15. Contact: Dr. M. D. Schroeder, Dean of Admissions and Records, (602) 523-2108.

SOUTHWESTERN BAPTIST BIBLE COLLEGE

Phoenix 85032. Private; suburban. Awards C, B. Enrolls 215 T (46% women, 60% state res.). Application deadline: 8/15. Contact: Mr. Kenneth A. Epp, Registrar, (602) 992-6101.

UNIVERSITY OF ARIZONA

Tucson 85721. Public; urban. Awards B, M, D. Enrolls 31,970 T, 24,155 U (48% women, 74% state res., 38% on fin. aid). Entrance difficulty: moderately difficult. Application deadline: 7/15. Contact: Mr. David L. Windsor, Dean of Admissions, (602) 626-3432.

ARKANSAS

ARKANSAS BAPTIST COLLEGE

Little Rock 72202.

ARKANSAS COLLEGE

Batesville 72501. Private; small town. Awards B. Enrolls 496 T (60% women, 65% state res., 80% on fin. aid). Entrance difficulty: moderately difficult. Application deadline: rolling. Contact: Mr. John A. Thompson, (501) 793-9813.

ARKANSAS STATE UNIVERSITY

State University 72467. Public; small town. Awards C, A, B, M. Enrolls 7,300 T, 6,641 U (53% women, 88% state res., 51% on fin. aid). Entrance difficulty: noncompetitive. Application deadline: 9/1. Contact: Dr. Greta Mack, (501) 972-3024.

ARKANSAS TECH UNIVERSITY

Russellville 72801. Public; small town. Awards A, B, M. Enrolls 2,998 T, 2,846 U (50% women, 85% state res., 50% on fin. aid). Entrance difficulty: less difficult. Application deadline: 9/15. Contact: Dr. Dix Stallings, (501) 968-0343.

CENTRAL BAPTIST COLLEGE

Conway 72032. Private; small town. Awards C, A, B. Enrolls 231 T (40% women, 60% state res., 80% on fin. aid). Entrance difficulty: less difficult. Application deadline: rolling. Contact: Mrs. Norma Tio, Registrar.

COLLEGE OF THE OZARKS

Clarksville 72830. Private; small town. Awards A, B. Enrolls 543 T (50% women, 57% state res., 67% on fin. aid). Entrance difficulty: moderately difficult. Application deadline: 8/15. Contact: Mr. Greg Blackburn, (501) 754-8715.

HARDING UNIVERSITY

Searcy 72143. Private; small town. Awards A, B, M. Enrolls 3,001 T, 2,979 U (53% women, 28% state res., 74% on fin. aid). Entrance difficulty: less difficult. Application deadline: 6/1. Contact: Mr. Durward McGaha, Associate Director of Admissions.

HENDERSON STATE UNIVERSITY

Arkadelphia 71923. Public; small town. Awards A, B, M. Enrolls 3,014 T, 2,611 U (53% women, 95% state res., 50% on fin. aid). Entrance difficulty: less difficult. Application deadline: rolling. Contact: Mr. Hershel F. Lucht, Registrar, (501) 246-5511.

HENDRIX COLLEGE

Conway 72032. Private; small town. Awards B. Enrolls 980 T (47% women, 85% state res., 65% on fin. aid). Entrance difficulty: moderately difficult. Application deadline: rolling. Contact: Mr. Rudy R. Pollan, (501) 329-6811.

JOHN BROWN UNIVERSITY

Siloam Springs 72761. Private; rural. Awards A, B. Enrolls 742 T (52% women, 25% state res., 70% on fin. aid). Entrance difficulty: moderately difficult. Application deadline: rolling. Contact: Mr. Bob Bethell, (501) 524-3131.

OUACHITA BAPTIST UNIVERSITY

Arkadelphia 71923. Private; small town. Awards B, M. Enrolls 1,642 T, 1,438 U (46% women, 81% state res., 80% on fin. aid). Entrance difficulty: noncompetitive. Application deadline: 8/15. Contact: Mr. Frank Taylor, Registrar and Director of Admissions, (501) 246-4531.

PHILANDER SMITH COLLEGE

Little Rock 72203. Private; urban. Awards B. Enrolls 600 T (47% women, 75% state res., 72% on fin. aid). Application deadline: 8/15. Contact: Mrs. Henrietta H. Torrence, Registrar.

SOUTHERN ARKANSAS UNIVERSITY

Magnolia 71753. Public; small town. Awards A, B, M. Enrolls 1,932 T, 1,825 U (60% women, 75% state res., 50% on fin. aid). Entrance difficulty: noncompetitive. Application deadline: 8/15. Contact: Dr. D. A. Haefner, Vice President for Student Affairs, (501) 234-5120.

UNIVERSITY OF ARKANSAS

Fayetteville 72701. Public; small town. Awards A, B, M, D. Enrolls 15,189 T, 12,645 U (41% women, 85% state res., 35% on fin. aid). Entrance difficulty: non-competitive; moderately difficult for architecture. Application deadline: rolling. Contact: Mr. Larry F. Matthews, (501) 575-5346.

UNIVERSITY OF ARKANSAS AT LITTLE ROCK

Little Rock 72204. Public; urban. Awards A, B, M. Enrolls 10,038 T, 8,982 U (54% women, 96% state res., 20% on fin. aid). Entrance difficulty: less difficult. Application deadline: rolling. Contact: Mrs. Sue Pine, (501) 569-3127.

UNIVERSITY OF ARKANSAS AT MONTICELLO

Monticello 71655. Public; small town. Awards C, A, B. Enrolls 1,800 T (53% women, 89% state res., 50% on fin. aid). Entrance difficulty: noncompetitive. Application deadline: 8/18. Contact: Mrs. Ernestine B. Brooks, Admissions Counselor, (501) 367-6811 Ext. 56.

UNIVERSITY OF ARKANSAS AT PINE BLUFF

Pine Bluff 71601. Public; urban. Awards A, B. Enrolls 2,999 T (58% women, 90% state res., 90% on fin. aid). Entrance difficulty: noncompetitive. Application deadline: 9/1. Contact: Dr. Clyde N. Toney, (501) 535-6700 Ext. 453.

UNIVERSITY OF CENTRAL ARKANSAS

Conway 72032. Public; small town. Awards A, B, M. Enrolls 5,538 T, 4,921 U (59% women, 96% state res., 50% on fin. aid). Entrance difficulty: noncompetitive. Application deadline: rolling. Contact: Mr. Tommy G. Smith, (501) 329-2931.

CALIFORNIA

AMBASSADOR COLLEGE

Pasadena 91123. Private; urban. Awards C, B, M. Enrolls 370 T, 331 U (47% women, 18% state res., 25% on fin. aid). Entrance difficulty: moderately difficult. Application deadline: 7/1. Contact: Miss Linda J. Baldwin, Recorder, (213) 577-5503.

ARMSTRONG COLLEGE

Berkeley 94704. Private; urban. Awards C, A, B, M. Enrolls 385 T, 362 U (52% women, 50% state res., 20% on fin. aid). Entrance difficulty: noncompetitive. Application deadline: rolling. Contact: Miss Kate W. Higgins, Admission Officer, (415) 848-2500.

ART CENTER COLLEGE OF DESIGN

Pasadena 91103. Private; suburban. Awards B, M. Enrolls 1,059 T, 1,057 U (34% women, 50% state res., 34% on fin. aid). Entrance difficulty: moderately difficult. Application deadline: rolling. Contact: Miss Olive M. Gardiner, Registrar, (213) 577-1700.

AZUSA PACIFIC COLLEGE

Azusa 91702. Private; suburban. Awards B, M. Enrolls 2,069 T, 1,230 U (55% women, 85% state res., 80% on fin. aid). Entrance difficulty: moderately difficult. Application deadline: 8/15. Contact: Mr. Larry R. Brooks, (213) 969-3434.

BETHANY BIBLE COLLEGE

Santa Cruz 95066. Private; rural. Awards C, B. Enrolls 598 T (44% women, 60% state res., 68% on fin. aid). Entrance difficulty: less difficult. Application deadline: 8/1. Contact: Mr. Paul Huffey, Director of Admissions Information, (408) 438-3800 Ext. 407.

BIOLA COLLEGE

La Mirada 90639. Private; suburban. Awards B, M, D. Enrolls 3,202 T, 2,384 U (53% women, 73% state res., 50% on fin. aid). Entrance difficulty: moderately difficult. Application deadline: 8/15. Contact: Mr. Wayne Chute, Dean of Admissions and Records, (213) 944-0351.

BROOKS INSTITUTE

Santa Barbara 93108. Private; urban. Awards A, B, M. Enrolls 793 T, 785 U (15% women). Entrance difficulty: noncompetitive. Application deadline: rolling. Contact: Mr. Eugene C. Streeter, Vice President.

CALIFORNIA BAPTIST COLLEGE

Riverside 92504. Private; suburban. Awards B. Enrolls 746 T (51% women, 78% state res., 80% on fin. aid). Entrance difficulty: moderately difficult. Application deadline: rolling. Contact: Mr. Walter Grubb, (714) 689-5771.

CALIFORNIA COLLEGE OF ARTS AND CRAFTS

Oakland 94618. Private; urban. Awards C, B, M. Enrolls 1,123 T, 906 U (67% women, 60% state res., 67% on fin. aid). Entrance difficulty: moderately difficult. Application deadline: rolling. Contact: Ms. Jean T. Thomma, (415) 653-8118.

CALIFORNIA INSTITUTE OF TECHNOLOGY

Pasadena 91125. Private; suburban. Awards B, M, D. Enrolls 1,715 T, 817 U (14% women, 45% state res., 70% on fin. aid). Entrance difficulty: most difficult. Application deadlines: 1/15, early decision 10/15. Contact: Dr. Stirling L. Huntley, (213) 795-6811.

CALIFORNIA INSTITUTE OF THE ARTS

Valencia 91355. Private; suburban. Awards C, B, M. Enrolls 715 T, 543 U (39% women, 54% state res., 70% on fin. aid). Entrance difficulty: very difficult. Application deadline: rolling. Contact: Ms. Renee W. Levine, (805) 255-1050.

CALIFORNIA LUTHERAN COLLEGE

Thousand Oaks 91360. Private; suburban. Awards B, M. Enrolls 2,494 T, 1,435 U (50% women, 87% state res., 75% on fin. aid). Entrance difficulty: moderately difficult. Application deadlines: 8/1, early decision 12/1. Contact: Mr. Ronald G. Timmons, (805) 492-2411.

CALIFORNIA MARITIME ACADEMY

Vallejo 94590. Public; urban. Awards B. Enrolls 485 T (3% women, 85% state res., 45% on fin. aid). Entrance difficulty: moderately difficult. Application deadline: 3/15. Contact: Mr. David G. Buchanan, (707) 644-5601.

CALIFORNIA POLYTECHNIC STATE UNIVERSITY

San Luis Obispo 93407. Public; small town. Awards C, B, M. Enrolls 15,592 T, 14,669 U (39% women, 98% state res., 20% on fin. aid). Entrance difficulty: very difficult. Application deadline: 11/30. Contact: Mr. David H. Snyder, Admissions Officer, (805) 546-2311.

CALIFORNIA STATE COLLEGE, BAKERSFIELD

Bakersfield 93309. Public; rural. Awards B, M. Enrolls 3,111 T, 2,272 U (52% women, 85% state res., 40% on fin. aid). Entrance difficulty: moderately difficult. Application deadline: 9/15. Contact: Dr. Homer S. Montalvo, (805) 833-2160.

CALIFORNIA STATE COLLEGE, SAN BERNARDINO

San Bernardino 92407. Public; suburban. Awards C, B, M. Enrolls 4,210 T, 2,752 U (52% women, 93% state res., 40% on fin. aid). Entrance difficulty: moderately difficult. Application deadline: rolling. Contact: Ms. Cheryl Weese, Admissions Officer, (714) 887-7319.

CALIFORNIA STATE COLLEGE, STANISLAUS

Turlock 95380. Public; small town. Awards B, M. Enrolls 3,612 T, 2,474 U (53% women, 93% state res., 20% on fin. aid). Entrance difficulty: moderately difficult. Application deadline: rolling. Contact: Mr. Edward J. Aubert, (209) 633-2261.

CALIFORNIA STATE POLYTECHNIC UNIVERSITY, POMONA

Pomona 91768. Public; suburban. Awards B, M. Enrolls 14,448 T, 12,879 U (37% women, 88% state res., 25% on fin. aid). Entrance difficulty: moderately difficult. Application deadline: rolling. Contact: Mr. Arthur G. Covarrubias, Admissions Officer.

CALIFORNIA STATE UNIVERSITY, CHICO

Chico 95929. Public; small town. Awards B, M. Enrolls 13,552 T, 11,390 U (53% women, 97% state res., 31% on fin. aid). Entrance difficulty: moderately difficult. Application deadline: rolling. Contact: Dr. Ken Edson, Acting Director of Admissions, (916) 895-6321.

CALIFORNIA STATE UNIVERSITY, DOMINGUEZ HILLS

Carson 90747. Public; urban. Awards B, M. Enrolls 7,173 T, 6,121 U (53% women, 35% state res., 20% on fin. aid). Entrance difficulty: moderately difficult. Application deadline: 8/15. Contact: Dr. Kenneth W. Finlay, Director of Admissions and Records, (213) 515-3600.

CALIFORNIA STATE UNIVERSITY, FRESNO

Fresno 93740. Public; urban. Awards B, M. Enrolls 14,819 T, 11,954 U (50% women, 90% state res., 33% on fin. aid). Entrance difficulty: moderately difficult; very difficult for physical therapy program. Application deadline: 9/7. Contact: Dr. T. Russell Mitchell, Coordinator, Relations with Schools, (209) 487-2191.

CALIFORNIA STATE UNIVERSITY, FULLERTON

Fullerton 92634. Public; suburban. Awards B, M. Enrolls 21,997 T, 17,153 U (53% women, 97% state res., 13% on fin. aid). Entrance difficulty: moderately difficult. Application deadline: 8/15. Contact: Dr. Ralph E. Bigelow, Dean of Admissions, (714) 773-2300.

CALIFORNIA STATE UNIVERSITY, HAYWARD

Hayward 94542. Public; urban. Awards C, B, M. Enrolls 10,976 T, 7,970 U (52% women, 98% state res., 6% on fin. aid). Entrance difficulty: very difficult. Application deadline: 8/15. Contact: Miss Judith L. Hirsch, (415) 881-3817.

CALIFORNIA STATE UNIVERSITY, LONG BEACH

Long Beach 90840. Public; urban. Awards B, M. Enrolls 30,500 T, 24,143 U (49% women, 90% state res.). Entrance difficulty: moderately difficult. Application deadline: rolling. Contact: Mr. Leonard Kreutner, Director of Admissions, (213) 498-4141.

CALIFORNIA STATE UNIVERSITY, LOS ANGELES

Los Angeles 90032. Public; urban. Awards B, M, D. Enrolls 22,570 T, 15,420 U (52% women, 95% state res., 45% on fin. aid). Entrance difficulty: moderately difficult. Application deadline: 9/5. Contact: Mr. Ronald L. Gibson, Admissions Officer, (213) 224-2172.

CALIFORNIA STATE UNIVERSITY, NORTHRIDGE

Northridge 91330. Public; suburban. Awards B, M. Enrolls 28,152 T, 22,302 U (47% women, 98% state res., 31% on fin. aid). Entrance difficulty: moderately difficult. Application deadline: 7/15. Contact: Mr. Ned Reynolds, (213) 885-3700.

CALIFORNIA STATE UNIVERSITY, SACRAMENTO

Sacramento 95819. Public; urban. Awards B, M. Enrolls 21,222 T, 16,191 U (52% women, 95% state res., 37% on fin. aid). Entrance difficulty: moderately difficult. Application deadline: rolling. Contact: Dr. Duane Anderson, (916) 454-6723.

CHAPMAN COLLEGE

Orange 92666. Private; suburban. Awards B, M. Enrolls 1,695 T, 1,259 U (51% women, 70% state res., 60% on fin. aid). Entrance difficulty: moderately difficult. Application deadline: rolling. Contact: Mr. Anthony Garcia, Dean of Admissions, (714) 997-6711.

CLAREMONT MEN'S COLLEGE

Claremont 91711. Private; suburban. Awards B. Enrolls 849 T (22% women, 60% state res., 65% on fin. aid). Entrance difficulty: very difficult. Application deadlines: 3/1, early decision 12/15. Contact: Mr. Emery R. Walker Jr, Dean of Admission, (714) 621-8088.

COGSWELL COLLEGE

San Francisco 94108. Private; urban. Awards A, B. Enrolls 425 T (9% women, 100% state res., 40% on fin. aid). Entrance difficulty: noncompetitive. Application deadline: rolling. Contact: Miss Ginny Porter, Admissions Counselor.

COLLEGE OF NOTRE DAME

Belmont 94002. Private; suburban. Awards A, B, M. Enrolls 1,357 T, 910 U (60% women, 64% state res., 60% on fin. aid). Entrance difficulty: moderately difficult. Application deadline: 8/15. Contact: Ms. Kris Crowe Zavoli, (415) 593-1601 Ext. 41.

DOMINICAN COLLEGE OF SAN RAFAEL

San Rafael 94901. Private; suburban. Awards B, M. Enrolls 645 T, 451 U (74% women, 81% state res., 40% on fin. aid). Entrance difficulty: moderately difficult. Application deadlines: rolling, early decision 12/1. Contact: Mr. Charles Lavaroni, Dean of Admissions, (415) 457-4440.

FRESNO PACIFIC COLLEGE

Fresno 93702. Private; suburban. Awards C, A, B, M. Enrolls 700 T, 450 U (55% women, 84% state res., 75% on fin. aid). Entrance difficulty: less difficult. Application deadlines: rolling, early decision 1/1. Contact: Mrs. Joan Martens, Admissions Counselor, (209) 251-7194 Ext. 57.

GOLDEN GATE UNIVERSITY

San Francisco 94105. Private; urban. Awards C, A, B, M, D. Enrolls 9,541 T, 2,847 U (35% women, 15% on fin. aid). Entrance difficulty: moderately difficult. Application deadline: rolling. Contact: Mrs. Char Hamada, (415) 442-7000.

HARVEY MUDD COLLEGE

Claremont 91711. Private; suburban. Awards B, M. Enrolls 493 T, 489 U (14% women, 60% state res., 70% on fin. aid). Entrance difficulty: most difficult. Application deadlines: 3/1, early decision 12/15. Contact: Mr. Emery R. Walker Jr, Dean of Admissions, (714) 621-8088.

HOLY NAMES COLLEGE

Oakland 94619. Private; urban. Awards C, B, M. Enrolls 628 T, 415 U (65% women, 8% state res., 60% on fin. aid). Entrance difficulty: moderately difficult. Application deadline: rolling. Contact: Miss Julie Atkinson, Acting Director of Admissions, (415) 436-1321.

HUMBOLDT STATE UNIVERSITY

Arcata 95521. Public; small town. Awards B, M. Enrolls 7,662 T, 6,677 U (44% women, 98% state res., 25% on fin. aid). Entrance difficulty: moderately difficult. Application deadline: rolling. Contact: Mr. Donald G. Clancy, (707) 826-4101.

INTERNATIONAL COLLEGE

Los Angeles 90024. Private; urban. Awards A, B, M, D. Enrolls 90 T, 60 U (60% women, 85% state res., 80% on fin. aid). Entrance difficulty: noncompetitive. Application deadline: rolling. Contact: Mr. Toby Hartman, Dean, (213) 451-1636.

JOHNSTON COLLEGE OF THE UNIVERSITY OF REDLANDS

Redlands 92373. Private; small town. Awards B, M. Enrolls 1,276 T, 1,124 U (55% women, 67% state res., 70% on fin. aid). Entrance difficulty: moderately difficult. Application deadlines: 3/1, early decision 12/1. Contact: Mr. C. Stephen Hankins, (714) 793-2121.

LINCOLN UNIVERSITY

San Francisco 94118. Private; urban. Awards B, M. Enrolls 365 T, 216 U (0% state res., 0% on fin. aid). Entrance difficulty: moderately difficult. Contact: Miss Paciencia Balonon, (415) 221-1212.

LOMA LINDA UNIVERSITY

Loma Linda 92354. Private; small town. Awards C, A, B, M, D. Enrolls 5,127 T, 3,108 U (50% women, 58% state res., 70% on fin. aid). Entrance difficulty: less difficult. Contact: Dr. Arno Kutzner, Director of Admissions and Records, (714) 796-7311 Ext. 2911.

LOMA LINDA UNIVERSITY, LA SIERRA CAMPUS

Riverside 92515. Private; suburban. Awards A, B, M. Enrolls 2,560 T, 2,212 U (52% women, 78% state res., 70% on fin. aid). Entrance difficulty: moderately difficult. Application deadline: 8/15. Contact: Dr. Arno Kutzner, (714) 785-2176.

LOS ANGELES BAPTIST COLLEGE

Newhall 91322. Private; small town. Awards C, A, B. Enrolls 393 T (50% women, 75% state res., 60% on fin. aid). Entrance difficulty: moderately difficult. Application deadline: 8/1. Contact: Mr. Paul S. Berry, Director of College Relations and Admissions, (805) 259-3540.

LOYOLA MARYMOUNT UNIVERSITY

Los Angeles 90045. Private; suburban. Awards B, M, D. Enrolls 5,896 T, 3,459 U (49% women, 92% state res., 74% on fin. aid). Entrance difficulty: moderately difficult. Application deadlines: 8/1, early decision 12/1. Contact: Mr. M. E. L'Heureux, (213) 642-2750.

MENLO COLLEGE

Menlo Park 94025. Private; suburban. Awards A, B. Enrolls 681 T (33% women, 56% state res., 20% on fin. aid). Entrance difficulty: moderately difficult. Application deadlines: rolling, early decision 12/1. Contact: Mrs. Suzy Charney, Associate Director of Admissions, (415) 323-6141.

MILLS COLLEGE

Oakland 94613. Private; urban. Awards B, M. Enrolls 973 T, 822 U (100% women, 60% state res., 51% on fin. aid). Entrance difficulty: very difficult. Application deadlines: 2/1, early decision 4/1. Contact: Ms. Gail Berson Weaver, Acting Dean of Admissions, (415) 632-2700.

MOUNT ST MARY'S COLLEGE

Los Angeles 90049. Private; urban. Awards A, B, M. Enrolls 1,047 T, 944 U (98% women, 86% state res., 58% on fin. aid). Application deadline: rolling. Contact: Dr. Irene Kelly, (213) 476-2237.

NATIONAL UNIVERSITY

San Diego 92106. Private; urban. Awards A, B, M. Enrolls 4,626 T, 2,687 U (29% women, 25% on fin. aid). Entrance difficulty: noncompetitive. Application deadline: rolling. Contact: Mr. David K. Costello, Dean of Records and Special Services, (714) 563-0100.

NEW COLLEGE OF CALIFORNIA

San Francisco 94110. Private; urban. Awards A, B, M. Enrolls 400 T, 200 U (55% women, 40% state res., 70% on fin. aid). Entrance difficulty: noncompetitive. Application deadline: rolling. Contact: Mr. Thomas Kunhardt, Admissions Director, (415) 626-1694.

NORTHROP UNIVERSITY

Inglewood 90306. Private; suburban. Awards C, A, B, M. Enrolls 1,893 T, 1,705 U (8% women, 25% state res., 25% on fin. aid). Entrance difficulty: moderately difficult. Application deadline: rolling. Contact: Mr. Judson W. Staples, Dean of Student Services, (213) 641-3470 Ext. 249.

OCCIDENTAL COLLEGE

Los Angeles 90041. Private; urban. Awards B, M. Enrolls 1,636 T, 1,602 U (50% women, 60% state res., 52% on fin. aid).

Occidental College (continued)
Entrance difficulty: very difficult. Application deadlines: 2/1, early decision 11/15. Contact: Mr. John A. Williams, (213) 259-2700.

OTIS ART INSTITUTE OF PARSONS SCHOOL OF DESIGN

Los Angeles 90057. Private; urban. Awards A, B, M. Enrolls 232 T, 143 U (60% women, 6% state res., 60% on fin. aid). Entrance difficulty: very difficult. Application deadline: rolling. Contact: Miss Nina Sadek, Assistant Director of Admissions, (213) 387-5288.

PACIFIC CHRISTIAN COLLEGE

Fullerton 92631. Private; urban. Awards A, B, M. Enrolls 345 T, 315 U (55% women, 83% state res., 67% on fin. aid). Entrance difficulty: less difficult. Application deadline: 9/22. Contact: Mr. Lloyd Hosman, (714) 879-3901.

PACIFIC UNION COLLEGE

Angwin 94508. Private; rural. Awards C, A, B, M. Enrolls 2,127 T, 2,108 U (59% women, 79% state res., 62% on fin. aid). Entrance difficulty: moderately difficult. Application deadline: rolling. Contact: Mr. Charles T. Smith Jr, Associate Director of Admissions.

PATTEN BIBLE COLLEGE

Oakland 94601. Private; urban. Awards A, B. Enrolls 125 T (60% women, 95% state res., 20% on fin. aid). Entrance difficulty: noncompetitive. Application deadline: rolling. Contact: Miss Christine Haynes, (415) 533-8300.

PEPPERDINE UNIVERSITY

Malibu 90265. Private; suburban. Awards B, M, D. Enrolls 2,781 T, 2,099 U (51% women, 68% state res., 65% on fin. aid). Entrance difficulty: moderately difficult. Application deadlines: 6/1, early decision 12/1. Contact: Mr. Robert L. Fraley, Dean of Admissions, (213) 456-4391.

PITZER COLLEGE

Claremont 91711. Private; suburban. Awards B. Enrolls 708 T (55% women, 45% state res., 51% on fin. aid). Entrance difficulty: very difficult. Application deadlines: 2/1, early decision 12/1. Contact:

Miss Alice H. Love, Admission Officer, (714) 621-8129.

POINT LOMA COLLEGE

San Diego 92106. Private; urban. Awards B, M. Enrolls 1,770 T, 1,511 U (54% women, 89% state res., 70% on fin. aid). Entrance difficulty: moderately difficult. Application deadlines: 8/15, early decision 4/15. Contact: Dr. Cecil W. Miller, (714) 222-6474.

POMONA COLLEGE

Claremont 91711. Private; suburban. Awards B. Enrolls 1,362 T (48% women, 58% state res., 47% on fin. aid). Entrance difficulty: very difficult. Application deadlines: 2/1, early decision 11/15. Contact: Mr. John E. Quinlan, Dean of Admissions, (714) 621-8134.

ST JOHN'S COLLEGE

Camarillo 93010. Contact: Rev. Stafford Poole, C.M, Director of Admissions.

SAINT MARY'S COLLEGE OF CALIFORNIA

Moraga 94575. Private; suburban. Awards C, B, M. Enrolls 1,890 T, 1,545 U (45% women, 80% state res., 65% on fin. aid). Entrance difficulty: moderately difficult. Application deadlines: 6/1, early decision 8/15. Contact: Mr. Peter J. Mohorko, Dean of Admissions, (415) 376-0197.

ST PATRICK'S COLLEGE

Mountain View 94042. Private; suburban. Awards B. Enrolls 52 T (0% women, 84% state res., 50% on fin. aid). Application deadline: 6/1. Contact: Rev. Gerald L. Brown, (415) 967-9501.

SAN DIEGO STATE UNIVERSITY

San Diego 92182. Public; urban. Awards B, M, D. Enrolls 31,495 T, 24,787 U (50% women, 96% state res., 25% on fin. aid). Entrance difficulty: moderately difficult. Application deadline: 8/31. Contact: Dr. Frank Medeiros, (714) 286-5384.

SAN FRANCISCO ART INSTITUTE

San Francisco 94133. Private; urban. Awards B, M. Enrolls 800 T, 625 U (45% women, 26% state res., 85% on fin. aid). Entrance difficulty: noncompetitive. Application deadline: rolling. Contact: Mrs. Alice Erskine, (415) 771-7020.

SAN FRANCISCO CONSERVATORY OF MUSIC

San Francisco 94122. Private; urban. Awards C, B, M. Enrolls 215 T, 150 U (43% women, 60% state res., 55% on fin. aid). Entrance difficulty: moderately difficult. Application deadline: 7/1. Contact: Mrs. Colleen Katzowitz, Director of Student Services, (415) 564-8086.

SAN FRANCISCO STATE UNIVERSITY

San Francisco 94132. Public; urban. Awards B, M, D. Enrolls 36,377 T, 11,210 U (52% women, 97% state res.). Entrance difficulty: moderately difficult. Application deadline: rolling. Contact: Mr. Charles A. Stone, (415) 469-2164.

SAN JOSE BIBLE COLLEGE

San Jose 95108. Private; urban. Awards A, B. Enrolls 238 T (40% women, 70% state res., 60% on fin. aid). Entrance difficulty: moderately difficult. Application deadline: 8/15. Contact: Miss Leeanna Meserve, Director of Admissions, (408) 293-9058.

SAN JOSE STATE UNIVERSITY

San Jose 95192. Public; urban. Awards B, M. Enrolls 26,951 T, 21,426 U (50% women, 40% on fin. aid). Entrance difficulty: moderately difficult. Application deadline: rolling. Contact: Mr. Clyde Brewer, Director of Admissions, (408) 277-3266.

SCRIPPS COLLEGE

Claremont 91711. Private; suburban. Awards B. Enrolls 560 T (100% women, 61% state res., 50% on fin. aid). Entrance difficulty: moderately difficult. Application deadline: 2/15. Contact: Miss Janet E. A. Burback, (714) 621-8149.

SIMPSON COLLEGE

San Francisco 94134. Private; urban. Awards C, B, M. Enrolls 245 T, 220 U (46% women, 60% state res., 40% on fin. aid). Entrance difficulty: less difficult. Application deadline: 8/12. Contact: Mr. Laurence Dorman, (415) 334-7400.

SONOMA STATE UNIVERSITY

Rohnert Park 94928. Public; rural. Awards B, M. Enrolls 5,505 T, 3,982 U (55% women, 97% state res.). Entrance difficulty: moderately difficult. Contact: Dr. Frank Tansey, (707) 664-2326.

SOUTHERN CALIFORNIA COLLEGE

Costa Mesa 92626. Private; suburban. Awards B. Enrolls 670 T (47% women, 80% state res., 78% on fin. aid). Entrance difficulty: less difficult. Application deadlines: 7/31, early decision 5/31. Contact: Mr. Robert E. Wilson, Director of Admissions, (714) 556-3610.

STANFORD UNIVERSITY

Stanford 94305. Private; suburban. Awards B, M, D. Enrolls 11,865 T, 6,638 U (43% women, 52% state res., 53% on fin. aid). Entrance difficulty: most difficult. Application deadline: 1/1. Contact: Mr. Fred A. Hargadon, Dean of Admissions, (415) 497-2091.

UNITED STATES INTERNATIONAL UNIVERSITY, SAN DIEGO CAMPUS

San Diego 92131. Private; suburban. Awards A, B, M, D. Enrolls 3,585 T, 1,565 U (33% women, 52% state res., 40% on fin. aid). Entrance difficulty: moderately difficult. Application deadline: 8/15. Contact: Ms. Judith A. Lewis, Director of Admissions Evaluation and Financial Aid, (714) 271-4300.

UNIVERSITY OF CALIFORNIA, BERKELEY

Berkeley 94720. Public; urban. Awards B, M, D. Enrolls 28,820 T, 19,850 U (42% women, 95% state res., 65% on fin. aid). Entrance difficulty: most difficult. Application deadline: 11/30. Contact: Mr. Robert E. Brownell, Associate Director of Admissions.

UNIVERSITY OF CALIFORNIA, DAVIS

Davis 95616. Public; small town. Awards B, M, D. Enrolls 17,987 T, 12,974 U (51% women, 88% state res., 39% on fin. aid). Entrance difficulty: very difficult. Application deadline: 11/30. Contact: Mr. Gary Tudor, (916) 752-2971.

UNIVERSITY OF CALIFORNIA, IRVINE

Irvine 92664. Public; suburban. Awards B, M, D. Enrolls 10,033 T, 7,689 U (47% women, 96% state res., 35% on fin. aid). Entrance difficulty: moderately difficult. Application deadline: rolling. Contact: Mr. James E. Dunning, (714) 833-6706.

UNIVERSITY OF CALIFORNIA, LOS ANGELES

Los Angeles 90024. Public; urban. Awards B, M, D. Enrolls 32,977 T, 21,082 U (49% women, 93% state res., 42% on fin. aid). Entrance difficulty: moderately difficult. Application deadline: rolling. Contact: Mr. Rae Lee Siporin, (213) 825-3101.

UNIVERSITY OF CALIFORNIA, RIVERSIDE

Riverside 92521. Public; suburban. Awards B, M, D. Enrolls 4,571 T, 3,199 U (50% women, 97% state res., 46% on fin. aid). Entrance difficulty: very difficult. Application deadline: rolling. Contact: Mr. Robert B. Herschler, (714) 787-3405.

UNIVERSITY OF CALIFORNIA, SAN DIEGO

La Jolla 92093. Public; suburban. Awards B, M, D. Enrolls 11,183 T, 8,818 U (40% women, 90% state res., 65% on fin. aid). Entrance difficulty: very difficult. Application deadline: 12/1. Contact: Mr. Ronald J. Bowker, Registrar, (714) 452-3192.

UNIVERSITY OF CALIFORNIA, SANTA BARBARA

Santa Barbara 93106. Public; suburban. Awards B, M, D. Enrolls 14,473 T, 12,623 U (49% women, 92% state res., 25% on fin. aid). Entrance difficulty: very difficult. Application deadline: rolling. Contact: Mr. Charles W. McKinney, Dean of Admissions and Registrar, (805) 961-2987.

UNIVERSITY OF CALIFORNIA, SANTA CRUZ

Santa Cruz 95064. Public; small town. Awards B, M, D. Enrolls 6,093 T, 5,695 U (53% women, 90% state res., 52% on fin. aid). Entrance difficulty: very difficult. Application deadline: 8/1. Contact: Mr. Richard Moll, (408) 429-2131.

UNIVERSITY OF JUDAISM

Los Angeles 90024. Private; urban. Awards A, B, M, D. Enrolls 220 T, 108 U (60% women, 80% state res., 30% on fin. aid). Entrance difficulty: moderately difficult. Application deadlines: 5/15, early decision 2/1. Contact: Dr. Joel Rembaum, Registrar, (213) 476-9777.

UNIVERSITY OF LA VERNE

La Verne 91750. Private; small town. Awards C, B, M, D. Enrolls 2,244 T, 1,557 U (52% women, 98% state res., 80% on fin. aid). Entrance difficulty: moderately difficult. Application deadline: rolling. Contact: Mr. Michael D. Welch, Director of Admissions and Financial Aid, (714) 593-3511.

UNIVERSITY OF REDLANDS

Redlands 92373. Private; small town. Awards B, M. Enrolls 1,276 T, 1,124 U (55% women, 69% state res., 70% on fin. aid). Entrance difficulty: moderately difficult. Application deadlines: 3/1, early decision 12/1. Contact: Mr. Steven Hankins, Dean of Admission and Financial Aid, (714) 793-2121 Ext. 457.

UNIVERSITY OF SAN DIEGO

San Diego 92110. Private; urban. Awards C, B, M, D. Enrolls 4,123 T, 2,636 U (52% women, 65% state res., 60% on fin. aid). Entrance difficulty: moderately difficult. Application deadlines: 5/1, early decision 11/1. Contact: Mrs. Kathy Estey, (714) 293-4506.

UNIVERSITY OF SAN FRANCISCO

San Francisco 94117. Private; urban. Awards B, M, D. Enrolls 6,339 T, 3,272 U (54% women, 63% state res., 72% on fin. aid). Entrance difficulty: moderately difficult. Application deadline: 3/15. Contact: Mr. Gabriel P. Capeto, Director of Admissions, (415) 666-6563.

UNIVERSITY OF SANTA CLARA

Santa Clara 95053. Private; suburban. Awards B, M, D. Enrolls 7,089 T, 3,600 U (43% women, 78% state res., 61% on fin. aid). Entrance difficulty: moderately difficult. Application deadline: 3/1. Contact: Mr. Daniel J. Saracino, (408) 984-4288.

UNIVERSITY OF SOUTHERN CALIFORNIA

Los Angeles 90007. Private; urban. Awards C, B, M, D. Enrolls 26,902 T, 15,404 U (41% women, 73% state res., 60% on fin. aid). Entrance difficulty: moderately difficult. Application deadline: 5/1. Contact: Mr. Jay V. Berger, (213) 743-6750.

UNIVERSITY OF THE PACIFIC

Stockton 95211. Private; suburban. Awards B, M, D. Enrolls 5,859 T, 3,654 U (49% women, 70% state res., 62% on fin. aid). Entrance difficulty: moderately difficult. Application deadline: rolling. Contact: Mr. E. Leslie Medford Jr, (209) 946-2211.

UNIVERSITY OF WEST LOS ANGELES

Culver City 90230. Private; suburban. Awards C, B. Enrolls 45 T (95% women, 95% state res., 15% on fin. aid). Entrance difficulty: less difficult. Application deadline: 9/1. Contact: Mrs. Sherry Avmack, Director of Admissions, (213) 204-0000.

WEST COAST BIBLE COLLEGE

Fresno 93710. Private; urban. Awards A, B. Enrolls 253 T (50% women, 50% state res., 80% on fin. aid). Entrance difficulty: less difficult. Application deadline: rolling. Contact: Miss Pamela Williams, Registrar, (209) 299-7205.

WEST COAST UNIVERSITY

Los Angeles 90020. Private. Awards A, B, M. Enrolls 1,417 T, 734 U (16% women, 80% state res., 5% on fin. aid). Entrance difficulty: noncompetitive. Application deadline: rolling. Contact: Ms. Maxine R. McCarty, (213) 487-4433.

WESTMONT COLLEGE

Santa Barbara 93108. Private; suburban. Awards B. Enrolls 1,021 T (55% women, 75% state res., 68% on fin. aid). Entrance difficulty: moderately difficult. Application deadline: rolling. Contact: Ms. Anita Perez Ferguson, Director of Admissions, (805) 969-5051.

WHITTIER COLLEGE

Whittier 90608. Private; suburban. Awards C, B, M. Enrolls 1,750 T, 1,340 U (51% women, 62% state res., 64% on fin. aid). Entrance difficulty: moderately difficult.

Application deadline: 6/1. Contact: Mr. Michael Adams, (213) 693-0771.

WOODBURY UNIVERSITY

Los Angeles 90017. Private; urban. Awards C, B, M. Enrolls 1,314 T, 1,243 U (35% state res., 15% on fin. aid). Entrance difficulty: moderately difficult. Application deadline: rolling. Contact: Mr. Biff Green, Dean of Students, (213) 482-8491.

WORLD COLLEGE WEST

San Rafael 94902. Private; suburban. Awards B. Enrolls 51 T (45% women, 60% state res., 68% on fin. aid). Entrance difficulty: moderately difficult. Application deadline: rolling. Contact: Ms. Christine A. Elbel, (415) 332-8412.

COLORADO

ADAMS STATE COLLEGE

Alamosa 81102. Public; small town. Awards A, B, M. Enrolls 1,924 T, 1,679 U (53% women, 87% state res., 80% on fin. aid). Entrance difficulty: moderately difficult; noncompetitive for associate's programs. Application deadline: 8/1. Contact: Miss Joyce Jantzer, Assistant Director of Admissions and Records, (303) 589-7321 Ext. 8.

COLORADO COLLEGE

Colorado Springs 80903. Private; urban. Awards B, M. Enrolls 1,885 T, 1,940 U (49% women, 33% state res., 40% on fin. aid). Entrance difficulty: moderately difficult. Application deadline: 2/15. Contact: Mr. Richard E. Wood, (303) 473-2233 Ext. 219.

COLORADO SCHOOL OF MINES

Golden 80401. Public; small town. Awards B, M, D. Enrolls 2,845 T, 2,166 U (16% women, 70% state res., 35% on fin. aid). Entrance difficulty: very difficult. Application deadline: 8/15. Contact: Mr. A. William Young, (303) 279-0300.

COLORADO STATE UNIVERSITY

Fort Collins 80523. Public; small town. Awards B, M, D. Enrolls 18,223 T, 15,346 U (45% women, 75% state res., 35% on fin. aid). Entrance difficulty: mod-

Colorado State University (continued) erately difficult. Application deadline: rolling. Contact: Dr. John Kennedy, (303) 491-7201.

COLORADO TECHNICAL COLLEGE

Colorado Springs 80907. Private; suburban. Awards C, A, B. Enrolls 433 T (15% women, 87% state res., 66% on fin. aid). Entrance difficulty: noncompetitive. Application deadline: rolling. Contact: Mr. Roy Wade, (303) 598-0200.

COLORADO WOMEN'S COLLEGE

Denver 80220. Private; urban. Awards B. Enrolls 500 T (100% women, 40% state res., 55% on fin. aid). Entrance difficulty: moderately difficult. Application deadlines: rolling, early decision 12/15. Contact: Dr. Elayne M. Donahue, (303) 394-6818.

FORT LEWIS COLLEGE

Durango 81301. Public; small town. Awards A, B. Enrolls 3,028 T (46% women, 70% state res., 40% on fin. aid). Entrance difficulty: less difficult. Application deadline: 8/1. Contact: Mr. Harlan Steinle, Supervisor of Admissions, (303) 247-7185.

LORETTO HEIGHTS COLLEGE

Denver 80236. Private; suburban. Awards B. Enrolls 850 T (70% women, 65% state res., 65% on fin. aid). Entrance difficulty: moderately difficult. Contact: Mr. William E. Fain, (303) 936-8441.

MESA COLLEGE

Grand Junction 81501. Public; small town. Awards C, A, B. Enrolls 4,259 T (56% women, 95% state res., 52% on fin. aid). Entrance difficulty: noncompetitive. Application deadline: 8/15. Contact: Mr. Jack Scott, (303) 248-1376.

METROPOLITAN STATE COLLEGE

Denver 80204. Public; urban. Awards A, B. Enrolls 13,350 T (55% women, 95% state res., 22% on fin. aid). Entrance difficulty: noncompetitive. Application deadline: 8/31. Contact: Mr. Al Rodriguez, (303) 629-3058.

REGIS COLLEGE

Denver 80221. Private; suburban. Awards B, M. Enrolls 1,220 T, 1,100 U (40% women, 45% state res., 35% on fin. aid). Entrance difficulty: moderately difficult. Application deadline: 8/15. Contact: Mr. William R. Regan, (303) 458-4900.

ROCKMONT COLLEGE

Denver 80226. Private; suburban. Awards A, B. Enrolls 311 T (48% women, 61% state res., 40% on fin. aid). Entrance difficulty: moderately difficult. Application deadline: rolling. Contact: Mr. Richard G. Meyers, (303) 238-5386.

UNITED STATES AIR FORCE ACADEMY

USAF Academy 80840. Public; rural. Awards B. Enrolls 4,400 T (8% women, 5% state res., 100% on fin. aid). Entrance difficulty: very difficult. Application deadline: 1/30. Contact: Col. Warren L. Simmons, (303) 472-3070.

UNIVERSITY OF COLORADO AT BOULDER

Boulder 80309. Public; suburban. Awards B, M, D. Enrolls 21,727 T, 17,965 U (45% women, 66% state res., 50% on fin. aid). Entrance difficulty: moderately difficult except for business, engineering, and environmental design. Application deadline: rolling. Contact: Mr. A. Dwight Grotewold, (303) 492-6301.

UNIVERSITY OF COLORADO AT COLORADO SPRINGS

Colorado Springs 80907. Public; suburban. Awards B, M. Enrolls 4,664 T, 3,263 U (53% women, 90% state res., 11% on fin. aid). Entrance difficulty: moderately difficult; very difficult for business and engineering. Application deadline: 7/1. Contact: Mr. Douglas R. Johnson, Director of Admissions and Records, (303) 593-3116.

UNIVERSITY OF COLORADO AT DENVER

Denver 80220. Public; urban. Awards B, M, D. Enrolls 8,744 T, 5,371 U (46% women, 91% state res., 14% on fin. aid). Entrance difficulty: moderately difficult. Application deadline: 7/1. Contact: Mr. George Burnham, (303) 629-2703.

UNIVERSITY OF DENVER

Denver 80208. Private; suburban. Awards B, M, D. Enrolls 8,038 T, 4,522 U (45% women, 39% state res., 48% on fin. aid). Entrance difficulty: moderately difficult. Application deadline: rolling. Contact: Dr. Steven R. Antonoff, Dean of Admissions and Financial Aid, (303) 753-2036.

UNIVERSITY OF NORTHERN COLORADO

Greeley 80639. Public; small town. Awards B, M, D. Enrolls 11,000 T, 8,500 U (60% women, 80% state res., 70% on fin. aid). Entrance difficulty: moderately difficult. Application deadline: 8/15. Contact: Mr. Robert J. Powers, (303) 351-2881.

UNIVERSITY OF SOUTHERN COLORADO

Pueblo 81001. Public; suburban. Awards A, B, M. Enrolls 4,500 T, 4,500 U (43% women, 88% state res., 50% on fin. aid). Entrance difficulty: less difficult. Application deadline: rolling. Contact: Mr. Harold J. Pope, Assistant Director of Admissions, (303) 549-2461.

WESTERN BIBLE COLLEGE

Morrison 80465. Private; suburban. Awards A, B. Enrolls 214 T (44% women, 64% state res., 50% on fin. aid). Entrance difficulty: moderately difficult. Application deadline: 8/15. Contact: Mr. Jess Mahon, Admissions Counselor, (303) 697-8135.

WESTERN STATE COLLEGE OF COLORADO

Gunnison 81230. Public; rural. Awards B, M. Enrolls 2,940 T, 2,843 U (42% women, 80% state res., 35% on fin. aid). Entrance difficulty: moderately difficult. Contact: Mr. Wes Lazenby, (303) 943-2119.

CONNECTICUT

ALBERTUS MAGNUS COLLEGE

New Haven 06511. Private; suburban. Awards A, B. Enrolls 561 T (98% women, 82% state res., 67% on fin. aid). Entrance difficulty: moderately difficult. Application deadline: rolling. Contact: Sr. Michele Ryan, Assistant Director of Admissions, (203) 865-3445.

BRIDGEPORT ENGINEERING INSTITUTE

Bridgeport 06606. Private; suburban. Awards A, B. Enrolls 630 T (15% women, 95% state res., 20% on fin. aid). Entrance difficulty: less difficult. Application deadline: 9/5. Contact: Mr. Ernest L. Greenhill, Dean of Admissions, (203) 372-4395.

CENTRAL CONNECTICUT STATE COLLEGE

New Britain 06050. Public; suburban. Awards B, M. Enrolls 12,061 T, 9,886 U (46% women, 97% state res., 30% on fin. aid). Entrance difficulty: moderately difficult. Application deadline: rolling. Contact: Mr. Johnie M. Floyd, Director of Admissions, (203) 827-7548.

CONNECTICUT COLLEGE

New London 06320. Private; suburban. Awards B, M. Enrolls 1,690 T, 1,627 U (58% women, 25% state res., 33% on fin. aid). Entrance difficulty: very difficult. Application deadlines: 2/1, early decision 1/1. Contact: Ms. Jeanette Hersey, Dean of Admissions, (203) 443-2141.

EASTERN CONNECTICUT STATE COLLEGE

Willimantic 06226. Public; small town. Awards A, B, M. Enrolls 2,900 T, 2,200 U (55% women, 95% state res., 60% on fin. aid). Entrance difficulty: moderately difficult. Application deadline: rolling. Contact: Ms. Claudette S. Milner, Assistant Director of Admissions, (203) 456-2231 Ext. 286.

FAIRFIELD UNIVERSITY

Fairfield 06430. Private; suburban. Awards B, M. Enrolls 4,713 T, 2,772 U (49% women, 50% state res., 30% on fin. aid). Entrance difficulty: very difficult. Application deadlines: 3/1, early decision 12/1/. Contact: Mr. David Flynn, (203) 255-5411.

HOLY APOSTLES COLLEGE

Cromwell 06416. Private; suburban. Awards A, B, M. Enrolls 95 T, 72 U (20% women, 25% state res., 80% on fin. aid). Entrance difficulty: noncompetitive. Application deadline: 8/1. Contact: Rev. Edward B. Reiter, Dean of Admissions, (203) 635-5311.

POST COLLEGE

Waterbury 06708. Private; suburban. Awards A, B. Enrolls 1,527 T (60% women, 80% state res., 73% on fin. aid). Entrance difficulty: less difficult. Application deadline: rolling. Contact: Mr. Joseph J. Martinkovic, Dean of Admissions, (203) 755-0121.

QUINNIPIAC COLLEGE

Hamden 06518. Private; suburban. Awards A, B, M. Enrolls 3,217 T, 2,936 U (60% women, 50% state res., 40% on fin. aid). Entrance difficulty: moderately difficult; very difficult for allied health programs. Application deadlines: 6/30, early decision 11/1. Contact: Mr. Russell J. Ryan, Director of Admissions and Student Records, (203) 288-5251.

SACRED HEART UNIVERSITY

Bridgeport 06606. Private; suburban. Awards C, A, B, M. Enrolls 2,912 T, 1,180 U (59% women, 99% state res., 60% on fin. aid). Entrance difficulty: moderately difficult. Application deadline: 9/1. Contact: Mrs. Sharon Brennan Browne, (203) 374-9441.

SAINT JOSEPH COLLEGE

West Hartford 06117. Private; suburban. Awards B, M. Enrolls 1,371 T, 771 U (100% women, 74% state res., 56% on fin. aid). Entrance difficulty: moderately difficult. Application deadlines: 5/1, early decision 11/1. Contact: Miss Anne M. Murphy, (203) 232-9608.

SOUTHERN CONNECTICUT STATE COLLEGE

New Haven 06515. Public; urban. Awards B, M. Enrolls 8,502 T, 6,620 U (63% women, 94% state res., 67% on fin. aid). Entrance difficulty: moderately difficult. Application deadline: rolling. Contact: Mr. Robert Porter, Director of Admissions, (203) 397-4451.

TRINITY COLLEGE

Hartford 06106. Private; urban. Awards B, M. Enrolls 2,030 T, 1,840 U (48% women, 22% state res., 29% on fin. aid). Entrance difficulty: very difficult. Application deadlines: 1/1, early decision 3/1. Contact: Mr. W. Howie Muir, (203) 527-3151.

UNITED STATES COAST GUARD ACADEMY

New London 06320. Public; suburban. Awards B. Enrolls 831 T (10% women, 7% state res., 100% on fin. aid). Entrance difficulty: very difficult. Application deadline: 12/15. Contact: Capt. R. T. Getman, (203) 444-8503.

UNIVERSITY OF BRIDGEPORT

Bridgeport 06602. Private; urban. Awards C, A, B, M, D. Enrolls 6,956 T, 4,837 U (55% women, 69% state res., 40% on fin. aid). Entrance difficulty: moderately difficult. Application deadline: rolling. Contact: Mr. Gerald N. Davis, Associate Dean of Admissions, (203) 576-4555.

UNIVERSITY OF CONNECTICUT

Stamford 06903.

UNIVERSITY OF CONNECTICUT

Storrs 06268. Public; rural. Awards B, M, D. Enrolls 21,042 T, 15,131 U (48% women, 90% state res.). Entrance difficulty: moderately difficult. Application deadline: 2/15. Contact: Mr. John W. Vlandis, (203) 486-3137.

UNIVERSITY OF HARTFORD

West Hartford 06117. Private; suburban. Awards C, A, B, M, D. Enrolls 9,890 T, 7,012 U (47% women, 70% state res., 40% on fin. aid). Entrance difficulty: moderately difficult. Application deadlines: 2/1, early decision 12/1. Contact: Mr. Charles F. Nelson Jr, (203) 243-4296.

UNIVERSITY OF NEW HAVEN

West Haven 06516. Private; urban. Awards C, A, B, M. Enrolls 7,254 T, 2,399 U (26% women, 75% state res., 64% on fin. aid). Entrance difficulty: less difficult. Application deadline: 8/15. Contact: Mr. John E. Benevento, Dean of Admissions and Financial Aid, (203) 934-6321 Ext. 315.

WESLEYAN UNIVERSITY

Middletown 06457. Private; small town. Awards B, M, D. Enrolls 2,550 T, 2,400 U (48% women, 20% state res., 40% on fin. aid). Entrance difficulty: most difficult. Application deadlines: 1/15, early decision 11/15. Contact: Mr. Karl M. Furstenberg, Dean of Admissions, (203) 347-9411.

WESTERN CONNECTICUT STATE COLLEGE

Danbury 06810. Public; urban. Awards A, B, M. Enrolls 5,454 T, 2,732 U (57% women, 90% state res., 49% on fin. aid). Entrance difficulty: moderately difficult. Application deadlines: 8/15, early decision 2/1. Contact: Mr. Delmore Kinney Jr, (203) 797-4298.

YALE UNIVERSITY

New Haven 06520. Private; urban. Awards B, M, D. Enrolls 9,954 T, 5,170 U (41% women, 11% state res., 36% on fin. aid). Entrance difficulty: most difficult. Application deadlines: 1/2, early decision 11/1. Contact: Mr. Worth David, Dean of Admissions, (203) 436-2405.

DELAWARE

DELAWARE STATE COLLEGE

Dover 19901. Public; rural. Awards B. Enrolls 2,153 T (50% women, 62% state res., 56% on fin. aid). Entrance difficulty: moderately difficult. Application deadline: 7/1. Contact: Mr. Jethro Williams, Admissions Officer, (302) 678-4916.

GOLDEY BEACOM COLLEGE

Wilmington 19808. Private; suburban. Awards C, A, B. Enrolls 1,460 T (71% women, 56% state res., 20% on fin. aid). Entrance difficulty: less difficult. Application deadline: rolling. Contact: Miss Margaret H. Juhl, (302) 998-8814.

UNIVERSITY OF DELAWARE

Newark 19711. Public; small town. Awards A, B, M, D. Enrolls 15,449 T, 13,525 U (54% women, 52% state res., 60% on fin. aid). Entrance difficulty: moderately difficult. Application deadline: 3/1. Contact: Mr. Douglas McConkey, (302) 738-8123.

WESLEY COLLEGE

Dover 19901. Private; small town. Awards C, A, B. Enrolls 1,345 T (50% women, 95% state res., 58% on fin. aid). Entrance difficulty: moderately difficult. Application deadlines: rolling, early decision 11/15. Contact: Mr. Joseph R. Slights Jr, Dean of Admissions, (302) 736-2400.

WILMINGTON COLLEGE

New Castle 19720. Private; suburban. Awards A, B, M. Enrolls 774 T, 683 U (40% women, 63% state res., 23% on fin. aid). Entrance difficulty: noncompetitive. Application deadline: rolling. Contact: Mr. Larry Crum, Director of Admissions, (302) 328-9401.

DISTRICT OF COLUMBIA

AMERICAN UNIVERSITY

Washington 20016. Private; suburban. Awards C, A, B, M, D. Enrolls 12,824 T, 5,717 U (48% women, 27% state res., 33% on fin. aid). Entrance difficulty: moderately difficult. Application deadline: 8/1. Contact: Mrs. Jennifer Hantho, (202) 686-2211.

BEACON COLLEGE

Washington 20009. Private; urban. Awards A, B, M. Enrolls 143 T, 43 U (45% women, 77% on fin. aid). Entrance difficulty: less difficult. Application deadline: rolling. Contact: Miss Ursula Poetzschke, (202) 797-9270.

CATHOLIC UNIVERSITY OF AMERICA

Washington 20064. Private; suburban. Awards B, M, D. Enrolls 7,100 T, 2,700 U (50% women, 41% on fin. aid). Entrance difficulty: moderately difficult. Application deadline: 7/1. Contact: Mr. Robert J. Talbot, (202) 635-5305.

GALLAUDET COLLEGE

Washington 20002. Contact: Bernard P. Greenberg, Director of Admissions.

GEORGETOWN UNIVERSITY

Washington 20057. Private; suburban. Awards B, M, D. Enrolls 11,615 T, 5,612 U (53% women, 50% on fin. aid). Entrance difficulty: very difficult. Application deadlines: 1/15, early decision 11/1. Contact: Mr. Charles A. Deacon, (202) 625-3051.

GEORGE WASHINGTON UNIVERSITY

Washington 20052.

HOWARD UNIVERSITY

Washington 20059. Private; urban. Awards C, B, M, D. Enrolls 10,706 T, 7,107 U (54% women, 31% state res., 69% on fin. aid). Entrance difficulty: moderately difficult. Application deadline: 4/1. Contact: Mrs. Adrienne W. McMurdock, (202) 636-6205.

MOUNT VERNON COLLEGE

Washington 20007. Private; urban. Awards A, B. Enrolls 462 T (100% women, 14% state res., 23% on fin. aid). Entrance difficulty: less difficult. Application deadlines: rolling, early decision 11/1. Contact: Mrs. Elaine B. Liles, (202) 331-3444.

SOUTHEASTERN UNIVERSITY

Washington 20024. Private; urban. Awards A, B, M. Enrolls 1,341 T, 650 U (50% women, 40% on fin. aid). Entrance difficulty: noncompetitive. Application deadline: rolling. Contact: Ms. Krystyna Jankowski, (202) 488-8162.

STRAYER COLLEGE

Washington 20005. Private; urban. Awards C, A, B. Enrolls 1,807 T (67% women, 55% state res., 60% on fin. aid). Entrance difficulty: less difficult. Application deadline: rolling. Contact: Ms. Shirley Stepro, Assistant to the Director, (202) 783-5180.

TRINITY COLLEGE

Washington 20017. Private; suburban. Awards B, M. Enrolls 850 T, 600 U (100% women, 6% state res., 48% on fin. aid). Entrance difficulty: very difficult. Application deadline: rolling. Contact: Miss Mary T. Conner, Assistant Director of Admissions, (202) 269-2201.

UNIVERSITY OF THE DISTRICT OF COLUMBIA

Washington 20004. Public; urban. Awards C, A, B, M. Enrolls 15,096 T, 14,434 U (56% women, 91% state res., 32% on fin. aid). Entrance difficulty: noncompetitive. Application deadline: 8/1. Contact: Mr. LaHugh Bankston, (202) 727-2271.

WASHINGTON INTERNATIONAL COLLEGE

Washington 20005. Private; urban. Awards A, B. Enrolls 280 T (70% women, 90% state res., 60% on fin. aid). Application deadline: rolling. Contact: Dr. Talmadge T. Williams, (202) 466-7220.

FLORIDA

BARRY COLLEGE

Miami Shores 33161. Private; suburban. Awards B, M. Enrolls 1,781 T, 1,249 U (73% women, 79% state res., 52% on fin. aid). Entrance difficulty: moderately difficult. Application deadline: 8/15. Contact: Miss Deborah Blaisdell, Director of Freshman Admissions, (305) 758-3392.

BETHUNE-COOKMAN COLLEGE

Daytona Beach 32015. Private; urban. Awards B. Enrolls 1,736 T (58% women, 84% state res., 89% on fin. aid). Entrance difficulty: moderately difficult. Application deadline: 7/30. Contact: Mr. James C. Wymes, (904) 255-1401 Ext. 362.

BISCAYNE COLLEGE

Miami 33054. Private; suburban. Awards B, M. Enrolls 2,400 T, 2,109 U (48% women, 65% state res., 70% on fin. aid). Entrance difficulty: moderately difficult. Application deadlines: 8/15, early decision 11/1. Contact: Dr. James T. Parker, (305) 625-6000.

ECKERD COLLEGE

St Petersburg 33733. Private; suburban. Awards B. Enrolls 1,060 T (48% women, 32% state res., 70% on fin. aid). Entrance difficulty: moderately difficult. Application deadline: 8/15. Contact: Dr. Richard R. Hallin, Dean of Admissions, (813) 867-1166.

EDWARD WATERS COLLEGE

Jacksonville 32209. Private; urban. Awards B. Enrolls 660 T (62% women, 90% state res., 72% on fin. aid). Entrance difficulty: noncompetitive. Application deadline: rolling. Contact: Mr. Bernard Clay, Dean of Admissions, (904) 355-6116.

EMBRY-RIDDLE AERONAUTICAL UNIVERSITY

Daytona Beach 32014. Private; urban. Awards A, B, M. Enrolls 7,543 T, 7,115 U (2% women, 10% state res., 60% on fin. aid). Entrance difficulty: noncompetitive;

moderately difficult for aeronautical engineering. Application deadline: rolling. Contact: Mr. Robert Pihlaja, Dean of Admissions and Records, (904) 252-5561 Ext. 326.

FLAGLER COLLEGE

St Augustine 32084. Private; small town. Awards B. Enrolls 745 T (55% women, 40% state res., 55% on fin. aid). Entrance difficulty: moderately difficult. Application deadline: rolling. Contact: Mr. William T. Abare Jr, (904) 829-6481 Ext. 220.

FLORIDA A&M UNIVERSITY

Tallahassee 32307. Public; small town. Awards A, B, M. Enrolls 5,489 T, 5,223 U (51% women, 88% state res., 88% on fin. aid). Entrance difficulty: less difficult. Application deadline: 8/20. Contact: Mr. Samuel Washington Jr, (904) 599-3796.

FLORIDA INSTITUTE OF TECHNOLOGY

Melbourne 32901. Private; suburban. Awards A, B, M, D. Enrolls 4,744 T, 2,626 U (20% women, 20% state res., 80% on fin. aid). Entrance difficulty: moderately difficult. Application deadline: 6/30. Contact: Mr. Robert S. Heidinger, Dean of Admissions, (305) 723-3701.

FLORIDA MEMORIAL COLLEGE

Miami 33054. Private; urban. Awards B. Enrolls 794 T (52% women, 59% state res., 80% on fin. aid). Entrance difficulty: noncompetitive. Contact: Mr. Roberto Barragan, (305) 625-4141.

FLORIDA SOUTHERN COLLEGE

Lakeland 33802. Private; small town. Awards B. Enrolls 1,735 T (52% women, 67% state res., 42% on fin. aid). Entrance difficulty: moderately difficult. Application deadline: 8/1. Contact: Mr. William B. Stephens Jr, (813) 683-5521 Ext. 311.

FLORIDA STATE UNIVERSITY

Tallahassee 32306. Public; urban. Awards A, B, M, D. Enrolls 21,531 T, 15,765 U (51% women, 90% state res., 50% on fin. aid). Entrance difficulty: moderately difficult. Application deadline: 8/22. Contact: Dr. Peter F. Metarko, (904) 644-6200.

FORT LAUDERDALE COLLEGE

Ft Lauderdale 33301. Private; urban. Awards C, A, B. Enrolls 1,087 T (19% women, 85% state res., 26% on fin. aid). Entrance difficulty: noncompetitive. Application deadline: rolling. Contact: Miss Judi McBride, (305) 462-3761.

HEED UNIVERSITY

Hollywood 33020. Contact: Dr. Russel Grenon, Chairman.

JACKSONVILLE UNIVERSITY

Jacksonville 32211. Private; suburban. Awards B, M. Enrolls 2,217 T, 2,141 U (43% women, 51% state res., 41% on fin. aid). Entrance difficulty: moderately difficult. Application deadline: 8/1. Contact: Mr. J. Bradford Sargent III, (904) 744-3950.

JONES COLLEGE

Jacksonville 32211. Private; suburban. Awards C, A, B. Enrolls 1,088 T (25% women, 92% state res., 46% on fin. aid). Entrance difficulty: noncompetitive. Application deadline: rolling. Contact: Mr. Barry B. Durden, (904) 743-1122.

JONES COLLEGE

Orlando 32803. Private; urban. Awards C, A, B. Enrolls 1,350 T (25% women, 96% state res., 59% on fin. aid). Entrance difficulty: noncompetitive. Application deadline: rolling. Contact: Mr. Robert W. Miller, Admissions Coordinator, (305) 896-2407.

MIAMI CHRISTIAN COLLEGE

Miami 33167. Private; urban. Awards C, A, B. Enrolls 190 T (44% women, 81% state res., 68% on fin. aid). Entrance difficulty: less difficult. Application deadline: 7/15. Contact: Mr. David E. Wiles, Registrar and Financial Aid Director, (305) 685-7431.

NOVA UNIVERSITY

Ft Lauderdale 33314. Private; suburban. Awards B, M, D. Enrolls 5,998 T, 638 U (40% women, 100% state res.). Entrance difficulty: noncompetitive. Application deadline: rolling. Contact: Mr. Donald E. Halter, Registrar, (305) 475-8300.

PALM BEACH ATLANTIC COLLEGE

West Palm Beach 33401. Private; urban. Awards A, B. Enrolls 580 T (52% women, 76% state res., 50% on fin. aid). Entrance difficulty: less difficult. Application deadline: 8/1. Contact: Mr. Michael Duduit, Director of Public Affairs, (305) 833-8592.

RINGLING SCHOOL OF ART

Sarasota 33580. Private; suburban. Awards B. Enrolls 465 T (50% women, 30% state res., 35% on fin. aid). Entrance difficulty: moderately difficult. Application deadline: rolling. Contact: Miss Lisa Redling Kaplan, (813) 355-5259.

ROLLINS COLLEGE

Winter Park 32789. Private; small town. Awards B, M. Enrolls 1,375 T, 1,350 U (50% women, 30% state res., 34% on fin. aid). Entrance difficulty: moderately difficult. Application deadlines: 4/15, early decision 11/1. Contact: Ms. Cynthia G. Grubbs, (305) 646-2161.

ST JOHN VIANNEY COLLEGE SEMINARY

Miami 33165. Private; urban. Awards A, B. Enrolls 70 T (0% women, 65% state res., 95% on fin. aid). Entrance difficulty: moderately difficult. Application deadline: rolling. Contact: Rev. Sean M. Sullivan, Academic Dean, (305) 223-4561.

SAINT LEO COLLEGE

Saint Leo 33574. Private; rural. Awards A, B. Enrolls 1,053 T (35% women, 50% state res., 40% on fin. aid). Entrance difficulty: less difficult. Application deadline: rolling. Contact: Fr. J. Dennis Murphy, OSB, (904) 588-8283.

SOUTHEASTERN COLLEGE OF THE ASSEMBLIES OF GOD

Lakeland 33801. Private; suburban. Awards C, B. Enrolls 1,232 T (44% women, 29% state res., 58% on fin. aid). Entrance difficulty: noncompetitive. Application deadline: rolling. Contact: Dr. C. Eugene Pansler, (813) 665-4404.

STETSON UNIVERSITY

Deland 32720. Private; suburban. Awards B, M. Enrolls 2,900 T, 1,950 U (45% women, 60% state res., 42% on fin. aid). Entrance difficulty: moderately difficult.

Application deadlines: 3/15, early decision 11/15. Contact: Mr. Gary A. Meadows, (904) 734-4121.

TAMPA COLLEGE

Tampa 33607. Private; urban. Awards C, A, B. Enrolls 1,413 T (52% women, 90% state res., 35% on fin. aid). Entrance difficulty: noncompetitive. Application deadline: rolling. Contact: Mr. Ted Whitworth, Director of Admissions, (813) 879-6000.

TAMPA COLLEGE, CLEARWATER CAMPUS

Clearwater 33515.

TAMPA COLLEGE, SAINT PETERSBURG CAMPUS

St Petersburg 33714.

UNIVERSITY OF CENTRAL FLORIDA

Orlando 32816. Private; suburban. Awards A, B, M, D. Enrolls 11,594 T, 9,929 U (44% women, 94% state res., 75% on fin. aid). Entrance difficulty: moderately difficult. Application deadline: 8/20. Contact: Mr. Ralph Boston, (305) 275-2511.

UNIVERSITY OF FLORIDA

Gainesville 32611. Public; suburban. Awards B, M, D. Enrolls 32,314 T, 25,989 U (44% women, 93% state res., 58% on fin. aid). Entrance difficulty: moderately difficult. Application deadlines: 3/1, early decision 12/1. Contact: Mr. James B. Parrish, Director of Admissions, (904) 392-1365.

UNIVERSITY OF MIAMI

Coral Gables 33124. Private; urban. Awards B, M, D. Enrolls 14,388 T, 10,325 U (44% women, 45% state res., 51% on fin. aid). Entrance difficulty: moderately difficult. Application deadline: rolling. Contact: Mr. George Giampetro, (305) 284-4323.

UNIVERSITY OF SOUTH FLORIDA

St Petersburg 33701. Public; suburban. Awards B, M, D. Enrolls 1,700 T (50% women). Contact: Mrs. Evelyn Mohler, Administrative Assistant.

UNIVERSITY OF SOUTH FLORIDA

Tampa 33620. Public; suburban. Awards A, B, M, D. Enrolls 20,011 T, 17,214 U (50% women, 91% state res., 45% on fin. aid). Entrance difficulty: moderately difficult. Application deadline: 8/12. Contact: Mr. Robert Levitt, (813) 974-4016.

UNIVERSITY OF SOUTH FLORIDA, NEW COLLEGE

Sarasota 33580. Public; suburban. Awards B. Enrolls 508 T (48% women, 50% state res., 50% on fin. aid). Entrance difficulty: very difficult. Application deadline: rolling. Contact: Mrs. Mildred P. Ellis, (813) 355-7671 Ext. 201.

UNIVERSITY OF TAMPA

Tampa 33606. Private; urban. Awards A, B, M. Enrolls 2,420 T, 1,845 U (40% women, 25% state res., 51% on fin. aid). Entrance difficulty: moderately difficult. Application deadlines: rolling, early decision 11/25. Contact: Mr. Walter M. Turner, (813) 253-8861.

WARNER SOUTHERN COLLEGE

Lake Wales 33853. Private; suburban. Awards C, A, B. Enrolls 264 T (50% women, 30% state res., 63% on fin. aid). Entrance difficulty: less difficult. Application deadline: rolling. Contact: Mr. Perry Grubbs, (813) 638 1426.

GEORGIA

AGNES SCOTT COLLEGE

Decatur 30030. Private; suburban. Awards B. Enrolls 544 T (100% women, 50% state res., 45% on fin. aid). Entrance difficulty: very difficult. Application deadline: rolling. Contact: Mrs. Judith Maguire Tindel, (404) 373-2571.

ALBANY STATE COLLEGE

Albany 31705. Public; urban. Awards B. Enrolls 4,962 T (61% women, 90% state res., 89% on fin. aid). Contact: Ms. Dorothy Hubbard, (912) 439-4107.

ARMSTRONG STATE COLLEGE

Savannah 31406. Public; suburban. Awards A, B, M. Enrolls 2,854 T (55% women, 95% state res., 40% on fin. aid). Entrance difficulty: less difficult. Application deadline: 9/15. Contact: Mr. Thomas P. Miller, Director of Admissions, (912) 927-5275.

ATLANTA CHRISTIAN COLLEGE

East Point 30344. Private; suburban. Awards C, B. Enrolls 207 T (40% women, 56% state res., 60% on fin. aid). Entrance difficulty: noncompetitive. Application deadline: rolling. Contact: Mr. David K. Akers, Director of Admissions and Registrar, (404) 761-8861.

ATLANTA COLLEGE OF ART

Atlanta 30309. Private; urban. Awards B. Enrolls 260 T (55% women, 40% state res., 40% on fin. aid). Entrance difficulty: less difficult. Application deadlines: 6/15, early decision 12/1. Contact: Mr. William W. Linthicum, (404) 892-3600 Ext. 163.

AUGUSTA COLLEGE

Augusta 30904. Public; urban. Awards A, B, M. Enrolls 3,685 T, 3,378 U (55% women, 90% state res., 28% on fin. aid). Entrance difficulty: moderately difficult. Application deadline: 8/15. Contact: Mr. Bart Snead, Admissions Counselor.

BERRY COLLEGE

Mount Berry 30149. Private; suburban. Awards A, B, M. Enrolls 1,540 T, 1,384 U (45% women, 60% state res., 65% on fin. aid). Entrance difficulty: moderately difficult. Application deadline: rolling. Contact: Mr. Thomas C. Glover, Dean of Admissions, (404) 235-4494.

BRENAU COLLEGE

Gainesville 30501. Private; small town. Awards B, M. Enrolls 806 T, 686 U (82% women, 75% state res., 40% on fin. aid). Entrance difficulty: less difficult. Application deadline: rolling. Contact: Mr. Jeff Saeli, Director of Admissions, (404) 534-6100.

CLARK COLLEGE

Atlanta 30314. Private; urban. Awards B. Enrolls 2,031 T (72% women, 60% state res., 94% on fin. aid). Entrance difficulty: moderately difficult. Application deadline: rolling. Contact: Mr. Clifton Rawles, (404) 681-3080.

COLUMBUS COLLEGE

Columbus 31907. Public; suburban. Awards C, A, B, M. Enrolls 4,665 T, 4,070 U (54% women, 88% state res., 33% on fin. aid). Entrance difficulty: noncompetitive. Application deadline: 8/29. Contact: Mr. Terry J. Bailey, Associate Director of Admissions, (404) 568-2035.

COVENANT COLLEGE

Lookout Mountain 37350. Private; suburban. Awards A, B. Enrolls 494 T (50% women, 15% state res., 80% on fin. aid). Entrance difficulty: moderately difficult. Application deadline: rolling. Contact: Mrs. Arline Cadwell, Director of Admissions Counseling, (404) 820-1560.

DEVRY INSTITUTE OF TECHNOLOGY

Atlanta 30341. Private; urban. Awards C, A, B. Enrolls 1,019 T (7% women, 18% state res., 46% on fin. aid). Entrance difficulty: noncompetitive. Application deadline: 10/1. Contact: Ms. Marjorie Coffing, (404) 452-0045.

EMORY UNIVERSITY

Atlanta 30322. Private; suburban. Awards C, B, M, D. Enrolls 8,037 T, 3,041 U (45% women, 25% state res., 28% on fin. aid). Entrance difficulty: very difficult. Application deadlines: 3/1, early decision 11/1. Contact: Miss Linda S. Davis, (404) 329-6036.

FORT VALLEY STATE COLLEGE

Fort Valley 31030. Public; small town. Awards A, B, M. Enrolls 1,813 T, 1,778 U (51% women, 84% state res., 91% on fin. aid). Entrance difficulty: less difficult. Application deadline: 8/27. Contact: Mrs. Delia W. Taylor, Acting Director of Admissions, (912) 825-6307.

GEORGIA COLLEGE

Milledgeville 31061. Public; small town. Awards A, B, M. Enrolls 3,362 T, 2,810 U (56% women, 95% state res., 40% on fin. aid). Entrance difficulty: less difficult. Application deadline: rolling. Contact: Mr. R. Linton Cox Jr, (912) 453-4558.

GEORGIA INSTITUTE OF TECHNOLOGY

Atlanta 30332. Public; urban. Awards B, M, D. Enrolls 11,246 T, 9,429 U (19% women, 20% on fin. aid). Entrance difficulty: very difficult. Application deadline: 4/1. Contact: Mr. Jerry L. Hitt, (404) 894-4157.

GEORGIA SOUTHERN COLLEGE

Statesboro 30458. Public; small town. Awards A, B, M. Enrolls 6,723 T, 5,735 U (49% women, 91% state res., 85% on fin. aid). Entrance difficulty: moderately difficult. Application deadline: 9/15. Contact: Mr. R. Scott MacLachlan, Assistant Director of Admissions, (912) 681-5531.

GEORGIA SOUTHWESTERN COLLEGE

Americus 31709. Public; small town. Awards C, A, B, M. Enrolls 2,367 T, 1,784 U (59% women, 97% state res., 39% on fin. aid). Entrance difficulty: less difficult. Application deadline: rolling. Contact: Dr. O. J. Cliett III, Acting Director of Admissions, (912) 928-1273.

GEORGIA STATE UNIVERSITY

Atlanta 30303. Public; urban. Awards A, B, M, D. Enrolls 20,338 T, 13,389 U (55% women, 89% state res., 16% on fin. aid). Entrance difficulty: moderately difficult. Application deadline: 8/15. Contact: Dr. George W. Stansbury, Dean of Admissions, (404) 658-2365.

KENNESAW COLLEGE

Marietta 30061. Public; suburban. Awards A, B. Enrolls 4,132 T (51% women, 95% state res., 10% on fin. aid). Entrance difficulty: less difficult. Application deadline: 9/1. Contact: Mr. Thomas H. Rogers Jr, Registrar and Director of Admissions, (404) 422-8770.

LA GRANGE COLLEGE

La Grange 30240. Private; small town. Awards A, B, M. Enrolls 876 T, 847 U (59% women, 90% state res., 29% on fin. aid). Entrance difficulty: moderately difficult. Application deadline: 8/15. Contact: Mr. Tom Helton, (404) 882-2911.

MERCER UNIVERSITY

Macon 31207. Private; urban. Awards B, M, D. Enrolls 2,327 T, 2,070 U (47% women,

50% state res., 55% on fin. aid). Entrance difficulty: moderately difficult. Application deadline: rolling. Contact: Mr. Larry J. Shertz, (912) 745-6811.

MERCER UNIVERSITY IN ATLANTA

Atlanta 30341. Private; suburban. Awards B, M. Enrolls 1,390 T, 1,177 U (45% women, 95% state res., 45% on fin. aid). Entrance difficulty: less difficult. Application deadline: 9/1. Contact: Mr. Richard V. Swindle, (404) 451-0331.

MOREHOUSE COLLEGE

Atlanta 30314. Private; urban. Awards B. Enrolls 1,805 T, 1,754 U (0% women, 30% state res., 70% on fin. aid). Entrance difficulty: moderately difficult. Application deadline: 4/15. Contact: Mr. Gary T. M. Bussey, (404) 681-2800.

MORRIS BROWN COLLEGE

Atlanta 30314.

NORTH GEORGIA COLLEGE

Dahlonega 30533. Public; small town. Awards C, A, B, M. Enrolls 1,885 T, 1,609 U (57% women, 95% state res., 55% on fin. aid). Entrance difficulty: moderately difficult. Application deadline: 9/1. Contact: Mr. Gary R. Steffey, (404) 864-3391.

OGLETHORPE UNIVERSITY

Atlanta 30319. Private; suburban. Awards B, M. Enrolls 1,060 T, 1,030 U (48% women, 51% state res., 70% on fin. aid). Entrance difficulty: moderately difficult. Application deadline: 8/1. Contact: Mr. Charles P. Sullivan, (404) 233-6864.

PAINE COLLEGE

Augusta 30901. Private; urban. Awards B. Enrolls 828 T (66% women, 82% state res., 99% on fin. aid). Entrance difficulty: less difficult. Application deadline: 9/1. Contact: Miss Christine Crockett, (404) 722-4471.

PIEDMONT COLLEGE

Demorest 30535. Private; rural. Awards B. Enrolls 406 T (38% women, 90% state res., 85% on fin. aid). Entrance difficulty: less difficult. Application deadline: 8/15. Contact: Mr. Robert K. Gregory, Financial Aid Director.

SAVANNAH STATE COLLEGE

Savannah 31404. Public; urban. Awards B, M. Enrolls 2,180 T, 2,140 U (55% women, 75% state res., 85% on fin. aid). Entrance difficulty: less difficult. Application deadlines: 9/1, early decision 8/1. Contact: Mr. David E. Foye, Director of Admissions, (912) 356-2181.

SHORTER COLLEGE

Rome 30161. Private; urban. Awards B. Enrolls 840 T (55% women, 78% state res.). Entrance difficulty: moderately difficult. Application deadline: rolling. Contact: Miss Patricia Y. Hart, (404) 291-2121.

SOUTHERN SCHOOL OF PHARMACY, MERCER UNIVERSITY

Atlanta 30312. Contact: Mr. Laddie R. Olterman, Director of Admissions.

SOUTHERN TECHNICAL INSTITUTE

Marietta 30060. Public; suburban. Awards A, B. Enrolls 2,380 T (11% women, 85% state res., 30% on fin. aid). Entrance difficulty: moderately difficult. Application deadlines: 8/15, early decision 7/15. Contact: Miss Virginia Smith, Assistant Director of Admissions.

SPELMAN COLLEGE

Atlanta 30314. Private; urban. Awards B. Enrolls 1,257 T (100% women, 29% state res., 60% on fin. aid). Entrance difficulty: moderately difficult. Application deadline: 3/1. Contact: Mrs. Leah Creque-Harris, (404) 681-3643 Ext. 300.

TIFT COLLEGE

Forsyth 31029. Private; small town. Awards B. Enrolls 489 T (100% women, 70% state res., 85% on fin. aid). Entrance difficulty: less difficult. Application deadline: rolling. Contact: Mr. Joe F. Head, (912) 994-6594.

TOCCOA FALLS COLLEGE

Toccoa Falls 30577. Private; small town. Awards C, A, B. Enrolls 582 T (50% women, 19% state res., 80% on fin. aid). Entrance difficulty: less difficult. Application deadline: 8/5. Contact: Mr. Michael Scales, Director of Admissions/Registrar, (404) 886-6831.

UNIVERSITY OF GEORGIA

Athens 30602. Public; small town. Awards B, M, D. Enrolls 23,359 T, 17,730 U (48% women, 82% state res., 40% on fin. aid). Entrance difficulty: moderately difficult. Application deadline: 9/1. Contact: Dr. M. O. Phelps, (404) 542-2112.

VALDOSTA STATE COLLEGE

Valdosta 31601. Public; suburban. Awards C, A, B, M. Enrolls 4,952 T, 3,903 U (56% women, 87% state res., 30% on fin. aid). Entrance difficulty: less difficult. Application deadline: 9/20. Contact: Mr. Gary Bass, (912) 247-3233.

WESLEYAN COLLEGE

Macon 31297. Private; suburban. Awards B. Enrolls 500 T (100% women, 50% state res., 60% on fin. aid). Entrance difficulty: moderately difficult. Application deadline: 8/15. Contact: Mr. James L. Brown, Dean of Admissions, (912) 477-1110.

WEST GEORGIA COLLEGE

Carrollton 30118. Public; small town. Awards A, B, M. Enrolls 5,051 T, 3,808 U (56% women, 96% state res., 57% on fin. aid). Entrance difficulty: less difficult. Application deadline: rolling. Contact: Mr. Doyle Bickers, (404) 834-1290.

HAWAII

BRIGHAM YOUNG UNIVERSITY–HAWAII CAMPUS

Laie, Oahu 96762. Contact: Mr. Charles W. H. Goo, Coordinator of Admissions.

CHAMINADE UNIVERSITY OF HONOLULU

Honolulu 96816. Private; suburban. Awards A, B, M. Enrolls 2,361 T, 1,059 U (44% women, 68% state res., 33% on fin. aid). Entrance difficulty: moderately difficult. Application deadline: 8/1. Contact: Miss Tana Hogan, Admissions Counselor.

HAWAII LOA COLLEGE

Kaneohe 96744. Suburban. Awards B. Enrolls 327 T (50% women, 40% state res., 61% on fin. aid). Entrance difficulty: moderately difficult. Application deadline:

8/15. Contact: Miss Janie Bossert, (808) 235-3641.

HAWAII PACIFIC COLLEGE

Honolulu 96813. Contact: Dr. Andrew J. Papageorge, Academic Vice President.

UNIVERSITY OF HAWAII AT HILO

Hilo 96720. Public; small town. Awards C, A, B. Enrolls 2,976 T (49% women, 87% state res., 27% on fin. aid). Entrance difficulty: less difficult; noncompetitive for 2-year programs. Application deadline: rolling. Contact: Miss Peggy Yorita, Associate Specialist, (808) 961-9325.

UNIVERSITY OF HAWAII AT MANOA

Honolulu 96822. Public; urban. Awards C, A, B, M, D. Enrolls 20,833 T, 15,173 U (52% women, 87% state res., 20% on fin. aid). Entrance difficulty: moderately difficult. Application deadline: 5/1. Contact: Mr. Donald R. Fukuda, Director of Admissions, (808) 948-8975.

IDAHO

BOISE STATE UNIVERSITY

Boise 83725. Public; urban. Awards C, A, B, M. Enrolls 10,575 T, 8,825 U (51% women, 95% state res., 26% on fin. aid). Entrance difficulty: noncompetitive. Application deadline: 8/22. Contact: Dr. Guy L. Hunt, Dean of Admissions, (208) 385-1177.

COLLEGE OF IDAHO

Caldwell 83605. Private; small town. Awards B, M. Enrolls 615 T, 482 U (48% women, 52% state res., 76% on fin. aid). Entrance difficulty: moderately difficult. Application deadline: 7/31. Contact: Mr. Steven W. Pochard, Director of Admissions, (208) 459-5305.

IDAHO STATE UNIVERSITY

Pocatello 83201. Public; small town. Awards C, A, B, M, D. Enrolls 6,323 T, 5,569 U (51% women, 95% state res., 66% on fin. aid). Entrance difficulty: noncompetitive. Application deadline: 8/15. Contact: Mr. Tim Hayhurst, Director of Admissions, (208) 236-2475.

LEWIS-CLARK STATE COLLEGE

Lewiston 83501. Public; small town. Awards C, A, B. Enrolls 1,454 T (58% women, 80% state res., 48% on fin. aid). Entrance difficulty: noncompetitive; moderately difficult for nursing. Application deadline: rolling. Contact: Ms. M. Elizabeth Ware, (208) 746-2341.

NORTHWEST NAZARENE COLLEGE

Nampa 83651. Private; small town. Awards A, B, M. Enrolls 1,332 T, 1,284 U (56% women, 30% state res., 82% on fin. aid). Entrance difficulty: noncompetitive. Application deadline: 8/15. Contact: Mr. Bruce Webb, (208) 467-8496.

UNIVERSITY OF IDAHO

Moscow 83843. Public; small town. Awards B, M, D. Enrolls 7,931 T, 6,662 U (38% women, 83% state res., 60% on fin. aid). Entrance difficulty: moderately difficult. Application deadline: 8/1. Contact: Mr. Matt E. Telin, Director of Admissions, (208) 885-6731.

ILLINOIS

AMERICAN CONSERVATORY OF MUSIC

Chicago 60603. Private; urban. Awards B, M, D. Enrolls 380 T, 311 U (51% women, 90% state res., 65% on fin. aid). Entrance difficulty: less difficult. Application deadlines: 8/1, early decision 3/1. Contact: Miss Carolyn Peters, Director of Admissions, (312) 263-4161.

AUGUSTANA COLLEGE

Rock Island 61201. Private; urban. Awards B, M. Enrolls 2,232 T, 2,220 U (50% women, 80% state res., 80% on fin. aid). Entrance difficulty: very difficult. Application deadline: rolling. Contact: Mr. Ralph Starenko, Director of Admissions, (309) 794-7341.

AURORA COLLEGE

Aurora 60507. Private; suburban. Awards B, M. Enrolls 1,058 T (45% women, 90%

state res., 83% on fin. aid). Entrance difficulty: moderately difficult. Application deadline: 8/30. Contact: Mr. Charles E. Coughlin, Director of Admissions, (312) 896-1975.

BARAT COLLEGE

Lake Forest 60045. Private; suburban. Awards B. Enrolls 737 T (99% women, 88% state res., 61% on fin. aid). Entrance difficulty: less difficult. Application deadline: rolling. Contact: Miss Doranne G. Polcrack, Director of Admissions, (312) 234-3000 Ext. 370.

BLACKBURN COLLEGE

Carlinville 62626. Private; small town. Awards B. Enrolls 531 T (60% women, 85% state res., 78% on fin. aid). Entrance difficulty: moderately difficult. Application deadline: rolling. Contact: Mr. Donald J. Gix, (217) 854-3231 Ext. 215.

BRADLEY UNIVERSITY

Peoria 61625. Private; suburban. Awards B, M, D. Enrolls 5,284 T, 4,780 U (43% women, 78% state res., 75% on fin. aid). Entrance difficulty: moderately difficult. Application deadline: rolling. Contact: Mr. Robert Voss, (309) 676-7611.

CHICAGO CONSERVATORY COLLEGE

Chicago 60605. Private. Awards B, M. Enrolls 70 T, 65 U.

CHICAGO STATE UNIVERSITY

Chicago 60628. Public; urban. Awards B, M. Enrolls 7,213 T, 5,165 U (63% women, 99% state res., 80% on fin. aid). Entrance difficulty: less difficult; moderately difficult for nursing and radiation therapy. Application deadlines: 8/1, early decision 3/15. Contact: Mr. B. J. Holloway, (312) 995-2513.

CHICAGO TECHNICAL COLLEGE

Chicago 60616. Contact: Ward J. Brady, Director of Admissions.

COLLEGE OF ST FRANCIS

Joliet 60435. Private; suburban. Awards B, M. Enrolls 745 T (60% women, 90% state res., 80% on fin. aid). Entrance difficulty: moderately difficult. Application deadlines:

College of St Francis (continued)
8/15, early decision 9/15. Contact: Miss Sally Feehan, Assistant Director of Admissions, (815) 740-3400.

COLUMBIA COLLEGE

Chicago 60605. Private; urban. Awards B. Enrolls 3,200 T (50% women, 90% state res., 64% on fin. aid). Entrance difficulty: noncompetitive. Application deadline: rolling. Contact: Dr. Edward H. Navakas, Director of Admissions, (312) 663-1600 Ext. 521.

CONCORDIA COLLEGE

River Forest 60305. Private; suburban. Awards B, M. Enrolls 1,141 T, 984 U (65% women, 55% state res., 80% on fin. aid). Entrance difficulty: moderately difficult. Application deadline: 9/1. Contact: Mr. Robert Preloger, (312) 771-8300.

DANIEL HALE WILLIAMS UNIVERSITY

Chicago 60644.

DEPAUL UNIVERSITY

Chicago 60604. Private; urban. Awards C, B, M, D. Enrolls 12,677 T, 8,101 U (46% women, 90% state res., 62% on fin. aid). Entrance difficulty: moderately difficult. Application deadline: 6/1. Contact: Rev. Thomas P. Munster, CM, (312) 321-7600.

DEVRY INSTITUTE OF TECHNOLOGY

Chicago 60618. Private; urban. Awards C, A, B. Enrolls 2,497 T (6% women, 84% state res., 58% on fin. aid). Entrance difficulty: noncompetitive. Application deadline: 10/1. Contact: Mr. Lawrence McHugh, (312) 929-6550.

EASTERN ILLINOIS UNIVERSITY

Charleston 61920. Public; small town. Awards B, M. Enrolls 9,717 T, 8,858 U (55% women, 98% state res., 62% on fin. aid). Entrance difficulty: moderately difficult. Application deadline: rolling. Contact: Mr. John Beacon, (217) 581-2223.

ELMHURST COLLEGE

Elmhurst 60126. Private; suburban. Awards B. Enrolls 3,317 T (58% women, 94% state res., 50% on fin. aid). Entrance difficulty:

moderately difficult. Application deadline: 8/15. Contact: Mr. Michael Dessimoz, (312) 279-4100.

EUREKA COLLEGE

Eureka 61530. Private; small town. Awards B. Enrolls 463 T (40% women, 88% state res., 75% on fin. aid). Entrance difficulty: moderately difficult. Application deadline: rolling. Contact: Mr. George A. Hearne, (309) 467-3721.

GEORGE WILLIAMS COLLEGE

Downers Grove 60515. Private; suburban. Awards B, M. Enrolls 1,811 T, 686 U (65% women, 88% state res., 67% on fin. aid). Entrance difficulty: moderately difficult. Application deadline: rolling. Contact: Mr. Russell Corey, Acting Director of Admissions, (312) 964-3113.

GREENVILLE COLLEGE

Greenville 62246. Private; small town. Awards B. Enrolls 879 T (53% women, 62% state res., 90% on fin. aid). Entrance difficulty: moderately difficult. Application deadline: rolling. Contact: Mr. Norman D. Swanson, Director of Admissions, (618) 664-1840.

ILLINOIS BENEDICTINE COLLEGE

Lisle 60532. Private; suburban. Awards B, M. Enrolls 1,951 T, 1,669 U (35% women, 98% state res., 81% on fin. aid). Entrance difficulty: moderately difficult. Application deadline: rolling. Contact: Mr. Thomas F. Rich, (312) 968-7270.

ILLINOIS COLLEGE

Jacksonville 62650. Private; small town. Awards B. Enrolls 760 T (43% women, 88% state res., 55% on fin. aid). Entrance difficulty: moderately difficult. Application deadline: 8/15. Contact: Mr. James M. Downer, (217) 245-7126.

ILLINOIS COLLEGE OF OPTOMETRY

Chicago 60616. Contact: Mr. Sheldon L. Siegel, Director of Admissions.

ILLINOIS INSTITUTE OF TECHNOLOGY

Chicago 60616. Private; urban. Awards C, B, M, D. Enrolls 7,196 T, 4,002 U (21%

women, 76% state res., 86% on fin. aid).
Entrance difficulty: moderately difficult.
Application deadline: rolling. Contact: Mr.
William Shackelford, (312) 567-3025.

ILLINOIS STATE UNIVERSITY

Normal 61761. Public; small town. Awards
B, M, D. Enrolls 19,576 T, 17,605 U (56%
women, 98% state res., 70% on fin. aid).
Entrance difficulty: moderately difficult.
Application deadline: rolling. Contact: Dr.
Wilbur R. Venerable, (309) 438-2181.

ILLINOIS WESLEYAN UNIVERSITY

Bloomington 61701. Private; small town.
Awards B. Enrolls 1,638 T (55% women,
94% state res., 70% on fin. aid). Entrance
difficulty: very difficult. Application deadline: 5/1. Contact: Mr. James R. Ruoti,
(309) 556-3031.

JUDSON COLLEGE

Elgin 60120. Private; urban. Awards B. Enrolls 486 T (50% women, 60% state res.,
90% on fin. aid). Entrance difficulty: moderately difficult. Application deadline:
8/15. Contact: Mr. Wendell P. Webster,
(312) 695-2500.

KENDALL COLLEGE

Evanston 60201. Private; suburban.
Awards A, B. Enrolls 416 T (45% women,
97% state res., 45% on fin. aid). Entrance
difficulty: less difficult except for nursing.
Application deadline: rolling. Contact: Mr.
Michael J. Alexander, Director of Admissions and Financial Aid, (312) 866-1305.

KNOX COLLEGE

Galesburg 61401. Private; small town.
Awards B. Enrolls 1,042 T (43% women,
80% state res., 70% on fin. aid). Entrance
difficulty: moderately difficult. Application
deadline: 8/15. Contact: Mr. William S.
McIlrath, (309) 343-0112.

LAKE FOREST COLLEGE

Lake Forest 60045. Private; suburban.
Awards B. Enrolls 1,067 T (49% women,
41% state res., 46% on fin. aid). Entrance
difficulty: moderately difficult. Application
deadlines: rolling, early decision 2/15.
Contact: Mr. Francis B. Gummere Jr, (312)
234-3100.

LEWIS UNIVERSITY

Romeoville 60441. Private; suburban.
Awards C, A, B, M. Enrolls 2,790 T,
2,437 U (42% women, 99% state res., 85%
on fin. aid). Entrance difficulty: less difficult. Application deadline: rolling. Contact:
Mr. Bob Brusich, Admissions Counselor,
(815) 838-0500 Ext. 250.

LOYOLA UNIVERSITY OF CHICAGO

Chicago 60611. Private; urban. Awards C,
B, M, D. Enrolls 13,851 T, 8,593 U (53%
women, 95% state res., 70% on fin. aid).
Entrance difficulty: moderately difficult.
Application deadline: 8/15. Contact: Mr.
John W. Christian, (312) 670-2900.

MACMURRAY COLLEGE

Jacksonville 62650. Private; small town.
Awards A, B. Enrolls 686 T (65% women,
90% state res., 80% on fin. aid). Entrance
difficulty: moderately difficult. Application
deadline: rolling. Contact: Mr. Louis Fon-
taine, (217) 245-6151 Ext. 230.

MCKENDREE COLLEGE

Lebanon 62254. Private; suburban. Awards
B. Enrolls 805 T (44% women, 81% state
res., 92% on fin. aid). Entrance difficulty:
moderately difficult. Application deadline:
9/1. Contact: Mr. Daniel B. Baker, Dean of
Admissions, (618) 537-4481.

MIDWEST COLLEGE OF ENGINEERING

Lombard 60148. Private; suburban.
Awards B, M. Enrolls 230 T, 179 U (5%
women, 95% state res., 10% on fin. aid).
Entrance difficulty: moderately difficult.
Application deadline: 8/15. Contact: Ms.
Marie C. Piet, Registrar, (312) 627-6850.

MILLIKIN UNIVERSITY

Decatur 62522. Private; suburban. Awards
B. Enrolls 1,358 T (5% women, 93% state
res., 64% on fin. aid). Entrance difficulty:
moderately difficult. Application deadline:
rolling. Contact: Mr. James F. Kettelkamp,
(217) 424-6210.

MONMOUTH COLLEGE

Monmouth 61462. Private; small town.
Awards A, B. Enrolls 700 T (44% women,
86% state res., 68% on fin. aid). Entrance
difficulty: moderately difficult. Application

Monmouth College (continued)
deadline: rolling. Contact: Mr. John M. Fettig, (309) 457-2131.

MOODY BIBLE INSTITUTE

Chicago 60610. Private; urban. Awards C, B. Enrolls 1,363 T (48% women, 25% state res., 100% on fin. aid). Entrance difficulty: moderately difficult. Application deadline: 8/1. Contact: Mr. Roy Shervy, (312) 329-4162.

MUNDELEIN COLLEGE

Chicago 60660. Private; urban. Awards B, M. Enrolls 1,463 T, 1,400 U (99% women, 88% state res., 72% on fin. aid). Entrance difficulty: moderately difficult. Application deadline: rolling. Contact: Miss Betty Miller, (312) 262-8100.

NATIONAL COLLEGE OF EDUCATION

Evanston 60201. Private; suburban. Awards B, M. Enrolls 823 T, 532 U (80% women, 65% state res., 88% on fin. aid). Entrance difficulty: moderately difficult. Application deadline: rolling. Contact: Mrs. Gail Kligerman-Straus, (312) 256-5150.

NATIONAL COLLEGE OF EDUCATION, URBAN CAMPUS

Chicago 60603. Private; urban. Awards C, B, M. Enrolls 882 T, 257 U (90% women, 100% state res., 86% on fin. aid). Entrance difficulty: moderately difficult. Application deadline: 9/1. Contact: Mrs. Gail Kligerman Straus, (312) 256-5150.

NORTH CENTRAL COLLEGE

Naperville 60540. Private; suburban. Awards B. Enrolls 1,111 T (44% women, 96% state res., 88% on fin. aid). Entrance difficulty: moderately difficult. Application deadline: rolling. Contact: Mr. Lloyd Krumlauf, (312) 420-3422.

NORTHEASTERN ILLINOIS UNIVERSITY

Chicago 60625. Public; urban. Awards B, M. Enrolls 10,061 T, 7,752 U (57% women, 99% state res., 37% on fin. aid). Entrance difficulty: moderately difficult. Application deadline: 8/15. Contact: Mr. Eric B. Moch, (312) 583-4050 Ext. 383.

NORTHERN ILLINOIS UNIVERSITY

DeKalb 60115. Public; small town. Awards B, M, D. Enrolls 22,130 T, 17,411 U (54% women, 99% state res., 67% on fin. aid). Entrance difficulty: moderately difficult. Application deadline: rolling. Contact: Dr. Daniel S. Oborn, (815) 753-0446.

NORTH PARK COLLEGE

Chicago 60625. Private; urban. Awards B. Enrolls 1,284 T (53% women, 40% state res., 80% on fin. aid). Entrance difficulty: moderately difficult. Application deadline: rolling. Contact: Mr. James Lundeen, (312) 583-2700.

NORTHWESTERN UNIVERSITY

Evanston 60201. Private; suburban. Awards B, M, D. Enrolls 15,725 T, 6,800 U (45% women, 30% state res., 60% on fin. aid). Entrance difficulty: very difficult. Application deadline: 10/15. Contact: Mr. Roger Campbell, (312) 492-7271.

OLIVET NAZARENE COLLEGE

Kankakee 60901. Private; suburban. Awards A, B, M. Enrolls 2,002 T, 1,905 U (57% women, 40% state res., 75% on fin. aid). Entrance difficulty: moderately difficult. Application deadline: 8/1. Contact: Mr. Roy F. Quanstrom, (815) 939-5011.

PARKS COLLEGE OF SAINT LOUIS UNIVERSITY

Cahokia 62206. Private; suburban. Awards C, A, B. Enrolls 958 T (9% women, 45% state res., 55% on fin. aid). Entrance difficulty: moderately difficult. Application deadline: rolling. Contact: Mr. Edward Affsprung, (618) 337-7500.

PRINCIPIA COLLEGE

Elsah 62028. Private; rural. Awards C, B. Enrolls 866 T (55% women, 11% state res., 36% on fin. aid). Entrance difficulty: moderately difficult. Application deadline: 8/25. Contact: Ms. Martha Quirk, (618) 374-2131 Ext. 254.

QUINCY COLLEGE

Quincy 62301. Private; suburban. Awards A, B. Enrolls 1,715 T (53% women, 83% state res., 80% on fin. aid). Entrance difficulty: moderately difficult. Application deadline: 8/20. Contact: Mr. Richard J. Smith, (217) 222-8020 Ext. 321.

ROCKFORD COLLEGE

Rockford 61101. Private; suburban. Awards B, M. Enrolls 1,620 T, 1,600 U (50% women, 75% state res., 70% on fin. aid). Entrance difficulty: moderately difficult. Application deadline: rolling. Contact: Miss Martha B. Beal, Director of Admissions and Financial Aid, (815) 226-4050.

ROOSEVELT UNIVERSITY

Chicago 60605. Private; urban. Awards C, B, M. Enrolls 6,788 T, 4,152 U (57% women, 90% state res., 45% on fin. aid). Entrance difficulty: moderately difficult. Application deadline: 8/15. Contact: Mrs. Lily S. Rose, (312) 341-3515.

ROSARY COLLEGE

River Forest 60305. Private; suburban. Awards B, M. Enrolls 1,575 T, 924 U (80% women, 94% state res., 75% on fin. aid). Entrance difficulty: moderately difficult. Application deadline: rolling. Contact: Mr. John Bellheim, Dean of Admissions, (312) 366-2490.

SAINT XAVIER COLLEGE

Chicago 60655. Private; urban. Awards B, M. Enrolls 2,140 T, 1,900 U (71% women, 96% state res., 76% on fin. aid). Entrance difficulty: moderately difficult. Application deadline: 8/1. Contact: Mr. Robert J. Fitzpatrick, (312) 779-3300.

SCHOOL OF THE ART INSTITUTE OF CHICAGO

Chicago 60603. Private; urban. Awards B, M. Enrolls 1,179 T, 934 U (61% women, 75% state res., 78% on fin. aid). Application deadline: rolling. Contact: Mrs. Lynn Gardner Tomko, (312) 443-3718.

SHERWOOD MUSIC SCHOOL

Chicago 60605. Private; urban. Awards B. Enrolls 35 T (50% women, 80% state res., 60% on fin. aid). Entrance difficulty: moderately difficult. Application deadline: 7/15. Contact: Mr. Ralph E. Sunden, Vice President and Musical Director, (312) 427-6267.

SHIMER COLLEGE

Waukegan 60085. Private; urban. Awards B. Enrolls 70 T (50% women, 50% state res., 99% on fin. aid). Entrance difficulty: moderately difficult. Application deadline:

rolling. Contact: Miss Mary Buckley, Admissions Counselor, (312) 623-8400.

SOUTHERN ILLINOIS UNIVERSITY AT CARBONDALE

Carbondale 62901. Public; rural. Awards A, B, M, D. Enrolls 22,537 T, 18,836 U (43% women, 89% state res., 70% on fin. aid). Entrance difficulty: moderately difficult. Application deadline: rolling. Contact: Mr. Jerre C. Pfaff, Associate Director of Admissions, (618) 453-4381.

SOUTHERN ILLINOIS UNIVERSITY AT EDWARDSVILLE

Edwardsville 62026. Public; rural. Awards B, M, D. Enrolls 9,790 T, 7,895 U (53% women, 90% state res., 65% on fin. aid). Entrance difficulty: moderately difficult. Application deadline: rolling. Contact: Mr. Eugene J. Magac, (618) 692-2010.

SPERTUS COLLEGE OF JUDAICA

Chicago 60605. Private; urban. Awards B, M. Enrolls 355 T, 337 U (52% women, 95% state res., 20% on fin. aid). Entrance difficulty: noncompetitive. Application deadline: rolling. Contact: Mr. Sheldon L. Siegel, Director, Admissions and Records, (312) 922-9012.

TRINITY CHRISTIAN COLLEGE

Palos Heights 60463. Private; suburban. Awards B. Enrolls 383 T (50% women, 85% state res., 78% on fin. aid). Entrance difficulty: moderately difficult. Application deadline: 8/15. Contact: Mr. Keith Vander Pol, (312) 597-3000 Ext. 34.

TRINITY COLLEGE

Deerfield 60015. Private; suburban. Awards B. Enrolls 780 T (54% women, 64% state res., 80% on fin. aid). Entrance difficulty: moderately difficult. Application deadline: rolling. Contact: Mr. Ray R. Frederick Jr, (312) 945-6700 Ext. 205.

UNIVERSITY OF CHICAGO

Chicago 60637. Private; urban. Awards B, M, D. Enrolls 7,781 T, 2,670 U (35% women, 36% state res., 65% on fin. aid). Entrance difficulty: most difficult. Application deadlines: 1/15, early decision 10/15. Contact: Mr. Fred R. Brooks Jr, (312) 753-4581.

UNIVERSITY OF ILLINOIS AT CHICAGO CIRCLE

Chicago 60680. Public; urban. Awards B, M, D. Enrolls 20,285 T, 17,036 U (44% women, 50% on fin. aid). Entrance difficulty: moderately difficult. Application deadline: 9/1. Contact: Dr. William Bain, (312) 996-4377.

UNIVERSITY OF ILLINOIS AT THE MEDICAL CENTER

Chicago 60612.

UNIVERSITY OF ILLINOIS AT URBANA-CHAMPAIGN

Urbana 61801. Public; small town. Awards C, B, M, D. Enrolls 34,376 T, 26,127 U (42% women, 97% state res., 50% on fin. aid). Entrance difficulty: very difficult. Application deadlines: early decision 11/1. Contact: Dr. Jane Loeb, (217) 333-2033.

VANDERCOOK COLLEGE OF MUSIC

Chicago 60616. Private; urban. Awards B, M. Enrolls 113 T, 92 U (23% women, 75% state res., 60% on fin. aid). Entrance difficulty: moderately difficult. Application deadline: rolling. Contact: Mr. George Zafros, Registrar, (312) 225-6288.

WESTERN ILLINOIS UNIVERSITY

Macomb 61455. Public; small town. Awards B, M. Enrolls 11,484 T, 10,514 U (45% women, 98% state res., 60% on fin. aid). Entrance difficulty: moderately difficult. Application deadline: rolling. Contact: Dr. Donald F. Totten, Assistant Dean of Admissions and Records, (309) 298-1891.

WHEATON COLLEGE

Wheaton 60187. Private; suburban. Awards B, M. Enrolls 2,410 T, 2,044 U (50% women, 25% state res., 36% on fin. aid). Entrance difficulty: very difficult. Application deadlines: 1/15, early decision 12/1. Contact: Mr. Bill Miller, Admissions Counselor, (313) 682-6082.

INDIANA

ANDERSON COLLEGE

Anderson 46011. Private; suburban. Awards A, B, M. Enrolls 2,038 T, 1,858 U (54% women, 40% state res., 80% on fin. aid). Entrance difficulty: moderately difficult. Application deadline: 8/15. Contact: Mr. George Nalywaiko, (317) 649-9071.

BALL STATE UNIVERSITY

Muncie 47306. Public; suburban. Awards A, B, M, D. Enrolls 17,557 T, 15,205 U (55% women, 93% state res., 80% on fin. aid). Entrance difficulty: moderately difficult. Application deadline: rolling. Contact: Dr. Richard D. Rowray, Director of Admissions, (317) 285-8282.

BETHEL COLLEGE

Mishawaka 46544. Private; urban. Awards A, B. Enrolls 464 T (51% women, 97% state res., 65% on fin. aid). Entrance difficulty: moderately difficult. Application deadline: rolling. Contact: Mr. Robert L. Beyler, Director of Admissions/Financial Aid, (219) 259-8511 Ext. 33.

BUTLER UNIVERSITY

Indianapolis 46208. Private; suburban. Awards A, B, M. Enrolls 3,737 T, 2,516 U (59% women, 75% state res., 79% on fin. aid). Entrance difficulty: moderately difficult. Application deadline: rolling. Contact: Mr. Robert Burnett, Assistant Director of Admissions, (317) 283-9255.

CALUMET COLLEGE

Whiting 46394. Private; urban. Awards C, A, B. Enrolls 1,460 T (60% women, 68% state res., 58% on fin. aid). Entrance difficulty: less difficult. Application deadline: rolling. Contact: Mr. John J. Jaros, Director of Admissions, (219) 473-4217.

DEPAUW UNIVERSITY

Greencastle 46135. Private; small town. Awards B, M. Enrolls 2,373 T, 2,251 U (50% women, 48% state res., 67% on fin. aid). Entrance difficulty: moderately difficult. Application deadline: 4/1. Contact: Mr. David C. Murray, Director of Admissions/Financial Aid, (317) 653-9721.

EARLHAM COLLEGE

Richmond 47374. Private; suburban. Awards B, M. Enrolls 1,015 T (53% women, 20% state res., 65% on fin. aid). Entrance difficulty: moderately difficult. Application deadlines: 3/15, early decision

12/1. Contact: Miss Lynette Robinson-Weening, (317) 962-6561.

FORT WAYNE BIBLE COLLEGE

Fort Wayne 46807. Private; suburban. Awards A, B. Enrolls 510 T (50% women, 50% state res., 70% on fin. aid). Entrance difficulty: moderately difficult. Application deadline: 8/25. Contact: Mr. Jeffrey R. Ling, (219) 456-2111.

FRANKLIN COLLEGE OF INDIANA

Franklin 46131. Private; small town. Awards B. Enrolls 653 T (49% women, 90% state res., 85% on fin. aid). Entrance difficulty: moderately difficult. Application deadlines: 8/30, early decision 12/1. Contact: Mr. Nolan C. Cooper, Vice-President for Admissions, (317) 736-8441.

GOSHEN COLLEGE

Goshen 46526. Private; small town. Awards C, B. Enrolls 1,209 T (59% women, 37% state res., 64% on fin. aid). Entrance difficulty: moderately difficult. Application deadline: rolling. Contact: Ms. June Yoder, (219) 533-3161.

GRACE COLLEGE

Winona Lake 46590. Private; small town. Awards A, B. Enrolls 804 T (54% women, 99% state res., 80% on fin. aid). Entrance difficulty: less difficult. Application deadline: 8/1. Contact: Mr. Ron Henry, (219) 267-8191.

HANOVER COLLEGE

Hanover 47243. Private; rural. Awards B. Enrolls 1,000 T (45% women, 50% state res., 63% on fin. aid). Entrance difficulty: moderately difficult. Application deadlines: 4/15, early decision 12/15. Contact: Mr. C. Eugene McLemore, (812) 866-2151.

HUNTINGTON COLLEGE

Huntington 46750. Private; small town. Awards C, A, B, M. Enrolls 581 T, 544 U (48% women, 80% state res., 80% on fin. aid). Entrance difficulty: moderately difficult. Application deadline: 8/15. Contact: Mr. John Schafer, Director of Admissions, (219) 356-6000.

INDIANA CENTRAL UNIVERSITY

Indianapolis 46227. Private; suburban. Awards A, B, M. Enrolls 3,144 T, 2,892 U (60% women, 96% state res., 85% on fin. aid). Entrance difficulty: moderately difficult. Application deadline: 8/15. Contact: Dr. David J. Huffman, (317) 788-3216.

INDIANA INSTITUTE OF TECHNOLOGY

Fort Wayne 46803. Private; urban. Awards C, A, B. Enrolls 430 T (15% women, 30% state res., 69% on fin. aid). Entrance difficulty: moderately difficult. Application deadline: 8/1. Contact: Mrs. Evelyn Bowyer, Registrar, (219) 422-5561.

INDIANA STATE UNIVERSITY

Terre Haute 47809. Public; urban. Awards A, B, M, D. Enrolls 11,474 T, 9,738 U (50% women, 83% state res., 55% on fin. aid). Entrance difficulty: moderately difficult. Application deadline: rolling. Contact: Mr. John F. Bush, Director of Admissions, (812) 232-6311.

INDIANA STATE UNIVERSITY AT EVANSVILLE

Evansville 47712. Public; suburban. Awards C, A, B. Enrolls 2,863 T (48% women, 95% state res., 70% on fin. aid). Entrance difficulty: noncompetitive. Application deadline: 8/15. Contact: Mr. Timothy K. Buecher, (812) 464-1765.

INDIANA UNIVERSITY

Bloomington 47405. Public; small town. Awards C, A, B, M, D. Enrolls 31,526 T, 22,816 U (48% women, 80% state res., 50% on fin. aid). Entrance difficulty: moderately difficult. Application deadline: 7/15. Contact: Mr. Robert S. Magee, Acting Director, Office of Records and Admissions, (812) 337-0661.

INDIANA UNIVERSITY AT KOKOMO

Kokomo 46901. Public; urban. Awards C, A, B. Enrolls 2,240 T, 1,950 U (60% women, 98% state res., 50% on fin. aid). Entrance difficulty: moderately difficult. Application deadline: 7/1. Contact: Dr. Raymond P. Echols, Dean of Student Services, (317) 453-2000.

INDIANA UNIVERSITY AT SOUTH BEND

South Bend 46615. Public; urban. Awards C, A, B, M. Enrolls 5,780 T, 4,303 U (53% women, 97% state res., 25% on fin. aid). Entrance difficulty: moderately difficult. Application deadline: 7/15. Contact: Ms. Connie Harton, (219) 237-4454.

INDIANA UNIVERSITY NORTHWEST

Gary 46408. Public; urban. Awards C, A, B, M. Enrolls 4,018 T, 3,364 U (60% women, 99% state res., 16% on fin. aid). Entrance difficulty: less difficult. Application deadline: rolling. Contact: Mr. Bill Lee, Director of Admissions and Financial Aid, (219) 980-6821.

INDIANA UNIVERSITY-PURDUE UNIVERSITY AT FORT WAYNE

Fort Wayne 46805. Public; urban. Awards C, A, B, M. Enrolls 9,015 T, 7,781 U (54% women, 97% state res., 40% on fin. aid). Entrance difficulty: moderately difficult. Application deadline: 7/15. Contact: Dr. Phillip A. Kennell, (219) 482-5626.

INDIANA UNIVERSITY-PURDUE UNIVERSITY AT INDIANAPOLIS

Indianapolis 46202. Public; urban. Awards C, A, B, M, D. Enrolls 21,453 T, 12,889 U (56% women, 95% state res., 60% on fin. aid). Entrance difficulty: less difficult except for 2-year nursing and some allied health programs. Application deadline: rolling. Contact: Mr. John C. Krivacs, (317) 264-4591.

INDIANA UNIVERSITY SCHOOL OF OPTOMETRY

Bloomington 47401. Public; small town. Awards C, A, B, M, D. Enrolls 262 T, 50 U (30% women, 80% state res.). Entrance difficulty: very difficult. Application deadline: 11/1. Contact: Mrs. Elena F. Bastin, Registrar, (812) 337-1917.

INDIANA UNIVERSITY SOUTHEAST

New Albany 47150. Public; suburban. Awards C, A, B, M. Enrolls 4,008 T, 3,868 U (55% women, 97% state res., 25% on fin. aid). Entrance difficulty: noncompetitive. Application deadline: 7/15. Contact: Dr. Kela Adams, (812) 945-2731.

MANCHESTER COLLEGE

North Manchester 46962. Private; small town. Awards A, B, M. Enrolls 1,237 T, 1,226 U (50% women, 80% state res., 50% on fin. aid). Entrance difficulty: moderately difficult. Application deadline: rolling. Contact: Mrs. Doraleen Scheetz-Hollar, (219) 982-2141 Ext. 218.

MARIAN COLLEGE

Indianapolis 46222. Private; suburban. Awards A, B. Enrolls 748 T (35% women, 86% state res., 60% on fin. aid). Entrance difficulty: moderately difficult. Application deadline: 8/15. Contact: Mr. Kevin H. Ryan, (317) 924-3291.

MARION COLLEGE

Marion 46952. Private; suburban. Awards A, B, M. Enrolls 1,119 T, 1,088 U (64% women, 67% state res.). Entrance difficulty: moderately difficult. Application deadline: rolling. Contact: Dr. James C. Blackburn, (317) 674-6901 Ext. 216.

OAKLAND CITY COLLEGE

Oakland City 47660. Private; small town. Awards C, A, B. Enrolls 545 T (40% women, 71% state res., 90% on fin. aid). Entrance difficulty: noncompetitive. Application deadline: rolling. Contact: Mrs. Paula Pendergrass, Dean of Student Services, (812) 749-4781 Ext. 28.

PURDUE UNIVERSITY

West Lafayette 47907. Public; small town. Awards A, B, M, D. Enrolls 31,554 T, 26,407 U (40% women, 75% state res.). Entrance difficulty: moderately difficult. Application deadline: rolling. Contact: Mr. James R. Kraynak, (317) 749-2681.

PURDUE UNIVERSITY–CALUMET

Hammond 46323. Public; urban. Awards C, A, B, M. Enrolls 6,630 T, 5,783 U (44% women, 87% state res., 65% on fin. aid). Entrance difficulty: noncompetitive. Application deadline: rolling. Contact: Mr. John P. Fruth, Director of Admissions and Financial Aid, (219) 844-0520 Ext. 214.

PURDUE UNIVERSITY–NORTH CENTRAL CAMPUS

Westville 46391. Public; rural. Awards C, A, B. Enrolls 2,015 T, 1,884 U (60% women, 99% state res., 15% on fin. aid).

Entrance difficulty: moderately difficult. Application deadline: 8/25. Contact: Mr. David P. Konzelmann, (219) 785-2541.

ROSE-HULMAN INSTITUTE OF TECHNOLOGY

Terre Haute 47803. Private; small town. Awards B, M. Enrolls 1,226 T, 1,221 U (0% women, 61% state res., 83% on fin. aid). Entrance difficulty: very difficult. Application deadline: rolling. Contact: Mr. Duncan C. Murdoch, (812) 877-1511.

SAINT FRANCIS COLLEGE

Fort Wayne 46808. Private; suburban. Awards C, A, B, M. Enrolls 1,364 T, 872 U (70% women, 75% state res., 85% on fin. aid). Entrance difficulty: moderately difficult. Application deadline: rolling. Contact: Mr. Wayne Klebe, Admissions Counselor, (219) 432-3551.

SAINT JOSEPH'S COLLEGE

Rensselaer 47978. Private; small town. Awards A, B, M. Enrolls 1,030 T (41% women, 46% state res., 62% on fin. aid). Entrance difficulty: moderately difficult. Contact: Mr. William T. Craig, (219) 866-7111.

SAINT MARY-OF-THE-WOODS COLLEGE

St Mary-of-the-Woods 47876. Private; small town. Awards A, B. Enrolls 625 T (100% women, 44% state res., 65% on fin. aid). Entrance difficulty: moderately difficult. Application deadlines; rolling, early decision 11/1. Contact: Sr. Terri Grasso, SP, (812) 535-4141.

SAINT MARY'S COLLEGE

Notre Dame 46556. Private; suburban. Awards B. Enrolls 1,817 T (99% women, 16% state res., 53% on fin. aid). Entrance difficulty: moderately difficult. Application deadline: 3/1. Contact: Mrs. Elisa Brooks, (219) 284-4305.

SAINT MEINRAD COLLEGE

St Meinrad 47577. Private; rural. Awards B. Enrolls 210 T (0% women, 20% state res., 70% on fin. aid). Entrance difficulty: moderately difficult. Application deadline: 7/30. Contact: Rev. Jonathan Fassero, (812) 357-6575.

TAYLOR UNIVERSITY

Upland 46989. Private; rural. Awards A, B. Enrolls 1,540 T (52% women, 30% state res., 70% on fin. aid). Entrance difficulty: moderately difficult. Application deadline: rolling. Contact: Mr. Ron Keller, (317) 998-2751 Ext. 206.

TRI-STATE UNIVERSITY

Angola 46703. Private; small town. Awards A, B. Enrolls 1,298 T (17% women, 39% state res., 71% on fin. aid). Entrance difficulty: moderately difficult. Application deadline: 9/1. Contact: Mr. Kent Myers, (219) 665-3141.

UNIVERSITY OF EVANSVILLE

Evansville 47702. Private; suburban. Awards A, B, M. Enrolls 4,817 T, 4,206 U (58% women, 75% state res., 75% on fin. aid). Entrance difficulty: moderately difficult. Application deadline: 9/1. Contact: Mr. John Oberhelman, (812) 479-2468.

UNIVERSITY OF NOTRE DAME

Notre Dame 46556. Private; urban. Awards B, M, D. Enrolls 8,700 T, 6,900 U (25% women, 8% state res., 66% on fin. aid). Entrance difficulty: very difficult. Application deadline: 3/1. Contact: Mr. John T. Goldrick, (219) 283-7505.

VALPARAISO UNIVERSITY

Valparaiso 46383. Private; small town. Awards A, B, M. Enrolls 4,206 T, 3,678 U (51% women, 29% state res., 60% on fin. aid). Entrance difficulty: moderately difficult. Application deadline: rolling. Contact: Mr. Warren W. Muller, (219) 464-5011.

WABASH COLLEGE

Crawfordsville 47933. Private; small town. Awards B. Enrolls 803 T (0% women, 80% state res., 80% on fin. aid). Entrance difficulty: very difficult. Application deadline: rolling. Contact: Mr. Paul M. Garman, (317) 362-0978.

IOWA

BRIAR CLIFF COLLEGE

Sioux City 51104. Private; urban. Awards A, B. Enrolls 1,258 T (63% women, 93%

Briar Cliff College (continued)
state res., 80% on fin. aid). Entrance difficulty: less difficult; moderately difficult for nursing. Application deadline: 9/1. Contact: Mr. James J. Hoffman, (712) 279-5422.

BUENA VISTA COLLEGE

Storm Lake 50588. Private; small town. Awards B. Enrolls 899 T (47% women, 94% state res., 88% on fin. aid). Entrance difficulty: moderately difficult. Application deadline: rolling. Contact: Mr. Kent McElvania, (712) 749-2235.

CENTRAL UNIVERSITY OF IOWA

Pella 50219. Private; small town. Awards B. Enrolls 1,545 T (54% women, 68% state res., 89% on fin. aid). Entrance difficulty: moderately difficult. Application deadline: 8/1. Contact: Mr. James M. Brandl, Dean of Admission, (515) 628-1434.

CLARKE COLLEGE

Dubuque 52001. Private; suburban. Awards A, B, M. Enrolls 666 T, 606 U (91% women, 75% state res., 60% on fin. aid). Entrance difficulty: moderately difficult. Application deadline: rolling. Contact: Mr. Edwin B. Reger, (319) 588-6316.

COE COLLEGE

Cedar Rapids 52402. Private; urban. Awards B. Enrolls 1,320 T (45% women, 62% state res., 70% on fin. aid). Entrance difficulty: moderately difficult. Application deadlines: rolling, early decision 12/15. Contact: Mrs. Christine Galloway, Director of Admissions, (319) 399-8500.

CORNELL COLLEGE

Mount Vernon 52314. Private; small town. Awards B. Enrolls 898 T (47% women, 30% state res., 62% on fin. aid). Entrance difficulty: very difficult. Application deadlines: rolling, early decision 12/15. Contact: Mr. Frank G. Krivo, Dean of Admissions, (319) 895-8811.

DIVINE WORD COLLEGE

Epworth 52045. Private; rural. Awards A, B. Enrolls 92 T (0% women, 21% state res., 68% on fin. aid). Entrance difficulty: less difficult. Application deadline: 8/1. Contact: Rev. Ed Herberger, (319) 876-3332.

DORDT COLLEGE

Sioux Center 51250. Private; rural. Awards A, B. Enrolls 1,218 T (56% women, 28% state res., 80% on fin. aid). Application deadline: 9/1. Contact: Mr. Howard J. Hall, (712) 722-3771 Ext. 140.

DRAKE UNIVERSITY

Des Moines 50311. Private; suburban. Awards B, M, D. Enrolls 6,568 T, 4,871 U (49% women, 40% state res., 40% on fin. aid). Entrance difficulty: moderately difficult. Application deadline: rolling. Contact: Mr. Everett Hadley, Executive Director of Admissions, (515) 271-3181.

FAITH BAPTIST BIBLE COLLEGE

Ankeny 50021. Private; small town. Awards A, B. Enrolls 530 T (51% women, 42% state res., 70% on fin. aid). Entrance difficulty: noncompetitive. Application deadline: 8/1. Contact: Mr. David Stout, Registrar, (515) 964-0601.

GRACELAND COLLEGE

Lamoni 50140. Private; small town. Awards B. Enrolls 1,345 T (56% women, 26% state res., 75% on fin. aid). Entrance difficulty: moderately difficult. Application deadline: 9/1. Contact: Mr. Robert L. Watts, (515) 784-3311 Ext. 223.

GRAND VIEW COLLEGE

Des Moines 50316. Private; urban. Awards A, B. Enrolls 1,186 T (55% women, 90% state res., 48% on fin. aid). Entrance difficulty: noncompetitive. Application deadline: rolling. Contact: Mr. Kenneth Paulsen, Registrar, (515) 266-2651.

GRINNELL COLLEGE

Grinnell 50112. Private; small town. Awards B. Enrolls 1,258 T (43% women, 14% state res., 49% on fin. aid). Entrance difficulty: very difficult. Application deadlines: rolling, early decision 12/15. Contact: Mr. John R. Hopkins, Director of Admissions and Financial Aid, (515) 236-7545.

IOWA STATE UNIVERSITY

Ames 50011. Public; small town. Awards C, B, M, D. Enrolls 23,486 T, 18,558 U (40% women, 79% state res., 50% on fin. aid). Entrance difficulty: moderately difficult; most difficult for veterinary medicine. Application deadline: rolling. Contact: Mr. Karsten Smedal, (515) 294-5836.

IOWA WESLEYAN COLLEGE

Mount Pleasant 52641. Private; small town. Awards A, B. Enrolls 730 T (62% women, 72% state res., 68% on fin. aid). Entrance difficulty: moderately difficult. Application deadline: rolling. Contact: Mr. Howard Martin, (319) 385-8021.

LORAS COLLEGE

Dubuque 52001. Private; urban. Awards A, B, M. Enrolls 1,795 T, 1,700 U (42% women, 60% state res., 70% on fin. aid). Entrance difficulty: moderately difficult. Application deadline: rolling. Contact: Mr. Dan Conry, (319) 588-7235.

LUTHER COLLEGE

Decorah 52101. Private; small town. Awards B. Enrolls 1,999 T (56% women, 56% state res., 70% on fin. aid). Entrance difficulty: moderately difficult. Application deadline: 8/1. Contact: Mr. David H. Snow, (319) 387-1287.

MAHARISHI INTERNATIONAL UNIVERSITY

Fairfield 52556. Private; small town. Awards C, A, B, M. Enrolls 769 T, 582 U (33% women, 5% state res., 66% on fin. aid). Entrance difficulty: noncompetitive. Application deadline: rolling. Contact: Ms. Bonnie Schneider, Co-Director of Admissions, (515) 472-5031.

MARYCREST COLLEGE

Davenport 52804. Private; suburban. Awards A, B, M. Enrolls 869 T, 708 U (85% women, 54% state res., 61% on fin. aid). Entrance difficulty: moderately difficult. Application deadline: rolling. Contact: Sr. Rae Elwood, Dean of Admissions and Financial Aid, (319) 326-9226.

MORNINGSIDE COLLEGE

Sioux City 51106. Private; suburban. Awards A, B, M. Enrolls 1,574 T, 1,520 U (52% women, 75% state res., 88% on fin. aid). Entrance difficulty: moderately difficult. Application deadline: rolling. Contact: Mr. Fred Erbes, (712) 277-5111.

MOUNT MERCY COLLEGE

Cedar Rapids 52402. Private; urban. Awards B. Enrolls 1,042 T (65% women, 90% state res., 85% on fin. aid). Entrance difficulty: moderately difficult. Application deadline: rolling. Contact: Mr. Don McCormick, (319) 363-8213.

NORTHWESTERN COLLEGE

Orange City 51041. Private; rural. Awards B. Enrolls 861 T, 861 U (52% women, 65% state res., 86% on fin. aid). Entrance difficulty: moderately difficult. Application deadline: rolling. Contact: Mr. Ronald K. DeJong, (712) 737-4821.

OPEN BIBLE COLLEGE

Des Moines 50321. Private; urban. Awards A, B. Enrolls 117 T (49% women, 70% state res., 52% on fin. aid). Entrance difficulty: noncompetitive. Application deadline: rolling. Contact: Mr. Steve Brant, Director of Admissions, (515) 283-0476.

ST AMBROSE COLLEGE

Davenport 52803. Private; urban. Awards B, M. Enrolls 1,818 T (33% women, 70% state res., 60% on fin. aid). Entrance difficulty: moderately difficult. Application deadline: rolling. Contact: Mr. James T. Barry, (319) 322-0989.

SIMPSON COLLEGE

Indianola 50125. Private; suburban. Awards B. Enrolls 850 T (45% women, 75% state res., 70% on fin. aid). Entrance difficulty: moderately difficult. Application deadline: 8/15. Contact: Mr. John Kellogg, (515) 961-6251.

UNIVERSITY OF DUBUQUE

Dubuque 52001. Private; suburban. Awards A, B, M. Enrolls 1,034 T (19% women, 63% state res., 65% on fin. aid). Entrance difficulty: moderately difficult. Application deadline: rolling. Contact: Mr. Clifford D. Bunting, Director of Student Services, (319) 589-3200.

UNIVERSITY OF IOWA

Iowa City 52242. Public; small town. Awards B, M, D. Enrolls 23,349 T, 15,449 U (51% women, 79% state res., 55% on fin. aid). Entrance difficulty: moderately difficult. Application deadline:

University of Iowa (continued)
8/15. Contact: Mr. John Moore, (319) 353-3361.

UNIVERSITY OF NORTHERN IOWA

Cedar Falls 50613. Public; small town. Awards B, M, D. Enrolls 10,382 T, 9,169 U (56% women, 97% state res., 66% on fin. aid). Entrance difficulty: moderately difficult. Application deadline: rolling. Contact: Mr. Jack Wielenga, (319) 273-2281.

UPPER IOWA UNIVERSITY

Fayette 52142. Private; small town. Awards B. Enrolls 580 T (45% women, 70% state res., 86% on fin. aid). Entrance difficulty: moderately difficult. Application deadline: 8/15. Contact: Mr. Paul Jones, (319) 425-3311.

VENNARD COLLEGE

University Park 52595. Private; small town. Awards C, A, B. Enrolls 211 T (51% women, 20% state res., 80% on fin. aid). Entrance difficulty: noncompetitive. Application deadline: rolling. Contact: Mr. Howard Ledford, (515) 673-8391.

WARTBURG COLLEGE

Waverly 50677. Private; small town. Awards B. Enrolls 1,086 T (50% women, 65% state res., 91% on fin. aid). Entrance difficulty: moderately difficult. Application deadline: rolling. Contact: Mr. Drew R. Boster, (319) 352-1200.

WESTMAR COLLEGE

Le Mars 51031. Private; small town. Awards B. Enrolls 646 T (47% women, 76% state res., 78% on fin. aid). Entrance difficulty: less difficult. Application deadline: rolling. Contact: Mrs. Valda Embree, (712) 546-7081 Ext. 213.

WILLIAM PENN COLLEGE

Oskaloosa 52577. Private; small town. Awards B. Enrolls 617 T (38% women, 65% state res., 86% on fin. aid). Entrance difficulty: moderately difficult. Contact: Mr. Eric Otto, (515) 673-8311.

KANSAS

BAKER UNIVERSITY

Baldwin City 66006. Private; small town. Awards B, M. Enrolls 977 T, 872 U (51% women, 55% state res., 71% on fin. aid). Entrance difficulty: moderately difficult. Application deadline: rolling. Contact: Mr. Ken Snow, Dean of Admissions, (913) 594-6451.

BENEDICTINE COLLEGE

Atchison 66002. Private; small town. Awards A, B. Enrolls 1,045 T (50% women, 60% state res., 70% on fin. aid). Entrance difficulty: moderately difficult. Application deadline: 8/15. Contact: Mr. Thomas V. Herriage, (913) 367-5340 Ext. 225.

BETHANY COLLEGE

Lindsborg 67465. Private; small town. Awards B. Enrolls 827 T (50% women, 73% state res., 80% on fin. aid). Entrance difficulty: moderately difficult. Application deadline: rolling. Contact: Mr. Leon Burch, Dean of Admissions, (913) 227-3311.

BETHEL COLLEGE

North Newton 67117. Private; small town. Awards C, A, B. Enrolls 638 T (48% women, 63% state res., 91% on fin. aid). Entrance difficulty: moderately difficult. Application deadline: 8/15. Contact: Mr. Jerry Weaver, (316) 283-2500.

EMPORIA STATE UNIVERSITY

Emporia 66801. Public; small town. Awards A, B, M. Enrolls 6,429 T, 4,473 U (57% women, 94% state res., 65% on fin. aid). Entrance difficulty: noncompetitive. Application deadline: rolling. Contact: Mr. Jan Jantzen, (316) 343-1200 Ext. 465.

FORT HAYS STATE UNIVERSITY

Hays 67601. Public; small town. Awards C, A, B, M. Enrolls 5,644 T, 4,050 U (53% women, 92% state res., 65% on fin. aid). Entrance difficulty: noncompetitive. Application deadline: rolling. Contact: Mr. James V. Kellerman, Registrar and Director of Admissions, (913) 628-4222.

FRIENDS BIBLE COLLEGE

Haviland 67059. Private; small town. Awards B. Enrolls 167 T (53% women, 37% state res., 75% on fin. aid). Entrance difficulty: noncompetitive. Application deadline: 9/1. Contact: Mr. Herbert Frazier, (316) 862-5252.

FRIENDS UNIVERSITY

Wichita 67213. Private; suburban. Awards A, B. Enrolls 908 T (50% women, 92% state res., 75% on fin. aid). Entrance difficulty: less difficult. Application deadline: rolling. Contact: Dr. George Potts, (316) 261-5842.

KANSAS NEWMAN COLLEGE

Wichita 67213. Private; suburban. Awards A, B. Enrolls 660 T (50% women, 91% state res., 72% on fin. aid). Entrance difficulty: moderately difficult. Application deadline: 8/15. Contact: Mr. Michael Stewart, (316) 942-4291.

KANSAS STATE UNIVERSITY

Manhattan 66506. Public; small town. Awards A, B, M, D. Enrolls 18,420 T, 14,525 U (45% women, 85% state res., 40% on fin. aid). Entrance difficulty: moderately difficult. Application deadline: rolling. Contact: Mr. Richard N. Elkins, (913) 532-6250.

KANSAS WESLEYAN

Salina 67401. Private; suburban. Awards A, B. Enrolls 470 T (50% women, 83% state res., 77% on fin. aid). Entrance difficulty: moderately difficult. Application deadline: rolling. Contact: Mr. Bill Stevens, (913) 827-5541.

MARYMOUNT COLLEGE OF KANSAS

Salina 67401. Private; small town. Awards A, B. Enrolls 787 T (65% women, 87% state res., 84% on fin. aid). Entrance difficulty: less difficult. Application deadline: rolling. Contact: Mr. Sam Rawdon, (913) 825-2101.

MCPHERSON COLLEGE

McPherson 67460. Private; rural. Awards A, B. Enrolls 493 T (40% women, 56% state res., 76% on fin. aid). Entrance difficulty: moderately difficult. Application deadline: rolling. Contact: Mr. Donald Hatword, (316) 241-0731.

MID-AMERICA NAZARENE COLLEGE

Olathe 66061. Private; suburban. Awards A, B. Enrolls 1,292 T (52% women, 46% state res., 80% on fin. aid). Entrance difficulty: noncompetitive. Application deadline: rolling. Contact: Mr. Paul M. Clem, Director of Recruitment, (913) 782-3750.

OTTAWA UNIVERSITY

Ottawa 66067. Private; small town. Awards B. Enrolls 555 T (45% women, 50% state res., 95% on fin. aid). Entrance difficulty: moderately difficult. Application deadline: rolling. Contact: Miss Cathy E. Duderstadt, Assistant Director of Admissions, (913) 242-6445.

PITTSBURG STATE UNIVERSITY

Pittsburg 66762. Public; small town. Awards C, A, B, M. Enrolls 5,268 T, 3,846 U (51% women, 84% state res., 74% on fin. aid). Entrance difficulty: noncompetitive. Application deadline: rolling. Contact: Mr. James E. Parker, (316) 231-7000 Ext. 381.

SAINT MARY COLLEGE

Leavenworth 66048. Private; small town. Awards A, B. Enrolls 798 T (73% women, 74% state res., 53% on fin. aid). Entrance difficulty: moderately difficult. Application deadline: rolling. Contact: Ms. Danielle Barr, (913) 682-5151.

SAINT MARY OF THE PLAINS COLLEGE

Dodge City 67801. Private; rural. Awards B. Enrolls 616 T (56% women, 60% state res., 90% on fin. aid). Entrance difficulty: moderately difficult. Application deadline: rolling. Contact: Mr. Maurice Werner, Dean of Admissions, (316) 225-4171.

SOUTHWESTERN COLLEGE

Winfield 67156. Private; small town. Awards C, B. Enrolls 656 T (54% women, 74% state res., 93% on fin. aid). Entrance difficulty: moderately difficult. Application deadline: rolling. Contact: Mr. Carl A. Pagles, (316) 221-4150 Ext. 36.

STERLING COLLEGE

Sterling 67579. Private; small town. Awards B. Enrolls 534 T (50% women, 45% state res., 75% on fin. aid). Entrance difficulty: less difficult. Application deadline: 8/15.

Sterling College (continued)
Contact: Mr. Robert M. Reed, Director of Admissions and Records, (316) 278-2173.

TABOR COLLEGE

Hillsboro 67063. Private; small town. Awards A, B. Enrolls 434 T (52% women, 58% state res., 60% on fin. aid). Entrance difficulty: moderately difficult. Application deadline: rolling. Contact: Mr. Phil Plett, (316) 947-3121.

UNIVERSITY OF KANSAS

Lawrence 66045. Public; small town. Awards B, M, D. Enrolls 24,125 T, 16,898 U (47% women, 74% state res.). Entrance difficulty: noncompetitive. Application deadline: 8/15. Contact: Mr. John A. Myers, (913) 864-3911.

WASHBURN UNIVERSITY OF TOPEKA

Topeka 66621. Public; urban. Awards A, B, M. Enrolls 5,763 T, 5,049 U (50% women, 97% state res., 35% on fin. aid). Entrance difficulty: noncompetitive. Application deadline: 8/6. Contact: Mr. John E. Triggs, Registrar and Director of Admissions, (913) 295-6574.

WICHITA STATE UNIVERSITY

Wichita 67208. Public; urban. Awards C, A, B, M, D. Enrolls 16,749 T, 12,700 U (51% women, 93% state res., 70% on fin. aid). Entrance difficulty: noncompetitive. Application deadline: rolling. Contact: Mr. Stanley E. Henderson, (316) 686-3409.

KENTUCKY

ALICE LLOYD COLLEGE

Pippa Passes 41844. Private; rural. Awards C, A, B. Enrolls 231 T (66% women, 93% state res., 100% on fin. aid). Entrance difficulty: moderately difficult. Application deadline: rolling. Contact: Mr. Billy C. Melton, (606) 368-2101.

ASBURY COLLEGE

Wilmore 40390. Private; small town. Awards B. Enrolls 1,273 T (51% women, 12% state res., 51% on fin. aid). Entrance difficulty: moderately difficult. Application deadline: 8/15. Contact: Dr. William E.

Eddy, Director of Admissions, (606) 858-3511 Ext. 112.

BELLARMINE COLLEGE

Louisville 40205. Private; suburban. Awards A, B, M. Enrolls 2,095 T, 1,820 U (52% women, 85% state res., 65% on fin. aid). Entrance difficulty: moderately difficult. Application deadline: rolling. Contact: Mr. Robert G. Pfaadt, Dean of Admissions and Educational Services, (502) 452-8131.

BEREA COLLEGE

Berea 40403. Private; small town. Awards B. Enrolls 1,438 T (56% women, 38% state res., 100% on fin. aid). Entrance difficulty: moderately difficult. Application deadline: rolling. Contact: Mr. John S. Cook, (606) 986-9341 Ext. 468.

BRESCIA COLLEGE

Owensboro 42301. Private; urban. Awards A, B. Enrolls 832 T (61% women, 91% state res., 59% on fin. aid). Entrance difficulty: moderately difficult. Application deadlines: rolling, early decision 10/15. Contact: Mr. John Wilbur, Director of Admissions, (502) 685-3131.

CAMPBELLSVILLE COLLEGE

Campbellsville 42718. Private; small town. Awards C, A, B. Enrolls 674 T (56% women, 76% state res., 80% on fin. aid). Entrance difficulty: less difficult. Application deadline: 8/25. Contact: Dr. James Coates, (502) 465-8158 Ext. 218.

CENTRE COLLEGE OF KENTUCKY

Danville 40422. Private; small town. Awards B. Enrolls 760 T (45% women, 55% state res., 40% on fin. aid). Entrance difficulty: very difficult. Application deadline: 5/1. Contact: Mr. Harold Smith, Dean of Admissions, (606) 236-5211.

CUMBERLAND COLLEGE

Williamsburg 40769. Private; small town. Awards A, B. Enrolls 2,000 T (52% women, 62% state res., 90% on fin. aid). Entrance difficulty: noncompetitive. Application deadline: rolling. Contact: Mr. Michael B. Colegrove, Director of Admissions, (606) 549-3967.

EASTERN KENTUCKY UNIVERSITY

Richmond 40475. Public; small town. Awards C, A, B, M. Enrolls 13,668 T, 11,366 U (54% women, 84% state res., 53% on fin. aid). Entrance difficulty: noncompetitive. Application deadline: rolling. Contact: Dr. Charles F. Ambrose, Dean of Admissions, (606) 622-2106.

GEORGETOWN COLLEGE

Georgetown 40324. Private; small town. Awards B, M. Enrolls 1,189 T, 1,031 U (48% women, 57% state res., 68% on fin. aid). Entrance difficulty: moderately difficult. Application deadline: 8/15. Contact: Mr. Donald DeBorde, (502) 863-8493.

KENTUCKY CHRISTIAN COLLEGE

Grayson 41143. Private; rural. Awards B. Enrolls 441 T (49% women, 23% state res., 50% on fin. aid). Entrance difficulty: noncompetitive. Application deadline: rolling. Contact: Dr. Benic P. Hampton Jr, Dean, (606) 474-6613.

KENTUCKY STATE UNIVERSITY

Frankfort 40601. Public; suburban. Awards C, A, B, M. Enrolls 2,300 T, 2,167 U (50% women, 74% state res., 85% on fin. aid). Entrance difficulty: noncompetitive. Application deadline: rolling. Contact: Mr. Charles Edington, Dean of Admissions and Registrar, (502) 564-5813.

KENTUCKY WESLEYAN COLLEGE

Owensboro 42301. Private; suburban. Awards A, B. Enrolls 852 T (57% women, 87% state res., 88% on fin. aid). Entrance difficulty: moderately difficult. Application deadline: 8/1. Contact: Mr. W. Steve Stocks, (502) 926-3111.

MOREHEAD STATE UNIVERSITY

Morehead 40351. Contact: Mr. Bill Bradford, Director of Admissions.

MURRAY STATE UNIVERSITY

Murray 42071. Public; small town. Awards A, B, M. Enrolls 7,841 T, 6,023 U (56% women, 80% state res., 50% on fin. aid). Entrance difficulty: noncompetitive. Application deadline: rolling. Contact: Mr. Wilson Gantt, Dean of Admissions, (502) 762-3741.

NORTHERN KENTUCKY UNIVERSITY

Highland Heights 41076. Public; suburban. Awards A, B, M. Enrolls 7,017 T, 6,567 U (48% women, 90% state res., 29% on fin. aid). Entrance difficulty: noncompetitive. Application deadline: rolling. Contact: Dr. Joseph Griffin, Acting Director of Admissions, (606) 292-5220.

PIKEVILLE COLLEGE

Pikeville 41501. Private; small town. Awards C, A, B. Enrolls 615 T (46% women, 78% state res., 75% on fin. aid). Entrance difficulty: noncompetitive. Application deadline: 9/12. Contact: Mr. William R. Little, Dean of Admissions, (606) 432-9332.

SPALDING COLLEGE

Louisville 40203. Private; urban. Awards B, M. Enrolls 928 T, 664 U (92% women, 88% state res., 60% on fin. aid). Entrance difficulty: moderately difficult. Application deadline: 8/15. Contact: Ms. Mary Pat Nolan, (502) 585-9201.

THOMAS MORE COLLEGE

Fort Mitchell 41017. Private; suburban. Awards C, A, B. Enrolls 1,270 T (55% women, 65% state res., 65% on fin. aid). Entrance difficulty: moderately difficult. Application deadline: 8/15. Contact: Miss Catherine M. Grady, (606) 341-5800.

TRANSYLVANIA UNIVERSITY

Lexington 40508. Private; urban. Awards B. Enrolls 810 T (51% women, 75% state res., 62% on fin. aid). Entrance difficulty: moderately difficult. Application deadline: rolling. Contact: Mr. Mike Delong, (606) 233-8242.

UNION COLLEGE

Barbourville 40906. Private; small town. Awards C, A, B, M. Enrolls 894 T, 660 U (61% women, 72% state res., 76% on fin. aid). Entrance difficulty: noncompetitive. Application deadline: 7/31. Contact: Mr. John E. Shappell, (606) 546-4151 Ext. 172.

UNIVERSITY OF KENTUCKY

Lexington 40506. Public; urban. Awards B, M, D. Enrolls 22,615 T, 17,694 U (47% women, 89% state res., 25% on fin. aid). Entrance difficulty: moderately difficult.

University of Kentucky (continued)
Application deadline: 6/1. Contact: Mr. Richard Stofer, (606) 257-1606.

UNIVERSITY OF LOUISVILLE

Louisville 40208. Public; urban. Awards C, A, B, M, D. Enrolls 19,343 T, 13,931 U (46% women, 92% state res., 40% on fin. aid). Entrance difficulty: noncompetitive. Application deadline: 8/15. Contact: Mr. Ray A. Stines, (502) 588-6531.

WESTERN KENTUCKY UNIVERSITY

Bowling Green 42101. Public; small town. Awards C, A, B, M. Enrolls 13,417 T, 8,984 U (52% women, 84% state res., 50% on fin. aid). Entrance difficulty: noncompetitive. Application deadline: 8/1. Contact: Mr. Thomas L. Updike Jr, (502) 745-2551.

LOUISIANA

CENTENARY COLLEGE OF LOUISIANA

Shreveport 71104. Private; urban. Awards A, B, M. Enrolls 940 T, 808 U (44% women, 63% state res., 60% on fin. aid). Entrance difficulty: moderately difficult. Application deadline: rolling. Contact: Mr. John Lambert, Director of Financial Aid, (318) 869-5104.

DILLARD UNIVERSITY

New Orleans 70122. Private; urban. Awards B. Enrolls 1,217 T (74% women, 60% state res., 80% on fin. aid). Entrance difficulty: moderately difficult. Application deadline: 7/15. Contact: Mrs. Vernese B. O'Neal, Director of Admissions, (504) 944-8751.

GRAMBLING STATE UNIVERSITY

Grambling 71245. Public; small town. Awards A, B, M. Enrolls 3,639 T, 3,293 U (52% women, 79% state res., 98% on fin. aid). Entrance difficulty: noncompetitive. Application deadline: rolling. Contact: Mrs. Irene S. A. Thomas, (318) 247-8608.

LOUISIANA COLLEGE

Pineville 71360. Private; small town. Awards C, A, B. Enrolls 1,314 T (56% women, 90% state res., 75% on fin. aid).

Entrance difficulty: moderately difficult. Application deadline: 8/1. Contact: Mr. David Pulling, Admissions Counselor, (318) 487-7386.

LOUISIANA STATE UNIVERSITY AND AGRICULTURAL AND MECHANICAL COLLEGE

Baton Rouge 70803. Public; suburban. Awards B, M, D. Enrolls 26,586 T, 21,504 U (47% women, 88% state res., 52% on fin. aid). Entrance difficulty: noncompetitive. Application deadline: rolling. Contact: Mr. Ordell Griffith, (504) 388-1175.

LOUISIANA STATE UNIVERSITY IN SHREVEPORT

Shreveport 71115. Public; suburban. Awards A, B, M. Enrolls 3,178 T, 3,103 U (54% women, 98% state res., 28% on fin. aid). Entrance difficulty: noncompetitive. Application deadline: 8/10. Contact: Mrs. Fabia E. Thomas, Registrar, (318) 797-7121 Ext. 204.

LOUISIANA TECH UNIVERSITY

Ruston 71272. Public; small town. Awards A, B, M, D. Enrolls 9,363 T, 8,476 U (42% women, 85% state res., 60% on fin. aid). Entrance difficulty: noncompetitive. Application deadline: rolling. Contact: Mrs. Patsy Lewis, (318) 257-3036.

LOYOLA UNIVERSITY

New Orleans 70118. Private; suburban. Awards A, B, M. Enrolls 4,403 T, 3,216 U (51% women, 75% state res., 70% on fin. aid). Entrance difficulty: moderately difficult. Application deadline: rolling. Contact: Dr. Rebecca Brectel, (504) 865-3240.

MCNEESE STATE UNIVERSITY

Lake Charles 70609. Public; suburban. Awards A, B, M. Enrolls 5,156 T, 4,435 U (53% women, 94% state res., 33% on fin. aid). Entrance difficulty: noncompetitive. Application deadline: 7/15. Contact: Miss Linda Finley, Registrar, (318) 477-2520 Ext. 207.

NICHOLLS STATE UNIVERSITY

Thibodaux 70301. Public; small town. Awards A, B, M. Enrolls 6,481 T, 5,652 U (54% women, 97% state res., 33% on fin. aid). Entrance difficulty: noncompetitive.

Application deadline: rolling. Contact: Mr. S. Dan Montz Jr, Dean of Admissions and Registrar, (504) 446-8111 Ext. 411.

NORTHEAST LOUISIANA UNIVERSITY

Monroe 71209. Public; urban. Awards C, A, B, M, D. Enrolls 9,175 T, 8,108 U (55% women, 92% state res., 55% on fin. aid). Entrance difficulty: noncompetitive. Application deadline: rolling. Contact: Mr. Barry M. Delcambre, Registrar.

NORTHWESTERN STATE UNIVERSITY OF LOUISIANA

Natchitoches 71457. Public; small town. Awards C, A, B, M, D. Enrolls 5,894 T, 4,653 U. Entrance difficulty: noncompetitive. Application deadline: rolling. Contact: Mr. Austin Temple, (318) 357-6171.

OUR LADY OF HOLY CROSS COLLEGE

New Orleans 70114. Private; suburban. Awards A, B. Enrolls 783 T (70% women, 100% state res., 21% on fin. aid). Entrance difficulty: noncompetitive. Application deadline: rolling. Contact: Miss Marianne Terrebonne Kerner, (504) 394-7744.

SAINT JOSEPH SEMINARY COLLEGE

St Benedict 70457. Private; small town. Awards B. Enrolls 110 T (0% women, 85% state res., 80% on fin. aid). Entrance difficulty: less difficult. Application deadline: rolling. Contact: Rev. Scott Underwood, OSB, Registrar, (504) 892-1800.

ST MARY'S DOMINICAN COLLEGE

New Orleans 70118. Private; urban. Awards A, B. Enrolls 805 T (95% women, 83% state res., 64% on fin. aid). Entrance difficulty: less difficult. Application deadline: 8/1. Contact: Mrs. Jane C. Chauvin, Executive Director of Admissions/Recruitment, (504) 865-7761.

SOUTHEASTERN LOUISIANA UNIVERSITY

Hammond 70402. Public; small town. Awards A, B, M. Enrolls 7,200 T, 6,346 U (56% women, 95% state res., 55% on fin. aid). Entrance difficulty: noncompetitive. Application deadline: rolling. Contact: Mrs. Iris S. Wiggins, (504) 549-2187.

SOUTHERN UNIVERSITY AND AGRICULTURAL AND MECHANICAL COLLEGE

Baton Rouge 70813. Public; suburban. Awards A, B, M. Enrolls 8,097 T, 7,231 U (53% women, 81% state res., 86% on fin. aid). Contact: Col. Johnson, (504) 771-2430.

SOUTHERN UNIVERSITY IN NEW ORLEANS

New Orleans 70126. Public; urban. Awards A, B. Enrolls 2,700 T (65% women, 99% state res., 69% on fin. aid). Entrance difficulty: noncompetitive. Application deadline: 7/1. Contact: Mr. Herman F. Plunkett, (504) 282-4401 Ext. 314.

TULANE UNIVERSITY

New Orleans 70118. Private; urban. Awards B, M, D. Enrolls 7,500 T, 5,000 U (36% women, 22% state res., 25% on fin. aid). Entrance difficulty: moderately difficult. Application deadlines: 2/1, early decision 11/1. Contact: Mr. R. Fred Zuker, Dean of Admissions, (504) 865-5731.

TULANE UNIVERSITY, NEWCOMB COLLEGE

New Orleans 70118. Private; urban. Awards B. Enrolls 1,629 T (100% women, 26% state res., 23% on fin. aid). Entrance difficulty: moderately difficult. Application deadlines: 2/1, early decision 11/1. Contact: Ms. Lois V. Conrad, (504) 865-4578.

UNIVERSITY OF NEW ORLEANS

New Orleans 70122. Public; urban. Awards A, B, M, D. Enrolls 14,431 T, 12,452 U (50% women, 96% state res., 45% on fin. aid). Entrance difficulty: noncompetitive. Application deadline: 8/1. Contact: Mr. Stanley P. Orvis, (504) 283-0595.

UNIVERSITY OF SOUTHWESTERN LOUISIANA

Lafayette 70504. Public; urban. Awards C, A, B, M, D. Enrolls 13,341 T, 12,070 U (50% women, 87% state res., 40% on fin. aid). Entrance difficulty: noncompetitive. Application deadline: rolling. Contact: Mr. Jacob Koehl, (318) 264-6457.

XAVIER UNIVERSITY OF LOUISIANA

New Orleans 70125. Private; urban. Awards B, M. Enrolls 1,904 T, 1,797 U (60% women, 80% state res., 98% on fin. aid). Entrance difficulty: moderately difficult. Application deadline: 8/1. Contact: Dr. Alfred J. Guillaume Jr, Dean of Admissions, (504) 486-7411.

MAINE

BATES COLLEGE

Lewiston 04240. Private; small town. Awards B. Enrolls 1,450 T (46% women, 11% state res., 35% on fin. aid). Entrance difficulty: very difficult. Application deadlines: 2/1, early decision 1/15. Contact: Mr. William C. Hiss, Dean of Admissions, (207) 784-0181.

BOWDOIN COLLEGE

Brunswick 04011. Private; small town. Awards B. Enrolls 1,340 T (45% women, 11% state res., 33% on fin. aid). Entrance difficulty: most difficult. Application deadlines: 2/1, early decision 11/1. Contact: Ms. Nancy A. Bellhouse, Assistant Director of Admissions, (207) 725-8731.

COLBY COLLEGE

Waterville 04901. Private; small town. Awards B. Enrolls 1,677 T (47% women, 18% state res., 29% on fin. aid). Entrance difficulty: very difficult. Application deadlines: 2/1, early decision 1/15. Contact: Mr. Harry R. Carroll, Dean of Admissions, (207) 873-1131.

COLLEGE OF THE ATLANTIC

Bar Harbor 04609. Private; small town. Awards B. Enrolls 170 T (55% women, 15% state res., 50% on fin. aid). Entrance difficulty: moderately difficult. Application deadline: 5/15. Contact: Mr. Jim Frick, (207) 288-5015.

HUSSON COLLEGE

Bangor 04401. Private; suburban. Awards C, A, B, M. Enrolls 1,212 T, 812 U (40% women, 65% state res., 70% on fin. aid). Entrance difficulty: noncompetitive. Application deadline: 8/30. Contact: Mr. Paul E. Husson, (207) 945-5641.

MAINE MARITIME ACADEMY

Castine 04421. Public; small town. Awards B. Enrolls 643 T (1% women, 70% state res., 38% on fin. aid). Entrance difficulty: moderately difficult. Application deadline: 6/1. Contact: Mr. Leonard Tyler, (207) 326-4311.

NASSON COLLEGE

Springvale 04083. Private; small town. Awards A, B. Enrolls 643 T (44% women, 16% state res., 42% on fin. aid). Entrance difficulty: moderately difficult. Application deadline: rolling. Contact: Mr. Richard Lolatte, (207) 324-5340.

PORTLAND SCHOOL OF ART

Portland 04101. Private; urban. Awards B. Enrolls 230 T (65% women, 49% state res., 60% on fin. aid). Entrance difficulty: moderately difficult. Application deadline: rolling. Contact: Mrs. Eudolia T. Gross, Registrar.

ST JOSEPH'S COLLEGE

North Windham 04062. Private; rural. Awards B. Enrolls 500 T (75% women, 44% state res., 65% on fin. aid). Entrance difficulty: moderately difficult. Application deadline: rolling. Contact: Mr. Daniel E. Small, (207) 892-6766 Ext. 15.

THOMAS COLLEGE

Waterville 04901. Private; small town. Awards A, B, M. Enrolls 1,058 T, 962 U (50% women, 72% state res., 67% on fin. aid). Entrance difficulty: moderately difficult. Application deadlines: 5/1, early decision 11/1. Contact: Mr. L. Lincoln Brown Jr, Dean of Admissions, (207) 873-0771.

UNITY COLLEGE

Unity 04988. Private; rural. Awards A, B. Enrolls 427 T (25% women, 18% state res., 66% on fin. aid). Entrance difficulty: noncompetitive. Application deadline: rolling. Contact: Miss Paula J. Meiers, Acting Director of Admissions, (207) 948-3131.

UNIVERSITY OF MAINE AT FARMINGTON

Farmington 04938. Public; small town. Awards A, B. Enrolls 1,590 T (70% women, 85% state res., 65% on fin. aid). Entrance difficulty: moderately difficult. Application deadline: rolling. Contact: Mr.

J. Anthony McLaughlin, (207) 778-3501 Ext. 350.

UNIVERSITY OF MAINE AT FORT KENT

Fort Kent 04743. Public; small town. Awards A, B. Enrolls 325 T (43% women, 63% state res., 70% on fin. aid). Entrance difficulty: noncompetitive. Application deadline: rolling. Contact: Miss Glenys Sayward, Acting Director of Admissions, (207) 834-3162.

UNIVERSITY OF MAINE AT MACHIAS

Machias 04654. Public; small town. Awards C, A, B. Enrolls 698 T (50% women, 80% state res., 60% on fin. aid). Entrance difficulty: moderately difficult. Application deadline: rolling. Contact: Mr. Daniel Molinsky, Admissions Counselor, (207) 255-3313.

UNIVERSITY OF MAINE AT ORONO

Orono 04469. Public; small town. Awards C, A, B, M, D. Enrolls 11,574 T, 10,566 U (46% women, 77% state res., 35% on fin. aid). Entrance difficulty: moderately difficult. Application deadline: 3/1. Contact: Mr. James A. Harmon, (207) 581-7568.

UNIVERSITY OF MAINE AT PRESQUE ISLE

Presque Isle 04769. Public; rural. Awards C, A, B. Enrolls 1,027 T (54% women, 88% state res., 85% on fin. aid). Entrance difficulty: moderately difficult. Application deadlines: 8/1, early decision 12/1. Contact: Mr. Fredric V. Stone, (207) 764-0311.

UNIVERSITY OF NEW ENGLAND

Biddeford 04005. Private; small town. Awards B, D. Enrolls 504 T, 406 U (34% women, 18% state res., 56% on fin. aid). Entrance difficulty: moderately difficult. Application deadlines: rolling, early decision 11/1. Contact: Ms. Judith L. Evrard, (207) 282-1515.

UNIVERSITY OF SOUTHERN MAINE

Gorham 04038. Public; suburban. Awards A, B, M. Enrolls 5,944 T, 5,084 U (55% women, 89% state res., 32% on fin. aid). Entrance difficulty: moderately difficult; very difficult for nursing and business. Ap-

plication deadline: rolling. Contact: Mr. William J. Munsey, (207) 780-4141.

WESTBROOK COLLEGE

Portland 04103. Private; suburban. Awards A, B. Enrolls 500 T (60% women, 58% state res., 75% on fin. aid). Entrance difficulty: moderately difficult; very difficult for dental hygiene. Application deadlines: 9/1, early decision 10/15. Contact: Ms. Ruth Ann Brooks, (207) 797-7261.

MARYLAND

ANTIOCH UNIVERSITY–MARYLAND AT BALTIMORE

Baltimore 21201. Public; urban. Awards B, M. Enrolls 190 T, 100 U (72% women, 95% state res., 75% on fin. aid). Entrance difficulty: moderately difficult. Application deadline: rolling. Contact: Miss Catherine E.P. Holland, Acting Director of Admissions, (301) 837-6965.

ANTIOCH UNIVERSITY–MARYLAND AT COLUMBIA

Columbia 21044. Contact: Miss Joyce Murray, Director of Admissions.

BALTIMORE HEBREW COLLEGE

Baltimore 21215. Private; suburban. Awards B, M, D. Enrolls 247 T, 95 U (73% women, 96% state res., 13% on fin. aid). Entrance difficulty: moderately difficult. Application deadline: 4/15. Contact: Dr. Jerome Gilison, Dean, (301) 466-7900.

BOWIE STATE COLLEGE

Bowie 20715. Public; suburban. Awards B, M. Enrolls 2,879 T, 2,049 U (54% women, 85% state res., 48% on fin. aid). Entrance difficulty: less difficult. Application deadline: rolling. Contact: Mrs. Patricia A. Wilson, (301) 464-3211.

CAPITOL INSTITUTE OF TECHNOLOGY

Kensington 20795. Private; suburban. Awards C, A, B. Enrolls 525 T (14% women, 75% state res., 26% on fin. aid). Entrance difficulty: noncompetitive. Application deadline: rolling. Contact: Mr.

Capitol Institute of Technology (continued)
Derick A. Veenstra, Director of Admissions, (301) 933-3300.

COLLEGE OF NOTRE DAME OF MARYLAND

Baltimore 21210. Private; suburban. Awards B. Enrolls 540 T (100% women, 75% state res., 55% on fin. aid). Entrance difficulty: moderately difficult. Application deadlines: 8/15, early decision 11/15. Contact: Mrs. Marion Bowers, Acting Director of Admissions, (301) 435-0100.

COLUMBIA UNION COLLEGE

Takoma Park 20012. Private; suburban. Awards C, A, B. Enrolls 956 T (60% women, 40% state res.). Entrance difficulty: moderately difficult. Application deadline: 8/1. Contact: Mr. Joseph E. Gurubatham, Registrar, (301) 270-9200 Ext. 320.

COPPIN STATE COLLEGE

Baltimore 21216. Public; urban. Awards B, M. Enrolls 2,918 T, 2,638 U (67% women, 97% state res., 92% on fin. aid). Entrance difficulty: noncompetitive. Application deadline: 7/30. Contact: Mr. Clyde W. Hatcher, (301) 383-5990 Ext. 91.

FROSTBURG STATE COLLEGE

Frostburg 21533. Public; small town. Awards B, M. Enrolls 3,600 T, 3,200 U (47% women, 93% state res., 35% on fin. aid). Entrance difficulty: moderately difficult. Contact: Mr. David L. Sanford, Dean of Admissions, (301) 689-4201.

GOUCHER COLLEGE

Towson 21204. Private; suburban. Awards B, M. Enrolls 1,020 T, 1,000 U (100% women, 39% state res., 47% on fin. aid). Entrance difficulty: moderately difficult. Application deadlines: 4/1, early decision 11/15. Contact: Miss B. Barbara Boerner, (301) 825-3300 Ext. 204.

HOOD COLLEGE

Frederick 21701. Private; suburban. Awards B, M. Enrolls 1,783 T, 1,145 U (93% women, 53% state res., 53% on fin. aid). Entrance difficulty: moderately difficult. Application deadlines: 7/1, early decision 10/31. Contact: Mr. George M. Hanold, (301) 663-3131.

JOHNS HOPKINS UNIVERSITY

Baltimore 21218. Private; urban. Awards B, M, D. Enrolls 2,963 T, 2,156 U (29% women, 32% state res., 55% on fin. aid). Entrance difficulty: most difficult. Application deadlines: 2/1, early decision 11/1. Contact: Mr. Jerome D. Schnydman, (301) 338-8171.

LOYOLA COLLEGE

Baltimore 21210. Private; suburban. Awards B, M. Enrolls 5,217 T, 2,111 U (45% women, 75% state res., 56% on fin. aid). Entrance difficulty: moderately difficult. Application deadline: rolling. Contact: Mrs. Martha E. Gagnon, (301) 323-1010.

MARYLAND INSTITUTE COLLEGE OF ART

Baltimore 21217. Private; urban. Awards C, B, M. Enrolls 825 T, 780 U (60% women, 55% state res., 65% on fin. aid). Entrance difficulty: moderately difficult. Application deadline: 5/1. Contact: Ms. Theresa M. Lynch, Director of Admissions, (301) 669-9200.

MORGAN STATE UNIVERSITY

Baltimore 21239. Public; urban. Awards B, M, D. Enrolls 5,299 T, 4,779 U (57% women, 63% state res., 74% on fin. aid). Entrance difficulty: noncompetitive. Application deadline: rolling. Contact: Ms. Chelseia H. Williams, Acting Director of Admissions, (301) 444-3000.

MOUNT SAINT MARY'S COLLEGE

Emmitsburg 21727. Private; rural. Awards B, M. Enrolls 1,550 T, 1,400 U (45% women, 38% state res., 65% on fin. aid). Entrance difficulty: moderately difficult. Application deadline: rolling. Contact: Mr. Lawrence J. Riordan, (301) 447-6122.

PEABODY CONSERVATORY OF JOHNS HOPKINS UNIVERSITY

Baltimore 21202. Private; urban. Awards B, M, D. Enrolls 448 T, 260 U (46% women, 35% state res., 60% on fin. aid). Entrance difficulty: very difficult. Application deadline: 5/1. Contact: Mr. Edward J. Weaver III, (301) 837-0600.

ST JOHN'S COLLEGE

Annapolis 21404. Private; small town. Awards B. Enrolls 350 T (47% women,

20% state res., 50% on fin. aid). Entrance difficulty: very difficult. Application deadline: rolling. Contact: Mr. John Christensen, (301) 263-2371.

ST MARY'S COLLEGE OF MARYLAND

St Mary's City 20686. Public; rural. Awards B. Enrolls 1,318 T (55% women, 93% state res., 32% on fin. aid). Entrance difficulty: moderately difficult. Application deadlines: 8/15, early decision 11/15. Contact: Miss Florence V. Curran, Director of Institutional Research.

SALISBURY STATE COLLEGE

Salisbury 21801. Public; small town. Awards B, M. Enrolls 4,361 T, 3,644 U (50% women, 86% state res., 35% on fin. aid). Entrance difficulty: moderately difficult. Application deadline: rolling. Contact: Malvin P. Minton III, (301) 546-3261 Ext. 301.

TOWSON STATE UNIVERSITY

Baltimore 21204. Public; urban. Awards B, M. Enrolls 15,340 T, 13,499 U (56% women, 96% state res., 9% on fin. aid). Entrance difficulty: moderately difficult. Application deadlines: 3/1, early decision 12/1. Contact: Miss Vivienne M. Lee, (301) 321-3112.

UNITED STATES NAVAL ACADEMY

Annapolis 21402. Public; small town. Awards B. Enrolls 4,300 T (5% women, 2% state res., 100% on fin. aid). Entrance difficulty: very difficult. Application deadline: 1/31. Contact: Rear Adm. Robert W. McNitt, (301) 267-2188.

UNIVERSITY OF MARYLAND AT COLLEGE PARK

College Park 20742. Public; suburban. Awards C, B, M, D. Enrolls 37,192 T, 29,835 U (47% women, 81% state res., 39% on fin. aid). Entrance difficulty: moderately difficult. Application deadline: 6/15. Contact: Dr. Wayne Sigler, (301) 454-2106.

UNIVERSITY OF MARYLAND BALTIMORE COUNTY

Catonsville 21228. Public; suburban. Awards C, B, M, D. Enrolls 5,396 T, 5,000 U (54% women, 96% state res., 50%

on fin. aid). Entrance difficulty: moderately difficult. Application deadline: 701. Contact: Dr. Michael L. Mahoney, Director of Academic Services, (301) 455-2097.

UNIVERSITY OF MARYLAND EASTERN SHORE

Princess Anne 21853. Public; rural. Awards B, M. Enrolls 1,117 T, 1,069 U (56% women, 63% state res., 90% on fin. aid). Entrance difficulty: moderately difficult. Application deadline: rolling. Contact: Mr. James B. Ewers, Director of Admissions and Registrations, (301) 651-2200.

WASHINGTON BIBLE COLLEGE

Lanham 20801. Private; suburban. Awards B, M. Enrolls 606 T, 506 U (40% women, 45% state res., 55% on fin. aid). Entrance difficulty: noncompetitive. Application deadline: rolling. Contact: Mr. William M. Curtis, Registrar, (301) 552-1400.

WASHINGTON COLLEGE

Chestertown 21620. Private; small town. Awards B, M. Enrolls 825 T, 783 U (48% women, 44% state res., 22% on fin. aid). Entrance difficulty: moderately difficult. Application deadline: rolling. Contact: Mr. A. M. Di Maggio, (301) 778-2800.

WESTERN MARYLAND COLLEGE

Westminster 21157. Private; small town. Awards B, M. Enrolls 1,665 T, 1,359 U (50% women, 70% state res., 50% on fin. aid). Entrance difficulty: moderately difficult. Application deadline: 8/1. Contact: Mr. L. Leslie Bennett Jr, (301) 848-7000.

MASSACHUSETTS

AMERICAN INTERNATIONAL COLLEGE

Springfield 01109. Private; suburban. Awards B, M. Enrolls 2,007 T, 1,463 U (42% women, 60% state res., 67% on fin. aid). Entrance difficulty: moderately difficult. Application deadlines: rolling, early decision 11/1. Contact: Mr. John R. Fallon, Director of Admissions, (413) 737-7000.

AMHERST COLLEGE

Amherst 01002. Private; small town. Awards B. Enrolls 1,541 T (37% women, 18% state res., 34% on fin. aid). Entrance difficulty: most difficult. Application deadlines: 1/15, early decision 11/1. Contact: Mr. Donald Dietrich, Assistant Dean of Admissions.

ANNA MARIA COLLEGE

Paxton 01612. Private; suburban. Awards A, B, M. Enrolls 1,320 T, 580 U (80% women, 75% state res., 65% on fin. aid). Entrance difficulty: moderately difficult. Application deadline: 7/15. Contact: Mr. F. Duane Quinn, Director of Admissions, (617) 757-4586 Ext. 45.

ASSUMPTION COLLEGE

Worcester 01609. Private; suburban. Awards B, M. Enrolls 1,885 T, 1,400 U (50% women, 50% state res., 48% on fin. aid). Entrance difficulty: moderately difficult. Application deadlines: 3/1, early decision 11/1. Contact: Mr. Thomas E. Dunn, (617) 752-5615.

ATLANTIC UNION COLLEGE

South Lancaster 01561. Private; small town. Awards A, B. Enrolls 640 T (55% women, 38% state res., 75% on fin. aid). Entrance difficulty: noncompetitive. Application deadline: 7/15. Contact: Mr. J. D. Mustard, Registrar, (617) 365-4561.

BABSON COLLEGE

Babson Park 02157. Private; suburban. Awards B, M. Enrolls 2,859 T, 1,335 U (26% women, 75% state res., 27% on fin. aid). Entrance difficulty: very difficult. Application deadlines: 2/1, early decision 12/1. Contact: Mr. Joseph B. Carver, Director of Admissions, (617) 235-1200.

BENTLEY COLLEGE

Waltham 02154. Private; suburban. Awards C, A, B, M. Enrolls 6,683 T, 4,950 U (30% women, 60% state res., 45% on fin. aid). Entrance difficulty: moderately difficult. Application deadline: 3/14. Contact: Mr. Charles S. Nolan, Director of Admissions, (617) 891-2244.

BERKLEE COLLEGE OF MUSIC

Boston 02215. Private; urban. Awards C, B. Enrolls 2,583 T (15% women, 20% state res., 55% on fin. aid). Entrance difficulty: moderately difficult. Application deadline: rolling. Contact: Mr. Steven Lipman, (617) 266-1400.

BERKSHIRE CHRISTIAN COLLEGE

Lenox 01240. Private; small town. Awards A, B. Enrolls 136 T (46% women, 33% state res., 75% on fin. aid). Entrance difficulty: moderately difficult. Application deadline: rolling. Contact: Mr. David L. Bowden, Director of Admissions, (413) 637-0838.

BOSTON COLLEGE

Chestnut Hill 02167. Private; suburban. Awards B, M, D. Enrolls 13,313 T, 10,185 U (56% women, 52% state res., 34% on fin. aid). Entrance difficulty: very difficult. Application deadlines: 1/15, early decision 11/1. Contact: Ms. Patricia Casey, Acting Director of Admissions, (617) 969-0100 Ext. 3290.

BOSTON CONSERVATORY OF MUSIC

Boston 02215. Private; urban. Awards B, M. Enrolls 539 T, 481 U (67% women, 86% on fin. aid). Entrance difficulty: moderately difficult. Application deadline: rolling. Contact: Dr. LeRoy Johnston, Dean of Admissions, (617) 536-6340.

BOSTON STATE COLLEGE

Boston 02115. Public; urban. Awards B, M. Enrolls 7,508 T, 5,241 U (48% women, 90% state res., 40% on fin. aid). Entrance difficulty: less difficult. Application deadline: 3/1. Contact: Mr. Edward Zaleskas, (617) 731-3300 Ext. 435.

BOSTON UNIVERSITY

Boston 02215. Private; urban. Awards C, A, B, M, D. Enrolls 26,011 T, 11,279 U (53% women, 25% state res., 40% on fin. aid). Entrance difficulty: moderately difficult. Application deadlines: rolling, early decision 11/15. Contact: Mr. Anthony T. G. Pallett, Director of Admissions, (617) 353-2300.

BRADFORD COLLEGE

Bradford 01830. Private; suburban. Awards A, B. Enrolls 341 T (57% women, 31% state res., 44% on fin. aid). Entrance difficulty: less difficult. Application deadlines:

rolling, early decision 11/15. Contact: Dr. Anthony R. DeLuca, (617) 372-7161.

BRANDEIS UNIVERSITY

Waltham 02154. Private; suburban. Awards B, M, D. Enrolls 3,377 T, 2,798 U (50% women, 22% state res., 46% on fin. aid). Entrance difficulty: very difficult. Application deadlines: 2/1, early decision 1/1. Contact: Mr. David L. Gould, (617) 647-2878.

BRIDGEWATER STATE COLLEGE

Bridgewater 02324. Public; small town. Awards B, M. Enrolls 4,600 T, 4,358 U (60% women, 96% state res., 60% on fin. aid). Entrance difficulty: moderately difficult. Application deadline: 3/1. Contact: Mr. James F. Plotner Jr, (617) 697-8321.

CENTRAL NEW ENGLAND COLLEGE

Worcester 01608. Private; urban. Awards A, B. Entrance difficulty: noncompetitive. Application deadline: rolling. Contact: Mr. Donald J. Shanley, (617) 755-4314.

CLARK UNIVERSITY

Worcester 01610. Private; urban. Awards B, M, D. Enrolls 3,000 T, 1,810 U (50% women, 25% state res., 45% on fin. aid). Entrance difficulty: very difficult. Application deadlines: 2/15, early decision 1/15. Contact: Mr. Richard W. Pierson, Director of Admissions, (617) 793-7431.

COLLEGE OF OUR LADY OF THE ELMS

Chicopee 01013. Private; suburban. Awards B. Enrolls 425 T (100% women, 65% state res., 50% on fin. aid). Entrance difficulty: moderately difficult. Application deadline: rolling. Contact: Mr. Peter J. Miller, Director of Admissions, (413) 598-8351 Ext. 38.

COLLEGE OF THE HOLY CROSS

Worcester 01610. Private; suburban. Awards B, M. Enrolls 2,500 T (43% women, 47% state res., 45% on fin. aid). Entrance difficulty: very difficult. Application deadlines: 2/1, early decision 11/1. Contact: Mr. James R. Halpin, Director of Admissions, (617) 793-2443.

CURRY COLLEGE

Milton 02186. Private; suburban. Awards B. Enrolls 831 T (51% women, 58% state res., 60% on fin. aid). Entrance difficulty: moderately difficult. Application deadlines: rolling, early decision 11/1. Contact: Mr. Dana Denault, Director of Admissions, (617) 333-0500.

EASTERN NAZARENE COLLEGE

Quincy 02170. Private; suburban. Awards A, B, M. Enrolls 775 T, 771 U (57% women, 32% state res., 85% on fin. aid). Entrance difficulty: less difficult. Application deadline: rolling. Contact: Mr. Robert M. Hubbard, (617) 773-6350.

EMERSON COLLEGE

Boston 02116. Private; urban. Awards B, M. Enrolls 1,587 T, 1,476 U (53% women, 45% state res., 23% on fin. aid). Entrance difficulty: moderately difficult. Application deadline: rolling. Contact: Ms. Helen M. Cross, (617) 262-2010.

EMMANUEL COLLEGE

Boston 02115. Private; urban. Awards A, B, M. Enrolls 1,200 T, 542 U (100% women, 65% state res., 60% on fin. aid). Entrance difficulty: moderately difficult. Application deadlines: rolling, early decision 11/1. Contact: Mr. Edward Gillis, (617) 277-9340 Ext. 115.

FITCHBURG STATE COLLEGE

Fitchburg 01420. Public; urban. Awards B, M. Enrolls 4,846 T, 3,719 U (65% women, 97% state res., 37% on fin. aid). Entrance difficulty: moderately difficult. Application deadline: 3/1. Contact: Mr. Joseph A. Angelini, (617) 345-2151 Ext. 129.

FRAMINGHAM STATE COLLEGE

Framingham 01701. Public; suburban. Awards B, M. Enrolls 3,225 T, 3,125 U (60% women, 97% state res., 50% on fin. aid). Entrance difficulty: moderately difficult. Application deadline: 3/1. Contact: Dr. Philip M. Dooher, (617) 620-1220.

GORDON COLLEGE

Wenham 01984. Private; suburban. Awards B. Enrolls 1,000 T (57% women, 60% on fin. aid). Entrance difficulty: moderately difficult. Application deadlines: rolling,

Gordon College (continued)
early decision 11/15. Contact: Mr. David MacMillan, (617) 927-2300.

HAMPSHIRE COLLEGE

Amherst 01002. Private; rural. Awards B. Enrolls 1,200 T (50% women, 11% state res., 25% on fin. aid). Entrance difficulty: very difficult. Application deadlines: 2/15, early decision 12/1. Contact: Mr. Robert de Veer, (413) 549-4640.

HARVARD AND RADCLIFFE COLLEGES

Cambridge 02138. Private; urban. Awards B, M, D. Enrolls 15,716 T, 6,557 U (37% women, 21% state res., 67% on fin. aid). Entrance difficulty: most difficult. Application deadlines: 1/1, early decision 11/1. Contact: Mr. William R. Fitzsimmons, (617) 495-1551.

HEBREW COLLEGE

Brookline 02146. Private; urban. Awards C, B, M. Enrolls 141 T, 112 U (74% women, 90% state res., 52% on fin. aid). Application deadline: 5/15. Contact: Mr. Martin Rabinovitz, Registrar, (617) 232-8710.

HELLENIC COLLEGE

Brookline 02146. Private; suburban. Awards B. Enrolls 78 T (10% women, 5% state res., 60% on fin. aid). Entrance difficulty: less difficult. Application deadline: rolling. Contact: Mr. Chris Metropolus, (617) 731-3500 Ext. 59.

LESLEY COLLEGE

Cambridge 02138. Private; urban. Awards B, M. Enrolls 1,190 T, 815 U (100% women, 58% state res., 51% on fin. aid). Entrance difficulty: moderately difficult; noncompetitive for minority students. Application deadline: 4/1. Contact: Mrs. Martha B. Ackerson, (617) 868-9600 Ext. 166.

MASSACHUSETTS COLLEGE OF ART

Boston 02215. Public; urban. Awards B, M. Enrolls 1,129 T, 1,050 U (60% women, 85% state res., 35% on fin. aid). Entrance difficulty: very difficult. Application deadline: 4/15. Contact: Miss Kay Ransdell, (617) 731-2340.

MASSACHUSETTS COLLEGE OF PHARMACY AND ALLIED HEALTH SCIENCES

Boston 02115. Private; urban. Awards C, B, M, D. Enrolls 1,300 T, 1,200 U (43% women, 64% state res., 44% on fin. aid). Entrance difficulty: moderately difficult. Application deadlines: 6/1, early decision 1/1. Contact: Mr. Bruce D. Grigsby, (617) 732-2850.

MASSACHUSETTS INSTITUTE OF TECHNOLOGY

Cambridge 02139. Private; urban. Awards B, M, D. Enrolls 8,247 T, 4,232 U (18% women, 17% state res., 55% on fin. aid). Entrance difficulty: most difficult. Application deadlines: 1/1, early decision 11/1. Contact: Mr. Peter H. Richardson, (617) 253-4791.

MASSACHUSETTS MARITIME ACADEMY

Buzzards Bay 02532. Public; small town. Awards B. Enrolls 850 T (7% women, 85% state res., 70% on fin. aid). Entrance difficulty: very difficult. Application deadline: 3/1. Contact: CDR Thomas S. Lee, (617) 759-5761 Ext. 213.

MERRIMACK COLLEGE

North Andover 01845. Private; suburban. Awards A, B. Enrolls 2,196 T (41% women, 74% state res., 33% on fin. aid). Entrance difficulty: moderately difficult. Application deadlines: 3/31, early decision 11/30. Contact: Mr. E. Joseph Lee, Dean of Admissions, (617) 683-7111 Ext. 121.

MOUNT HOLYOKE COLLEGE

South Hadley 01075. Private; small town. Awards B, M. Enrolls 1,850 T (100% women, 20% state res., 50% on fin. aid). Entrance difficulty: very difficult. Application deadlines: 2/1, early decision 11/15. Contact: Miss Clara R. Ludwig, (413) 538-2023.

NEW ENGLAND CONSERVATORY OF MUSIC

Boston 02115. Private; urban. Awards C, B, M. Enrolls 762 T, 508 U (37% women, 35% state res., 40% on fin. aid). Entrance difficulty: very difficult. Application deadline: 3/1. Contact: Mr. Lawrence Murphy, (617) 262-1120 Ext. 244.

NICHOLS COLLEGE

Dudley 01570. Private; small town. Awards B, M. Enrolls 896 T, 776 U (18% women, 50% state res., 54% on fin. aid). Entrance difficulty: moderately difficult. Application deadlines: 8/1, early decision 11/15. Contact: Mr. Dan S. Ramsey, (617) 943-2055.

NORTH ADAMS STATE COLLEGE

North Adams 01247. Public; small town. Awards B, M. Enrolls 2,920 T, 2,350 U (52% women, 90% state res., 37% on fin. aid). Entrance difficulty: moderately difficult. Application deadlines: 3/1, early decision 12/1. Contact: Mr. William T. West Jr, (413) 664-4511.

NORTHEASTERN UNIVERSITY

Boston 02115. Private; urban. Awards C, A, B, M, D. Enrolls 25,598 T, 19,275 U (36% women, 65% state res., 82% on fin. aid). Entrance difficulty: moderately difficult. Application deadline: rolling. Contact: Mr. Philip R. McCabe, (617) 437-2222.

PINE MANOR COLLEGE

Chestnut Hill 02167. Private; suburban. Awards A, B. Enrolls 494 T (100% women, 17% state res., 20% on fin. aid). Entrance difficulty: less difficult. Application deadlines: rolling, early decision 11/25. Contact: Mr. C. Richard Plank, (617) 731-7104.

REGIS COLLEGE

Weston 02193. Private; suburban. Awards B, M. Enrolls 1,266 T, 1,099 U (100% women, 80% state res., 72% on fin. aid). Entrance difficulty: moderately difficult. Application deadline: rolling. Contact: Mr. Marshall Raucci, (617) 893-1820.

ST HYACINTH COLLEGE AND SEMINARY

Granby 01033. Private; small town. Awards B. Enrolls 51 T (0% women, 30% state res., 10% on fin. aid). Entrance difficulty: moderately difficult. Application deadline: rolling. Contact: Fr. Martin Kobos, Director of Admissions, (301) 988-9833.

SALEM STATE COLLEGE

Salem 01970. Public; suburban. Awards B, M. Enrolls 9,481 T, 5,580 U (60% women, 98% state res., 70% on fin. aid). Entrance difficulty: moderately difficult; very difficult for nursing, business administration pro-

grams. Application deadline: 3/1. Contact: Mr. David Sartwell, (617) 745-0556.

SCHOOL OF THE MUSEUM OF FINE ARTS

Boston 02115.

SCHOOL OF THE WORCESTER ART MUSEUM

Worcester 01608. Private; urban. Awards C. Enrolls 112 T (66% women, 95% state res., 45% on fin. aid). Entrance difficulty: moderately difficult. Application deadline: rolling. Contact: Ms. Charlene Lowell, Director of Student Relations, (617) 799-4406.

SIMMONS COLLEGE

Boston 02115. Private; urban. Awards C, B, M, D. Enrolls 2,766 T, 1,797 U (100% women, 51% state res., 40% on fin. aid). Entrance difficulty: moderately difficult. Application deadline: 3/15. Contact: Ms. Linda Cox Maguire, (617) 738-2107.

SIMON'S ROCK OF BARD COLLEGE

Great Barrington 01230. Private; small town. Awards A, B. Enrolls 212 T (60% women, 20% state res., 40% on fin. aid). Entrance difficulty: moderately difficult. Application deadline: rolling. Contact: Ms. Sharon K. Pinkerton, (413) 528-0771.

SMITH COLLEGE

Northampton 01063. Private; small town. Awards C, B, M, D. Enrolls 2,737 T, 2,651 U (100% women, 23% state res., 35% on fin. aid). Entrance difficulty: very difficult. Application deadlines: 2/1, early decision 11/15. Contact: Miss Lorna R. Blake, (413) 584-0515.

SOUTHEASTERN MASSACHUSETTS UNIVERSITY

North Dartmouth 02747. Public; suburban. Awards B, M. Enrolls 5,079 T, 5,063 U (49% women, 96% state res., 62% on fin. aid). Entrance difficulty: moderately difficult. Application deadline: rolling. Contact: Mr. Barrie G. Phelps, (617) 999-8605.

SPRINGFIELD COLLEGE

Springfield 01109. Private; suburban. Awards B, M, D. Enrolls 2,428 T, 2,146 U (50% women, 38% state res., 36% on fin.

Springfield College (continued)
aid). Entrance difficulty: moderately difficult. Application deadline: 4/1. Contact: Mr. Robert B. Palmer, Dean of Admissions, (413) 787-2030.

STONEHILL COLLEGE

North Easton 02356. Private; rural. Awards B. Enrolls 1,687 T (50% women, 60% state res., 35% on fin. aid). Entrance difficulty: moderately difficult. Application deadlines: 3/1, early decision 11/1. Contact: Mr. Brian P. Murphy, (617) 238-1081.

SUFFOLK UNIVERSITY

Boston 02114. Private; urban. Awards C, A, B, M. Enrolls 4,707 T, 1,954 U (49% women, 98% state res., 33% on fin. aid). Entrance difficulty: moderately difficult. Application deadline: 6/1. Contact: Mr. William F. Coughlin, (617) 723-4700 Ext. 220.

SWAIN SCHOOL OF DESIGN

New Bedford 02740. Private; suburban. Awards B. Enrolls 167 T (50% women, 71% state res., 75% on fin. aid). Entrance difficulty: less difficult. Application deadline: rolling. Contact: Mr. Peter W. Newport, (617) 997-7831.

TUFTS UNIVERSITY

Medford 02155. Private; suburban. Awards B, M, D. Enrolls 6,700 T, 4,576 U (49% women, 33% state res., 32% on fin. aid). Entrance difficulty: very difficult. Application deadline: 1/15. Contact: Isable B. Abbott, Assistant Director of Admissions, (617) 628-5000 Ext. 374.

UNIVERSITY OF LOWELL

Lowell 01854. Public; urban. Awards A, B, M, D. Enrolls 7,564 T, 6,866 U (37% women, 93% state res., 37% on fin. aid). Entrance difficulty: moderately difficult. Application deadline: 4/1. Contact: Mr. Lawrence R. Martin, (617) 452-5000.

UNIVERSITY OF MASSACHUSETTS AT AMHERST

Amherst 01003. Public; small town. Awards A, B, M, D. Enrolls 24,012 T, 18,481 U (48% women, 88% state res., 75% on fin. aid). Entrance difficulty: moderately difficult. Application deadline: 3/1. Contact: Miss Deirdre Kedesdy, (413) 545-0222.

UNIVERSITY OF MASSACHUSETTS AT BOSTON

Boston 02125. Public; urban. Awards C, B, M. Enrolls 7,948 T, 7,848 U (50% women, 96% state res., 60% on fin. aid). Entrance difficulty: moderately difficult. Application deadline: rolling. Contact: Mr. Douglas Hartnagel, (617) 287-8100.

WELLESLEY COLLEGE

Wellesley 02181. Private; suburban. Awards B. Enrolls 2,147 T (100% women, 26% state res., 50% on fin. aid). Entrance difficulty: very difficult. Application deadlines: 2/1, early decision 11/15. Contact: Mrs. Mary Ellen Ames, (617) 235-0320 Ext. 201.

WENTWORTH INSTITUTE OF TECHNOLOGY

Boston 02115. Private; urban. Awards C, A, B. Enrolls 2,300 T (5% women, 75% state res., 33% on fin. aid). Entrance difficulty: moderately difficult. Application deadline: 9/1. Contact: Mr. Charles P. Oppvall, Dean of Admissions, (617) 442-9010.

WESTERN NEW ENGLAND COLLEGE

Springfield 01119. Private; suburban. Awards B, M. Enrolls 3,508 T, 2,634 U (33% women, 64% state res., 65% on fin. aid). Entrance difficulty: moderately difficult. Application deadline: rolling. Contact: Mr. Rae James Malcolm, (413) 782-3111.

WESTFIELD STATE COLLEGE

Westfield 01085. Public; suburban. Awards B, M. Enrolls 3,117 T, 2,862 U (63% women, 97% state res., 50% on fin. aid). Entrance difficulty: moderately difficult. Application deadline: rolling. Contact: Mr. William Crean, (413) 568-3311.

WHEATON COLLEGE

Norton 02766. Private; small town. Awards B. Enrolls 1,227 T (100% women, 33% state res., 55% on fin. aid). Entrance difficulty: moderately difficult. Application deadlines: 2/1, early decision 11/1. Contact: Ms. Niki Janus, (617) 285-7722.

WHEELOCK COLLEGE

Boston 02215. Private; urban. Awards A, B, M. Enrolls 993 T, 600 U (98% women, 41% state res., 33% on fin. aid). Entrance difficulty: moderately difficult. Application deadlines: 2/15, early decision 12/1. Contact: Miss Melanie J. Horton, Admissions Counselor, (617) 734-5200.

WILLIAMS COLLEGE

Williamstown 01267. Private; small town. Awards B, M. Enrolls 2,048 T, 1,987 U (44% women, 17% state res., 31% on fin. aid). Entrance difficulty: most difficult. Application deadlines: 1/15, early decision 11/15. Contact: Mr. Philip F. Smith, (413) 597-2211.

WORCESTER POLYTECHNIC INSTITUTE

Worcester 01609. Private; urban. Awards B, M, D. Enrolls 2,573 T, 2,388 U (18% women, 49% state res., 65% on fin. aid). Entrance difficulty: very difficult. Application deadlines: 2/15, early decision 1/1. Contact: Mr. John Brandon, (617) 753-1411.

WORCESTER STATE COLLEGE

Worcester 01602. Public; urban. Awards B, M. Enrolls 3,465 T, 3,125 U (57% women, 98% state res., 20% on fin. aid). Entrance difficulty: less difficult. Application deadline: rolling. Contact: Mr. Joseph P. Scannell, (617) 752-7700.

MICHIGAN

ADRIAN COLLEGE

Adrian 49221. Private; small town. Awards A, B. Enrolls 946 T (52% women, 84% state res., 76% on fin. aid). Entrance difficulty: moderately difficult. Application deadline: 8/15. Contact: Mr. Thomas E. Williams, Director of Admissions, (517) 265-5161.

ALBION COLLEGE

Albion 49224. Private; small town. Awards B. Enrolls 1,800 T (45% women, 85% state res., 51% on fin. aid). Entrance difficulty: moderately difficult. Application deadline: rolling. Contact: Mr. Frank Bonta, Dean of Admissions, (517) 629-5511 Ext. 321.

ALMA COLLEGE

Alma 48801. Private; small town. Awards B. Enrolls 1,210 T (51% women, 74% state

res., 81% on fin. aid). Entrance difficulty: very difficult. Application deadline: rolling. Contact: Mr. Stephen Bushouse, (517) 463-2141.

ANDREWS UNIVERSITY

Berrien Springs 49104. Private; small town. Awards C, A, B, M, D. Enrolls 2,983 T, 2,087 U (52% women, 38% state res., 86% on fin. aid). Entrance difficulty: moderately difficult. Application deadline: 9/15. Contact: Mr. Douglas K. Brown, (616) 471-3303.

AQUINAS COLLEGE

Grand Rapids 49506. Private; suburban. Awards A, B, M. Enrolls 2,172 T, 1,907 U (54% women, 89% state res., 89% on fin. aid). Entrance difficulty: moderately difficult. Application deadlines: 8/1, early decision 12/1. Contact: Mr. James L. Schultz, Dean of Admissions, (616) 459-8281.

CALVIN COLLEGE

Grand Rapids 49506. Private; suburban. Awards B, M. Enrolls 4,024 T, 3,900 U (52% women, 57% state res., 75% on fin. aid). Entrance difficulty: moderately difficult. Application deadline: rolling. Contact: Mr. Donald Lautenbach, (616) 949-4000.

CENTER FOR CREATIVE STUDIES– COLLEGE OF ART AND DESIGN

Detroit 48202. Private; urban. Awards B. Enrolls 756 T (50% women, 92% state res., 75% on fin. aid). Entrance difficulty: moderately difficult. Application deadline: rolling. Contact: Miss Lorraine Smith, Secretary to Director of Admissions, (313) 872-3118.

CENTRAL MICHIGAN UNIVERSITY

Mount Pleasant 48858. Public; small town. Awards B, M, D. Enrolls 16,281 T, 14,556 U (55% women, 98% state res., 60% on fin. aid). Entrance difficulty: moderately difficult. Application deadline: rolling. Contact: Mr. Michael Owens, Director of Admissions, (517) 774-3076.

CLEARY COLLEGE

Ypsilanti 48197. Private; urban. Awards C, A, B. Enrolls 453 T (74% women, 95% state res., 22% on fin. aid). Application deadline: rolling. Contact: Mrs. Marsha Ellard, (313) 483-4400.

CONCORDIA COLLEGE

Ann Arbor 48105. Private; small town. Awards A, B. Enrolls 560 T (40% women, 50% state res., 50% on fin. aid). Entrance difficulty: moderately difficult. Application deadline: 8/15. Contact: Mr. Eugene L. Krentz, (313) 665-3691.

CRANBROOK ACADEMY OF ART

Bloomfield Hills 48013. Contact: Miss Lucille Harper, Director of Admissions.

DETROIT BIBLE COLLEGE

Farmington Hills 48018. Private; suburban. Awards C, B. Enrolls 345 T (38% women, 98% state res., 10% on fin. aid). Entrance difficulty: moderately difficult. Application deadline: 8/11. Contact: Miss Margaret Barron, (313) 553-7200.

DETROIT INSTITUTE OF TECHNOLOGY

Detroit 48201. Private; urban. Awards C, A, B. Enrolls 800 T (38% women, 84% state res., 90% on fin. aid). Entrance difficulty: less difficult. Application deadlines: 9/1, early decision 12/31. Contact: Mr. Walter Williamson, (313) 962-0830.

DUNS SCOTUS COLLEGE

Southfield 48075.

EASTERN MICHIGAN UNIVERSITY

Ypsilanti 48197. Public; small town. Awards B, M. Enrolls 20,079 T, 14,502 U (57% women, 96% state res., 50% on fin. aid). Entrance difficulty: moderately difficult. Application deadline: rolling. Contact: Mr. Don Kajcienski, (313) 487-3060.

FERRIS STATE COLLEGE

Big Rapids 49307. Public; small town. Awards C, A, B. Enrolls 10,486 T (39% women, 96% state res., 50% on fin. aid). Entrance difficulty: less difficult. Application deadline: rolling. Contact: Mr. Karl S. Walker, (616) 796-9971 Ext. 221.

GENERAL MOTORS INSTITUTE

Flint 48502. Private; urban. Awards B. Enrolls 2,241 T (34% women, 42% state res., 18% on fin. aid). Entrance difficulty: very difficult. Contact: Mrs. Sandra Urquhart Brown, (313) 766-9870.

GRACE BIBLE COLLEGE

Grand Rapids 49509. Private; suburban. Awards C, A, B. Enrolls 210 T (47% women, 25% state res., 66% on fin. aid). Entrance difficulty: moderately difficult. Application deadline: 7/15. Contact: Miss Evlyne Beyer, Admissions Director and Registrar, (616) 538-2330.

GRAND RAPIDS BAPTIST COLLEGE

Grand Rapids 49505. Private; suburban. Awards C, A, B, M. Enrolls 1,135 T, 935 U (47% women, 47% state res., 70% on fin. aid). Entrance difficulty: less difficult. Application deadline: rolling. Contact: Mr. Daniel Mead, (616) 949-5300 Ext. 267.

GRAND VALLEY STATE COLLEGES

Allendale 49401. Public; rural. Awards C, B, M. Enrolls 7,142 T, 6,170 U (50% women, 97% state res., 70% on fin. aid). Entrance difficulty: less difficult. Application deadline: 8/27. Contact: Mr. Carl Wallman, (616) 895-6611.

HILLSDALE COLLEGE

Hillsdale 49242. Private; small town. Awards B. Enrolls 1,025 T (47% women, 48% state res., 50% on fin. aid). Entrance difficulty: moderately difficult. Application deadline: rolling. Contact: Dr. Russell L. Nichols, (517) 437-7341.

HOPE COLLEGE

Holland 49423. Private; suburban. Awards B. Enrolls 2,371 T (48% women, 67% state res., 73% on fin. aid). Entrance difficulty: moderately difficult. Application deadline: rolling. Contact: Dr. Philip Fredrickson, Dean for Admissions, (616) 392-5111 Ext. 2200.

JOHN WESLEY COLLEGE

Owosso 48867. Private; small town. Awards A, B. Enrolls 80 T (50% women, 60% state res.). Entrance difficulty: moderately difficult. Application deadline: rolling. Contact: Ms. Mary Herrguth, (517) 723-8141.

KALAMAZOO COLLEGE

Kalamazoo 49007. Private; suburban. Awards B. Enrolls 1,440 T (48% women, 70% state res., 42% on fin. aid). Entrance difficulty: very difficult. Application deadline: rolling. Contact: Mr. Paul M. Lane, (616) 383-8408.

LAKE SUPERIOR STATE COLLEGE

Sault Ste Marie 49783. Public; small town. Awards C, A, B. Enrolls 2,309 T (46% women, 90% state res., 84% on fin. aid). Entrance difficulty: moderately difficult. Application deadline: rolling. Contact: Dr. James E. Honkanen, (906) 632-6841 Ext. 231.

LAWRENCE INSTITUTE OF TECHNOLOGY

Southfield 48075. Private; suburban. Awards A, B. Enrolls 4,991 T (15% women, 90% state res., 60% on fin. aid). Entrance difficulty: moderately difficult. Application deadline: rolling. Contact: Mr. S. F. Harris, (313) 356-0200.

MADONNA COLLEGE

Livonia 48150. Private; suburban. Awards C, A, B. Enrolls 3,011 T (68% women, 98% state res., 40% on fin. aid). Entrance difficulty: noncompetitive; moderately difficult for nursing and science programs. Application deadline: rolling. Contact: Mr. Louis E. Brohl III, (313) 591-5052.

MARYGROVE COLLEGE

Detroit 48221. Private; urban. Awards A, B, M. Enrolls 958 T, 752 U (82% women, 98% state res., 84% on fin. aid). Entrance difficulty: moderately difficult. Application deadline: rolling. Contact: Mr. Charles Donaldson, (313) 862-8000 Ext. 234.

MERCY COLLEGE OF DETROIT

Detroit 48219. Private; urban. Awards C, A, B, M. Enrolls 2,454 T (74% women, 95% state res., 80% on fin. aid). Entrance difficulty: moderately difficult; very difficult for applicants to medical technology and nursing programs. Application deadline: 8/15. Contact: Ms. Jeanne Umholtz, (313) 592-6030.

MICHIGAN STATE UNIVERSITY

East Lansing 48824. Public; small town. Awards B, M, D. Enrolls 44,756 T, 36,372 U (50% women, 86% state res., 50% on fin. aid). Entrance difficulty: moderately difficult. Application deadline: 8/15. Contact: Mr. Charles F. Seeley, Director of Admissions and Scholarships, (517) 355-8332.

MICHIGAN TECHNOLOGICAL UNIVERSITY

Houghton 49931. Public; small town. Awards C, A, B, M, D. Enrolls 7,603 T, 7,341 U (23% women, 85% state res., 72% on fin. aid). Entrance difficulty: very difficult. Application deadline: 8/1. Contact: Mr. Ernest R. Griff, Director of Admissions and School Services, (906) 487-2335.

NAZARETH COLLEGE

Nazareth 49074. Private; small town. Awards B. Enrolls 540 T (81% women, 97% state res., 54% on fin. aid). Entrance difficulty: less difficult; moderately difficult for health programs. Application deadline: rolling. Contact: Sr. Virginia Jones, (616) 349-7783.

NORTHERN MICHIGAN UNIVERSITY

Marquette 49855. Public; urban. Awards C, A, B, M. Enrolls 8,756 T, 7,524 U (49% women, 94% state res., 56% on fin. aid). Entrance difficulty: less difficult. Application deadline: 8/15. Contact: Mr. Jack M. Kunkel, (906) 227-2650.

NORTHWOOD INSTITUTE– MIDLAND CAMPUS

Midland 48640. Private; suburban. Awards C, A, B. Enrolls 1,770 T (33% women, 50% state res., 42% on fin. aid). Entrance difficulty: moderately difficult. Application deadline: rolling. Contact: Mr. Jack King, (517) 631-1600.

OAKLAND UNIVERSITY

Rochester 48063. Public; suburban. Awards C, B, M, D. Enrolls 11,729 T, 9,331 U (57% women, 99% state res., 30% on fin. aid). Entrance difficulty: moderately difficult. Application deadline: rolling. Contact: Mr. Jerry W. Rose, (313) 377-3360.

OLIVET COLLEGE

Olivet 49076. Private; small town. Awards B, M. Enrolls 630 T, 629 U (39% women, 96% state res., 90% on fin. aid). Entrance difficulty: moderately difficult. Application deadline: 8/1. Contact: Mr. John J. Bart, (616) 749-7635.

REFORMED BIBLE COLLEGE

Grand Rapids 49506. Private; urban. Awards C, A, B. Enrolls 230 T (48% women, 50% state res., 36% on fin. aid). Entrance difficulty: noncompetitive. Application deadline: rolling. Contact: Mr. Jeffrey Stam, Director of Admissions, (616) 458-0404.

SACRED HEART SEMINARY

Detroit 48206. Contact: Rev. Francis R. Reiss, Director of Admissions.

SAGINAW VALLEY STATE COLLEGE

University Center 48710. Public; suburban. Awards B, M. Enrolls 3,855 T, 3,275 U (50% women, 99% state res., 48% on fin. aid). Entrance difficulty: less difficult. Application deadline: rolling. Contact: Mr. Richard P. Thompson, (517) 790-4200.

SAINT MARY'S COLLEGE

Orchard Lake 48034. Private; suburban. Awards C, A, B. Enrolls 225 T (52% women, 85% state res., 70% on fin. aid). Entrance difficulty: less difficult. Application deadline: rolling. Contact: Ms. Shirley Zytell, Associate Director of Admissions, (313) 682-1885.

SHAW COLLEGE AT DETROIT

Detroit 48202. Private; urban. Awards C, A, B. Enrolls 603 T (59% women, 99% state res., 92% on fin. aid). Entrance difficulty: noncompetitive. Application deadline: rolling. Contact: Dr. Shana Sharma, Director of Institutional Research, (313) 873-7920.

SIENA HEIGHTS COLLEGE

Adrian 49221. Private; small town. Awards C, A, B, M. Enrolls 1,131 T, 1,039 U (67% women, 87% state res., 63% on fin. aid). Entrance difficulty: moderately difficult. Application deadline: rolling. Contact: Sr. Anne Marie Brown, O.P, (517) 263-0731 Ext. 217.

SPRING ARBOR COLLEGE

Spring Arbor 49283. Private; rural. Awards A, B. Enrolls 847 T (54% women, 87% state res., 85% on fin. aid). Entrance difficulty: very difficult. Application deadline: rolling. Contact: Mr. Karl Somerville, (517) 750-1200.

UNIVERSITY OF DETROIT

Detroit 48221. Private; urban. Awards B, M, D. Enrolls 8,087 T, 6,005 U (41% women, 80% state res., 70% on fin. aid). Entrance difficulty: moderately difficult. Application deadline: 8/15. Contact: Mr. James M. Masuga, (313) 927-1245.

UNIVERSITY OF MICHIGAN

Ann Arbor 48109. Public; small town. Awards B, M, D. Enrolls 35,423 T, 22,057 U (45% women, 78% state res., 50% on fin. aid). Entrance difficulty: very difficult. Application deadline: 3/1. Contact: Dr. Clifford Sjogren, (313) 764-2573.

UNIVERSITY OF MICHIGAN—DEARBORN

Dearborn 48128. Public; urban. Awards B, M. Enrolls 6,400 T, 5,913 U (43% women, 99% state res., 25% on fin. aid). Entrance difficulty: moderately difficult. Application deadline: rolling. Contact: Mr. Edward J. Bagale, (313) 593-5100.

UNIVERSITY OF MICHIGAN—FLINT

Flint 48503. Public; urban. Awards B, M. Enrolls 4,122 T, 4,054 U (55% women, 99% state res., 35% on fin. aid). Entrance difficulty: moderately difficult. Application deadline: rolling. Contact: Mr. Charles Rickard, (313) 762-3300.

WAYNE STATE UNIVERSITY

Detroit 48202. Public; urban. Awards B, M, D. Enrolls 34,337 T, 23,883 U (51% women, 99% state res., 19% on fin. aid). Entrance difficulty: moderately difficult. Application deadline: 8/25. Contact: Mr. J. Richard Thorderson, (313) 577-3505.

WESTERN MICHIGAN UNIVERSITY

Kalamazoo 49008. Public; suburban. Awards B, M, D. Enrolls 20,689 T, 17,070 U (49% women, 91% state res., 83% on fin. aid). Entrance difficulty: moderately difficult. Application deadline: rolling. Contact: Mr. Duncan Clarkson, (616) 383-1950.

MINNESOTA

AUGSBURG COLLEGE

Minneapolis 55454. Private; urban. Awards B. Enrolls 1,625 T (54% women, 88% state res., 85% on fin. aid). Entrance difficulty: moderately difficult. Application deadlines: 8/1, early decision 11/15. Contact: Miss Kathryn E. Lange, (612) 330-1004.

BEMIDJI STATE UNIVERSITY

Bemidji 56601. Public; rural. Awards A, B, M. Enrolls 4,284 T, 4,014 U (47% women, 93% state res., 75% on fin. aid). Entrance difficulty: moderately difficult. Application deadline: 8/15. Contact: Mr. Theodore P. Kuryla, (218) 755-2021.

BETHEL COLLEGE

St Paul 55112. Private; suburban. Awards A, B. Enrolls 1,989 T (55% women, 59% state res., 75% on fin. aid). Entrance difficulty: moderately difficult. Application deadline: 8/15. Contact: Mr. Phillip Kimball, (612) 638-6242.

CARLETON COLLEGE

Northfield 55057. Private; small town. Awards B. Enrolls 1,850 T (48% women, 25% state res., 46% on fin. aid). Entrance difficulty: very difficult. Application deadlines: 2/1, early decision 1/1. Contact: Mr. Jon M. Nicholson, (507) 663-4190.

COLLEGE OF SAINT BENEDICT

Saint Joseph 56374. Private; rural. Awards A, B. Enrolls 1,620 T (100% women, 88% state res., 82% on fin. aid). Entrance difficulty: moderately difficult. Application deadline: rolling. Contact: Mr. Michael Ryan, (612) 363-5308.

COLLEGE OF ST CATHERINE

St Paul 55105. Private; urban. Awards B. Enrolls 2,004 T (100% women, 75% state res., 58% on fin. aid). Entrance difficulty: moderately difficult. Application deadlines: rolling, early decision 11/1. Contact: Mrs. Lorraine Jensen, (612) 690-6505.

COLLEGE OF ST SCHOLASTICA

Duluth 55811. Private; urban. Awards B, M. Enrolls 1,082 T (79% women, 72% state res., 72% on fin. aid). Entrance difficulty: moderately difficult. Application deadline: rolling. Contact: Mr. James Buxton, (218) 723-6046.

COLLEGE OF SAINT TERESA

Winona 55987. Private; small town. Awards B. Enrolls 791 T (97% women, 97% state res., 68% on fin. aid). Entrance difficulty: moderately difficult. Application deadline: rolling. Contact: Ms. Gloria McPeak, Acting Director of Admissions, (507) 452-1000.

COLLEGE OF SAINT THOMAS

St Paul 55105. Private; suburban. Awards B, M. Enrolls 4,784 T, 3,183 U (31% women, 89% state res., 70% on fin. aid). Entrance difficulty: moderately difficult. Application deadline: rolling. Contact: Mr. Charles E. Murphy, (612) 647-5265.

CONCORDIA COLLEGE

Moorhead 56560. Private; suburban. Awards B. Enrolls 2,607 T (57% women, 66% state res., 76% on fin. aid). Entrance difficulty: moderately difficult. Application deadline: 6/1. Contact: Mr. James L. Hausmann, (218) 299-3004.

CONCORDIA COLLEGE

St Paul 55104. Private; urban. Awards A, B. Enrolls 664 T (52% women, 60% state res., 98% on fin. aid). Entrance difficulty: moderately difficult. Application deadline: 8/15. Contact: Ms. Myrtle Shira, Director of Admissions, (612) 641-8231.

DR MARTIN LUTHER COLLEGE

New Ulm 56073. Private; small town. Awards B. Enrolls 849 T (70% women, 15% state res., 66% on fin. aid). Entrance difficulty: noncompetitive. Application deadline: 8/1. Contact: Dr. Conrad Frey, President, (507) 354-8221 Ext. 211.

GUSTAVUS ADOLPHUS COLLEGE

St Peter 56082. Private; small town. Awards B. Enrolls 2,278 T (52% women, 70% state res., 62% on fin. aid). Entrance difficulty: very difficult. Application deadlines: 4/1, early decision 11/15. Contact: Mr. Owen E. Sammelson, (507) 931-4300 Ext. 323.

HAMLINE UNIVERSITY

St Paul 55104. Private; urban. Awards B, M. Enrolls 1,750 T, 1,189 U (50% women,

Hamline University (continued)
80% state res., 63% on fin. aid). Entrance difficulty: moderately difficult. Contact: Mr. Daniel J. Murray, (612) 641-2208.

MACALESTER COLLEGE

St Paul 55105. Private; urban. Awards B. Enrolls 1,763 T (51% women, 35% state res., 51% on fin. aid). Entrance difficulty: very difficult. Application deadlines: 3/15, early decision 12/15. Contact: Ms. Carol A. Stack, (612) 647-6357.

MANKATO STATE UNIVERSITY

Mankato 56001. Public; urban. Awards C, A, B, M. Enrolls 10,613 T, 9,048 U (52% women, 88% state res., 54% on fin. aid). Entrance difficulty: moderately difficult. Application deadline: rolling. Contact: Mr. Joseph R. Farnham, (507) 389-1823.

MINNEAPOLIS COLLEGE OF ART AND DESIGN

Minneapolis 55404. Private; urban. Awards B. Enrolls 591 T (51% women, 50% state res., 54% on fin. aid). Entrance difficulty: moderately difficult. Application deadline: 7/31. Contact: Mr. Tom Reeve, Director of Admissions and Records, (612) 870-3260.

MINNESOTA BIBLE COLLEGE

Rochester 55901. Private; urban. Awards A, B. Enrolls 128 T (50% women, 55% state res., 58% on fin. aid). Entrance difficulty: noncompetitive. Contact: Mr. Earl E. Grice, Academic Dean, (507) 288-4563.

MOORHEAD STATE UNIVERSITY

Moorhead 56560. Public; suburban. Awards A, B, M. Enrolls 6,999 T, 6,414 U (58% women, 67% state res., 45% on fin. aid). Entrance difficulty: moderately difficult. Application deadline: 8/15. Contact: Mr. Floyd W. Brown, (218) 236-2161.

NORTH CENTRAL BIBLE COLLEGE

Minneapolis 55404. Contact: Rev. G. L. Strom, Director of Admissions.

NORTHWESTERN COLLEGE

Roseville 55113. Private; suburban. Awards C, A, B. Enrolls 706 T (50% women, 65% state res., 50% on fin. aid). Entrance difficulty: noncompetitive. Application dead-line: rolling. Contact: Dr. Robert D. Pose-gate, (612) 636-4840 Ext. 237.

ST CLOUD STATE UNIVERSITY

St Cloud 56301. Public; urban. Awards A, B, M. Enrolls 11,591 T, 9,970 U (51% women, 98% state res., 56% on fin. aid). Entrance difficulty: moderately difficult. Application deadline: 8/15. Contact: Mr. Sherwood Reid, Director, High School and Community College Relations, (612) 255-2243.

SAINT JOHN'S UNIVERSITY

Collegeville 56321. Private; rural. Awards B, M. Enrolls 1,975 T, 1,860 U (0% women, 74% state res., 65% on fin. aid). Entrance difficulty: moderately difficult. Application deadlines: rolling, early decision 11/1. Contact: Mr. Roger C. Young, (612) 363-2196.

SAINT MARY'S COLLEGE

Winona 55987. Private; small town. Awards B, M. Enrolls 1,400 T, 1,250 U (47% women, 30% state res., 65% on fin. aid). Entrance difficulty: moderately difficult. Application deadline: 6/1. Contact: Mr. Anthony M. Piscitiello, (507) 452-4430.

ST OLAF COLLEGE

Northfield 55057. Private; small town. Awards B. Enrolls 2,971 T (52% women, 60% state res., 44% on fin. aid). Entrance difficulty: moderately difficult. Application deadlines: 2/15, early decision 11/1. Contact: Mr. Bruce K. Moe, (507) 663-3025.

ST PAUL BIBLE COLLEGE

Bible College 55375. Private; rural. Awards C, A, B. Enrolls 656 T (54% women, 54% state res., 80% on fin. aid). Entrance difficulty: less difficult. Application deadline: rolling. Contact: Mr. Richard Porter, (612) 446-1411.

SOUTHWEST STATE UNIVERSITY

Marshall 56258. Public; rural. Awards A, B. Enrolls 2,040 T (48% women, 79% state res., 72% on fin. aid). Entrance difficulty: moderately difficult. Application deadline: rolling. Contact: Mr. Michael L. Akin, (507) 537-6286.

UNIVERSITY OF MINNESOTA, DULUTH

Duluth 55812. Public; urban. Awards A, B, M. Enrolls 6,855 T, 6,507 U (49% women, 87% state res., 60% on fin. aid). Entrance difficulty: noncompetitive. Application deadline: rolling. Contact: Mr. Gerald R. Allen, (218) 726-7171.

UNIVERSITY OF MINNESOTA, MINNEAPOLIS-ST PAUL

Minneapolis 55455. Public; urban. Awards C, A, B, M, D. Enrolls 45,765 T, 31,404 U (46% women, 88% state res., 60% on fin. aid). Entrance difficulty: moderately difficult. Application deadline: 7/15. Contact: Mr. Leo D. Abbott, (612) 373-2144.

UNIVERSITY OF MINNESOTA, MORRIS

Morris 56267. Public; small town. Awards B. Enrolls 1,450 T (45% women, 95% state res., 80% on fin. aid). Entrance difficulty: moderately difficult. Application deadlines: 9/15, early decision 12/30. Contact: Mr. Robert J. Vikander, (612) 589-2116.

WINONA STATE UNIVERSITY

Winona 55987. Public; small town. Awards C, A, B, M. Enrolls 4,400 T, 4,000 U (57% women, 75% state res., 55% on fin. aid). Entrance difficulty: moderately difficult. Application deadline: rolling. Contact: Dr. J. A. Mootz, (507) 457-2065.

MISSISSIPPI

ALCORN STATE UNIVERSITY

Lorman 39096. Public; rural. Awards C, A, B, M. Enrolls 2,500 T (55% women, 92% state res., 95% on fin. aid). Entrance difficulty: less difficult. Application deadline: 8/15. Contact: Mrs. Alice Davis Gill, (601) 877-3711 Ext. 168.

BELHAVEN COLLEGE

Jackson 39202. Private; suburban. Awards B. Enrolls 886 T (55% women, 85% state res., 50% on fin. aid). Entrance difficulty: less difficult. Application deadline: rolling. Contact: Mr. R. Douglas Mickey, Director of Admissions, (601) 969-7400.

BLUE MOUNTAIN COLLEGE

Blue Mountain 38610. Private; small town. Awards B. Enrolls 340 T (72% women, 82% state res., 60% on fin. aid). Entrance difficulty: moderately difficult. Application deadline: 8/15. Contact: Mr. Gerald Fowler, (601) 685-5711.

DELTA STATE UNIVERSITY

Cleveland 38733. Public; small town. Awards B, M. Enrolls 3,172 T, 2,521 U (56% women, 97% state res., 81% on fin. aid). Entrance difficulty: less difficult. Contact: Dr. Mac G. McRaney, (601) 843-9441.

JACKSON STATE UNIVERSITY

Jackson 39217. Public; urban. Awards B, M. Enrolls 7,646 T, 6,013 U (56% women, 92% state res., 89% on fin. aid). Entrance difficulty: less difficult. Application deadline: 8/1. Contact: Mr. Oscar C. Williams, (601) 968-2100.

MILLSAPS COLLEGE

Jackson 39210. Private; urban. Awards B, M. Enrolls 972 T (46% women, 74% state res., 62% on fin. aid). Entrance difficulty: moderately difficult. Application deadline: rolling. Contact: Mr. John H. Christmas, (601) 355-2929.

MISSISSIPPI COLLEGE

Clinton 39058. Private; small town. Awards B, M. Enrolls 3,190 T, 1,871 U (48% women, 90% state res., 75% on fin. aid). Entrance difficulty: moderately difficult. Application deadline: rolling. Contact: Mr. Rory Lee, (601) 924-6082.

MISSISSIPPI INDUSTRIAL COLLEGE

Holly Springs 38635. Contact: Mr. W. F. Thompson, Admissions Officer.

MISSISSIPPI STATE UNIVERSITY

Mississippi State 39762. Public; small town. Awards B, M, D. Enrolls 11,374 T, 9,752 U (38% women, 95% state res., 34% on fin. aid). Entrance difficulty: moderately difficult. Application deadline: 8/3. Contact: Mr. Jerry Inmon, (601) 325-2224.

MISSISSIPPI UNIVERSITY FOR WOMEN

Columbus 39701. Public; small town. Awards C, A, B, M. Enrolls 2,260 T,

Mississippi University for Women (continued)
1,970 U (100% women, 75% state res., 65% on fin. aid). Entrance difficulty: moderately difficult. Application deadline: 8/15. Contact: Mr. James B. Alinder, (601) 328-5891.

MISSISSIPPI VALLEY STATE UNIVERSITY

Itta Bena 38941. Public; small town. Awards C, A, B, M. Enrolls 2,734 T, 2,675 U (59% women, 88% state res., 89% on fin. aid). Entrance difficulty: less difficult. Application deadline: rolling. Contact: Miss Sarah White, Director of Admissions, (601) 254-9041 Ext. 6391.

RUST COLLEGE

Holly Springs 38635. Private; rural. Awards A, B. Enrolls 734 T (90% women, 76% state res., 98% on fin. aid). Entrance difficulty: less difficult. Application deadline: rolling. Contact: Mrs. Rubye Owens, (601) 252-4661 Ext. 281.

SOUTHEASTERN BAPTIST COLLEGE

Laurel 39440. Private; urban. Awards C, B. Enrolls 58 T (8% women, 75% state res., 10% on fin. aid). Entrance difficulty: less difficult. Application deadline: rolling. Contact: Mr. Earle Knight, (601) 426-6346.

TOUGALOO COLLEGE

Tougaloo 39174. Private; suburban. Awards B. Enrolls 1,031 T (66% women, 73% state res., 92% on fin. aid). Application deadline: rolling. Contact: Mr. Halbert E. Dockins, (601) 956-4941 Ext. 253.

UNIVERSITY OF MISSISSIPPI

University 38677. Public; small town. Awards B, M, D. Enrolls 9,655 T, 7,865 U (45% women, 74% state res., 51% on fin. aid). Entrance difficulty: moderately difficult. Application deadline: 8/5. Contact: Dr. Kenneth L. Wooten, (601) 232-7226.

UNIVERSITY OF MISSISSIPPI MEDICAL CENTER

Jackson 39216.

UNIVERSITY OF SOUTHERN MISSISSIPPI

Hattiesburg 39401. Public; small town. Awards C, B, M, D. Enrolls 12,298 T,
9,560 U (54% women, 88% state res., 40% on fin. aid). Entrance difficulty: less difficult. Application deadline: rolling. Contact: Mr. Charles McNeill, (601) 266-7111.

WILLIAM CAREY COLLEGE

Hattiesburg 39401. Private; small town. Awards B, M. Enrolls 1,761 T, 1,460 U (60% women, 65% state res., 75% on fin. aid). Entrance difficulty: moderately difficult. Application deadline: rolling. Contact: Mr. Antonio Pascale, (601) 582-5051.

MISSOURI

AVILA COLLEGE

Kansas City 64145. Private; suburban. Awards C, A, B, M. Enrolls 2,050 T, 1,980 U (56% women, 31% state res., 63% on fin. aid). Entrance difficulty: moderately difficult. Application deadline: rolling. Contact: Mr. Ronald N. Van Fleet II, Coordinator of Admissions, (816) 942-8400.

CALVARY BIBLE COLLEGE

Kansas City 64111. Private; urban. Awards A, B, M. Enrolls 496 T, 454 U (46% women, 33% state res., 0% on fin. aid). Entrance difficulty: noncompetitive. Application deadline: rolling. Contact: Mr. Jesse Hensarling, Registrar, (816) 753-4511.

CARDINAL GLENNON COLLEGE

St Louis 63119. Private; suburban. Awards B. Enrolls 94 T (0% women, 73% state res., 100% on fin. aid). Entrance difficulty: moderately difficult. Application deadline: 8/1. Contact: Rev. Donald Brinkman, Director of Vocations, (314) 647-5270.

CENTRAL BIBLE COLLEGE

Springfield 65802. Private; suburban. Awards A, B. Enrolls 1,115 T (38% women, 14% state res., 48% on fin. aid). Entrance difficulty: noncompetitive. Application deadline: rolling. Contact: Mr. David B. Drake, Director of Admissions and Records, (417) 833-2551 Ext. 35.

CENTRAL METHODIST COLLEGE

Fayette 65248. Private; rural. Awards A, B. Enrolls 667 T (51% women, 88% state res., 80% on fin. aid). Entrance difficulty:

moderately difficult. Application deadline: rolling. Contact: Mr. Anthony Boes, Director of New Student Relations, (816) 248-3391.

CENTRAL MISSOURI STATE UNIVERSITY

Warrensburg 64093. Public; small town. Awards C, A, B, M. Enrolls 9,905 T, 8,319 U (52% women, 95% state res., 57% on fin. aid). Entrance difficulty: moderately difficult. Application deadline: 9/9. Contact: Dr. A. Louie Sosebee, Director of Admissions, (816) 429-4810.

COLUMBIA COLLEGE

Columbia 65201. Private; small town. Awards A, B. Enrolls 843 T (53% women, 45% state res., 62% on fin. aid). Entrance difficulty: less difficult. Application deadline: rolling. Contact: Mr. Robert B. Godfrey, Director of Admissions, (314) 449-0531 Ext. 273.

CONCEPTION SEMINARY COLLEGE

Conception 64433. Private; rural. Awards B. Enrolls 94 T (0% women, 43% state res., 92% on fin. aid). Entrance difficulty: less difficult. Application deadline: 7/31. Contact: Rev. Isaac True, OSB, Director of Admissions, (816) 944-2218.

CULVER-STOCKTON COLLEGE

Canton 63435. Private; small town. Awards A, B. Enrolls 443 T (51% women, 56% state res., 80% on fin. aid). Entrance difficulty: noncompetitive. Application deadline: rolling. Contact: Dr. John Terrill Hohman, (314) 288-5221 Ext. 31.

DRURY COLLEGE

Springfield 65802. Private; urban. Awards B, M. Enrolls 1,316 T, 1,087 U (51% women, 65% state res., 70% on fin. aid). Entrance difficulty: moderately difficult. Application deadline: rolling. Contact: Dr. Eltjen Flikkema, Dean of Admissions, (417) 862-0541.

EVANGEL COLLEGE

Springfield 65802. Private; small town. Awards A, B. Enrolls 1,612 T (56% women, 21% state res., 82% on fin. aid). Entrance difficulty: moderately difficult. Application deadline: 8/15. Contact: Mrs. Eva M. Box, (417) 865-2811 Ext. 262.

FONTBONNE COLLEGE

St Louis 63105. Private; suburban. Awards B, M. Enrolls 794 T, 757 U (87% women, 90% state res., 60% on fin. aid). Entrance difficulty: moderately difficult. Application deadline: 8/1. Contact: Mr. Charles E. Beech, (314) 862-3456 Ext. 208.

HANNIBAL-LAGRANGE COLLEGE

Hannibal 63401. Private; small town. Awards A, B. Enrolls 450 T (45% women, 60% state res., 85% on fin. aid). Entrance difficulty: moderately difficult. Application deadline: rolling. Contact: Mr. Bill Creech, Dean of Admissions, (314) 221-3113.

HARRIS-STOWE STATE COLLEGE

St Louis 63103. Public; urban. Awards B. Enrolls 1,102 T (74% women, 100% state res., 60% on fin. aid). Entrance difficulty: moderately difficult. Application deadline: rolling. Contact: Mrs. Valerie A. Beeson, (314) 533-3366.

KANSAS CITY ART INSTITUTE

Kansas City 64111. Private; urban. Awards B. Enrolls 590 T (46% women, 30% state res., 52% on fin. aid). Entrance difficulty: moderately difficult. Application deadline: rolling. Contact: Mr. Leonard B. Panar, Dean of Admissions, (816) 561-4852.

LINCOLN UNIVERSITY

Jefferson City 65101. Public; small town. Awards C, A, B, M. Enrolls 2,332 T, 2,085 U (45% women, 69% state res., 65% on fin. aid). Entrance difficulty: less difficult. Application deadline: 7/22. Contact: Dr. Joe Simmons, Director of Admissions, (314) 751-2325 Ext. 473.

LINDENWOOD COLLEGES

St Charles 63301. Private; small town. Awards A, B, M. Enrolls 1,727 T, 1,403 U (67% women, 21% state res., 56% on fin. aid). Entrance difficulty: moderately difficult. Application deadline: 8/15. Contact: Mr. Robert McKay, Acting Director of Admissions, (314) 723-7152.

MARYVILLE COLLEGE–SAINT LOUIS

St Louis 63141. Private; suburban. Awards C, A, B, M. Enrolls 1,391 T, 1,355 U (77% women, 85% state res., 60% on fin. aid). Entrance difficulty: moderately difficult.

Maryville College–Saint Louis (continued)
Application deadline: 9/1. Contact: Mr. Michael J. Gillick, (314) 434-4100 Ext. 204.

MISSOURI BAPTIST COLLEGE

St Louis 63141. Private; suburban. Awards C, A, B. Enrolls 434 T (50% women, 98% state res., 50% on fin. aid). Entrance difficulty: moderately difficult. Application deadline: rolling. Contact: Mr. M. E. Moser, Registrar, (314) 434-1115.

MISSOURI INSTITUTE OF TECHNOLOGY

Kansas City 64114. Private; urban. Awards A, B. Enrolls 740 T (3% women, 40% state res., 57% on fin. aid). Entrance difficulty: noncompetitive. Application deadline: 10/1. Contact: Mr. Joseph Buechner, (816) 363-7030.

MISSOURI SOUTHERN STATE COLLEGE

Joplin 64801. Public; small town. Awards C, A, B. Enrolls 3,790 T (50% women, 95% state res.). Entrance difficulty: noncompetitive. Application deadline: 9/3. Contact: Mr. Richard D. Humphrey, (417) 624-8100.

MISSOURI VALLEY COLLEGE

Marshall 65340. Private; small town. Awards A, B. Enrolls 376 T (30% women, 62% state res., 87% on fin. aid). Entrance difficulty: moderately difficult. Application deadline: rolling. Contact: Mrs. Thomazene Riley, Assistant Director of Admissions, (816) 886-6924.

MISSOURI WESTERN STATE COLLEGE

St Joseph 64507. Public; suburban. Awards C, A, B. Enrolls 3,777 T (50% women, 93% state res., 69% on fin. aid). Entrance difficulty: noncompetitive. Application deadline: rolling. Contact: Mr. George Ashworth, Director of Admissions and Records, (816) 271-4211.

NORTHEAST MISSOURI STATE UNIVERSITY

Kirksville 63501. Public; small town. Awards C, A, B, M. Enrolls 6,041 T, 5,380 U (56% women, 75% state res., 60% on fin. aid). Entrance difficulty: moderately difficult. Application deadline: 8/15. Contact: Mr. Terry Taylor, (816) 665-5121.

NORTHWEST MISSOURI STATE UNIVERSITY

Maryville 64468. Public; small town. Awards C, B, M. Enrolls 4,400 T, 3,860 U (51% women, 65% state res., 60% on fin. aid). Entrance difficulty: less difficult. Application deadline: rolling. Contact: Mr. Charles W. Veatch, (816) 582-7141.

PARK COLLEGE

Parkville 64152. Private; suburban. Awards A, B. Enrolls 460 T (48% women, 50% state res., 75% on fin. aid). Entrance difficulty: less difficult. Contact: Dr. Joseph H. Holst Jr, Dean of Admissions, (816) 741-2000.

ROCKHURST COLLEGE

Kansas City 64110. Private; urban. Awards B, M. Enrolls 1,919 T, 1,315 U (41% women, 73% state res.). Entrance difficulty: moderately difficult. Contact: Miss Geraldine L. Gumbel, Admissions Counselor, (816) 363-4010.

ST LOUIS COLLEGE OF PHARMACY

St Louis 63110. Private; urban. Awards B. Enrolls 710 T (42% women, 47% state res., 70% on fin. aid). Entrance difficulty: moderately difficult. Application deadline: 8/1. Contact: Dr. Taylor E. Lindhorst, Dean of Student Affairs, (314) 367-8700.

SAINT LOUIS CONSERVATORY OF MUSIC

St Louis 63130. Private; urban. Awards B, M. Enrolls 68 T (48% women, 52% state res., 35% on fin. aid). Entrance difficulty: very difficult. Application deadline: rolling. Contact: Mr. Michael Christopher, (314) 863-3033.

SAINT LOUIS UNIVERSITY

St Louis 63103. Private; urban. Awards C, A, B, M, D. Enrolls 10,496 T, 6,863 U (50% women, 60% state res., 65% on fin. aid). Entrance difficulty: moderately difficult. Application deadline: 8/1. Contact: Mr. Louis A. Menard, Dean of Admissions, (314) 658-2500.

ST MARY'S OF THE BARRENS SEMINARY COLLEGE

Perryville 63775. Private; small town. Awards B. Enrolls 56 T (0% women, 0% on fin. aid). Entrance difficulty: less difficult. Application deadline: 9/8. Contact: Rev. Ralph C. Pansza, CM, (314) 547-6533.

SCHOOL OF THE OZARKS

Point Lookout 65726. Public; small town. Awards B. Enrolls 1,200 T (50% women, 70% state res., 100% on fin. aid). Entrance difficulty: moderately difficult. Application deadline: rolling. Contact: Dr. M. Glen Cameron, (417) 334-6411.

SOUTHEAST MISSOURI STATE UNIVERSITY

Cape Girardeau 63701. Public; small town. Awards C, A, B, M. Enrolls 8,659 T, 7,893 U (53% women, 95% state res., 45% on fin. aid). Entrance difficulty: moderately difficult. Application deadline: rolling. Contact: Mr. John A. Behrens, (314) 651-2255.

SOUTHWEST BAPTIST COLLEGE

Bolivar 65613. Private; small town. Awards C, A, B. Enrolls 1,383 T (60% women, 75% state res., 90% on fin. aid). Entrance difficulty: noncompetitive. Application deadlines: 9/15, early decision 1/31. Contact: Mr. Jerald L. Andrews, (417) 326-5281.

SOUTHWEST MISSOURI STATE UNIVERSITY

Springfield 65802. Public; suburban. Awards C, A, B, M. Enrolls 13,818 T, 12,624 U (52% women, 96% state res., 47% on fin. aid). Entrance difficulty: moderately difficult. Application deadline: 8/1. Contact: Mr. Lyle B. Leisenring, (417) 836-5517.

STEPHENS COLLEGE

Columbia 65215. Private; small town. Awards C, A, B. Enrolls 1,402 T (100% women, 23% state res., 40% on fin. aid). Entrance difficulty: moderately difficult. Application deadline: rolling. Contact: Ms. Martha G. Wade, Vice President and Dean of Admissions, (314) 442-2212 Ext. 207.

TARKIO COLLEGE

Tarkio 64491. Private; rural. Awards B. Enrolls 585 T (42% women, 35% state res., 80% on fin. aid). Entrance difficulty: moderately difficult. Application deadlines: 8/15, early decision 11/1. Contact: Mr. A. L. Ruby, (816) 736-4131.

UNIVERSITY OF MISSOURI–COLUMBIA

Columbia 65211. Public; small town. Awards C, B, M, D. Enrolls 23,064 T, 17,497 U (47% women, 89% state res., 50% on fin. aid). Entrance difficulty: moderately difficult. Application deadline: 5/1. Contact: Dr. Gary L. Smith, (314) 882-7651.

UNIVERSITY OF MISSOURI–KANSAS CITY

Kansas City 64111. Public; urban. Awards C, B, M, D. Enrolls 10,824 T, 6,453 U (50% women, 88% state res., 25% on fin. aid). Entrance difficulty: moderately difficult. Application deadline: rolling. Contact: Mr. Leo J. Sweeney, (816) 276-1125.

UNIVERSITY OF MISSOURI–ROLLA

Rolla 65401. Public; small town. Awards B, M, D. Enrolls 5,535 T, 5,117 U (18% women, 84% state res., 35% on fin. aid). Entrance difficulty: moderately difficult. Application deadline: 7/1. Contact: Mr. Robert B. Lewis, Director of Admissions and Registrar, (314) 341-4164.

UNIVERSITY OF MISSOURI–ST LOUIS

St Louis 63121. Public; urban. Awards B, M, D. Enrolls 11,053 T, 9,409 U (46% women, 98% state res., 35% on fin. aid). Entrance difficulty: moderately difficult. Application deadline: rolling. Contact: Dr. H. E. Mueller, (314) 553-5460.

WASHINGTON UNIVERSITY

St Louis 63130. Private; suburban. Awards B, M, D. Enrolls 8,429 T, 5,631 U (41% women, 23% state res., 50% on fin. aid). Entrance difficulty: very difficult. Application deadlines: rolling, early decision 10/15. Contact: Mr. William H. Turner, (314) 889-6000.

WEBSTER COLLEGE

St Louis 63119. Private; suburban. Awards B, M. Enrolls 3,658 T, 950 U (67% women, 70% state res., 70% on fin. aid). Entrance difficulty: less difficult. Application deadline: 8/15. Contact: Dr. Jerry Davis, (314) 968-0500 Ext. 208.

WESTMINSTER COLLEGE

Fulton 65251. Private; small town. Awards B. Enrolls 664 T (5% women, 45% state res., 50% on fin. aid). Entrance difficulty: moderately difficult. Application deadline: rolling. Contact: Mr. Larry M. West, (314) 642-3361.

WILLIAM JEWELL COLLEGE

Liberty 64068. Private; suburban. Awards B. Enrolls 1,410 T (50% women, 70% state res., 76% on fin. aid). Entrance difficulty: very difficult. Application deadlines: rolling, early decision 11/1. Contact: Mr. Harley Wyatt Jr, (816) 781-3806.

WILLIAM WOODS COLLEGE

Fulton 65251. Private; small town. Awards B. Enrolls 1,000 T (100% women, 39% state res.). Entrance difficulty: moderately difficult. Application deadline: 9/1. Contact: Mr. Roy D. Love, (314) 642-2251.

MONTANA

CARROLL COLLEGE OF MONTANA

Helena 59601. Private; small town. Awards A, B. Enrolls 1,342 T (58% women, 74% state res., 52% on fin. aid). Entrance difficulty: moderately difficult. Application deadline: 8/15. Contact: Mr. John Grobe, (406) 442-3510.

COLLEGE OF GREAT FALLS

Great Falls 59405. Private; suburban. Awards A, B. Enrolls 1,200 T (50% women, 80% state res., 60% on fin. aid). Entrance difficulty: noncompetitive. Application deadline: rolling. Contact: Sr. Elizabeth Gress, (406) 761-8210.

EASTERN MONTANA COLLEGE

Billings 59101. Public; urban. Awards A, B, M. Enrolls 3,450 T, 3,103 U (60% women, 95% state res., 65% on fin. aid). Entrance

difficulty: moderately difficult. Application deadline: 9/15. Contact: Mr. Victor Signori, (406) 657-2158.

MONTANA COLLEGE OF MINERAL SCIENCE AND TECHNOLOGY

Butte 59701. Public; rural. Awards A, B, M. Enrolls 1,393 T, 1,283 U (35% women, 80% state res., 62% on fin. aid). Entrance difficulty: moderately difficult. Application deadline: rolling. Contact: Mr. Joseph E. Kasperick, Registrar, (406) 792-8321.

MONTANA STATE UNIVERSITY

Bozeman 59717. Public; small town. Awards B, M, D. Enrolls 9,920 T, 9,156 U (45% women, 84% state res., 60% on fin. aid). Entrance difficulty: noncompetitive; moderately difficult for nonresidents. Application deadline: rolling. Contact: Mr. Joseph E. Frazier, Director of Admissions, (406) 994-4361.

NORTHERN MONTANA COLLEGE

Havre 59501. Public; small town. Awards C, A, B, M. Enrolls 1,209 T, 1,114 U (46% women, 90% state res., 75% on fin. aid). Entrance difficulty: noncompetitive. Application deadline: 9/20. Contact: Miss Marilyn Garrahan, Acting Registrar, (406) 265-7821.

ROCKY MOUNTAIN COLLEGE

Billings 59102. Private; suburban. Awards B. Enrolls 503 T (46% women, 25% state res., 74% on fin. aid). Entrance difficulty: less difficult. Application deadline: rolling. Contact: Miss Mary Lou Stewart, Assistant Director of Admissions, (406) 245-6151.

UNIVERSITY OF MONTANA

Missoula 59812. Public; small town. Awards A, B, M, D. Enrolls 8,376 T, 6,972 U (47% women, 72% state res., 50% on fin. aid). Entrance difficulty: noncompetitive. Application deadline: rolling. Contact: Mr. Richard Hill, Director of Admissions, (406) 243-6266.

WESTERN MONTANA COLLEGE

Dillon 59725. Public; rural. Awards C, A, B, M. Enrolls 824 T, 679 U (55% women, 90% state res., 60% on fin. aid). Entrance difficulty: noncompetitive; moderately difficult for out-of-staters. Application deadline: rolling. Contact: Mr. Larry Hickethier, (406) 683-7331.

NEBRASKA

BELLEVUE COLLEGE

Bellevue 68005. Private; urban. Awards B. Enrolls 2,272 T (47% women, 20% on fin. aid). Entrance difficulty: less difficult. Application deadline: rolling. Contact: Mr. Pierre D. Flatowicz, Associate Director of Admissions.

CHADRON STATE COLLEGE

Chadron 69337. Public; small town. Awards C, A, B, M. Enrolls 1,954 T, 1,554 U (59% women, 85% state res., 72% on fin. aid). Entrance difficulty: noncompetitive. Application deadline: rolling. Contact: Mr. Randy Bauer, (308) 432-6263.

COLLEGE OF SAINT MARY

Omaha 68124. Private; urban. Awards A, B. Enrolls 592 T (95% women, 77% state res., 72% on fin. aid). Entrance difficulty: moderately difficult. Application deadline: rolling. Contact: Mr. Gary L. Johnson, (402) 393-8800 Ext. 200.

CONCORDIA TEACHERS COLLEGE

Seward 68434. Private; small town. Awards B, M. Enrolls 1,144 T, 1,137 U (55% women, 25% state res., 90% on fin. aid). Entrance difficulty: moderately difficult. Application deadline: rolling. Contact: Mr. Elden F. Duensing, (402) 643-3651.

CREIGHTON UNIVERSITY

Omaha 68178. Private; urban. Awards B, M, D. Enrolls 5,400 T, 3,520 U (47% women, 38% state res., 50% on fin. aid). Entrance difficulty: moderately difficult. Application deadline: 8/1. Contact: Mr. Howard J. Bachman, (402) 449-2703.

DANA COLLEGE

Blair 68008. Private; small town. Awards B. Enrolls 527 T (50% women, 40% state res., 87% on fin. aid). Entrance difficulty: moderately difficult. Application deadline: rolling. Contact: Mr. Lee E. Johnson, (402) 426-4101.

DOANE COLLEGE

Crete 68333. Private; small town. Awards B. Enrolls 689 T (50% women, 76% state res., 92% on fin. aid). Entrance difficulty: moderately difficult. Application deadline: 8/1. Contact: Mr. Steve Rasmussen, (402) 826-2161.

GRACE COLLEGE OF THE BIBLE

Omaha 68108. Private; urban. Awards C, A, B. Enrolls 458 T (45% women, 43% state res., 40% on fin. aid). Entrance difficulty: moderately difficult. Application deadline: rolling. Contact: Mr. Leo Thomas, (402) 342-3377.

HASTINGS COLLEGE

Hastings 68901. Private; small town. Awards B. Enrolls 780 T (56% women, 80% state res., 75% on fin. aid). Entrance difficulty: moderately difficult. Application deadlines: rolling, early decision 9/15. Contact: Mr. Gene Schuppan, (402) 463-2402.

KEARNEY STATE COLLEGE

Kearney 68847. Public; small town. Awards B, M. Enrolls 6,165 T, 5,865 U (18% women). Entrance difficulty: noncompetitive. Contact: Dr. Wayne Samuelson, (308) 236-4216.

MIDLAND LUTHERAN COLLEGE

Fremont 68025. Private; small town. Awards A, B. Enrolls 757 T (53% women, 70% state res., 86% on fin. aid). Entrance difficulty: moderately difficult. Application deadline: rolling. Contact: Mr. Roland R. Kahnk, (402) 721-5480.

NEBRASKA WESLEYAN UNIVERSITY

Lincoln 68504. Private; suburban. Awards A, B. Enrolls 1,160 T (54% women, 84% state res., 29% on fin. aid). Entrance difficulty: moderately difficult. Application deadline: rolling. Contact: Mr. Ken Sieg, (402) 466-2371.

PERU STATE COLLEGE

Peru 68421. Public; rural. Awards C, A, B. Enrolls 718 T (52% women, 75% state res., 71% on fin. aid). Entrance difficulty: noncompetitive. Application deadline: 9/4. Contact: Dr. Richard C. Muth, (402) 872-3815 Ext. 221.

UNION COLLEGE

Lincoln 68506. Private; suburban. Awards C, A, B. Enrolls 909 T (54% women, 25% state res., 35% on fin. aid). Entrance difficulty: noncompetitive except for nursing program. Application deadline: rolling. Contact: Miss Leona Murray, (402) 488-2331.

UNIVERSITY OF NEBRASKA–LINCOLN

Lincoln 68588. Public; urban. Awards C, B, M, D. Enrolls 23,661 T, 19,903 U (42% women, 93% state res., 35% on fin. aid). Entrance difficulty: noncompetitive. Application deadline: 8/15. Contact: Mr. Al Papik, (402) 472-3601.

UNIVERSITY OF NEBRASKA AT OMAHA

Omaha 68182. Public; urban. Awards C, A, B, M. Enrolls 14,873 T, 12,815 U (49% women, 94% state res., 25% on fin. aid). Entrance difficulty: noncompetitive. Application deadline: rolling. Contact: Dr. Duncan M. Sargent, (402) 554-2393.

WAYNE STATE COLLEGE

Wayne 68787. Public; small town. Awards B, M. Enrolls 2,589 T, 2,143 U (55% women, 85% state res., 50% on fin. aid). Entrance difficulty: noncompetitive. Application deadline: rolling. Contact: Mr. Jim Hummel, (402) 375-2200 Ext. 319.

NEVADA

SIERRA NEVADA COLLEGE

Incline Village 89450. Private; rural. Awards A, B. Enrolls 225 T (46% women, 52% state res., 22% on fin. aid). Entrance difficulty: noncompetitive. Application deadline: rolling. Contact: Ms. Nettie J. McClure, Registrar, (702) 831-1314.

UNIVERSITY OF NEVADA

Las Vegas 89154. Public; urban. Awards A, B, M, D. Enrolls 6,935 T, 6,223 U (47% women, 80% state res., 24% on fin. aid). Entrance difficulty: less difficult. Application deadline: 7/15. Contact: Mr. Robert A. Stephens, (702) 739-3443.

UNIVERSITY OF NEVADA

Reno 89557. Public; urban. Awards C, A, B, M, D. Enrolls 7,474 T, 5,890 U (47% women, 83% state res., 33% on fin. aid). Entrance difficulty: moderately difficult. Application deadline: 7/15. Contact: Dr. Jack H. Shirley, (702) 784-6866.

NEW HAMPSHIRE

COLBY-SAWYER COLLEGE

New London 03257. Private; small town. Awards A, B. Enrolls 700 T (100% women, 14% state res., 53% on fin. aid). Entrance difficulty: moderately difficult. Application deadlines: 4/15, early decision 11/15. Contact: Mr. Peter Dietrich, Dean of Admissions, (603) 526-2010.

DANIEL WEBSTER COLLEGE

Nashua 03060. Private; suburban. Awards A, B. Enrolls 500 T (20% women, 25% state res., 58% on fin. aid). Entrance difficulty: less difficult. Application deadlines: rolling, early decision 11/1. Contact: Ms. Hannah McCarthy, (603) 883-3556.

DARTMOUTH COLLEGE

Hanover 03755. Private; small town. Awards B, M, D. Enrolls 3,900 T, 3,200 U (32% women, 6% state res., 45% on fin. aid). Entrance difficulty: most difficult. Application deadlines: 1/1, early decision 11/15. Contact: Mr. Alfred Quirk, (603) 646-2875.

FRANKLIN PIERCE COLLEGE

Rindge 03461. Private; rural. Awards B. Enrolls 904 T (45% women, 10% state res., 60% on fin. aid). Entrance difficulty: moderately difficult. Application deadline: 8/15. Contact: Mr. Thomas E. Desrosiers, (603) 899-2228.

KEENE STATE COLLEGE

Keene 03431. Public; small town. Awards A, B, M. Enrolls 2,900 T, 2,700 U (62% women, 65% state res., 42% on fin. aid). Entrance difficulty: moderately difficult. Application deadline: 6/1. Contact: Mr. John J. Cunningham, (603) 352-1909 Ext. 340.

NATHANIEL HAWTHORNE COLLEGE

Antrim 03440. Private; rural. Awards A, B. Enrolls 500 T (25% women, 5% state res., 35% on fin. aid). Entrance difficulty: non-competitive. Application deadline: rolling. Contact: Mr. Edward A. Snell, (603) 588-6341.

NEW ENGLAND COLLEGE

Henniker 03242. Private; small town. Awards B. Enrolls 1,249 T (45% women, 15% state res., 50% on fin. aid). Entrance difficulty: less difficult. Application deadline: rolling. Contact: Mr. John J. Beaulieu, Dean of Admissions, (603) 428-2223.

NEW HAMPSHIRE COLLEGE

Manchester 03104. Private; suburban. Awards A, B, M. Enrolls 1,475 T (45% women, 30% state res., 63% on fin. aid). Entrance difficulty: moderately difficult. Application deadline: rolling. Contact: Miss Dianne V. Louis, (603) 668-2211.

NOTRE DAME COLLEGE

Manchester 03104. Private; suburban. Awards A, B, M. Enrolls 723 T, 581 U (90% women, 1% state res., 55% on fin. aid). Entrance difficulty: moderately difficult. Application deadlines: rolling, early decision 11/1. Contact: Barbara E. Schultze, Director of Admissions, (603) 669-4298.

PLYMOUTH STATE COLLEGE

Plymouth 03264. Public; small town. Awards A, B, M. Enrolls 2,750 T, 2,700 U (50% women, 70% state res., 50% on fin. aid). Entrance difficulty: moderately difficult. Application deadline: rolling. Contact: Mr. Clarence W. Bailey, (603) 536-1550.

RIVIER COLLEGE

Nashua 03060. Private; suburban. Awards C, A, B, M. Enrolls 1,850 T, 1,083 U (88% women, 43% state res., 55% on fin. aid). Entrance difficulty: moderately difficult. Application deadlines: rolling, early decision 10/15. Contact: Mrs. Janice Kenney Fortado, (603) 888-1311.

ST ANSELM'S COLLEGE

Manchester 03102. Private; suburban. Awards A, B. Enrolls 1,923 T (41% women, 99% state res., 65% on fin. aid).

Entrance difficulty: moderately difficult. Application deadline: rolling. Contact: Mr. Donald E. Healy, (603) 669-1030.

UNIVERSITY OF NEW HAMPSHIRE

Durham 03824. Public; small town. Awards A, B, M, D. Enrolls 10,500 T, 8,887 U (50% women, 65% state res., 50% on fin. aid). Entrance difficulty: moderately difficult. Application deadlines: 2/1, early decision 9/15. Contact: Mr. Eugene A. Savage, Dean of Admissions, (603) 862-1360.

NEW JERSEY

BLOOMFIELD COLLEGE

Bloomfield 07003. Private; suburban. Awards B. Enrolls 2,268 T (50% women, 99% state res., 85% on fin. aid). Entrance difficulty: less difficult. Application deadline: rolling. Contact: Mr. Peter H. Scudder, (201) 748-9000 Ext. 271.

CALDWELL COLLEGE

Caldwell 07006. Private; suburban. Awards B. Enrolls 723 T (100% women, 85% state res., 64% on fin. aid). Entrance difficulty: moderately difficult. Application deadline: rolling. Contact: Sr. Mary Joseph, (201) 226-0534.

CENTENARY COLLEGE

Hackettstown 07840. Private; small town. Awards A, B. Enrolls 705 T (99% women, 60% state res., 38% on fin. aid). Entrance difficulty: less difficult. Application deadline: rolling. Contact: Miss Barbara J. Edler, (201) 852-1400.

COLLEGE OF SAINT ELIZABETH

Convent Station 07961. Private; suburban. Awards B. Enrolls 581 T (98% women, 85% state res., 61% on fin. aid). Entrance difficulty: moderately difficult. Application deadlines: 8/15, early decision 11/15. Contact: Sr. Maureen Sullivan, (201) 539-1600.

DON BOSCO COLLEGE

Newton 07860. Private; rural. Awards B. Enrolls 83 T (0% women, 30% state res., 27% on fin. aid). Entrance difficulty: moderately difficult. Application deadline: 7/1.

Don Bosco College (continued)
Contact: Fr. Kenneth McAlice, Registrar, (201) 383-3900.

DREW UNIVERSITY

Madison 07940. Private; suburban. Awards B, M, D. Enrolls 2,294 T, 1,510 U (55% women, 50% state res., 45% on fin. aid). Entrance difficulty: very difficult. Application deadlines: 3/1, early decision 12/1. Contact: Mr. Daniel Boyer, (201) 377-3000 Ext. 252.

FAIRLEIGH DICKINSON UNIVERSITY, FLORHAM-MADISON CAMPUS

Madison 07940. Private; suburban. Awards A, B, M. Enrolls 4,961 T, 3,354 U (50% women, 80% state res., 50% on fin. aid). Entrance difficulty: moderately difficult. Application deadlines: rolling, early decision 11/1. Contact: Mr. George Lynes, Associate Director of Admissions, (201) 377-4700 Ext. 402.

FAIRLEIGH DICKINSON UNIVERSITY, RUTHERFORD CAMPUS

Rutherford 07070. Private; suburban. Awards B, M. Enrolls 5,062 T, 2,787 U (50% women, 85% state res., 50% on fin. aid). Entrance difficulty: moderately difficult. Application deadlines: rolling, early decision 11/1. Contact: Mr. Howard H. Hamilton, (201) 933-5000 Ext. 203.

FAIRLEIGH DICKINSON UNIVERSITY, TEANECK-HACKENSACK CAMPUS

Teaneck 07666. Private; suburban. Awards A, B, M, D. Enrolls 8,704 T, 5,532 U (45% women, 85% state res., 55% on fin. aid). Entrance difficulty: moderately difficult. Application deadlines: rolling, early decision 11/1. Contact: Ms. Shirley Leeds, (201) 836-6300 Ext. 253.

FELICIAN COLLEGE

Lodi 07644. Private; small town. Awards C, A, B. Enrolls 457 T (99% women, 99% state res., 55% on fin. aid). Entrance difficulty: less difficult. Application deadline: rolling. Contact: Miss Cynthia Seiss, (201) 778-1190.

GEORGIAN COURT COLLEGE

Lakewood 08701. Private; suburban. Awards B, M. Enrolls 1,200 T, 730 U (95% women, 80% state res., 70% on fin. aid). Application deadline: 8/15. Contact: Dr. Anthony A. D'Elia Jr, (201) 367-4440.

GLASSBORO STATE COLLEGE

Glassboro 08028. Public; small town. Awards B, M. Enrolls 10,950 T, 9,800 U (57% women, 97% state res., 58% on fin. aid). Entrance difficulty: moderately difficult. Application deadline: 3/15. Contact: Mr. John G. Davies, (609) 445-5346.

JERSEY CITY STATE COLLEGE

Jersey City 07305. Public; urban. Awards B, M. Enrolls 8,700 T, 7,700 U (55% women, 95% state res., 40% on fin. aid). Entrance difficulty: less difficult. Application deadline: rolling. Contact: Mr. Samuel T. McGhee, (201) 547-3234.

KEAN COLLEGE OF NEW JERSEY

Union 07083. Public; suburban. Awards B, M. Enrolls 13,533 T, 11,110 U (56% women, 96% state res., 43% on fin. aid). Entrance difficulty: moderately difficult. Application deadline: 6/15. Contact: Mr. E. Theodore Stier, (201) 527-2195.

MONMOUTH COLLEGE

West Long Branch 07764. Private; suburban. Awards C, A, B, M. Enrolls 3,900 T, 2,900 U (51% women, 90% state res., 70% on fin. aid). Entrance difficulty: moderately difficult. Application deadline: rolling. Contact: Mr. Robert N. Cristadoro, (201) 222-6600.

MONTCLAIR STATE COLLEGE

Upper Montclair 07043. Public; suburban. Awards B, M. Enrolls 15,246 T, 11,695 U (60% women, 95% state res., 40% on fin. aid). Entrance difficulty: moderately difficult. Application deadline: 2/1. Contact: Mr. Alan L. Buechler, (201) 893-5116.

NEW JERSEY INSTITUTE OF TECHNOLOGY

Newark 07102. Public; urban. Awards C, B, M, D. Enrolls 5,561 T, 4,531 U (8% women, 95% state res., 60% on fin. aid). Entrance difficulty: moderately difficult. Application deadline: 5/1. Contact: Mr. Neil Holtzman, (201) 645-5140.

NORTHEASTERN BIBLE COLLEGE

Essex Fells 07021. Private; suburban. Awards C, A, B. Enrolls 337 T (41% women, 74% state res., 38% on fin. aid). Entrance difficulty: moderately difficult. Application deadline: rolling. Contact: Miss Evelyn W. Richards, (201) 226-1074.

PRINCETON UNIVERSITY

Princeton 08544. Private; suburban. Awards B, M, D. Enrolls 5,877 T, 4,447 U (35% women, 20% state res., 45% on fin. aid). Entrance difficulty: most difficult. Application deadlines: 1/1, early decision 11/1. Contact: Mr. James W. Wickenden, (609) 452-3060.

RAMAPO COLLEGE OF NEW JERSEY

Mahwah 07430. Public; suburban. Awards B. Enrolls 4,318 T (49% women, 96% state res., 40% on fin. aid). Entrance difficulty: moderately difficult. Application deadline: 8/1. Contact: Mr. Wayne C. Marshall, (201) 825-2800.

RIDER COLLEGE

Lawrenceville 08648. Private; suburban. Awards C, A, B, M. Enrolls 6,083 T, 4,984 U (42% women, 76% state res., 60% on fin. aid). Entrance difficulty: moderately difficult. Application deadline: rolling. Contact: Mr. Earl L. Davis, Director of Admissions and Financial Aid, (609) 896-5042.

RUTGERS UNIVERSITY, CAMDEN COLLEGE OF ARTS AND SCIENCES

Camden 08102. Public; urban. Awards B. Enrolls 3,220 T (51% women, 98% state res., 52% on fin. aid). Application deadline: 3/15. Contact: Miss Natalie Aharonian, (201) 932-3770.

RUTGERS UNIVERSITY, COLLEGE OF ENGINEERING

New Brunswick 08903. Public; suburban. Awards B. Enrolls 2,307 T (13% women, 91% state res., 52% on fin. aid). Application deadline: 2/1. Contact: Miss Natalie Aharonian, (201) 932-3770.

RUTGERS UNIVERSITY, COLLEGE OF NURSING

Newark 07102. Public; urban. Awards B. Enrolls 564 T (93% women, 98% state res., 52% on fin. aid). Application deadline:
3/15. Contact: Miss Natalie Aharonian, (201) 932-3770.

RUTGERS UNIVERSITY, COLLEGE OF PHARMACY

New Brunswick 08903. Public; suburban. Awards B. Enrolls 699 T (56% women, 92% state res., 52% on fin. aid). Application deadline: 2/1. Contact: Miss Natalie Aharonian, (201) 932-3770.

RUTGERS UNIVERSITY, COOK COLLEGE

New Brunswick 08903. Public; suburban. Awards B. Enrolls 2,943 T (45% women, 90% state res., 52% on fin. aid). Application deadline: 2/1. Contact: Miss Natalie Aharonian, (201) 932-3770.

RUTGERS UNIVERSITY, DOUGLASS COLLEGE

New Brunswick 08903. Public; suburban. Awards B. Enrolls 3,718 T (100% women, 95% state res., 52% on fin. aid). Application deadline: 2/1. Contact: Miss Natalie Aharonian, (201) 932-3770.

RUTGERS UNIVERSITY, LIVINGSTON COLLEGE

New Brunswick 08903. Public; suburban. Awards B. Enrolls 3,717 T (39% women, 90% state res., 52% on fin. aid). Application deadline: 2/1. Contact: Miss Natalie Aharonian, (201) 932-3770.

RUTGERS UNIVERSITY, MASON GROSS SCHOOL OF THE ARTS

New Brunswick 08903. Public; suburban. Awards B, M. Enrolls 232 T (59% women, 100% state res., 52% on fin. aid). Application deadline: 2/1. Contact: Miss Natalie Aharonian, (201) 932-3770.

RUTGERS UNIVERSITY, NEWARK COLLEGE OF ARTS AND SCIENCES

Newark 07102. Public; urban. Awards B. Enrolls 4,085 T (39% women, 98% state res., 52% on fin. aid). Application deadline: 3/15. Contact: Miss Natalie Aharonian, (201) 932-3770.

RUTGERS UNIVERSITY, RUTGERS COLLEGE

New Brunswick 08903. Public; suburban. Awards B. Enrolls 8,389 T (44% women,

Rutgers University, Rutgers College (continued)
92% state res., 52% on fin. aid). Application deadline: 2/1. Contact: Miss Natalie Aharonian, (201) 932-3770.

SAINT PETER'S COLLEGE

Englewood Cliffs 07632.

SAINT PETER'S COLLEGE

Jersey City 07306. Private; urban. Awards C, A, B. Enrolls 2,790 T (48% women, 95% state res., 85% on fin. aid). Entrance difficulty: moderately difficult. Application deadlines: 3/1, early decision 12/1. Contact: Mr. Robert J. Nilan, Dean of Admissions, (201) 333-4400.

SETON HALL UNIVERSITY

South Orange 07079. Private; suburban. Awards B, M, D. Enrolls 10,420 T, 6,555 U (49% women, 90% state res., 60% on fin. aid). Entrance difficulty: moderately difficult. Application deadline: 3/1. Contact: Mr. Lee W. Cooke, (201) 762-9000 Ext. 444.

STEVENS INSTITUTE OF TECHNOLOGY

Hoboken 07030. Private; urban. Awards B, M, D. Enrolls 2,554 T, 1,476 U (13% women, 68% state res., 80% on fin. aid). Entrance difficulty: very difficult. Application deadlines: 3/1, early decision 11/1. Contact: Mr. Robert H. Seavy, (201) 420-5194.

STOCKTON STATE COLLEGE

Pomona 08240. Public; rural. Awards C, B. Enrolls 4,699 T (45% women, 95% state res., 69% on fin. aid). Entrance difficulty: moderately difficult. Application deadline: 6/1. Contact: Miss Nancy G. Iszard, (609) 652-1776.

TRENTON STATE COLLEGE

Trenton 08625. Public; suburban. Awards B, M. Enrolls 10,000 T, 7,500 U (60% women, 97% state res., 50% on fin. aid). Entrance difficulty: moderately difficult. Application deadlines: 3/1, early decision 11/1. Contact: Dr. Alfred Bridges, Director of Admissions, (609) 771-2131.

UPSALA COLLEGE

East Orange 07019. Private; urban. Awards B, M. Enrolls 1,849 T, 1,801 U (54% women, 85% state res., 80% on fin. aid). Entrance difficulty: moderately difficult. Application deadlines: rolling, early decision 11/15. Contact: Dr. Barry E. Abrams, (201) 266-7191.

WESTMINSTER CHOIR COLLEGE

Princeton 08540. Private; small town. Awards B, M. Enrolls 462 T, 376 U (56% women, 36% state res., 83% on fin. aid). Entrance difficulty: moderately difficult. Application deadline: 8/1. Contact: Mr. Steven Kreinberg, (609) 921-7144.

WILLIAM PATERSON COLLEGE OF NEW JERSEY

Wayne 07470. Public; suburban. Awards B, M. Enrolls 12,555 T, 10,732 U (43% women, 97% state res., 64% on fin. aid). Entrance difficulty: moderately difficult. Application deadline: 3/1. Contact: Mr. Dennis Seale, (201) 595-2126.

NEW MEXICO

COLLEGE OF SANTA FE

Santa Fe 87501. Private; urban. Awards A, B. Enrolls 1,203 T (56% women, 80% state res., 80% on fin. aid). Entrance difficulty: less difficult. Application deadline: rolling. Contact: Mr. Donald R. Weiss, Dean of Admissions, (505) 982-6131.

COLLEGE OF THE SOUTHWEST

Hobbs 88240. Private; suburban. Awards B. Enrolls 156 T (60% women, 87% state res., 26% on fin. aid). Entrance difficulty: noncompetitive. Application deadline: rolling. Contact: Mr. Chris W. McCormick, (505) 392-6561.

EASTERN NEW MEXICO UNIVERSITY, PORTALES CAMPUS

Portales 88130. Public; small town. Awards A, B, M. Enrolls 3,707 T, 3,100 U (51% women, 85% state res., 65% on fin. aid). Entrance difficulty: less difficult. Application deadline: rolling. Contact: Mr. Larry Fuqua, (505) 562-2178.

NEW MEXICO HIGHLANDS UNIVERSITY

Las Vegas 87701. Public; small town. Awards A, B, M. Enrolls 2,222 T, 1,680 U (52% women, 85% state res., 79% on fin. aid). Entrance difficulty: less difficult. Application deadline: 7/15. Contact: Dr. Stanley J. Hipwood, (505) 425-7511.

NEW MEXICO INSTITUTE OF MINING AND TECHNOLOGY

Socorro 87801. Public; small town. Awards A, B, M, D. Enrolls 1,021 T, 904 U (26% women, 86% state res., 83% on fin. aid). Entrance difficulty: moderately difficult. Application deadline: 8/15. Contact: Miss Louise E. Chamberlin, (505) 835-5424.

NEW MEXICO STATE UNIVERSITY

Las Cruces 88003. Public; suburban. Awards C, A, B, M, D. Enrolls 11,864 T, 10,469 U (45% women, 91% state res., 75% on fin. aid). Entrance difficulty: less difficult. Application deadline: 8/1. Contact: Mr. Bill J. Bruner, (505) 646-3121.

ST JOHN'S COLLEGE

Santa Fe 87501. Private; small town. Awards B, M. Enrolls 285 T, 270 U (45% women, 5% state res., 50% on fin. aid). Entrance difficulty: very difficult. Application deadline: rolling. Contact: Mr. Stephen R. Van Luchene, (505) 982-3691.

UNIVERSITY OF ALBUQUERQUE

Albuquerque 87140. Private; suburban. Awards C, A, B. Enrolls 2,084 T (50% women, 70% state res., 65% on fin. aid). Entrance difficulty: noncompetitive; moderately difficult for nursing, radiographic technology, respiratory therapy. Application deadline: 8/15. Contact: Miss Mary T. Gustas, Assistant Director of Admissions, (505) 831-1111.

UNIVERSITY OF NEW MEXICO

Albuquerque 87131. Public; urban. Awards C, A, B, M, D. Enrolls 22,033 T, 17,980 U (51% women, 92% state res., 60% on fin. aid). Entrance difficulty: less difficult. Application deadline: 8/18. Contact: Miss Lucille Morrow, Director of Admissions, (505) 277-3430.

WESTERN NEW MEXICO UNIVERSITY

Silver City 88061. Public; small town. Awards C, A, B, M. Enrolls 1,721 T, 1,463 U (54% women, 91% state res., 71% on fin. aid). Entrance difficulty: noncompetitive. Application deadline: rolling. Contact: Mr. Daniel R. Chacon, Director of Student Services, (505) 538-6106.

NEW YORK

ADELPHI UNIVERSITY

Garden City 11530. Private; suburban. Awards B, M, D. Enrolls 9,204 T, 5,517 U (67% women, 90% state res., 50% on fin. aid). Entrance difficulty: moderately difficult. Application deadline: rolling. Contact: Miss Virginia O'Brien, (516) 294-8700 Ext. 7225.

ALBANY COLLEGE OF PHARMACY OF UNION UNIVERSITY

Albany 12208. Private; urban. Awards B. Enrolls 596 T (53% women, 98% state res., 81% on fin. aid). Entrance difficulty: moderately difficult. Application deadline: rolling. Contact: Mr. H. Russell Denegar, Associate Dean, (518) 445-7221.

ALFRED UNIVERSITY

Alfred 14802. Private; rural. Awards B, M, D. Enrolls 2,100 T, 1,765 U (50% women, 75% state res., 80% on fin. aid). Entrance difficulty: moderately difficult. Application deadlines: 2/1, early decision 12/1. Contact: Mr. Paul P. Priggon, Director of Admissions, (607) 871-2115.

BARD COLLEGE

Annandale 12504. Private; rural. Awards B. Enrolls 700 T (51% women, 43% state res., 50% on fin. aid). Entrance difficulty: moderately difficult. Application deadline: 3/31. Contact: Mr. George Hanolb, Associate Director of Admissions.

BARNARD COLLEGE

New York 10027. Private; urban. Awards B. Enrolls 2,441 T (100% women, 45% state res., 44% on fin. aid). Entrance difficulty: very difficult. Application deadlines: 1/15, early decision 11/15. Contact: Miss R. Christine Royer, (212) 280-2014.

CANISIUS COLLEGE

Buffalo 14208. Private; urban. Awards C, B, M. Enrolls 4,069 T, 2,422 U (40% women, 95% state res., 79% on fin. aid). Entrance difficulty: moderately difficult. Application deadline: rolling. Contact: Miss Penelope H. Lips, Director of Admissions, (716) 883-7000 Ext. 204.

CATHEDRAL COLLEGE OF THE IMMACULATE CONCEPTION

Douglaston 11362. Private; urban. Awards B. Enrolls 147 T (0% women, 98% state res., 75% on fin. aid). Entrance difficulty: moderately difficult. Application deadline: rolling. Contact: Dr. Joseph W. Reisig, Academic Dean, (212) 631-4600.

CITY UNIVERSITY OF NEW YORK, BERNARD M BARUCH COLLEGE

New York 10010. Public; urban. Awards B, M. Enrolls 14,775 T, 12,425 U (51% women, 95% state res., 70% on fin. aid). Entrance difficulty: moderately difficult; very difficult for operations research, computer methodology, dual degree programs. Application deadline: rolling. Contact: Ms. Patricia Hassett, (212) 725-3158.

CITY UNIVERSITY OF NEW YORK, BROOKLYN COLLEGE

Brooklyn 11210. Public; urban. Awards B, M. Enrolls 15,895 T, 14,651 U (55% women, 98% state res., 70% on fin. aid). Entrance difficulty: less difficult. Contact: Mr. Justin L. Dunn, (212) 780-5485.

CITY UNIVERSITY OF NEW YORK, CITY COLLEGE

New York 10031. Public; urban. Awards B, M. Enrolls 13,375 T, 11,510 U (42% women, 96% state res., 85% on fin. aid). Entrance difficulty: moderately difficult. Contact: Dr. Saul Friedman, Acting Director of Admissions, (212) 690-6977.

CITY UNIVERSITY OF NEW YORK, COLLEGE OF STATEN ISLAND

Staten Island 10301. Public; urban. Awards A, B, M. Enrolls 10,500 T (53% women, 99% state res., 6% on fin. aid). Entrance difficulty: noncompetitive. Application deadline: rolling. Contact: Dr. Ann Merlino, Dean of Admissions, (212) 390-7733.

CITY UNIVERSITY OF NEW YORK, HERBERT H LEHMAN COLLEGE

Bronx 10468. Public; urban. Awards B, M. Enrolls 9,787 T, 9,076 U (63% women, 99% state res., 78% on fin. aid). Entrance difficulty: moderately difficult. Application deadline: rolling. Contact: Mr. Bernard Iantosca, (212) 960-8131.

CITY UNIVERSITY OF NEW YORK, HUNTER COLLEGE

New York 10021. Public; urban. Awards B, M. Enrolls 18,000 T, 14,872 U (70% women, 70% on fin. aid). Entrance difficulty: moderately difficult. Application deadline: rolling. Contact: Ms. Ruth Weisgal, (212) 570-5483.

CITY UNIVERSITY OF NEW YORK, JOHN JAY COLLEGE OF CRIMINAL JUSTICE

New York 10019. Public; urban. Awards A, B, M. Enrolls 5,960 T, 5,223 U (41% women, 97% state res., 90% on fin. aid). Entrance difficulty: moderately difficult; noncompetitive for associate's degree programs. Application deadline: rolling. Contact: Mr. Francis M. McHugh, Registrar, (212) 489-5080.

CITY UNIVERSITY OF NEW YORK, MEDGAR EVERS COLLEGE

Brooklyn 11225. Public; urban. Awards A, B. Enrolls 2,894 T (70% women, 97% state res., 70% on fin. aid). Entrance difficulty: noncompetitive. Application deadline: rolling. Contact: Miss Roberta Dannenfelser, Director of Admissions, (212) 735-1750.

CITY UNIVERSITY OF NEW YORK, QUEENS COLLEGE

Flushing 11367. Public; urban. Awards B, M. Enrolls 19,000 T, 13,000 U (58% women, 99% state res., 50% on fin. aid). Entrance difficulty: moderately difficult. Application deadline: rolling. Contact: Mr. Leo J. DeBartolo, Acting Director of Admissions, (212) 520-7385.

CITY UNIVERSITY OF NEW YORK, YORK COLLEGE

Jamaica 11451. Public; urban. Awards B. Enrolls 3,889 T (65% women, 95% state res., 75% on fin. aid). Entrance difficulty: noncompetitive. Application deadline: rolling. Contact: Ms. Ronnie Levitt, Director of Admissions, (212) 969-4215.

CLARKSON COLLEGE

Potsdam 13676. Private; small town. Awards B, M, D. Enrolls 3,420 T, 3,304 U (17% women, 84% state res., 90% on fin. aid). Entrance difficulty: very difficult. Application deadlines: 3/15, early decision 11/15. Contact: Mr. Robert A. Croot, Director of Admissions, (315) 268-6479.

COLGATE UNIVERSITY

Hamilton 13346. Private; small town. Awards B, M. Enrolls 2,680 T, 2,600 U (42% women, 50% state res., 80% on fin. aid). Entrance difficulty: very difficult. Application deadline: 1/15. Contact: Mr. David S. Perham, Dean of Admissions, (315) 824-1000.

COLLEGE FOR HUMAN SERVICES

New York 10014. Private; urban. Awards B. Enrolls 100 T (40% women). Contact: Ms. Constance Burrus, Admissions Coordinator, (212) 989-2002.

COLLEGE OF INSURANCE

New York 10038. Private; urban. Awards C, A, B, M. Enrolls 2,475 T, 1,825 U (50% women, 45% state res., 100% on fin. aid). Entrance difficulty: very difficult. Application deadline: rolling. Contact: Mr. Russell F. Whiting, Director, Work-Study Admissions, (212) 962-4111.

COLLEGE OF MOUNT SAINT VINCENT

Riverdale 10471. Private; suburban. Awards A, B. Enrolls 1,308 T (90% women, 90% state res., 75% on fin. aid). Entrance difficulty: moderately difficult. Application deadlines: rolling, early decision 11/1. Contact: Mr. William W. Hamilton, Director of Admissions, (212) 549-8000.

COLLEGE OF NEW ROCHELLE

New Rochelle 10801. Private; suburban. Awards B, M. Enrolls 4,484 T, 3,669 U (92% women, 75% state res., 62% on fin. aid). Entrance difficulty: noncompetitive; moderately difficult for School of Nursing, School of Arts and Sciences. Application deadlines: rolling, early decision 11/1.

Contact: Ms. Lynn McCaffrey, (914) 632-5300 Ext. 252.

COLLEGE OF SAINT ROSE

Albany 12203. Private; urban. Awards B, M. Enrolls 2,136 T, 1,627 U (70% women, 95% state res., 85% on fin. aid). Entrance difficulty: moderately difficult. Application deadline: rolling. Contact: Miss Genevieve Ann Flaherty, Director of Admissions, (518) 454-5150.

COLUMBIA COLLEGE

New York 10027. Private; urban. Awards B. Enrolls 2,800 T (0% women, 65% on fin. aid). Entrance difficulty: very difficult. Application deadlines: 1/15, early decision 11/15. Contact: Mr. Gary Cornog, (212) 280-2521.

CONCORDIA COLLEGE

Bronxville 10708. Private; suburban. Awards A, B. Enrolls 430 T (56% women, 65% state res., 75% on fin. aid). Entrance difficulty: moderately difficult. Application deadline: 9/1. Contact: Mr. Stephen F. Muller, (914) 337-9300 Ext. 116.

COOPER UNION FOR THE ADVANCEMENT OF SCIENCE AND ART

New York 10003. Private; urban. Awards C, B, M. Enrolls 890 T, 881 U (26% women, 78% state res., 17% on fin. aid). Entrance difficulty: very difficult. Application deadline: 1/1. Contact: Mr. Herbert Liebeskind, Dean of Admissions and Records, (212) 254-6300.

CORNELL UNIVERSITY

Ithaca 14853. Private; small town. Awards B, M, D. Enrolls 17,356 T, 11,945 U (43% women, 55% state res., 75% on fin. aid). Entrance difficulty: very difficult. Application deadlines: 1/15, early decision 11/1. Contact: Mr. Robert J. Storandt, (607) 256-3447.

C W POST CENTER OF LONG ISLAND UNIVERSITY

Greenvale 11548. Private; suburban. Awards A, B, M. Enrolls 12,532 T, 7,229 U (49% women, 93% state res., 80% on fin. aid). Entrance difficulty: moderately difficult. Application deadline: rolling. Contact: Mr. James F. Reilly, (516) 299-2413.

DAEMEN COLLEGE

Amherst 14226. Private; suburban. Awards C, B. Enrolls 1,317 T (60% women, 95% state res., 70% on fin. aid). Entrance difficulty: moderately difficult. Application deadline: rolling. Contact: Mr. Peter W. Stevens, Vice President for Admissions, (716) 839-3600 Ext. 225.

DOMINICAN COLLEGE

Orangeburg 10962. Private; suburban. Awards A, B. Enrolls 1,230 T (65% women, 74% state res., 55% on fin. aid). Entrance difficulty: less difficult. Application deadlines: 8/15, early decision 11/2. Contact: Mr. John Brennan Jr, (914) 359-7800.

DOWLING COLLEGE

Oakdale 11769. Private; suburban. Awards B, M. Enrolls 2,100 T, 1,500 U (50% women, 98% state res., 75% on fin. aid). Entrance difficulty: moderately difficult. Application deadline: rolling. Contact: Mr. William B. Galloway, Dean of Admissions, (516) 589-1040.

D'YOUVILLE COLLEGE

Buffalo 14201. Private; urban. Awards B. Enrolls 1,550 T (90% women, 98% state res., 85% on fin. aid). Entrance difficulty: less difficult. Application deadline: rolling. Contact: Mr. Kenneth Radig, Acting Director of Admissions, (716) 886-8100.

EISENHOWER COLLEGE OF ROCHESTER INSTITUTE OF TECHNOLOGY

Seneca Falls 13148. Private; small town. Awards B. Enrolls 550 T (50% women, 70% state res., 70% on fin. aid). Entrance difficulty: moderately difficult. Application deadlines: rolling, early decision 12/1. Contact: Mr. Robert C. French, Assistant Director of Admissions.

ELMIRA COLLEGE

Elmira 14901. Private; urban. Awards C, A, B, M. Enrolls 2,339 T, 1,913 U (57% women, 52% state res., 63% on fin. aid). Entrance difficulty: moderately difficult. Application deadlines: rolling, early decision 11/1. Contact: Mr. John Zeller, Director of Admissions, (607) 734-3911.

FASHION INSTITUTE OF TECHNOLOGY

New York 10001. Public; urban. Awards A, B. Enrolls 3,468 T (85% women, 71% state res., 68% on fin. aid). Entrance difficulty: moderately difficult. Application deadline: 3/15. Contact: Mr. Jim Pidgeon, (212) 760-7675.

FORDHAM UNIVERSITY

Bronx 10458. Private; urban. Awards B, M, D. Enrolls 14,626 T, 7,675 U (50% women, 86% state res., 84% on fin. aid). Entrance difficulty: moderately difficult. Application deadlines: 2/15, early decision 11/1. Contact: Mr. Richard T. Waldron, (212) 220-3020.

FORDHAM UNIVERSITY AT LINCOLN CENTER

New York 10023. Private; urban. Awards B, M, D. Enrolls 14,626 T, 3,042 U (66% women, 90% state res., 50% on fin. aid). Entrance difficulty: moderately difficult. Application deadlines: 2/15, early decision 11/1. Contact: Mr. Richard T. Waldron, (212) 220-3020.

FRIENDS WORLD COLLEGE

Huntington 11743. Private; suburban. Awards B. Enrolls 150 T (64% women, 35% state res., 75% on fin. aid). Entrance difficulty: moderately difficult. Application deadline: 9/1. Contact: Mr. Arthur Meyer, Director of Admissions, (516) 549-1102.

HAMILTON COLLEGE

Clinton 13323. Private; rural. Awards B. Enrolls 1,600 T (38% women, 50% state res., 43% on fin. aid). Entrance difficulty: very difficult. Application deadline: 2/1. Contact: Mr. Christopher W. Covert, Dean of Admissions, (315) 859-4421.

HARTWICK COLLEGE

Oneonta 13820. Private; small town. Awards B. Enrolls 1,418 T (57% women, 52% state res., 60% on fin. aid). Entrance difficulty: moderately difficult. Application deadlines: early decision 11/1. Contact: Mr. John Muyskens Jr, (607) 432-4200.

HEBREW UNION COLLEGE, JEWISH INSTITUTE OF RELIGION

New York 10023. Private; urban. Awards B. Enrolls 44 T (30% women, 60% on fin.

aid). Application deadline: 6/1. Contact: Rabbi Lawrence W. Raphael, Associate Dean of Admissions, (212) 674-5300.

HOBART COLLEGE

Geneva 14456. Private; urban. Awards B. Enrolls 1,050 T (0% women, 50% state res., 35% on fin. aid). Entrance difficulty: very difficult. Application deadlines: 2/1, early decision 1/1. Contact: Mr. Leonard A. Wood Jr, (315) 789-5500.

HOFSTRA UNIVERSITY

Hempstead 11550. Private; suburban. Awards B, M, D. Enrolls 10,981 T, 7,049 U (44% women, 80% state res., 78% on fin. aid). Entrance difficulty: moderately difficult. Application deadlines: 2/15, early decision 12/1. Contact: Mr. Marc K. Dion, (516) 560-3491.

HOUGHTON COLLEGE

Houghton 14744. Private; rural. Awards A, B. Enrolls 1,209 T (55% women, 60% state res., 36% on fin. aid). Entrance difficulty: very difficult. Application deadlines: 8/1, early decision 10/1. Contact: Mr. Richard J. Alderman, Director of Admissions and Records, (716) 567-2211.

IONA COLLEGE

New Rochelle 10801. Private; suburban. Awards B, M. Enrolls 5,988 T, 3,683 U (38% women, 90% state res., 70% on fin. aid). Entrance difficulty: moderately difficult. Application deadlines: rolling, early decision 11/1. Contact: Br. Francis I. Offer, (914) 636-2100.

ITHACA COLLEGE

Ithaca 14850. Private; small town. Awards B, M. Enrolls 4,698 T, 4,520 U (53% women, 48% state res., 40% on fin. aid). Entrance difficulty: moderately difficult; very difficult for physical therapy, television/radio studies. Application deadlines: 3/1, early decision 11/1. Contact: Mr. Matthew B. Wall, (607) 274-3124.

JUILLIARD SCHOOL

New York 10023. Private; urban. Awards B, M, D. Enrolls 1,220 T, 1,000 U (40% women, 40% state res., 60% on fin. aid). Application deadline: 4/15. Contact: Miss Irene W. Anderson, (212) 799-5000 Ext. 223.

KEUKA COLLEGE

Keuka Park 14478. Private; rural. Awards B. Enrolls 566 T (99% women, 85% state res., 78% on fin. aid). Entrance difficulty: moderately difficult. Application deadline: rolling. Contact: Mr. Bruce A. Westerdahl, (315) 536-4411.

KING'S COLLEGE

Briarcliff Manor 10510. Private; suburban. Awards A, B. Enrolls 853 T (59% women, 41% state res., 75% on fin. aid). Entrance difficulty: moderately difficult. Application deadline: rolling. Contact: Mr. Roy McCandless, (914) 941-7200 Ext. 241.

LADYCLIFF COLLEGE

Highland Falls 10928. Contact: Sr. Eileen Mary Halloran, Director of Admissions.

LE MOYNE COLLEGE

Syracuse 13214. Private; suburban. Awards B. Enrolls 1,947 T (45% women, 80% state res., 70% on fin. aid). Entrance difficulty: moderately difficult. Application deadlines: rolling, early decision 12/1. Contact: Mr. Edward J. Gorman, (315) 446-2882 Ext. 213.

LONG ISLAND UNIVERSITY, ARNOLD AND MARIE SCHWARTZ COLLEGE OF PHARMACY AND HEALTH SCIENCES

Brooklyn 11201. Private; urban. Awards B, M. Enrolls 1,340 T, 1,100 U (20% women, 80% state res., 60% on fin. aid). Entrance difficulty: moderately difficult. Application deadline: 5/1. Contact: Dr. James Keating, (212) 834-6364.

LONG ISLAND UNIVERSITY, BROOKLYN CENTER

Brooklyn 11201. Private; urban. Awards C, A, B, M, D. Enrolls 7,200 T, 4,365 U (63% women, 90% state res., 60% on fin. aid). Entrance difficulty: moderately difficult. Application deadline: rolling. Contact: Mr. Daniel T. Burke, (212) 834-6100.

LONG ISLAND UNIVERSITY, SOUTHAMPTON COLLEGE

Southampton 11968. Private; rural. Awards B, M. Enrolls 1,340 T, 1,298 U (46% women, 70% state res., 60% on fin. aid). Entrance difficulty: moderately difficult. Application deadline: rolling. Contact: Mr.

Long Island University, Southampton College (*continued*)
Kevin Coveney, Dean of Admissions, (516) 283-4000.

MANHATTAN COLLEGE

Bronx 10471. Private; suburban. Awards A, B, M. Enrolls 4,860 T, 4,090 U (26% women, 82% state res., 85% on fin. aid). Entrance difficulty: moderately difficult. Application deadline: 3/1. Contact: Br. William Batt, FSC, (212) 548-1400 Ext. 316.

MANHATTAN SCHOOL OF MUSIC

New York 10027. Private; urban. Awards B, M, D. Enrolls 668 T, 427 U (50% women, 55% state res., 60% on fin. aid). Entrance difficulty: very difficult. Application deadline: 4/15. Contact: Mr. Stanley Bednar, (212) 749-2802.

MANHATTANVILLE COLLEGE

Purchase 10577. Private; suburban. Awards B, M. Enrolls 1,000 T, 858 U (65% women, 50% state res., 54% on fin. aid). Entrance difficulty: moderately difficult. Application deadlines: 3/1, early decision 11/1. Contact: Mr. Robert H. Jones, Director of Admissions, (914) 946-9600.

MANNES COLLEGE OF MUSIC

New York 10021. Private; urban. Awards B. Enrolls 197 T, 195 U (47% women, 40% state res., 72% on fin. aid). Entrance difficulty: very difficult. Application deadline: 7/15. Contact: Miss Diane Newman, Admissions Adviser, (212) 737-0700.

MARIST COLLEGE

Poughkeepsie 12601. Private; suburban. Awards C, B, M. Enrolls 2,200 T, 1,850 U (40% women, 80% state res., 82% on fin. aid). Entrance difficulty: moderately difficult. Application deadline: rolling. Contact: Mr. James E. Daly, Dean of Admissions, (914) 471-3240.

MARYMOUNT COLLEGE

Tarrytown 10591. Private; suburban. Awards B. Enrolls 931 T (100% women, 51% state res., 68% on fin. aid). Entrance difficulty: moderately difficult. Application deadline: 3/15. Contact: Mrs. Micheileen Doran, (914) 631-3451.

MARYMOUNT MANHATTAN COLLEGE

New York 10021. Private; urban. Awards C, B. Enrolls 2,252 T (95% women, 94% state res., 78% on fin. aid). Entrance difficulty: moderately difficult. Application deadline: rolling. Contact: Mr. William DiBrienza, (212) 472-3800 Ext. 555.

MEDAILLE COLLEGE

Buffalo 14214. Private; urban. Awards A, B, M. Enrolls 700 T (66% women, 99% state res., 85% on fin. aid). Entrance difficulty: moderately difficult. Application deadline: 8/1. Contact: Miss Marilynn Propis, (716) 884-3281.

MERCY COLLEGE

Dobbs Ferry 10522. Private; small town. Awards C, A, B. Enrolls 10,500 T (49% women, 92% state res., 85% on fin. aid). Entrance difficulty: moderately difficult. Application deadline: 9/1. Contact: Mr. William W. Hitz, (914) 693-7600.

MOLLOY COLLEGE

Rockville Centre 11570. Private; suburban. Awards A, B. Enrolls 1,533 T (95% women, 100% state res., 60% on fin. aid). Entrance difficulty: moderately difficult. Application deadlines: 8/15, early decision 11/1. Contact: Mr. Francis A. Mullin, (516) 678-5018.

MOUNT SAINT MARY COLLEGE

Newburgh 12550. Private; urban. Awards B. Enrolls 1,046 T (80% women, 80% state res., 75% on fin. aid). Entrance difficulty: moderately difficult. Application deadline: 8/1. Contact: Mr. James L. Sagona, (914) 561-6321.

NAZARETH COLLEGE OF ROCHESTER

Rochester 14610. Private; suburban. Awards B, M. Enrolls 2,594 T, 1,678 U (74% women, 92% state res., 56% on fin. aid). Entrance difficulty: moderately difficult. Application deadline: rolling. Contact: Mr. Paul Buntich, (716) 586-2525.

NEW SCHOOL FOR SOCIAL RESEARCH

New York 10011. Private; urban. Awards B, M, D. Enrolls 3,000 T, 238 U (60% women, 67% state res., 20% on fin. aid). Entrance difficulty: very difficult. Application deadlines: 8/1, early decision 11/15. Contact: Ms. Barbara Hartung, (212) 741-5665.

NEW YORK COLLEGE OF PODIATRIC MEDICINE

New York 10035. Contact: Mr. Pedro H. Valdes, Vice Pres for Student Affairs.

NEW YORK INSTITUTE OF TECHNOLOGY, COMMACK COLLEGE CENTER

Commack 11725. Public. Awards A, B, M.

NEW YORK INSTITUTE OF TECHNOLOGY, METROPOLITAN CENTER

New York 10023. Private; urban. Awards A, B, M. Enrolls 2,720 T, 2,387 U (22% women, 59% state res., 43% on fin. aid). Entrance difficulty: less difficult. Application deadline: rolling. Contact: Mr. Kaspar Schroeter, Associate Director of Admissions.

NEW YORK INSTITUTE OF TECHNOLOGY, OLD WESTBURY

Old Westbury 11568. Private; suburban. Awards C, A, B, M. Enrolls 10,443 T (27% women, 95% state res., 82% on fin. aid). Entrance difficulty: moderately difficult. Application deadline: rolling. Contact: Mr. Arden H. deBrun, (516) 686-7520.

NEW YORK UNIVERSITY

New York 10003. Private; urban. Awards C, A, B, M, D. Enrolls 32,537 T, 12,685 U (54% women, 80% state res., 70% on fin. aid). Entrance difficulty: moderately difficult. Application deadlines: 2/1, early decision 11/15. Contact: Mr. Harold R. Doughty, (212) 598-3591.

NIAGARA UNIVERSITY

Niagara University 14109. Private; suburban. Awards A, B, M. Enrolls 3,924 T, 3,328 U (54% women, 88% state res., 85% on fin. aid). Entrance difficulty: moderately difficult. Application deadline: 8/1. Contact: Mr. George C. Pachter Jr, Dean of Admissions, (716) 285-1212.

NYACK COLLEGE

Nyack 10960. Private; suburban. Awards B, M. Enrolls 688 T, 602 U (52% women, 50% state res., 60% on fin. aid). Entrance difficulty: less difficult. Application deadline: 8/15. Contact: Miss Marj Goodwin, Director of Admissions and Financial Aid, (914) 358-1710 Ext. 200.

PACE UNIVERSITY

New York 10038. Private; urban. Awards C, A, B, M, D. Enrolls 9,193 T, 6,143 U (52% women, 91% state res., 90% on fin. aid). Entrance difficulty: moderately difficult. Application deadline: 8/15. Contact: Miss Emilie Bidlingmeyer, (212) 285-3323.

PACE UNIVERSITY, COLLEGE OF WHITE PLAINS

White Plains 10603. Private; suburban. Awards A, B. Enrolls 1,200 T (66% women, 86% state res., 75% on fin. aid). Entrance difficulty: moderately difficult. Application deadline: 8/15. Contact: Mr. Mark J. Brooks, (914) 682-7070.

PACE UNIVERSITY—PLEASANTVILLE/BRIARCLIFF

Pleasantville 10570. Private; suburban. Awards C, A, B, M, D. Enrolls 5,243 T, 4,214 U (59% women, 84% state res., 70% on fin. aid). Entrance difficulty: moderately difficult. Application deadlines: 8/15, early decision 12/1. Contact: Mr. Richard A. Avitabile, (914) 769-3788.

PARSONS SCHOOL OF DESIGN

New York 10011. Private; urban. Awards A, B, M. Enrolls 1,500 T, 1,400 U (60% women, 27% state res., 78% on fin. aid). Entrance difficulty: very difficult. Application deadline: 6/1. Contact: Mr. Thomas Heinegg, (212) 741-8910.

POLYTECHNIC INSTITUTE OF NEW YORK

Brooklyn 11201. Private; urban. Awards B, M, D. Enrolls 4,252 T, 2,253 U (10% women, 90% state res., 90% on fin. aid). Entrance difficulty: moderately difficult. Application deadline: rolling. Contact: Ms. Elizabeth Sharp Ross, (212) 643-2150.

PRATT INSTITUTE

Brooklyn 11205. Private; urban. Awards A, B, M. Enrolls 4,422 T, 3,294 U (48% women, 58% state res., 75% on fin. aid). Entrance difficulty: moderately difficult. Application deadline: 4/1. Contact: Mr.

Pratt Institute (continued)
Daniel Kimball, Director of Admissions and Financial Aid, (212) 636-3535.

RENSSELAER POLYTECHNIC INSTITUTE

Troy 12181. Private; suburban. Awards B, M, D. Enrolls 5,708 T, 4,155 U (13% women, 43% state res., 60% on fin. aid). Entrance difficulty: very difficult. Application deadlines: 1/1, early decision 11/1. Contact: Mr. Christopher Small, (518) 270-6216.

ROBERTS WESLEYAN COLLEGE

Rochester 14624. Private; suburban. Awards A, B. Enrolls 645 T (70% women, 74% state res., 85% on fin. aid). Entrance difficulty: moderately difficult. Application deadline: rolling. Contact: Mr. David C. Morrow, (716) 594-9471 Ext. 125.

ROCHESTER INSTITUTE OF TECHNOLOGY

Rochester 14623. Private; suburban. Awards A, B, M. Enrolls 13,000 T, 8,242 U (35% women, 60% state res., 80% on fin. aid). Entrance difficulty: moderately difficult. Application deadline: 7/1. Contact: Mr. E. Louis Guard, (716) 475-6636.

RUSSELL SAGE COLLEGE

Troy 12180. Private; urban. Awards B, M. Enrolls 1,430 T, 1,400 U (100% women, 62% state res., 55% on fin. aid). Entrance difficulty: moderately difficult; very difficult for some programs. Application deadlines: rolling, early decision 8/15. Contact: Ms. Meg Snyder, Admissions Counselor.

ST BONAVENTURE UNIVERSITY

St Bonaventure 14778. Private; rural. Awards B, M, D. Enrolls 2,781 T, 2,333 U (47% women, 79% state res., 78% on fin. aid). Entrance difficulty: moderately difficult. Application deadline: rolling. Contact: Mr. Donald C. Burkard, Director of Admissions, (716) 375-2400.

ST FRANCIS COLLEGE

Brooklyn 11201. Contact: Br. George Larkin OSF, Director of Admissions.

ST JOHN FISHER COLLEGE

Rochester 14618. Private; suburban. Awards B. Enrolls 3,007 T (45% women, 53% state res., 85% on fin. aid). Entrance difficulty: moderately difficult. Application deadline: rolling. Contact: Ms. Cynthia A. Moll, Admissions Counselor.

ST JOHN'S UNIVERSITY

Jamaica 11439. Private; urban. Awards A, B, M, D. Enrolls 16,200 T, 11,194 U (41% women, 92% state res., 75% on fin. aid). Entrance difficulty: moderately difficult. Application deadline: 8/1. Contact: Mr. Henry F. Rossi, Dean of Admissions and Registrar, (212) 969-8000.

ST JOSEPH'S COLLEGE

Brooklyn 11205. Private; urban. Awards B. Enrolls 388 T (84% women, 98% state res., 80% on fin. aid). Entrance difficulty: moderately difficult. Application deadline: 8/15. Contact: Ms. Sherrie Van Arnam, (212) 622-4696.

ST JOSEPH'S COLLEGE, SUFFOLK CAMPUS

Patchogue 11772. Private; suburban. Awards B. Enrolls 500 T (80% women, 100% state res., 80% on fin. aid). Entrance difficulty: moderately difficult. Application deadline: 8/15. Contact: Miss Marion E. Salgado, Director of Admissions, (516) 289-3479.

ST LAWRENCE UNIVERSITY

Canton 13617. Private; small town. Awards B, M. Enrolls 2,516 T, 2,440 U (50% women, 49% state res., 24% on fin. aid). Entrance difficulty: moderately difficult. Application deadlines: 2/1, early decision 1/1. Contact: Mr. Conrad J. Sharrow, (315) 379-5261.

ST THOMAS AQUINAS COLLEGE

Sparkill 10976. Private; suburban. Awards B. Enrolls 1,300 T (50% women, 80% state res., 45% on fin. aid). Entrance difficulty: moderately difficult. Application deadline: rolling. Contact: Ms. Andrea Kraeft, (914) 359-9500.

SARAH LAWRENCE COLLEGE

Bronxville 10708. Private; suburban. Awards B, M. Enrolls 976 T, 814 U (70% women, 48% state res., 40% on fin. aid).

Entrance difficulty: moderately difficult. Application deadlines: 2/1, early decision 12/1. Contact: Mr. Dudley F. Blodget, (914) 337-0700 Ext. 207.

SIENA COLLEGE

Loudonville 12211. Private; suburban. Awards C, B. Enrolls 3,054 T (39% women, 94% state res., 80% on fin. aid). Entrance difficulty: moderately difficult. Application deadlines: 3/1, early decision 12/15. Contact: Mr. Harry Wood, (518) 783-2423.

SKIDMORE COLLEGE

Saratoga Springs 12866. Private; small town. Awards B. Enrolls 2,082 T (79% women, 38% state res., 27% on fin. aid). Entrance difficulty: moderately difficult. Application deadlines: 2/1, early decision 12/15. Contact: Mrs. Louise B. Wise, (518) 584-5000 Ext. 213.

STATE UNIVERSITY OF NEW YORK AT ALBANY

Albany 12222. Public; suburban. Awards B, M, D. Enrolls 15,070 T, 10,730 U (50% women, 99% state res., 50% on fin. aid). Entrance difficulty: very difficult. Application deadline: 4/1. Contact: Mr. Rodney A. Hart, (518) 457-8996.

STATE UNIVERSITY OF NEW YORK AT BINGHAMTON

Binghamton 13901. Public; suburban. Awards C, B, M, D. Enrolls 10,636 T, 8,100 U (52% women, 97% state res., 83% on fin. aid). Entrance difficulty: very difficult. Application deadline: 2/15. Contact: Mr. Geoffrey G. Gould, Assistant Vice-President for Admissions and Financial Aid, (607) 798-2171.

STATE UNIVERSITY OF NEW YORK AT BUFFALO

Buffalo 14260. Public; suburban. Awards A, B, M, D. Enrolls 24,683 T, 16,960 U (42% women, 95% state res.). Entrance difficulty: moderately difficult. Application deadline: rolling. Contact: Mr. Michael Rivera, Associate Director of Admissions, (716) 831-2111.

STATE UNIVERSITY OF NEW YORK AT STONY BROOK

Stony Brook 11794. Public; suburban. Awards B, M, D. Enrolls 16,000 T, 11,000 U (47% women, 99% state res., 75% on fin. aid). Entrance difficulty: moderately difficult. Application deadline: rolling. Contact: Mr. Steven E. Kesman, Assistant Director of Admissions, (516) 246-8660.

STATE UNIVERSITY OF NEW YORK COLLEGE AT BROCKPORT

Brockport 14420. Public; small town. Awards B, M. Enrolls 9,785 T, 8,201 U (52% women, 99% state res., 70% on fin. aid). Entrance difficulty: moderately difficult. Application deadline: 8/15. Contact: Dr. Ralph R. Pascale, (716) 395-2751.

STATE UNIVERSITY OF NEW YORK COLLEGE AT BUFFALO

Buffalo 14222. Public; urban. Awards B, M. Enrolls 10,909 T, 9,291 U (55% women, 98% state res., 55% on fin. aid). Entrance difficulty: moderately difficult. Application deadline: 8/1. Contact: Mr. Kevin M. Durkin, (716) 878-5511.

STATE UNIVERSITY OF NEW YORK COLLEGE AT CORTLAND

Cortland 13045. Public; small town. Awards B, M. Enrolls 5,875 T, 5,274 U (60% women, 98% state res., 70% on fin. aid). Entrance difficulty: moderately difficult. Application deadline: 5/1. Contact: Mr. Thomas A. Syracuse, (607) 753-4711.

STATE UNIVERSITY OF NEW YORK COLLEGE AT FREDONIA

Fredonia 14063. Public; small town. Awards B, M. Enrolls 5,262 T, 4,776 U (50% women, 97% state res., 67% on fin. aid). Entrance difficulty: moderately difficult. Application deadline: rolling. Contact: Mr. William S. Clark, (716) 673-3251.

STATE UNIVERSITY OF NEW YORK COLLEGE AT GENESEO

Geneseo 14454. Public; small town. Awards B, M. Enrolls 5,551 T, 4,886 U (64% women, 99% state res., 60% on fin. aid). Entrance difficulty: moderately difficult. Application deadline: rolling. Contact: Dr. William L. Caren, (716) 245-5571.

STATE UNIVERSITY OF NEW YORK COLLEGE AT NEW PALTZ

New Paltz 12561. Public; rural. Awards B, M. Enrolls 6,750 T, 4,980 U (52% women, 95% state res., 80% on fin. aid). Entrance difficulty: moderately difficult. Application deadline: rolling. Contact: Dr. William S. Whittaker, (914) 257-2414.

STATE UNIVERSITY OF NEW YORK COLLEGE AT OLD WESTBURY

Old Westbury 11568. Public; suburban. Awards B. Enrolls 2,854 T (62% women, 96% state res., 80% on fin. aid). Entrance difficulty: noncompetitive. Application deadline: 8/30. Contact: Mr. Alan Chaves, (516) 876-3073.

STATE UNIVERSITY OF NEW YORK COLLEGE AT ONEONTA

Oneonta 13820. Public; small town. Awards B, M. Enrolls 6,204 T, 5,702 U (58% women, 98% state res., 75% on fin. aid). Entrance difficulty: moderately difficult. Application deadline: 4/1. Contact: Mr. Richard Burr, (607) 431-2524.

STATE UNIVERSITY OF NEW YORK COLLEGE AT OSWEGO

Oswego 13126. Public; small town. Awards B, M. Enrolls 7,200 T, 6,500 U (48% women, 90% state res., 75% on fin. aid). Entrance difficulty: moderately difficult. Application deadline: 3/15. Contact: Mr. Joseph F. Grant Jr, (315) 341-2250.

STATE UNIVERSITY OF NEW YORK COLLEGE AT PLATTSBURGH

Plattsburgh 12901. Public; small town. Awards B, M. Enrolls 5,355 T, 5,183 U (56% women, 98% state res., 85% on fin. aid). Entrance difficulty: moderately difficult; very difficult for nursing and accounting programs. Application deadline: rolling. Contact: Mr. David E. Truax, (518) 564-2040.

STATE UNIVERSITY OF NEW YORK COLLEGE AT POTSDAM

Potsdam 13676. Public; small town. Awards B, M. Enrolls 4,682 T, 3,927 U (54% women, 98% state res., 80% on fin. aid). Entrance difficulty: moderately difficult. Application deadline: 6/1. Contact: Mr. J. Butler Sullivan, (315) 268-2941.

STATE UNIVERSITY OF NEW YORK COLLEGE AT PURCHASE

Purchase 10577. Public; suburban. Awards B. Enrolls 2,100 T (55% women, 75% state res., 70% on fin. aid). Entrance difficulty: moderately difficult. Application deadline: rolling. Contact: Mr. Thomas R. Phillips, Acting Director of Admissions, (914) 253-5046.

STATE UNIVERSITY OF NEW YORK HEALTH SCIENCE CENTER AT BUFFALO

Buffalo 14214.

STATE UNIVERSITY OF NEW YORK MARITIME COLLEGE

Bronx 10465. Public; suburban. Awards B, M. Enrolls 1,060 T, 970 U (5% women, 80% state res., 40% on fin. aid). Entrance difficulty: very difficult. Application deadline: 5/1. Contact: Mr. R. Thomas Cerny, (212) 892-3000.

STERN COLLEGE FOR WOMEN

New York 10033. Private; urban. Awards B. Enrolls 523 T (100% women, 34% state res., 75% on fin. aid). Application deadlines: 4/15, early decision 11/15. Contact: Rabbi Abner H. Groff, Dean of Admissions, (212) 960-5277.

SYRACUSE UNIVERSITY

Syracuse 13210. Private; urban. Awards C, B, M, D. Enrolls 15,314 T, 11,044 U (50% women, 60% on fin. aid). Entrance difficulty: moderately difficult. Application deadlines: 2/1, early decision 12/1. Contact: Mr. Thomas F. Cummings Jr, Dean of Admissions and Financial Aid, (315) 423-3611.

SYRACUSE UNIVERSITY, UTICA COLLEGE

Utica 13502. Private; suburban. Awards A, B. Enrolls 1,312 T (54% women, 84% state res., 80% on fin. aid). Entrance difficulty: moderately difficult. Application deadlines: rolling, early decision 12/1. Contact: Mr. Dominic Passalacqua, (315) 792-3006.

TOURO COLLEGE

New York 10036. Private; urban. Awards A, B. Enrolls 1,957 T (60% women, 85% state res., 84% on fin. aid). Entrance difficulty: moderately difficult. Application deadline:

rolling. Contact: Mr. Norman Twersky, Dean of Admissions, (212) 575-0190.

UNION COLLEGE

Schenectady 12308. Private; suburban. Awards B, M, D. Enrolls 2,062 T (33% women, 71% state res., 37% on fin. aid). Entrance difficulty: moderately difficult; most difficult for 6-year medical and law programs. Application deadlines: 2/1, early decision 12/15. Contact: Mr. Kenneth A. Nourse, (518) 370-6112.

UNITED STATES MERCHANT MARINE ACADEMY

Kings Point 10024. Public; suburban. Awards B. Enrolls 1,100 T (9% women, 23% state res.). Entrance difficulty: most difficult. Application deadline: 3/1. Contact: Capt. Emmanuel L. Jenkins, Director of Admissions, (516) 482-8200.

UNITED STATES MILITARY ACADEMY

West Point 10996. Public; small town. Awards B. Enrolls 4,400 T (7% women, 12% state res., 100% on fin. aid). Entrance difficulty: very difficult. Application deadline: 1/15. Contact: Col. Manley E. Rogers, (914) 938-2162.

UNIVERSITY OF ROCHESTER

Rochester 14627. Private; suburban. Awards B, M, D. Enrolls 8,100 T, 4,288 U (41% women, 58% state res., 80% on fin. aid). Entrance difficulty: very difficult. Application deadlines: 1/15, early decision 11/15. Contact: Mr. Timothy W. Scholl, Dean of Admissions, (716) 275-3221.

VASSAR COLLEGE

Poughkeepsie 12601. Private; suburban. Awards B, M. Enrolls 2,298 T, 2,295 U (60% women, 41% state res., 60% on fin. aid). Entrance difficulty: very difficult. Application deadline: 2/1. Contact: Mr. Fred W. Brooks Jr, (914) 452-7000 Ext. 2020.

WAGNER COLLEGE

Staten Island 10301. Private; suburban. Awards B, M. Enrolls 2,539 T, 1,947 U (55% women, 80% state res., 61% on fin. aid). Entrance difficulty: moderately difficult. Application deadline: rolling. Contact: Mr. Frank Carnabuci, (212) 390-3011.

WEBB INSTITUTE OF NAVAL ARCHITECTURE

Glen Cove 11542. Private; suburban. Awards B. Enrolls 78 T (6% women, 39% state res., 37% on fin. aid). Entrance difficulty: very difficult. Application deadline: 2/15. Contact: Mr. William G. Murray, Registrar, (516) 671-2213.

WELLS COLLEGE

Aurora 13026. Private; small town. Awards B. Enrolls 529 T (100% women, 35% state res., 63% on fin. aid). Entrance difficulty: moderately difficult. Application deadline: 3/1. Contact: Mrs. Joan C. Irving, (315) 364-3264.

WILLIAM SMITH COLLEGE

Geneva 14456. Private; small town. Awards B. Enrolls 700 T (100% women, 50% state res., 35% on fin. aid). Entrance difficulty: very difficult. Application deadlines: 2/15, early decision 1/1. Contact: Miss Mara O'-Laughlin, (315) 789-5500.

YESHIVA COLLEGE

New York 10033. Private; urban. Awards B. Enrolls 809 T (0% women, 54% state res., 75% on fin. aid). Application deadline: 4/15. Contact: Mr. Paul Glasser, Dean of Admissions, (212) 960-5277.

NORTH CAROLINA

APPALACHIAN STATE UNIVERSITY

Boone 28608. Public; small town. Awards B, M. Enrolls 9,242 T, 8,277 U (52% women, 93% state res., 54% on fin. aid). Entrance difficulty: moderately difficult. Application deadline: rolling. Contact: Mr. C. H. Gilstrap, Director of Admissions, (704) 262-2120.

ATLANTIC CHRISTIAN COLLEGE

Wilson 27893. Private; suburban. Awards B. Enrolls 1,650 T (62% women, 80% state res., 55% on fin. aid). Entrance difficulty: moderately difficult. Application deadline: rolling. Contact: Miss Marie E. Deans, Associate Director of Admissions.

BARBER-SCOTIA COLLEGE

Concord 28025. Private; small town. Awards A, B. Enrolls 435 T (61% women, 61% state res., 98% on fin. aid). Entrance difficulty: noncompetitive. Application deadline: rolling. Contact: Mr. John Black, Acting Director, (704) 786-5171 Ext. 219.

BELMONT ABBEY COLLEGE

Belmont 28012. Private; suburban. Awards B. Enrolls 777 T (40% women, 37% state res., 83% on fin. aid). Entrance difficulty: less difficult. Application deadline: rolling. Contact: Mr. Robin R. Roberts, (704) 825-3711.

BENNETT COLLEGE

Greensboro 27420. Private; urban. Awards B. Enrolls 645 T (100% women). Entrance difficulty: less difficult. Application deadline: rolling. Contact: Mrs. Phyllis Johnson, Director of Admissions and Records, (919) 273-4431.

CAMPBELL UNIVERSITY

Buies Creek 27506. Private; small town. Awards A, B, M. Enrolls 2,420 T, 1,790 U (45% women, 75% state res., 80% on fin. aid). Entrance difficulty: moderately difficult. Application deadline: rolling. Contact: Mr. Allen J. Carter, (919) 893-4111.

CATAWBA COLLEGE

Salisbury 28144. Private; suburban. Awards B. Enrolls 1,000 T (48% women, 50% state res., 60% on fin. aid). Entrance difficulty: moderately difficult. Application deadline: rolling. Contact: Mr. J. William Hall, (704) 637-4402.

DAVIDSON COLLEGE

Davidson 28036. Private; small town. Awards B. Enrolls 1,352 T (30% women, 30% state res., 40% on fin. aid). Entrance difficulty: very difficult. Application deadlines: 2/15, early decision 11/1. Contact: Mr. John V. Griffith, Director of Admissions, (704) 892-2000.

DUKE UNIVERSITY

Durham 27710. Private; suburban. Awards B, M, D. Enrolls 9,100 T, 5,700 U (46% women, 16% state res., 30% on fin. aid). Entrance difficulty: very difficult. Application deadlines: 1/15, early decision 12/1.

Contact: Mr. Edward C. Lingenheld, (919) 684-3214.

DURHAM COLLEGE

Durham 27707. Private; urban. Awards C, A, B. Enrolls 275 T (85% women, 40% state res., 90% on fin. aid). Entrance difficulty: less difficult. Application deadline: rolling. Contact: Mrs. Lottie Killett, (919) 688-8813.

EAST CAROLINA UNIVERSITY

Greenville 27834. Public; rural. Awards B, M, D. Enrolls 12,874 T, 10,824 U (55% women, 89% state res., 55% on fin. aid). Entrance difficulty: moderately difficult. Application deadlines: 8/15, early decision 11/1. Contact: Mr. Walter Bortz, Dean of Admissions, (919) 757-6640.

ELIZABETH CITY STATE UNIVERSITY

Elizabeth City 27909. Public; small town. Awards C, B. Enrolls 1,600 T (57% women, 90% state res., 88% on fin. aid). Entrance difficulty: less difficult. Application deadline: rolling. Contact: Mrs. Wanda McLean, (919) 335-0551.

ELON COLLEGE

Elon College 27244. Private; small town. Awards C, A, B. Enrolls 2,501 T (45% women, 64% state res., 65% on fin. aid). Entrance difficulty: moderately difficult. Application deadline: rolling. Contact: Mrs. Marydell R. Bright, (919) 584-9711 Ext. 271.

FAYETTEVILLE STATE UNIVERSITY

Fayetteville 28301. Public; urban. Awards A, B. Enrolls 2,283 T (58% women, 87% state res., 77% on fin. aid). Entrance difficulty: less difficult. Application deadline: 7/1. Contact: Mr. Charles A. Darlington, Acting Director of Admissions, (919) 486-1371.

GARDNER-WEBB COLLEGE

Boiling Springs 28017. Private; small town. Awards A, B, M. Enrolls 1,354 T (49% women, 10% state res., 65% on fin. aid). Entrance difficulty: moderately difficult. Application deadline: 8/1. Contact: Mr. Richard M. Holbrook, (704) 434-2361.

GREENSBORO COLLEGE

Greensboro 27420. Private; suburban. Awards B. Enrolls 664 T (65% women, 60% state res., 65% on fin. aid). Entrance difficulty: moderately difficult. Application deadline: rolling. Contact: Mr. James Tucker, Assistant Director of Admissions, (919) 272-7102.

GUILFORD COLLEGE

Greensboro 27410. Private; suburban. Awards A, B. Enrolls 1,105 T (45% women, 40% state res., 51% on fin. aid). Entrance difficulty: very difficult. Application deadlines: 7/1, early decision 10/15. Contact: Mr. Herbert Poole, (919) 292-5511.

HIGH POINT COLLEGE

High Point 27262. Private; suburban. Awards B. Enrolls 1,228 T (56% women, 62% state res., 76% on fin. aid). Entrance difficulty: moderately difficult. Application deadline: rolling. Contact: Mr. Alfred S. Hassell, (919) 885-0414.

JOHNSON C SMITH UNIVERSITY

Charlotte 28216. Private; urban. Awards B. Enrolls 1,473 T (51% women, 37% state res., 90% on fin. aid). Entrance difficulty: less difficult. Application deadline: 8/1. Contact: Mr. Moses W. Jones, (704) 372-2370.

LENOIR-RHYNE COLLEGE

Hickory 28601. Private; suburban. Awards C, B, M. Enrolls 1,291 T (55% women, 70% state res., 54% on fin. aid). Entrance difficulty: moderately difficult. Application deadline: rolling. Contact: Mr. Richard P. Thompson, Dean of Admissions, (704) 328-1741.

LIVINGSTONE COLLEGE

Salisbury 28144. Contact: Mrs. Emily H. Harper, Registrar/Director of Admiss.

MARS HILL COLLEGE

Mars Hill 28754. Private; small town. Awards A, B. Enrolls 1,958 T (67% women, 71% state res., 67% on fin. aid). Entrance difficulty: less difficult. Application deadline: rolling. Contact: Mr. Dennis Hill, Associate Dean for Admissions, (704) 689-1201.

MEREDITH COLLEGE

Raleigh 27611. Private; urban. Awards B. Enrolls 1,427 T (100% women, 85% state res., 24% on fin. aid). Entrance difficulty: moderately difficult. Application deadlines: 2/15, early decision 10/15. Contact: Miss Mary Bland Josey, (919) 833-6461.

METHODIST COLLEGE

Fayetteville 28301. Private; suburban. Awards A, B. Enrolls 762 T (50% women, 70% state res., 84% on fin. aid). Entrance difficulty: moderately difficult. Application deadline: rolling. Contact: Mr. Thomas Dent, (919) 488-7110.

NORTH CAROLINA AGRICULTURAL AND TECHNICAL STATE UNIVERSITY

Greensboro 27411. Public; small town. Awards B, M. Enrolls 5,385 T, 4,863 U (49% women, 76% state res., 77% on fin. aid). Entrance difficulty: moderately difficult. Application deadline: rolling. Contact: Mr. W.H. Gamble, (919) 379-7946.

NORTH CAROLINA CENTRAL UNIVERSITY

Durham 27707. Public; urban. Awards B, M. Enrolls 4,810 T, 3,922 U (62% women, 90% state res., 87% on fin. aid). Entrance difficulty: less difficult. Application deadline: 8/1. Contact: Mrs. Maria B. Creed, (919) 683-6298.

NORTH CAROLINA SCHOOL OF THE ARTS

Winston-Salem 27107. Public; urban. Awards B. Enrolls 453 T (50% women, 45% state res., 30% on fin. aid). Entrance difficulty: very difficult. Application deadline: rolling. Contact: Mr. Dirk Dawson, (919) 784-7170.

NORTH CAROLINA STATE UNIVERSITY AT RALEIGH

Raleigh 27650. Public; suburban. Awards A, B, M, D. Enrolls 19,597 T, 15,539 U (32% women, 87% state res.). Entrance difficulty: moderately difficult. Application deadline: 5/1. Contact: Ms. Ann Lowery Yoest, Assistant Director of Admissions, (919) 737-2434.

NORTH CAROLINA WESLEYAN COLLEGE

Rocky Mount 27801. Private; suburban. Awards B. Enrolls 743 T (70% women, 74% state res., 72% on fin. aid). Entrance difficulty: less difficult. Application deadline: rolling. Contact: Mrs. Katrina Eatman, (919) 442-7121.

PEMBROKE STATE UNIVERSITY

Pembroke 28372. Public; rural. Awards B, M. Enrolls 2,231 T, 2,102 U (57% women, 97% state res., 65% on fin. aid). Entrance difficulty: less difficult. Application deadline: 6/15. Contact: Mr. Warren Baker, (919) 521-4214.

PFEIFFER COLLEGE

Misenheimer 28109. Private; rural. Awards B. Enrolls 844 T (52% women, 70% state res., 88% on fin. aid). Entrance difficulty: moderately difficult. Application deadline: rolling. Contact: Mr. Kenneth D. Holshouser, Director of Admissions/Registrar, (704) 463-7343.

PIEDMONT BIBLE COLLEGE

Winston-Salem 27101. Private; urban. Awards B. Enrolls 470 T (34% women, 48% state res., 9% on fin. aid). Entrance difficulty: noncompetitive. Application deadline: rolling. Contact: Mr. Shelby L. Harbour, Registrar, (919) 725-8344.

QUEENS COLLEGE

Charlotte 28274. Private; suburban. Awards B, M. Enrolls 640 T (95% women, 64% state res., 57% on fin. aid). Entrance difficulty: moderately difficult. Application deadline: rolling. Contact: Miss Donna M. Pugh, Admissions Director, (704) 332-7121.

SACRED HEART COLLEGE

Belmont 28012. Private; small town. Awards A, B. Enrolls 475 T (89% women, 76% state res., 66% on fin. aid). Entrance difficulty: moderately difficult. Application deadline: 6/1. Contact: Ms. Jo Singleton, (704) 825-5146 Ext. 219.

ST ANDREWS PRESBYTERIAN COLLEGE

Laurinburg 28352. Private; small town. Awards B. Enrolls 601 T (43% women, 52% state res., 60% on fin. aid). Entrance difficulty: moderately difficult. Application deadline: rolling. Contact: Mr. Dudley Crawford, (919) 276-3652.

SAINT AUGUSTINE'S COLLEGE

Raleigh 27611. Private; urban. Awards B. Enrolls 1,709 T (92% women, 61% state res., 92% on fin. aid). Entrance difficulty: moderately difficult. Application deadline: 8/10. Contact: Mr. Igal E. Spraggins, (919) 828-4451.

SALEM COLLEGE

Winston-Salem 27108. Private; urban. Awards B. Enrolls 530 T (100% women, 53% state res., 35% on fin. aid). Entrance difficulty: moderately difficult. Application deadline: rolling. Contact: Ms. Annette P. Lynch, Assistant Director of Admissions, (919) 721-2600.

SHAW UNIVERSITY

Raleigh 27611. Private; urban. Awards B. Enrolls 1,263 T (44% women, 50% state res.). Entrance difficulty: noncompetitive. Contact: Mrs. Barbara Sellars, Admissions Coordinator, (919) 755-2924.

UNIVERSITY OF NORTH CAROLINA AT ASHEVILLE

Asheville 28804. Public; suburban. Awards B. Enrolls 1,446 T (56% women, 95% state res., 25% on fin. aid). Entrance difficulty: moderately difficult. Application deadline: 8/10. Contact: Dr. James C. Blackburn, (704) 258-0200.

UNIVERSITY OF NORTH CAROLINA AT CHAPEL HILL

Chapel Hill 27514. Public; small town. Awards B, M, D. Enrolls 21,060 T, 14,661 U (55% women, 87% state res., 25% on fin. aid). Entrance difficulty: very difficult. Application deadline: 2/1. Contact: Mr. Richard G. Cashwell, (919) 933-2304.

UNIVERSITY OF NORTH CAROLINA AT CHARLOTTE

Charlotte 28223. Public; urban. Awards B, M. Enrolls 8,945 T, 7,703 U (46% women, 91% state res., 21% on fin. aid). Entrance difficulty: moderately difficult. Application deadline: 7/1. Contact: Mr. L. Robert Grogan, (704) 597-2115.

UNIVERSITY OF NORTH CAROLINA AT GREENSBORO

Greensboro 27412. Public; urban. Awards B, M, D. Enrolls 9,925 T, 7,082 U (69% women, 88% state res., 31% on fin. aid). Entrance difficulty: moderately difficult. Application deadlines: 8/10, early decision 10/10. Contact: Dr. Robert W. Hites, (919) 379-5243.

UNIVERSITY OF NORTH CAROLINA AT WILMINGTON

Wilmington 28401. Public; suburban. Awards A, B, M. Enrolls 4,258 T, 4,132 U (51% women, 94% state res., 31% on fin. aid). Entrance difficulty: less difficult. Application deadline: 8/15. Contact: Mrs. Dorothy P. Marshall, (919) 791-4330 Ext. 213.

WAKE FOREST UNIVERSITY

Winston-Salem 27109. Private; suburban. Awards B, M, D. Enrolls 3,386 T, 3,160 U (38% women, 47% state res., 40% on fin. aid). Entrance difficulty: very difficult. Application deadlines: 2/1, early decision 10/31. Contact: Mr. William G. Starling, (919) 761-5201.

WARREN WILSON COLLEGE

Swannanoa 28778. Private; rural. Awards B. Enrolls 527 T (55% women, 30% state res., 67% on fin. aid). Entrance difficulty: moderately difficult except for anesthesia program. Application deadline: 8/1. Contact: Mr. Robert B. Glass, (704) 298-3325.

WESTERN CAROLINA UNIVERSITY

Cullowhee 28723. Public; rural. Awards B, M. Enrolls 6,274 T, 5,350 U (48% women, 91% state res., 50% on fin. aid). Entrance difficulty: moderately difficult. Application deadline: 8/1. Contact: Mr. Tyree H. Kiser Jr, (704) 227-7317.

WINGATE COLLEGE

Wingate 28174. Private; small town. Awards C, A, B. Enrolls 1,501 T (47% women, 88% state res., 95% on fin. aid). Entrance difficulty: less difficult. Application deadlines: 8/15, early decision 12/31. Contact: Mr. William M. B. Fleming Jr, (704) 233-4061.

WINSTON-SALEM STATE UNIVERSITY

Winston-Salem 27102. Public; urban. Awards B. Enrolls 2,224 T (62% women, 91% state res., 91% on fin. aid). Entrance difficulty: less difficult. Application deadline: rolling. Contact: Mrs. Emily H. Harper, (919) 761-2070.

NORTH DAKOTA

DICKINSON STATE COLLEGE

Dickinson 58601. Public; small town. Awards C, A, B. Enrolls 1,062 T (55% women, 90% state res., 65% on fin. aid). Entrance difficulty: less difficult. Application deadline: 9/1. Contact: Mr. Richard A. Brown, Admissions Counselor.

JAMESTOWN COLLEGE

Jamestown 58401. Private; small town. Awards B. Enrolls 540 T (50% women, 55% state res., 85% on fin. aid). Entrance difficulty: moderately difficult. Application deadline: rolling. Contact: Mr. Dale R. Washburn, Assistant Director of Admissions, (701) 253-2562.

MARY COLLEGE

Bismarck 58501. Private; rural. Awards B. Enrolls 917 T (65% women, 92% state res., 75% on fin. aid). Entrance difficulty: moderately difficult. Application deadline: rolling. Contact: Mr. Leland D. Nagel, (701) 255-4681 Ext. 340.

MAYVILLE STATE COLLEGE

Mayville 58257. Public; small town. Awards C, A, B. Enrolls 746 T (66% women, 80% state res., 73% on fin. aid). Entrance difficulty: noncompetitive. Application deadline: 9/17. Contact: Mr. Larry A. Young, Director of Admissions, (701) 786-2301 Ext. 138.

MINOT STATE COLLEGE

Minot 58701. Public; small town. Awards C, A, B, M. Enrolls 2,443 T, 2,303 U (60% women, 92% state res., 75% on fin. aid). Entrance difficulty: noncompetitive. Application deadline: rolling. Contact: Mr. William Edwards, Registrar, (701) 857-3340.

NORTH DAKOTA STATE UNIVERSITY

Fargo 58102. Public; urban. Awards A, B, M, D. Enrolls 7,600 T, 6,882 U (43% women, 71% state res., 39% on fin. aid). Entrance difficulty: noncompetitive except for architecture, nursing, animal medical technology. Application deadline: rolling. Contact: Dr. George H. Wallman, (701) 237-8643.

NORTHWEST BIBLE COLLEGE

Minot 58701. Private; small town. Awards A, B. Enrolls 150 T (45% women, 32% state res., 80% on fin. aid). Entrance difficulty: noncompetitive. Application deadline: rolling. Contact: Mr. Calvin Eastham, Director of Admissions, (701) 852-3781.

UNIVERSITY OF NORTH DAKOTA

Grand Forks 58201. Public; rural. Awards A, B, M, D. Enrolls 9,705 T, 7,729 U (46% women, 80% state res., 65% on fin. aid). Contact: Miss Donna Bruce, Admissions Officer, (701) 777-3821.

VALLEY CITY STATE COLLEGE

Valley City 58072. Public; small town. Awards C, A, B. Enrolls 1,145 T (58% women, 93% state res., 70% on fin. aid). Entrance difficulty: noncompetitive. Application deadline: rolling. Contact: Mr. David A. Nelson, Director of Admissions and Records, (701) 845-7295.

OHIO

ANTIOCH COLLEGE

Yellow Springs 45387. Private; small town. Awards B. Enrolls 989 T (57% women, 12% state res., 57% on fin. aid). Entrance difficulty: moderately difficult. Contact: Mr. C. Robert Friedman, Associate Director of Admissions, (513) 767-7331.

ASHLAND COLLEGE

Ashland 44805. Private; small town. Awards C, A, B, M. Enrolls 2,598 T, 1,901 U (51% women, 75% state res., 52% on fin. aid). Entrance difficulty: moderately difficult. Application deadline: rolling. Contact: Mr. Carl Gerbasi, (419) 289-5079.

BALDWIN-WALLACE COLLEGE

Berea 44017. Private; suburban. Awards B, M. Enrolls 3,264 T, 2,656 U (49% women, 80% state res., 60% on fin. aid). Entrance difficulty: moderately difficult. Application deadline: rolling. Contact: Mr. John T. Amy, (216) 826-2222.

BLUFFTON COLLEGE

Bluffton 45817. Private; small town. Awards B. Enrolls 660 T (50% women, 90% state res., 75% on fin. aid). Entrance difficulty: moderately difficult. Application deadline: 8/15. Contact: Dr. Glenn Snyder, (419) 358-8015 Ext. 134.

BORROMEO COLLEGE OF OHIO

Wickliffe 44092. Private; suburban. Awards B. Enrolls 80 T (0% women, 90% state res., 55% on fin. aid). Entrance difficulty: moderately difficult. Application deadlines: 8/1, early decision 12/15. Contact: Rev. James F. Kramer, (216) 585-5900.

BOWLING GREEN STATE UNIVERSITY

Bowling Green 43403. Public; small town. Awards A, B, M, D. Enrolls 16,907 T, 14,868 U (58% women, 95% state res., 35% on fin. aid). Application deadline: rolling. Contact: Mr. John W. Martin, Director of Admissions, (419) 372-2086.

CAPITAL UNIVERSITY

Columbus 43209. Private; suburban. Awards B, M. Enrolls 2,625 T, 1,825 U (61% women, 87% state res., 70% on fin. aid). Entrance difficulty: moderately difficult. Application deadline: rolling. Contact: Miss Diane M. Kohlmeyer, Assistant Provost for Admissions, (614) 236-6101.

CASE WESTERN RESERVE UNIVERSITY

Cleveland 44106. Private; urban. Awards B, M, D. Enrolls 8,236 T, 3,158 U (34% women, 60% state res., 60% on fin. aid). Entrance difficulty: very difficult; most difficult for preprofessional Scholars Program in medicine. Application deadline: 3/15. Contact: Mr. N. Kip Howard, (216) 368-4450.

CEDARVILLE COLLEGE

Cedarville 45314. Private; small town. Awards B. Enrolls 1,185 T (52% women,

50% state res., 60% on fin. aid). Entrance difficulty: moderately difficult. Application deadline: rolling. Contact: Dr. L. Robert White, Registrar, (513) 766-2211.

CENTRAL STATE UNIVERSITY

Wilberforce 45384. Contact: Mrs. Edith W. Johnson, Director of Admissions.

CINCINNATI BIBLE COLLEGE

Cincinnati 45204. Private; urban. Awards C, A, B, M. Enrolls 666 T, 522 U (46% women, 55% state res.). Entrance difficulty: noncompetitive. Application deadline: 8/1. Contact: Dr. T. W. Mobley, (513) 471-4800.

CIRCLEVILLE BIBLE COLLEGE

Circleville 43113. Private; small town. Awards A, B. Enrolls 226 T (30% women, 65% state res.). Entrance difficulty: noncompetitive. Application deadline: rolling. Contact: Mr. Amos N. Henry, Registrar, (614) 474-8896.

CLEVELAND COLLEGE OF JEWISH STUDIES

Beachwood 44122. Private; suburban. Awards C, B, M. Enrolls 102 T, 84 U (72% women, 100% state res., 9% on fin. aid). Entrance difficulty: noncompetitive. Application deadline: 9/7. Contact: Mrs. Bea Stadtler, Registrar, (216) 464-4050.

CLEVELAND INSTITUTE OF ART

Cleveland 44106. Private; urban. Awards B. Enrolls 546 T (54% women, 74% state res., 51% on fin. aid). Entrance difficulty: moderately difficult. Application deadline: rolling. Contact: Catherine A. McLaughlin, Director of Admissions, (216) 421-4322.

CLEVELAND INSTITUTE OF MUSIC

Cleveland 44106. Private; urban. Awards B, M, D. Enrolls 253 T, 179 U (50% women, 25% state res., 66% on fin. aid). Entrance difficulty: very difficult. Application deadline: rolling. Contact: Mr. William Kurzban, (216) 791-5165.

CLEVELAND STATE UNIVERSITY

Cleveland 44115. Public; urban. Awards B, M, D. Enrolls 15,939 T, 12,396 U (43% women, 98% state res., 25% on fin. aid). Entrance difficulty: moderately difficult.

Application deadline: 9/10. Contact: Dr. Richard Dickerman, (216) 687-3755.

COLLEGE OF MOUNT ST JOSEPH ON-THE-OHIO

Mt St Joseph 45051. Private; suburban. Awards A, B, M. Enrolls 1,360 T, 1,311 U (96% women, 88% state res., 34% on fin. aid). Entrance difficulty: moderately difficult. Application deadline: rolling. Contact: Mr. Domenic N. Teti, (513) 244-4531.

COLLEGE OF WOOSTER

Wooster 44691. Private; small town. Awards B. Enrolls 1,760 T (48% women, 48% state res., 50% on fin. aid). Entrance difficulty: moderately difficult. Application deadline: rolling. Contact: Mr. A. Steven Graff, Director of Admissions Planning, (216) 264-1234 Ext. 323.

DEFIANCE COLLEGE

Defiance 43512. Private; small town. Awards A, B. Enrolls 800 T (48% women, 82% state res., 76% on fin. aid). Entrance difficulty: moderately difficult. Application deadline: rolling. Contact: Mr. Brian J. Lewis, (419) 784-4010.

DENISON UNIVERSITY

Granville 43023. Private; small town. Awards B. Enrolls 2,080 T (49% women, 26% state res., 21% on fin. aid). Entrance difficulty: moderately difficult. Application deadlines: 2/1, early decision 1/1. Contact: Mr. Richard F. Boyden, (614) 587-0810 Ext. 276.

DYKE COLLEGE

Cleveland 44114. Private; urban. Awards C, A, B. Enrolls 1,375 T (65% women, 98% state res., 85% on fin. aid). Entrance difficulty: moderately difficult. Application deadline: 9/1. Contact: Mr. Bruce T. Shields, (216) 696-9000 Ext. 48.

EDGECLIFF COLLEGE

Cincinnati 45206. Private; urban. Awards A, B. Enrolls 951 T (70% women, 75% state res., 55% on fin. aid). Entrance difficulty: moderately difficult. Application deadline: rolling. Contact: Miss Dawn Weiner, (513) 961-3770.

FINDLAY COLLEGE

Findlay 45840. Private; suburban. Awards A, B. Enrolls 926 T (54% women, 80% state res., 70% on fin. aid). Entrance difficulty: moderately difficult. Application deadline: rolling. Contact: Mr. Thomas S. Robinson, (419) 422-8313.

FRANKLIN UNIVERSITY

Columbus 43215. Private; urban. Awards A, B. Enrolls 4,214 T (50% women, 100% state res., 21% on fin. aid). Entrance difficulty: noncompetitive. Contact: Mr. Stuart B. Tennant, (614) 224-6237.

HEIDELBERG COLLEGE

Tiffin 44883. Private; small town. Awards B. Enrolls 790 T (50% women, 75% state res., 70% on fin. aid). Entrance difficulty: moderately difficult. Application deadline: 8/1. Contact: Ms. Anne Kear, (419) 448-2404.

HIRAM COLLEGE

Hiram 44234. Private; rural. Awards B. Enrolls 1,150 T (50% women, 66% state res., 70% on fin. aid). Entrance difficulty: moderately difficult. Application deadline: 8/15. Contact: Mr. John P. Pirozzi, Dean of Admissions, (216) 569-7964.

JOHN CARROLL UNIVERSITY

University Heights 44118. Private; suburban. Awards B, M. Enrolls 3,800 T, 3,133 U (40% women, 60% state res., 45% on fin. aid). Entrance difficulty: moderately difficult. Application deadline: 8/15. Contact: Mr. John P. Sammon, (216) 491-4294.

⟨ KENT STATE UNIVERSITY ⟩

Kent 44242. Public; small town. Awards B, M, D. Enrolls 17,796 T, 12,786 U (51% women, 93% state res., 62% on fin. aid). Entrance difficulty: noncompetitive except for some programs. Application deadline: 8/15. Contact: Mr. Bruce L. Riddle, (216) 672-2444.

KENYON COLLEGE

Gambier 43022. Private; rural. Awards B. Enrolls 1,445 T (44% women, 28% state res., 26% on fin. aid). Entrance difficulty: moderately difficult. Application deadlines: 3/1, early decision 12/1. Contact: Mr. John D. Kushan, (614) 427-2244.

LAKE ERIE COLLEGE

Painesville 44077. Private; suburban. Awards B, M. Enrolls 400 T (100% women, 50% state res., 48% on fin. aid). Entrance difficulty: moderately difficult. Contact: Miss Fran Cook, (216) 352-3361.

MALONE COLLEGE

Canton 44709. Private; suburban. Awards A, B. Enrolls 772 T (52% women, 89% state res., 80% on fin. aid). Entrance difficulty: moderately difficult. Application deadline: rolling. Contact: Mr. Scott Armstrong, (216) 489-0800.

MARIETTA COLLEGE

Marietta 45750. Private; small town. Awards B, M. Enrolls 1,488 T (36% women, 45% state res., 55% on fin. aid). Entrance difficulty: moderately difficult. Application deadline: rolling. Contact: Mr. Daniel J. Jones, (614) 373-4643.

MIAMI UNIVERSITY

Oxford 45056. Public; small town. Awards A, B, M, D. Enrolls 14,824 T, 12,828 U (51% women, 88% state res., 40% on fin. aid). Entrance difficulty: moderately difficult. Application deadline: 3/1. Contact: Mr. Charles R. Schuler, (513) 529-2531.

MOUNT UNION COLLEGE

Alliance 44601. Private; suburban. Awards B. Enrolls 1,020 T (44% women, 82% state res., 65% on fin. aid). Entrance difficulty: moderately difficult. Application deadline: 6/1. Contact: Mr. W. Edwin Seaver III, (216) 821-5320.

MOUNT VERNON NAZARENE COLLEGE

Mt Vernon 43050. Private; small town. Awards A, B. Enrolls 1,005 T (55% women, 75% state res., 70% on fin. aid). Entrance difficulty: noncompetitive. Application deadline: rolling. Contact: Miss Carolyn B. Learned, (614) 397-1244.

MUSKINGUM COLLEGE

New Concord 43762. Private; rural. Awards B. Enrolls 883 T (48% women, 80% state res., 56% on fin. aid). Entrance difficulty: moderately difficult. Application deadline: 8/1. Contact: Mr. Jay L. Leiendecker, (614) 826-8137.

NOTRE DAME COLLEGE OF OHIO

Cleveland 44121. Private; suburban. Awards A, B. Enrolls 604 T (100% women, 86% state res., 60% on fin. aid). Entrance difficulty: moderately difficult. Application deadline: 8/15. Contact: Mr. Frank L. Stephenson, Director of Admissions, (216) 381-1680.

OBERLIN COLLEGE

Oberlin 44074. Private; small town. Awards B, M. Enrolls 2,730 T, 2,724 U (52% women, 14% state res., 42% on fin. aid). Entrance difficulty: very difficult. Application deadlines: 2/15, early decision 2/1. Contact: Mr. Carl W. Bewig, (216) 775-8411.

OHIO DOMINICAN COLLEGE

Columbus 43219. Private; suburban. Awards A, B. Enrolls 849 T (63% women, 84% state res., 50% on fin. aid). Entrance difficulty: moderately difficult. Application deadline: 8/25. Contact: Sr. Thomas Albert Corbett, Director of Institutional Research.

OHIO INSTITUTE OF TECHNOLOGY

Columbus 43219. Private; urban. Awards A, B. Enrolls 2,327 T (6% women, 40% state res., 60% on fin. aid). Entrance difficulty: noncompetitive. Application deadline: 10/1. Contact: Mr. Louis Collins, (614) 253-7291.

OHIO NORTHERN UNIVERSITY

Ada 45810. Private; small town. Awards B. Enrolls 2,667 T, 2,174 U (40% women, 80% state res., 60% on fin. aid). Entrance difficulty: moderately difficult. Application deadline: 8/24. Contact: Mr. Ronald L. Knoble, (419) 634-9921.

⟨OHIO STATE UNIVERSITY⟩

Columbus 43210. Public; urban. Awards B, M, D. Enrolls 53,278 T, 40,715 U (46% women, 94% state res., 37% on fin. aid). Entrance difficulty: noncompetitive. Application deadline: 8/15. Contact: Dr. James J. Mager, (614) 422-3980.

OHIO STATE UNIVERSITY

Lima 45804. Public; small town. Awards A, B. Enrolls 851 T, 777 U (55% women, 99% state res., 30% on fin. aid). Entrance difficulty: noncompetitive. Application deadline: 8/15. Contact: Dr. Douglas E. Torrance, Coordinator of Admissions, (419) 228-2641.

OHIO STATE UNIVERSITY

Mansfield 44906. Public; small town. Awards A, B. Enrolls 1,143 T, 1,081 U (55% women, 99% state res., 17% on fin. aid). Entrance difficulty: noncompetitive. Application deadline: 8/15. Contact: Miss Margaret S. Warrick, Coordinator of Admissions, (419) 755-4011.

OHIO UNIVERSITY

Athens 45701. Public; small town. Awards C, A, B, M, D. Enrolls 13,853 T, 11,870 U (47% women, 80% state res., 46% on fin. aid). Entrance difficulty: noncompetitive. Application deadline: 5/1. Contact: Dr. James C. Walters, (614) 594-5174.

OHIO UNIVERSITY

Lancaster 43130. Public; suburban. Awards C, A, B, M. Enrolls 1,550 T, 1,450 U (50% women, 97% state res., 25% on fin. aid). Entrance difficulty: noncompetitive. Application deadline: rolling. Contact: Mr. Scott Shepherd, Director of Student Services, (614) 654-6711.

OHIO WESLEYAN UNIVERSITY

Delaware 43015. Private; small town. Awards B. Enrolls 2,250 T (47% women, 33% state res., 35% on fin. aid). Entrance difficulty: moderately difficult. Application deadlines: 3/1, early decision 11/1. Contact: Mr. Peter D. Feickert, Director of Admissions, (614) 369-4431 Ext. 550.

OTTERBEIN COLLEGE

Westerville 43081. Private; suburban. Awards A, B. Enrolls 1,687 T (51% women, 85% state res., 60% on fin. aid). Entrance difficulty: moderately difficult. Application deadline: rolling. Contact: Mr. Morris F. Briggs, Dean of Admissions, (614) 890-3000 Ext. 655.

PONTIFICAL COLLEGE JOSEPHINUM

Columbus 43085. Private; urban. Awards B, M. Enrolls 163 T, 80 U (1% women, 56% state res., 95% on fin. aid). Entrance difficulty: moderately difficult. Application deadline: rolling. Contact: Rev. Terence O'Shaughnessy, OP, Admissions Officer, (614) 885-5585.

RIO GRANDE COLLEGE/COMMUNITY COLLEGE

Rio Grande 45674. Private; rural. Awards C, A, B. Enrolls 1,144 T (54% women, 75% state res., 65% on fin. aid). Entrance difficulty: noncompetitive. Application deadline: rolling. Contact: Mr. Dean S. Brown, Director of Admissions and Records, (614) 245-5353.

TIFFIN UNIVERSITY

Tiffin 44883. Private; small town. Awards A, B. Enrolls 395 T (38% women, 97% state res., 66% on fin. aid). Entrance difficulty: noncompetitive. Application deadline: rolling. Contact: Mr. Thomas R. Moore, Admissions Coordinator, (419) 447-6442.

UNION FOR EXPERIMENTING COLLEGES AND UNIVERSITIES

Cincinnati 45201. Private; urban. Awards B, D. Enrolls 673 T, 196 U (70% women, 100% state res., 85% on fin. aid). Entrance difficulty: moderately difficult. Application deadline: rolling. Contact: Mr. Marcus L. Casbeer, Assistant Dean of Academic Services.

UNIVERSITY OF AKRON

Akron 44304. Public; urban. Awards C, A, B, M, D. Enrolls 23,364 T, 19,090 U (50% women, 98% state res., 45% on fin. aid). Entrance difficulty: noncompetitive. Application deadline: rolling. Contact: Mr. John W. Owen, (216) 375-7100.

UNIVERSITY OF CINCINNATI

Cincinnati 45221. Public; urban. Awards C, A, B, M, D. Enrolls 39,071 T, 32,836 U (47% women, 86% state res., 55% on fin. aid). Entrance difficulty: moderately difficult; noncompetitive for 2-year programs. Application deadline: rolling. Contact: Mr. Robert W. Neel, (513) 475-3420.

UNIVERSITY OF CINCINNATI, OHIO COLLEGE OF APPLIED SCIENCE

Cincinnati 45210.

UNIVERSITY OF DAYTON

Dayton 45469. Private; suburban. Awards A, B, M, D. Enrolls 9,611 T, 6,158 U (40% women, 59% state res., 70% on fin. aid). Entrance difficulty: moderately difficult; very difficult for engineering. Application deadline: rolling. Contact: Mr. Myron Achbach, (513) 229-4411.

UNIVERSITY OF STEUBENVILLE

Steubenville 43952. Private; small town. Awards A, B. Enrolls 900 T (56% women, 45% state res., 74% on fin. aid). Entrance difficulty: moderately difficult. Application deadline: rolling. Contact: Mr. John G. Burt, (614) 283-3771.

UNIVERSITY OF TOLEDO

Toledo 43606. Public; suburban. Awards C, A, B, M, D. Enrolls 17,257 T, 14,505 U (49% women, 95% state res., 45% on fin. aid). Entrance difficulty: noncompetitive. Application deadline: rolling. Contact: Mr. Richard J. Eastop, (419) 537-2696.

URBANA COLLEGE

Urbana 43078. Private; small town. Awards A, B. Enrolls 750 T (35% women, 95% state res., 64% on fin. aid). Entrance difficulty: less difficult. Application deadline: rolling. Contact: Mr. William Riska, (513) 652-1301.

URSULINE COLLEGE

Pepper Pike 44124. Private; suburban. Awards A, B. Enrolls 840 T (97% women, 95% state res., 65% on fin. aid). Entrance difficulty: moderately difficult. Application deadline: 8/28. Contact: August A. Napoli, Director of Admissions, (216) 449-4200.

WALSH COLLEGE

North Canton 44720. Private; suburban. Awards A, B. Enrolls 690 T (52% women, 90% state res., 75% on fin. aid). Entrance difficulty: moderately difficult. Application deadline: 8/15. Contact: Mr. John Latchic, Assistant to the Director of Admissions, (216) 499-7090 Ext. 56.

WILBERFORCE UNIVERSITY

Wilberforce 45384. Private; rural. Awards B. Enrolls 1,112 T (49% women, 31% state res., 95% on fin. aid). Entrance difficulty: less difficult. Application deadline: 6/1. Contact: Mr. Theodore Sherron, (513) 376-2911.

WILMINGTON COLLEGE

Wilmington 45177. Private; rural. Awards B. Enrolls 750 T (38% women, 65% state res., 75% on fin. aid). Entrance difficulty: moderately difficult. Application deadline: rolling. Contact: Miss Leslie S. Clark, (513) 382-6661 Ext. 260.

WITTENBERG UNIVERSITY

Springfield 45501. Private; suburban. Awards B, M. Enrolls 2,270 T (52% women, 60% state res., 40% on fin. aid). Entrance difficulty: moderately difficult. Application deadline: rolling. Contact: Mr. Kenneth G. Benne, (513) 327-6314.

WRIGHT STATE UNIVERSITY

Dayton 45435. Public; suburban. Awards A, B, M, D. Enrolls 14,735 T, 11,218 U (56% women, 97% state res., 12% on fin. aid). Entrance difficulty: noncompetitive. Application deadline: 9/1. Contact: Mr. Ken Davenport, (513) 873-2211.

WRIGHT STATE UNIVERSITY, PIQUA CENTER

Piqua 45356. Public; small town. Awards B, M. Enrolls Contact: Mr. J. Gatton, Director, (513) 773-4471.

XAVIER UNIVERSITY

Cincinnati 45207. Private; suburban. Awards A, B, M. Enrolls 6,643 T, 3,144 U (39% women, 80% state res., 60% on fin. aid). Entrance difficulty: moderately difficult. Application deadline: rolling. Contact: Mr. Rene A. Durand Jr, (513) 745-3301.

YOUNGSTOWN STATE UNIVERSITY

Youngstown 44555. Public; urban. Awards C, A, B, M. Enrolls 15,303 T, 13,736 U (47% women, 91% state res., 25% on fin. aid). Entrance difficulty: moderately difficult. Application deadline: 8/15. Contact: Mr. William Livosky, (216) 742-3150.

OKLAHOMA

BARTLESVILLE WESLEYAN COLLEGE

Bartlesville 74003. Private; suburban. Awards A, B. Enrolls 662 T (59% women, 51% state res.). Entrance difficulty: non-competitive. Application deadline: rolling. Contact: Mr. Wendell O. Rovenstine, Director of Public Relations/Recruitment, (918) 333-6151 Ext. 218.

BETHANY NAZARENE COLLEGE

Bethany 73008. Private; suburban. Awards A, B, M. Enrolls 1,339 T, 1,277 U (51% women, 30% state res., 60% on fin. aid). Entrance difficulty: noncompetitive. Application deadline: rolling. Contact: Mr. Vernon A. Snowbarger, (405) 789-6400.

CAMERON UNIVERSITY

Lawton 73501. Public; urban. Awards A, B. Enrolls 4,712 T (46% women, 99% state res., 40% on fin. aid). Entrance difficulty: less difficult. Application deadline: rolling. Contact: Mr. Raymond Chapman, Director of Admissions and Records, (405) 248-2200 Ext. 230.

CENTRAL STATE UNIVERSITY

Edmond 73034. Public; suburban. Awards C, B, M. Enrolls 11,876 T, 8,518 U (54% women, 95% state res., 30% on fin. aid). Entrance difficulty: noncompetitive. Application deadline: 9/10. Contact: Dr. Barbara J. Ryan, Director, Office of Institutional Research, (405) 341-2980 Ext. 516.

EAST CENTRAL OKLAHOMA STATE UNIVERSITY

Ada 74820. Public; suburban. Awards C, B, M. Enrolls 3,882 T, 3,517 U (57% women, 91% state res., 60% on fin. aid). Entrance difficulty: less difficult. Application deadline: 8/25. Contact: Mrs. Merle Boatwright, Registrar, (405) 332-8000.

HILLSDALE FREE WILL BAPTIST COLLEGE

Moore 73160. Private; suburban. Awards A, B. Enrolls 150 T (45% women, 59% state res., 67% on fin. aid). Entrance difficulty: noncompetitive. Application deadline: 9/1. Contact: Mr. Dan C. Arnold, Registrar, (405) 794-6661.

LANGSTON UNIVERSITY

Langston 73050. Public; small town. Awards C, A, B. Enrolls 1,087 T (47% women, 60% state res., 89% on fin. aid). Entrance difficulty: noncompetitive. Application deadline: rolling. Contact: Mr. Raymond E. Parker, (405) 466-2231 Ext. 214.

NORTHEASTERN OKLAHOMA STATE UNIVERSITY

Tahlequah 74464. Public; small town. Awards C, B, M. Enrolls 5,281 T, 4,323 U (54% women, 96% state res., 82% on fin. aid). Entrance difficulty: less difficult. Application deadline: 8/1. Contact: Mr. James A. Watkins, (918) 456-5511.

NORTHWESTERN OKLAHOMA STATE UNIVERSITY

Alva 73717. Public; small town. Awards B, M. Enrolls 2,180 T, 1,721 U (52% women, 92% state res.). Entrance difficulty: moderately difficult. Application deadline: rolling. Contact: Mrs. Doris Blue, Registrar, (405) 327-1700 Ext. 331.

OKLAHOMA BAPTIST UNIVERSITY

Shawnee 74801. Private; small town. Awards C, B. Enrolls 1,531 T (54% women, 69% state res., 89% on fin. aid). Entrance difficulty: moderately difficult except for Upward Bound. Application deadline: 8/1. Contact: Mr. Larry Smith, (405) 275-2850 Ext. 234.

OKLAHOMA CHRISTIAN COLLEGE

Oklahoma City 73111. Private; suburban. Awards B. Enrolls 1,522 T (55% women, 44% state res., 78% on fin. aid). Entrance difficulty: noncompetitive. Application deadline: rolling. Contact: Mr. Bob D. Smith, Dean of Admissions and Registrar, (405) 478-1661 Ext. 200.

OKLAHOMA CITY SOUTHWESTERN COLLEGE

Oklahoma City 73127. Private; urban. Awards A, B. Enrolls 824 T (27% women, 60% on fin. aid). Entrance difficulty: noncompetitive. Application deadline: rolling. Contact: Miss Liz Murray, Registrar, (405) 947-2331.

OKLAHOMA CITY UNIVERSITY

Oklahoma City 73106. Private; urban. Awards B, M. Enrolls 2,712 T, 1,496 U (50% women, 95% state res., 70% on fin. aid). Entrance difficulty: moderately difficult. Application deadline: 8/1. Contact: Dr. Kenneth Doake, (405) 521-5050.

OKLAHOMA PANHANDLE STATE UNIVERSITY

Goodwell 73939. Public; rural. Awards C, B. Enrolls 1,041 T (47% women, 80% state res., 35% on fin. aid). Entrance difficulty: noncompetitive. Application deadline: rolling. Contact: Mr. Jack V. Begley, Registrar, (405) 349-2611.

OKLAHOMA STATE UNIVERSITY

Stillwater 74074. Public; small town. Awards C, A, B, M, D. Enrolls 22,003 T, 18,714 U (42% women, 90% state res., 25% on fin. aid). Entrance difficulty: moderately difficult. Application deadline: rolling. Contact: Mr. Raymond Girod, Registrar, (405) 624-6857.

ORAL ROBERTS UNIVERSITY

Tulsa 74171. Private; suburban. Awards C, B, M. Enrolls 4,001 T, 3,880 U (50% women, 19% state res., 50% on fin. aid). Entrance difficulty: moderately difficult. Application deadline: rolling. Contact: Mr. Jim Cameron, (918) 492-6161.

PHILLIPS UNIVERSITY

Enid 73701. Private; small town. Awards A, B, M, D. Enrolls 1,284 T, 947 U (55% women, 30% state res., 65% on fin. aid). Entrance difficulty: moderately difficult. Application deadline: rolling. Contact: Mr. Rick Ziegler, (405) 237-4433.

SOUTHEASTERN OKLAHOMA STATE UNIVERSITY

Durant 74701. Public; small town. Awards C, B, M. Enrolls 4,391 T, 3,972 U (45% women, 85% state res., 50% on fin. aid). Entrance difficulty: less difficult. Application deadline: 8/15. Contact: Mrs. Lisa Kutait, (405) 924-0121 Ext. 264.

SOUTHWESTERN OKLAHOMA STATE UNIVERSITY

Weatherford 73096. Public; small town. Awards C, B, M. Enrolls 4,800 T, 4,143 U (52% women, 87% state res., 53% on fin. aid). Entrance difficulty: moderately difficult. Application deadline: 8/25. Contact: Mr. Bob Klaassen, (405) 772-6611 Ext. 5221.

UNIVERSITY OF OKLAHOMA

Norman 73019. Public; small town. Awards B, M, D. Enrolls 21,090 T, 16,252 U (41%

women, 85% state res., 28% on fin. aid).
Entrance difficulty: less difficult. Application deadline: rolling. Contact: Mr. Kenneth Conklin, Director, High School and College Relations, (405) 325-2151.

UNIVERSITY OF SCIENCE AND ARTS OF OKLAHOMA

Chickasha 73018. Public; small town. Awards B. Enrolls 1,289 T (57% women, 90% state res., 48% on fin. aid). Entrance difficulty: moderately difficult. Application deadline: rolling. Contact: Mr. Jack Hudson, Director of Admissions, (405) 224-3140.

UNIVERSITY OF TULSA

Tulsa 74104. Private; urban. Awards B, M, D. Enrolls 5,644 T, 4,592 U (47% women, 70% state res., 75% on fin. aid). Entrance difficulty: moderately difficult. Contact: Miss Sharon Mossberger, (918) 939-6351.

OREGON

COLEGIO CESAR CHAVEZ

Mount Angel 97362.

COLUMBIA CHRISTIAN COLLEGE

Portland 97220. Private; urban. Awards C, A, B. Enrolls 325 T (44% women, 34% state res., 64% on fin. aid). Entrance difficulty: noncompetitive. Application deadline: 9/15. Contact: Mr. Paul King, (503) 255-7060.

CONCORDIA COLLEGE

Portland 97211. Private; urban. Awards A, B. Enrolls 313 T (50% women, 40% state res., 85% on fin. aid). Entrance difficulty: moderately difficult. Application deadline: rolling. Contact: Mr. Stephen P. Dinger, Director of Admissions, (503) 288-9371.

EASTERN OREGON STATE COLLEGE

La Grande 97850. Public; small town. Awards A, B, M. Enrolls 1,591 T, 1,490 U (50% women, 80% state res., 50% on fin. aid). Entrance difficulty: less difficult. Application deadline: rolling. Contact: Ms. Sandra Downing, (503) 963-2171 Ext. 393.

GEORGE FOX COLLEGE

Newberg 97132. Private; small town. Awards B. Enrolls 734 T (56% women, 70% state res., 75% on fin. aid). Entrance difficulty: moderately difficult. Application deadline: rolling. Contact: Mr. James E. Settle, (503) 538-8383.

JUDSON BAPTIST COLLEGE

The Dalles 97058. Private; small town. Awards A, B. Enrolls 219 T (52% women, 64% state res., 85% on fin. aid). Entrance difficulty: moderately difficult. Application deadline: 9/5. Contact: Mr. Richard Ellsworth, Admissions Counselor, (503) 252-5563.

LEWIS AND CLARK COLLEGE

Portland 97219. Private; suburban. Awards B, M. Enrolls 3,085 T, 1,887 U (54% women, 42% state res., 34% on fin. aid). Entrance difficulty: moderately difficult. Application deadlines: 3/1, early decision 12/15. Contact: Mr. Robert H. Loeb III, Dean of Admissions, (503) 244-6161 Ext. 240.

LINFIELD COLLEGE

McMinnville 97128. Private; small town. Awards B, M. Enrolls 1,109 T, 1,072 U (40% women, 50% state res., 72% on fin. aid). Entrance difficulty: moderately difficult. Application deadlines: 1/15, early decision 11/30. Contact: Mr. Thomas Meicho, Dean of Admissions, (503) 472-4121 Ext. 213.

MARYLHURST EDUCATION CENTER

Marylhurst 97036. Private; suburban. Awards B. Enrolls 526 T (66% women, 97% state res., 49% on fin. aid). Entrance difficulty: noncompetitive. Application deadline: rolling. Contact: Miss Nancy Rich, (503) 636-8141 Ext. 26.

MOUNT ANGEL SEMINARY

St Benedict 97373. Private; rural. Awards B, M. Enrolls 114 T, 41 U (6% women, 70% state res., 55% on fin. aid). Entrance difficulty: moderately difficult. Application deadline: 8/1. Contact: Rev. James Ribble, (503) 845-3327.

MULTNOMAH SCHOOL OF THE BIBLE

Portland 97220. Private; urban. Awards C, B, M. Enrolls 736 T, 619 U (42% women, 30% state res.). Entrance difficulty: moderately difficult. Application deadline: 8/15. Contact: Miss Joyce L. Kehoe, Registrar, (503) 255-0332 Ext. 371.

MUSEUM ART SCHOOL

Portland 97205. Private; urban. Awards B. Enrolls 175 T (65% women, 60% state res., 50% on fin. aid). Application deadline: 5/15. Contact: Ms. Beverly Eppick, Assistant to the Dean.

NORTHWEST CHRISTIAN COLLEGE

Eugene 97401. Private; urban. Awards A, B. Enrolls 382 T (45% women, 35% state res., 75% on fin. aid). Entrance difficulty: noncompetitive. Application deadline: rolling. Contact: Mr. Dorral E. Campbell, (503) 343-1641.

OREGON COLLEGE OF EDUCATION

Monmouth 97361. Public; small town. Awards B, M. Enrolls 3,070 T, 2,290 U (55% women, 66% state res., 70% on fin. aid). Entrance difficulty: less difficult. Application deadline: 9/29. Contact: Dr. Marcelene Ling, (503) 838-1220.

OREGON INSTITUTE OF TECHNOLOGY

Klamath Falls 97601. Public; small town. Awards C, A, B. Enrolls 2,195 T (32% women, 87% state res., 25% on fin. aid). Application deadline: rolling. Contact: Mr. Alfred Roberson, (503) 882-6321.

OREGON STATE UNIVERSITY

Corvallis 97331. Public; small town. Awards B, M, D. Enrolls 17,181 T, 14,312 U (40% women, 86% state res., 40% on fin. aid). Entrance difficulty: moderately difficult. Application deadline: 8/15. Contact: Mr. Wallace E. Gibbs, Director of Admissions and Registrar, (503) 754-4331.

PACIFIC UNIVERSITY

Forest Grove 97116. Private; small town. Awards B, M. Enrolls 1,091 T, 889 U (41% women, 35% state res., 55% on fin. aid). Entrance difficulty: moderately difficult.

Application deadline: rolling. Contact: Mr. Paul B. Ranslow, (503) 357-6151.

PORTLAND STATE UNIVERSITY

Portland 97207. Public; urban. Awards C, B, M, D. Enrolls 16,841 T, 12,061 U (51% women, 89% state res., 32% on fin. aid). Entrance difficulty: moderately difficult. Application deadline: 9/15. Contact: Miss Eileen Rose, (503) 229-3511.

REED COLLEGE

Portland 97202. Private; suburban. Awards B, M. Enrolls 1,154 T, 1,139 U (41% women, 20% state res., 50% on fin. aid). Entrance difficulty: very difficult. Application deadlines: 3/1, early decision 11/1. Contact: Miss Ann V. York, Dean of Admissions, (503) 771-1112.

SOUTHERN OREGON STATE COLLEGE

Ashland 97520. Public; small town. Awards A, B, M. Enrolls 4,505 T, 4,177 U (53% women, 90% state res., 40% on fin. aid). Entrance difficulty: less difficult. Application deadline: rolling. Contact: Mr. Allen H. Blaszak, (503) 482-6411.

UNIVERSITY OF OREGON

Eugene 97403. Public; small town. Awards C, B, M, D. Enrolls 16,916 T, 12,534 U (48% women, 76% state res., 50% on fin. aid). Entrance difficulty: moderately difficult. Application deadline: rolling. Contact: Mr. James R. Buch, (503) 686-3201.

UNIVERSITY OF PORTLAND

Portland 97203. Private; urban. Awards B, M. Enrolls 2,708 T, 2,165 U (48% women, 40% state res., 65% on fin. aid). Entrance difficulty: moderately difficult. Application deadline: 8/15. Contact: Mr. Daniel B. Reilly, (503) 283-7147.

WARNER PACIFIC COLLEGE

Portland 97215. Private; urban. Awards A, B, M. Enrolls 420 T, 409 U (50% women, 49% state res., 75% on fin. aid). Entrance difficulty: moderately difficult. Application deadline: rolling. Contact: Mr. Mark Deffenbacher, Dean of Students, (503) 775-4366 Ext. 37.

WESTERN BAPTIST COLLEGE

Salem 97302. Private; small town. Awards A, B. Enrolls 394 T (50% women, 33% state res., 60% on fin. aid). Entrance difficulty: less difficult. Application deadline: 8/15. Contact: Mrs. Rita A. Wright, Registrar, (503) 581-8600.

WESTERN STATES CHIROPRACTIC COLLEGE

Portland 97230.

WILLAMETTE UNIVERSITY

Salem 97301. Private; small town. Awards B, M. Enrolls 1,829 T, 1,281 U (47% women, 49% state res., 53% on fin. aid). Entrance difficulty: moderately difficult. Application deadlines: rolling, early decision 12/15. Contact: Mr. Franklin Meyer, (503) 370-6303.

PENNSYLVANIA

ACADEMY OF THE NEW CHURCH

Bryn Athyn 19009. Private; suburban. Awards A, B. Enrolls 149 T (52% women, 42% state res., 51% on fin. aid). Entrance difficulty: noncompetitive. Application deadline: rolling. Contact: Dr. Robert W. Gladish, Dean, (215) 947-4200 Ext. 43.

ALBRIGHT COLLEGE

Reading 19604. Private; suburban. Awards B. Enrolls 1,275 T (51% women, 60% state res., 60% on fin. aid). Entrance difficulty: very difficult. Application deadlines: 3/15, early decision 11/1. Contact: Mrs. Susan Hutchinson-Jones, Admissions Counselor, (215) 921-2381.

ALLEGHENY COLLEGE

Meadville 16335. Private; small town. Awards B, M. Enrolls 1,870 T, 1,850 U (48% women, 50% state res., 43% on fin. aid). Entrance difficulty: very difficult. Application deadlines: 3/1, early decision 12/31. Contact: Mr. Richard A. Stewart, (814) 724-4351.

ALLENTOWN COLLEGE OF ST FRANCIS DE SALES

Center Valley 18034. Private; rural. Awards C, B. Enrolls 600 T (51% women, 70% state res., 70% on fin. aid). Entrance difficulty: moderately difficult. Application deadline: rolling. Contact: Rev. David Voellinger, Director of Admissions, (215) 282-1100.

ALLIANCE COLLEGE

Cambridge Springs 16403. Private; rural. Awards C, A, B. Enrolls 251 T (37% women, 53% state res., 80% on fin. aid). Entrance difficulty: less difficult. Application deadline: rolling. Contact: Mr. Paul A. Simpson, Director of Admissions, (814) 398-4611.

ALVERNIA COLLEGE

Reading 19607. Private; suburban. Awards A, B. Enrolls 750 T (50% women, 60% state res., 80% on fin. aid). Entrance difficulty: moderately difficult. Application deadline: rolling. Contact: Mr. Craig G. Neff, (215) 777-5411.

BAPTIST BIBLE COLLEGE OF PENNSYLVANIA

Clarks Summit 18411. Private; suburban. Awards C, A, B. Enrolls 780 T (50% women, 8% state res., 40% on fin. aid). Entrance difficulty: moderately difficult. Application deadline: 8/1. Contact: Mr. Leonard Vanderveld Jr, Director of Admissions, (717) 587-1172 Ext. 317.

BEAVER COLLEGE

Glenside 19038. Private; suburban. Awards A, B, M. Enrolls 1,925 T, 994 U (81% women, 69% state res., 49% on fin. aid). Entrance difficulty: moderately difficult. Application deadline: 8/1. Contact: Mr. T. Edwards Townsley, Dean of Admissions, (215) 572-0132.

BLOOMSBURG STATE COLLEGE

Bloomsburg 17815. Public; small town. Awards A, B, M. Enrolls 6,532 T, 5,803 U (59% women, 94% state res., 70% on fin. aid). Entrance difficulty: moderately difficult; very difficult for nursing. Application deadline: rolling. Contact: Mr. Thomas L. Cooper, (717) 389-3316.

BRYN MAWR COLLEGE

Bryn Mawr 19010. Private; suburban. Awards B, M, D. Enrolls 1,550 T, 1,026 U (100% women, 12% state res., 43% on fin. aid). Entrance difficulty: most difficult. Ap-

Bryn Mawr College (continued)
plication deadlines: 2/1, early decision 11/15. Contact: Miss Elizabeth G. Vermey, (215) 645-5152.

BUCKNELL UNIVERSITY

Lewisburg 17837. Private; small town. Awards B, M. Enrolls 3,210 T, 3,084 U (46% women, 35% state res., 25% on fin. aid). Entrance difficulty: very difficult. Application deadlines: 1/1, early decision 12/1. Contact: Mr. Richard C. Skelton, Director of Admissions, (717) 524-1101.

CABRINI COLLEGE

Radnor 19087. Private; suburban. Awards B. Enrolls 515 T (80% women, 75% state res., 80% on fin. aid). Entrance difficulty: moderately difficult. Application deadlines: rolling, early decision 11/15. Contact: Mrs. Estelle T. Oristaglio, (215) 687-2100.

CALIFORNIA STATE COLLEGE

California 15419. Public; small town. Awards A, B, M. Enrolls 4,250 T, 975 U (47% women, 98% state res., 70% on fin. aid). Entrance difficulty: moderately difficult. Application deadline: 8/30. Contact: Mr. Richard H. Webb, Director of Admissions, (412) 938-4404.

CARLOW COLLEGE

Pittsburgh 15213. Private; urban. Awards B. Enrolls 792 T (97% women, 91% state res., 80% on fin. aid). Entrance difficulty: moderately difficult. Application deadline: 8/15. Contact: Mr. John P. Hine Jr, Director of Admissions, (412) 578-6059.

CARNEGIE-MELLON UNIVERSITY

Pittsburgh 15213. Private; urban. Awards B, M, D. Enrolls 5,351 T, 3,880 U (35% women, 45% state res., 65% on fin. aid). Entrance difficulty: very difficult. Application deadlines: 3/1, early decision 11/1. Contact: Dr. William F. Elliott, Vice Provost for Enrollment Planning, (412) 578-2082.

CEDAR CREST COLLEGE

Allentown 18104. Private; suburban. Awards B. Enrolls 1,013 T (98% women, 65% state res., 50% on fin. aid). Entrance difficulty: moderately difficult. Application deadline: rolling. Contact: Mrs. Robin M. Huss, (215) 437-4471.

CHATHAM COLLEGE

Pittsburgh 15232. Private; urban. Awards B. Enrolls 615 T (100% women, 60% state res., 62% on fin. aid). Entrance difficulty: moderately difficult. Application deadline: rolling. Contact: Miss Marilyn Kimball, (412) 441-8200 Ext. 420.

CHESTNUT HILL COLLEGE

Philadelphia 19118. Private; urban. Awards B, M. Enrolls 650 T (65% on fin. aid). Application deadline: 5/1. Contact: Sr. Roberta Archibald, SSJ, Director of Admissions, (215) 248-7004.

CHEYNEY STATE COLLEGE

Cheyney 19319. Public; rural. Awards B, M. Enrolls 2,500 T, 2,300 U (51% women, 82% state res., 80% on fin. aid). Entrance difficulty: moderately difficult. Application deadline: 5/1. Contact: Mr. Christopher M. Roulhac, (215) 758-2275.

CLARION STATE COLLEGE

Clarion 16214. Public; small town. Awards A, B, M. Enrolls 5,100 T, 4,900 U (52% women, 85% state res., 65% on fin. aid). Entrance difficulty: moderately difficult. Application deadlines: 5/1, early decision 12/1. Contact: Mr. John S. Shropshire, (814) 226-2306.

COLLEGE MISERICORDIA

Dallas 18612. Private; suburban. Awards C, A, B, M. Enrolls 1,043 T (90% women, 80% state res., 80% on fin. aid). Entrance difficulty: moderately difficult. Application deadlines: rolling, early decision 9/1. Contact: Mr. David M. Payne, Director of Admissions, (717) 675-4449.

COMBS COLLEGE OF MUSIC

Philadelphia 19119. Private; urban. Awards B, M, D. Enrolls 98 T, 91 U (40% women, 70% state res., 50% on fin. aid). Entrance difficulty: moderately difficult. Application deadline: 6/1. Contact: Mrs. Sara E. Lelar, (215) 951-2250.

DELAWARE VALLEY COLLEGE OF SCIENCE AND AGRICULTURE

Doylestown 18901. Private; rural. Awards B. Enrolls 1,428 T (35% women, 65% state res., 67% on fin. aid). Entrance difficulty: moderately difficult; less difficult for business administration programs. Application deadline: rolling. Contact: Mr. H. William Craver, (215) 345-1500.

DICKINSON COLLEGE

Carlisle 17013. Private; small town. Awards B. Enrolls 1,650 T (51% women, 40% state res., 30% on fin. aid). Entrance difficulty: very difficult. Application deadlines: 3/1, early decision 12/15. Contact: Mr. J. Larry Mench, (717) 245-1231.

DREXEL UNIVERSITY

Philadelphia 19104. Private; urban. Awards B, M, D. Enrolls 11,153 T, 6,577 U (28% women, 65% state res., 70% on fin. aid). Entrance difficulty: moderately difficult. Application deadlines: 4/1, early decision 12/1. Contact: Mr. John R. McCullough, Dean of Admissions, (215) 895-2400.

DUQUESNE UNIVERSITY

Pittsburgh 15219. Private; urban. Awards B, M, D. Enrolls 7,188 T, 4,530 U (50% women, 85% state res., 70% on fin. aid). Entrance difficulty: moderately difficult. Application deadline: rolling. Contact: Mr. Frederick H. Lorensen, (412) 434-6220.

EASTERN COLLEGE

St Davids 19087. Private; suburban. Awards B. Enrolls 708 T (66% women, 68% state res., 70% on fin. aid). Entrance difficulty: moderately difficult. Application deadline: 8/15. Contact: Mr. David R. McBride, (215) 688-3300.

EAST STROUDSBURG STATE COLLEGE

East Stroudsburg 18301. Public; small town. Awards A, B, M. Enrolls 3,890 T, 3,568 U (56% women, 81% state res., 65% on fin. aid). Entrance difficulty: moderately difficult. Application deadline: rolling. Contact: Mr. Alan T. Chesterton, (717) 424-3542.

EDINBORO STATE COLLEGE

Edinboro 16444. Public; small town. Awards C, A, B, M. Enrolls 5,596 T, 4,556 U (53% women, 92% state res., 73% on fin. aid). Entrance difficulty: moderately difficult; very difficult for nursing program. Application deadline: rolling. Contact: Mr. Harold O. Umbarger, Dean of Admissions.

ELIZABETHTOWN COLLEGE

Elizabethtown 17022. Private; small town. Awards A, B. Enrolls 1,466 T (58% women, 68% state res., 60% on fin. aid). Entrance difficulty: moderately difficult; very difficult for occupational therapy. Application deadline: 4/1. Contact: Mr. Kevin J. Manning, (717) 367-1151.

FRANKLIN AND MARSHALL COLLEGE

Lancaster 17604. Private; small town. Awards B. Enrolls 2,094 T (40% women, 30% state res., 65% on fin. aid). Entrance difficulty: very difficult. Application deadlines: 2/9, early decision 12/1. Contact: Mr. Ronald D. Potier, (717) 291-3951.

GANNON UNIVERSITY

Erie 16541. Private; urban. Awards C, A, B, M. Enrolls 3,900 T, 3,200 U (40% women, 89% state res., 85% on fin. aid). Entrance difficulty: moderately difficult except for family medicine program. Application deadline: rolling. Contact: Mr. Richard E. Sukitsch, (814) 871-7240.

GENEVA COLLEGE

Beaver Falls 15010. Private; suburban. Awards A, B. Enrolls 1,500 T (45% women, 64% state res., 80% on fin. aid). Entrance difficulty: moderately difficult. Application deadline: rolling. Contact: Mr. Paul Sutcliffe, (412) 843-2400.

GETTYSBURG COLLEGE

Gettysburg 17325. Private; small town. Awards B. Enrolls 1,900 T (48% women, 30% state res., 28% on fin. aid). Entrance difficulty: moderately difficult. Application deadlines: 2/15, early decision 11/15. Contact: Mr. Delwin K. Gustafson, (717) 334-3131.

GRATZ COLLEGE

Philadelphia 19141. Private; urban. Awards B, M. Enrolls 165 T, 142 U (50% women, 95% state res., 50% on fin. aid). Entrance difficulty: moderately difficult. Application deadline: 9/15. Contact: Dr. Saul P. Wachs, Dean of Admissions, (215) 329-3363.

GROVE CITY COLLEGE

Grove City 16127. Private; small town. Awards B. Enrolls 2,211 T (47% women, 72% state res., 19% on fin. aid). Entrance

Grove City College (continued)
difficulty: moderately difficult. Application deadlines: rolling, early decision 11/1. Contact: Mr. John H. Moser, (412) 458-6600 Ext. 217.

GWYNEDD-MERCY COLLEGE

Gwynedd Valley 19437. Private; suburban. Awards C, A, B. Enrolls 1,573 T (94% women, 90% state res., 68% on fin. aid). Entrance difficulty: moderately difficult; very difficult for nursing and allied health programs. Application deadline: rolling. Contact: Sr. Helen Cahill, (215) 646-8632.

HAVERFORD COLLEGE

Haverford 19041. Private; suburban. Awards B. Enrolls 985 T (3% women, 19% state res., 40% on fin. aid). Entrance difficulty: very difficult. Application deadlines: 1/31, early decision 11/15. Contact: Mr. William W. Ambler, (215) 649-4950.

HOLY FAMILY COLLEGE

Philadelphia 19114. Private; suburban. Awards C, B. Enrolls 1,162 T (85% women, 99% state res., 72% on fin. aid). Entrance difficulty: moderately difficult. Application deadline: rolling. Contact: Miss Angela A. Godshall, Director of Admissions and Financial Aid, (215) 637-7700.

IMMACULATA COLLEGE

Immaculata 19345. Private; suburban. Awards B. Enrolls 581 T (100% women, 90% state res., 62% on fin. aid). Entrance difficulty: moderately difficult. Application deadline: 8/1. Contact: Sr. Loretta Mary, IHM, (215) 647-4400.

INDIANA UNIVERSITY OF PENNSYLVANIA

Indiana 15705. Public; small town. Awards A, B, M, D. Enrolls 12,019 T, 10,866 U (58% women, 97% state res., 75% on fin. aid). Entrance difficulty: moderately difficult. Application deadlines: 12/31, early decision 10/1. Contact: Dr. Fred Dakak, (412) 357-2230.

JUNIATA COLLEGE

Huntingdon 16652. Private; small town. Awards B. Enrolls 1,250 T (42% women, 73% state res., 70% on fin. aid). Entrance difficulty: moderately difficult. Application deadline: rolling. Contact: Mrs. Gayle W.

Kreider, Associate Director of Admissions, (814) 643-4310.

KING'S COLLEGE

Wilkes-Barre 18711. Private; urban. Awards A, B. Enrolls 1,717 T (40% women, 74% state res., 85% on fin. aid). Entrance difficulty: moderately difficult. Application deadlines: 8/1, early decision 11/1. Contact: Mr. George J. Machinchick, (717) 824-9931 Ext. 211.

KUTZTOWN STATE COLLEGE

Kutztown 19530. Public; small town. Awards B, M. Enrolls 5,154 T, 4,728 U (59% women, 90% state res., 68% on fin. aid). Entrance difficulty: moderately difficult. Application deadline: rolling. Contact: Mr. George McKinley, (215) 683-4060.

LAFAYETTE COLLEGE

Easton 18042. Private; suburban. Awards B. Enrolls 2,071 T (40% women, 30% state res., 30% on fin. aid). Entrance difficulty: very difficult. Application deadlines: 3/1, early decision 2/1. Contact: Mr. Richard W. Haines, (215) 258-0411.

LANCASTER BIBLE COLLEGE

Lancaster 17601. Private; suburban. Awards C, B. Enrolls 437 T (48% women, 82% state res., 80% on fin. aid). Entrance difficulty: moderately difficult. Application deadline: rolling. Contact: Mr. Gilbert G. Gregory, Director of Admissions, (717) 569-7071 Ext. 57.

LA ROCHE COLLEGE

Pittsburgh 15237. Private; suburban. Awards B, M. Enrolls 1,300 T, 1,122 U (64% women, 65% on fin. aid). Entrance difficulty: moderately difficult. Application deadline: rolling. Contact: Mr. Norman Hasbrouck, (412) 931-9333.

LA SALLE COLLEGE

Philadelphia 19141. Private; urban. Awards B, M. Enrolls 7,908 T, 6,318 U (43% women, 80% state res., 70% on fin. aid). Entrance difficulty: moderately difficult. Application deadline: 7/15. Contact: Br. Lewis Mullin, F.S.C, (215) 951-1500.

LEBANON VALLEY COLLEGE

Annville 17003. Private; small town. Awards B. Enrolls 938 T (53% women, 60% state res., 65% on fin. aid). Entrance difficulty: moderately difficult. Application deadline: rolling. Contact: Mr. Gregory G. Stanson, (717) 867-4411.

LEHIGH UNIVERSITY

Bethlehem 18015. Private; suburban. Awards B, M, D. Enrolls 6,240 T, 4,400 U (32% women, 43% state res., 31% on fin. aid). Entrance difficulty: very difficult. Application deadlines: 3/1, early decision 11/1. Contact: Mr. Samuel H. Missimer, (215) 691-7000.

LINCOLN UNIVERSITY

Lincoln University 19352. Public; small town. Awards A, B, M. Enrolls 1,250 T, 1,062 U (45% women, 10% state res., 95% on fin. aid). Entrance difficulty: less difficult. Application deadline: rolling. Contact: Mr. Darrell C. Davis, (215) 932-8300 Ext. 278.

LOCK HAVEN STATE COLLEGE

Lock Haven 17745. Public; small town. Awards B. Enrolls 2,416 T (52% women, 87% state res., 60% on fin. aid). Entrance difficulty: moderately difficult. Application deadline: 8/1. Contact: Mr. Joseph A. Coldren, (717) 893-2027.

LYCOMING COLLEGE

Williamsport 17701. Private; suburban. Awards B. Enrolls 1,159 T (42% women, 58% state res., 45% on fin. aid). Entrance difficulty: moderately difficult. Application deadline: 4/1. Contact: Mr. Robert A. Doyle, (717) 326-1951.

MANSFIELD STATE COLLEGE

Mansfield 16933. Public; small town. Awards A, B, M. Enrolls 2,688 T, 2,501 U (54% women, 90% state res., 68% on fin. aid). Entrance difficulty: moderately difficult. Application deadline: 7/1. Contact: Mr. John J. Abplanalp, Acting Director of Admissions, (717) 662-4205.

MARYWOOD COLLEGE

Scranton 18509. Private; suburban. Awards B, M. Enrolls 3,100 T, 2,100 U (87% women, 55% state res., 80% on fin. aid). Entrance difficulty: moderately difficult. Application deadlines: 3/1, early decision 11/1. Contact: Sr. M. Gabriel Kane, IHM, (717) 343-6521 Ext. 211.

MERCYHURST COLLEGE

Erie 16546. Private; suburban. Awards C, A, B, M. Enrolls 1,406 T, 1,300 U (59% women, 79% state res., 85% on fin. aid). Entrance difficulty: moderately difficult. Application deadline: rolling. Contact: Mrs. Karen S. Benzel, (814) 864-0681.

MESSIAH COLLEGE

Grantham 17027. Private; small town. Awards B. Enrolls 1,149 T (55% women, 60% state res., 72% on fin. aid). Entrance difficulty: moderately difficult. Application deadline: rolling. Contact: Mr. Ron E. Long, (717) 766-2511 Ext. 225.

MILLERSVILLE STATE COLLEGE

Millersville 17551. Public; small town. Awards B, M. Enrolls 6,029 T, 5,216 U (57% women, 96% state res., 68% on fin. aid). Entrance difficulty: moderately difficult. Application deadline: rolling. Contact: Mr. Blair E. Treasure, (717) 872-5411.

MOORE COLLEGE OF ART

Philadelphia 19103. Private; urban. Awards B. Enrolls 508 T (100% women, 56% state res., 45% on fin. aid). Entrance difficulty: moderately difficult. Application deadline: rolling. Contact: Ms. Linda K. Harper, (215) 568-4515.

MORAVIAN COLLEGE

Bethlehem 18018. Private; small town. Awards B. Enrolls 1,342 T (48% women, 56% state res., 50% on fin. aid). Entrance difficulty: moderately difficult. Application deadlines: 3/15, early decision 11/15. Contact: Mr. John T. McKeown, (215) 865-0741.

MUHLENBERG COLLEGE

Allentown 18104. Private; suburban. Awards B. Enrolls 1,530 T (45% women, 35% state res., 60% on fin. aid). Entrance difficulty: very difficult. Application deadlines: 2/15, early decision 1/1. Contact: Mr. George W. Gibbs, (215) 433-3191.

NEUMANN COLLEGE

Aston 19014. Private; suburban. Awards B. Enrolls 703 T (88% women, 83% state res., 65% on fin. aid). Entrance difficulty: moderately difficult. Application deadline: 8/15. Contact: Mr. Richard A. Nigro, (215) 459-0905 Ext. 9.

NEW SCHOOL OF MUSIC

Philadelphia 19103. Private; urban. Awards B. Enrolls 81 T (55% women, 45% state res., 43% on fin. aid). Entrance difficulty: noncompetitive. Application deadline: rolling. Contact: Mr. James F. Leitch, (215) 732-3966.

PENNSYLVANIA STATE UNIVERSITY–BEHREND COLLEGE

Erie 16563. Public; suburban. Awards A, B, M. Enrolls 1,827 T, 1,810 U (38% women, 96% state res., 52% on fin. aid). Entrance difficulty: moderately difficult. Application deadline: rolling. Contact: Mr. Benjamin A. Lane, Admissions Officer, (814) 899-1511.

PENNSYLVANIA STATE UNIVERSITY–UNIVERSITY PARK CAMPUS

University Park 16802. Public; small town. Awards C, A, B, M, D. Enrolls 31,961 T, 27,131 U (43% women, 91% state res., 76% on fin. aid). Entrance difficulty: very difficult. Application deadline: rolling. Contact: Mr. Donald G. Dickason, (814) 865-5471.

PHILADELPHIA COLLEGE OF ART

Philadelphia 19104. Private; urban. Awards B, M. Enrolls 1,154 T, 1,131 U (59% women, 57% state res., 65% on fin. aid). Entrance difficulty: moderately difficult. Application deadline: rolling. Contact: Miss Carolyn A. Connelly, Acting Director of Admissions, (215) 893-3174.

PHILADELPHIA COLLEGE OF BIBLE

Langhorne 19047. Private; suburban. Awards B. Enrolls 525 T (44% women, 49% state res., 56% on fin. aid). Entrance difficulty: moderately difficult. Application deadline: rolling. Contact: Miss Catherine P. Baird, (215) 752-5800.

PHILADELPHIA COLLEGE OF PHARMACY AND SCIENCE

Philadelphia 19104. Private; urban. Awards B, M, D. Enrolls 1,155 T, 1,043 U (44% women, 63% state res., 70% on fin. aid). Entrance difficulty: moderately difficult. Application deadline: rolling. Contact: Mr. Richard C. Kent, Registrar, (215) 596-8810.

PHILADELPHIA COLLEGE OF TEXTILES AND SCIENCE

Philadelphia 19144. Private; suburban. Awards A, B, M. Enrolls 1,948 T, 1,784 U (51% women, 80% state res., 75% on fin. aid). Entrance difficulty: moderately difficult. Application deadline: 6/1. Contact: Dr. Mott R. Linn, (215) 843-9700.

PHILADELPHIA COLLEGE OF THE PERFORMING ARTS

Philadelphia 19102. Private; urban. Awards A, B, M. Enrolls 372 T, 355 U (40% women, 69% state res., 68% on fin. aid). Entrance difficulty: moderately difficult. Application deadline: 6/1. Contact: Mr. Edward T. Brake, (215) 545-6200.

POINT PARK COLLEGE

Pittsburgh 15222. Private; urban. Awards A, B. Enrolls 2,072 T (46% women, 77% state res., 70% on fin. aid). Entrance difficulty: moderately difficult. Application deadline: 8/1. Contact: Mr. Richard K. Watson, Dean of Enrollment Planning, (412) 391-4100.

ROBERT MORRIS COLLEGE

Coraopolis 15108. Private; suburban. Awards A, B, M. Enrolls 4,561 T, 4,368 U (50% women, 60% on fin. aid). Entrance difficulty: moderately difficult. Application deadline: rolling. Contact: Dr. Helen Mullen, Dean of Admissions, (412) 264-9300.

ROSEMONT COLLEGE

Rosemont 19010. Private; suburban. Awards B. Enrolls 585 T (100% women, 40% state res., 50% on fin. aid). Entrance difficulty: moderately difficult. Application deadline: rolling. Contact: Miss Jane A. Maloney, (215) 527-0200 Ext. 248.

SAINT FRANCIS COLLEGE

Loretto 15940. Private; rural. Awards A, B, M. Enrolls 1,445 T, 1,226 U (45% women,

56% state res., 60% on fin. aid). Entrance difficulty: moderately difficult. Application deadline: rolling. Contact: Mr. Edward E. Kale Jr, (814) 472-7000.

SAINT JOSEPH'S UNIVERSITY

Philadelphia 19131. Private; urban. Awards C, A, B, M. Enrolls 2,291 T, 2,220 U (35% women, 70% state res., 64% on fin. aid). Entrance difficulty: moderately difficult. Application deadlines: 3/1, early decision 11/1. Contact: Mr. Dennis P. Farrell, (215) 879-7400.

SAINT VINCENT COLLEGE

Latrobe 15650. Private; rural. Awards B. Enrolls 896 T (0% women, 86% state res., 70% on fin. aid). Entrance difficulty: moderately difficult. Application deadline: rolling. Contact: Rev. Earl J. Henry, OSB, (412) 539-9761 Ext. 305.

SETON HILL COLLEGE

Greensburg 15601. Private; small town. Awards B. Enrolls 917 T (100% women, 84% state res., 85% on fin. aid). Entrance difficulty: moderately difficult. Application deadline: 7/30. Contact: Sr. Jean Boggs, SC, (412) 834-2200.

SHIPPENSBURG STATE COLLEGE

Shippensburg 17257. Public; small town. Awards B, M. Enrolls 5,915 T, 4,628 U (52% women, 94% state res., 75% on fin. aid). Entrance difficulty: moderately difficult. Application deadline: rolling. Contact: Mr. Albert Drachbar, Director of Admissions, (717) 532-1283.

SLIPPERY ROCK STATE COLLEGE

Slippery Rock 16057. Public; rural. Awards B, M. Enrolls 5,694 T, 5,042 U (49% women, 80% state res., 66% on fin. aid). Entrance difficulty: moderately difficult. Application deadline: rolling. Contact: Mr. Thomas L. Nesbit, (412) 794-7203.

SPRING GARDEN COLLEGE

Chestnut Hill 19118. Private; suburban. Awards C, A, B. Enrolls 1,103 T (31% women, 70% state res., 65% on fin. aid). Entrance difficulty: moderately difficult. Application deadline: rolling. Contact: Mr. Peter J. Bonasto, (215) 242-3700.

SUSQUEHANNA UNIVERSITY

Selinsgrove 17870. Private; small town. Awards A, B. Enrolls 1,478 T (44% women, 46% state res., 60% on fin. aid). Entrance difficulty: moderately difficult. Application deadlines: 3/15, early decision 12/15. Contact: Mr. Paul W. Beardslee, (717) 374-0101.

SWARTHMORE COLLEGE

Swarthmore 19081. Private; suburban. Awards B. Enrolls 1,280 T (46% women, 25% state res., 35% on fin. aid). Entrance difficulty: most difficult. Application deadlines: 2/1, early decision 11/15. Contact: Mr. Robert A. Barr Jr, Dean of Admissions, (215) 544-7900.

TEMPLE UNIVERSITY

Philadelphia 19122. Public; urban. Awards C, A, B, M, D. Enrolls 24,377 T, 17,444 U (35% women, 91% state res., 60% on fin. aid). Entrance difficulty: moderately difficult. Application deadlines: 6/15, early decision 11/15. Contact: Mr. R. Kenneth Haldeman, (215) 787-7201.

TEMPLE UNIVERSITY, AMBLER CAMPUS

Ambler 19002. Public; suburban. Awards C, A, B, M, D. Enrolls 5,902 T, 2,455 U (48% women, 95% state res., 37% on fin. aid). Entrance difficulty: moderately difficult. Application deadline: 6/15. Contact: Mr. Kenneth Haldeman, (215) 643-1200.

TEMPLE UNIVERSITY HEALTH SCIENCES CENTER

Philadelphia 19140. Public. Awards C, B, M, D. Enrolls 1,820 T, 925 U.

THIEL COLLEGE

Greenville 16125. Private; small town. Awards A, B. Enrolls 1,042 T (46% women, 77% state res., 87% on fin. aid). Entrance difficulty: moderately difficult. Application deadline: 8/1. Contact: Mr. John R. Hauser, (412) 588-7700 Ext. 212.

UNITED WESLEYAN COLLEGE

Allentown 18103. Private; urban. Awards A, B. Enrolls 206 T (40% women, 49% state res., 85% on fin. aid). Entrance difficulty: noncompetitive. Application deadline: 8/15. Contact: Dr. John P. Ragsdale, (215) 439-8709.

UNIVERSITY OF PENNSYLVANIA

Philadelphia 19104. Private; urban. Awards C, A, B, M, D. Enrolls 18,730 T, 8,730 U (38% women, 28% state res., 55% on fin. aid). Entrance difficulty: very difficult. Application deadlines: 1/1, early decision 11/1. Contact: Mr. Willis J. Stetson Jr, (215) 243-7502.

UNIVERSITY OF PITTSBURGH

Pittsburgh 15261. Public; urban. Awards C, B, M, D. Enrolls 28,069 T, 17,815 U (45% women, 95% state res., 70% on fin. aid). Entrance difficulty: moderately difficult. Application deadline: 7/1. Contact: Mr. Joseph A. Marante, (412) 624-5761.

UNIVERSITY OF PITTSBURGH AT BRADFORD

Bradford 16701. Public; rural. Awards A, B. Enrolls 1,100 T (40% women, 93% state res., 65% on fin. aid). Entrance difficulty: moderately difficult. Application deadlines: 7/1, early decision 11/1. Contact: Mr. Michael L. Mulvihill, Director of Admissions, (814) 362-3801.

UNIVERSITY OF PITTSBURGH AT JOHNSTOWN

Johnstown 15904. Public; suburban. Awards C, B. Enrolls 3,000 T (48% women, 90% state res., 80% on fin. aid). Entrance difficulty: moderately difficult. Application deadlines: 8/1, early decision 11/1. Contact: Mr. Thomas J. Wonders, (814) 266-9661 Ext. 331.

UNIVERSITY OF SCRANTON

Scranton 18510. Private; urban. Awards A, B, M. Enrolls 4,437 T, 3,542 U (37% women, 69% state res., 70% on fin. aid). Entrance difficulty: moderately difficult. Application deadline: rolling. Contact: Rev. Bernard R. McIlhenny, SJ, (717) 961-7540.

URSINUS COLLEGE

Collegeville 19426. Private; small town. Awards A, B. Enrolls 1,040 T (45% women, 66% state res., 68% on fin. aid). Entrance difficulty: moderately difficult. Application deadlines: rolling, early decision 11/1. Contact: Mr. H. Lloyd Jones Jr, Dean of Admissions, (215) 489-4111.

VILLA MARIA COLLEGE

Erie 16505. Private; suburban. Awards C, A, B. Enrolls 616 T (99% women, 93% state res., 69% on fin. aid). Entrance difficulty: moderately difficult. Application deadline: rolling. Contact: Mr. Patrick Ward, (814) 838-1966 Ext. 276.

VILLANOVA UNIVERSITY

Villanova 19085. Private; suburban. Awards A, B, M, D. Enrolls 9,500 T, 6,000 U (45% women, 44% state res., 40% on fin. aid). Entrance difficulty: very difficult. Application deadlines: 2/15, early decision 11/15. Contact: Rev. Harry J. Erdlen, OSA, (215) 645-4000.

WASHINGTON AND JEFFERSON COLLEGE

Washington 15301. Private; small town. Awards C, B. Enrolls 1,053 T (33% women, 55% on fin. aid). Entrance difficulty: very difficult. Application deadlines: 3/1, early decision 11/1. Contact: Mr. Thomas P. O'Connor, (412) 222-4400.

WAYNESBURG COLLEGE

Waynesburg 15370. Private; small town. Awards A, B. Enrolls 820 T (40% women, 70% state res., 80% on fin. aid). Entrance difficulty: less difficult. Contact: Mrs. Danielle D. Barr, (412) 627-8191.

WEST CHESTER STATE COLLEGE

West Chester 19380. Public; small town. Awards B, M. Enrolls 8,374 T, 7,016 U (59% women, 89% state res., 51% on fin. aid). Entrance difficulty: moderately difficult. Application deadline: 7/1. Contact: Mr. William E. Kipp, (215) 436-3411.

WESTMINSTER COLLEGE

New Wilmington 16142. Private; small town. Awards B, M. Enrolls 1,859 T, 1,540 U (50% women, 72% state res., 58% on fin. aid). Entrance difficulty: moderately difficult. Application deadline: rolling. Contact: Dr. Edwin G. Tobin, (412) 946-8761.

WIDENER UNIVERSITY

Chester 19013. Contact: Mr. Vincent F. Lindsley, Director of Admissions.

WILKES COLLEGE

Wilkes-Barre 18703. Private; urban. Awards A, B, M. Enrolls 2,527 T, 2,050 U (40% women, 80% state res., 75% on fin. aid). Entrance difficulty: moderately difficult. Application deadline: rolling. Contact: Mr. G. K. Wuori, Dean of Admissions, (717) 824-4651.

WILSON COLLEGE

Chambersburg 17201. Private; small town. Awards B. Enrolls 221 T (100% women, 58% on fin. aid). Entrance difficulty: moderately difficult. Application deadline: rolling. Contact: Frank Kamus, (717) 264-4141.

YORK COLLEGE OF PENNSYLVANIA

York 17405. Private; suburban. Awards A, B, M. Enrolls 3,628 T, 3,536 U (60% women, 74% state res., 72% on fin. aid). Entrance difficulty: less difficult. Application deadlines: 8/1, early decision 12/1. Contact: Miss Nancy C. Spruell, Admissions Director, (717) 846-7788.

RHODE ISLAND

BARRINGTON COLLEGE

Barrington 02806. Private; suburban. Awards A, B. Enrolls 456 T (56% women, 26% state res., 67% on fin. aid). Entrance difficulty: moderately difficult. Application deadline: rolling. Contact: Mr. Michael Wildeman, Assistant Director of Admissions, (401) 246-1200.

BROWN UNIVERSITY

Providence 02912. Private; urban. Awards B, M, D. Enrolls 6,900 T, 5,487 U (47% women, 7% state res., 35% on fin. aid). Entrance difficulty: most difficult. Application deadlines: 1/1, early decision 11/1. Contact: Mr. James H. Rogers, (401) 863-2378.

BRYANT COLLEGE

Smithfield 02917. Private; suburban. Awards A, B, M. Enrolls 5,518 T, 2,731 U (48% women, 24% state res., 65% on fin. aid). Entrance difficulty: moderately difficult. Application deadlines: rolling, early decision 11/15. Contact: Mr. Roy A. Nelson, (401) 231-1200.

JOHNSON AND WALES COLLEGE

Providence 02903. Private; urban. Awards C, A, B. Enrolls 4,000 T, 3,000 U (45% women, 20% state res., 70% on fin. aid). Entrance difficulty: less difficult. Application deadline: rolling. Contact: Mr. Manuel Pimentel Jr, (401) 456-1055.

NEWPORT COLLEGE–SALVE REGINA

Newport 02840. Private; small town. Awards C, A, B, M. Enrolls 1,719 T, 1,522 U (78% women, 51% state res., 50% on fin. aid). Entrance difficulty: moderately difficult. Application deadlines: rolling, early decision 11/1. Contact: Sr. Mary Audrey O'Donnell, (401) 847-6650 Ext. 233.

PROVIDENCE COLLEGE

Providence 02918. Private; urban. Awards B, M, D. Enrolls 4,232 T, 3,500 U (49% women, 27% state res., 65% on fin. aid). Entrance difficulty: moderately difficult. Application deadlines: 2/15, early decision 11/1. Contact: Mr. Michael G. Backes, (401) 865-2141.

RHODE ISLAND COLLEGE

Providence 02908. Public; suburban. Awards B, M. Enrolls 7,742 T, 6,093 U (68% women, 90% state res., 45% on fin. aid). Entrance difficulty: moderately difficult. Application deadlines: 5/1, early decision 12/1. Contact: Mr. James M. Colman, (401) 456-8234.

RHODE ISLAND SCHOOL OF DESIGN

Providence 02903. Private; urban. Awards B, M. Enrolls 1,509 T, 1,395 U (56% women, 10% state res., 60% on fin. aid). Entrance difficulty: very difficult. Application deadlines: 1/21, early decision 12/15. Contact: Mrs. Frances Innis, (401) 331-3511.

ROGER WILLIAMS COLLEGE

Bristol 02809. Private; small town. Awards A, B. Enrolls 2,000 T (45% women, 15% state res., 65% on fin. aid). Entrance difficulty: moderately difficult; very difficult for marine biology, electrical engineering technology programs. Application deadline: rolling. Contact: Mr. Michael E. Diffily, Dean of Admissions, (401) 255-2151.

UNIVERSITY OF RHODE ISLAND

Kingston 02881. Public; small town. Awards A, B, M, D. Enrolls 11,255 T, 9,280 U (48% women, 70% state res., 62% on fin. aid). Entrance difficulty: moderately difficult. Application deadlines: 3/1, early decision 11/15. Contact: Dr. Richard A. Edwards, (401) 792-2164.

SOUTH CAROLINA

ALLEN UNIVERSITY

Columbia 29204. Private; suburban. Awards B. Enrolls 419 T (60% women, 90% on fin. aid). Entrance difficulty: noncompetitive. Application deadline: rolling. Contact: Mrs. L. S. Grady, (803) 254-4165 Ext. 338.

BAPTIST COLLEGE AT CHARLESTON

Charleston 29411. Private; suburban. Awards A, B. Enrolls 2,420 T (51% women, 85% state res., 89% on fin. aid). Entrance difficulty: moderately difficult. Application deadline: rolling. Contact: Miss Barbara Mead, (803) 797-4326.

BENEDICT COLLEGE

Columbia 29204. Private; urban. Awards B. Enrolls 1,584 T (60% women, 90% state res., 97% on fin. aid). Entrance difficulty: noncompetitive. Application deadline: rolling. Contact: Ms. Vivian Counts, Interim Director of Admissions, (803) 256-4220.

CENTRAL WESLEYAN COLLEGE

Central 29630. Private; small town. Awards B. Enrolls 413 T (45% women, 60% state res., 75% on fin. aid). Entrance difficulty: less difficult. Application deadline: 8/20. Contact: Mr. James J. Kimble, Registrar, (803) 639-2991.

CITADEL

Charleston 29409. Public; urban. Awards B, M. Enrolls 3,353 T, 2,378 U (0% women, 65% state res., 67% on fin. aid). Entrance difficulty: moderately difficult. Application deadline: 7/1. Contact: Capt. Wallace I. West, Assistant Director of Admissions.

CLAFLIN COLLEGE

Orangeburg 29115. Private; small town. Awards B. Enrolls 866 T (64% women, 88% state res., 97% on fin. aid). Entrance difficulty: less difficult. Application deadline: rolling. Contact: Mr. George F. Lee, Admissions Officer, (803) 536-5635.

CLEMSON UNIVERSITY

Clemson 29631. Public; small town. Awards A, B, M, D. Enrolls 11,748 T, 9,240 U (39% women, 79% state res., 40% on fin. aid). Entrance difficulty: moderately difficult. Application deadline: rolling. Contact: Mr. William R. Mattox, (803) 656-2287.

COKER COLLEGE

Hartsville 29550. Private; small town. Awards B. Enrolls 321 T (66% women, 88% state res., 65% on fin. aid). Entrance difficulty: moderately difficult. Application deadline: rolling. Contact: Mr. Charlie Geren, (803) 332-1381.

COLLEGE OF CHARLESTON

Charleston 29401. Public; urban. Awards B, M. Enrolls 4,358 T, 4,137 U (60% women, 95% state res., 35% on fin. aid). Entrance difficulty: moderately difficult. Application deadline: rolling. Contact: Mr. Frederick W. Daniels, (803) 792-5671.

COLUMBIA BIBLE COLLEGE

Columbia 29203. Private; suburban. Awards A, B, M. Enrolls 539 T (44% women, 30% state res., 35% on fin. aid). Entrance difficulty: moderately difficult. Application deadline: rolling. Contact: Mr. Ralph E. Enlow Jr, Director of Admissions, (803) 754-4100.

COLUMBIA COLLEGE

Columbia 29203. Private; suburban. Awards B. Enrolls 1,103 T (100% women, 90% state res., 60% on fin. aid). Entrance difficulty: moderately difficult. Application deadline: rolling. Contact: Mr. Joe Mitchell, Dean of Admissions, (803) 786-3871.

CONVERSE COLLEGE

Spartanburg 29301. Private; urban. Awards B, M. Enrolls 933 T, 732 U (100% women, 40% state res., 42% on fin. aid). Entrance difficulty: moderately difficult. Application deadline: 8/1. Contact: Ms. Elizabeth F. Williford, (803) 585-6421.

ERSKINE COLLEGE

Due West 29639. Private; small town. Awards C, B, M. Enrolls 700 T, 653 U (45% women, 65% state res., 80% on fin. aid). Entrance difficulty: moderately difficult. Application deadline: rolling. Contact: Mr. Roddy Gray, (803) 379-8838.

FRANCIS MARION COLLEGE

Florence 29501. Public; rural. Awards A, B, M. Enrolls 2,818 T, 2,392 U (52% women, 99% state res., 37% on fin. aid). Entrance difficulty: moderately difficult. Contact: Mr. Marvin W. Lynch, (803) 669-4121 Ext. 231.

FURMAN UNIVERSITY

Greenville 29613. Private; suburban. Awards B, M. Enrolls 2,880 T, 2,698 U (49% women, 47% state res., 55% on fin. aid). Entrance difficulty: very difficult. Application deadlines: 2/1, early decision 12/1. Contact: Mr. Charles E. Brock, (803) 294-2034.

LANDER COLLEGE

Greenwood 29646. Public; small town. Awards A, B. Enrolls 1,696 T (63% women, 96% state res., 50% on fin. aid). Entrance difficulty: moderately difficult. Application deadline: rolling. Contact: Ms. Jacquelyn C. DeVore Roark, (803) 229-8307.

LIMESTONE COLLEGE

Gaffney 29340. Private; small town. Awards B. Enrolls 1,124 T (40% women, 85% state res., 30% on fin. aid). Entrance difficulty: moderately difficult. Application deadline: rolling. Contact: Miss Anslie J. Waters, (803) 489-7151.

MORRIS COLLEGE

Sumter 29150. Private. Awards B. Enrolls 727 T (555% women, 95% state res., 98% on fin. aid). Entrance difficulty: noncompetitive. Application deadline: rolling. Contact: Mrs. Gueen Spann, (803) 775-9371.

NEWBERRY COLLEGE

Newberry 29108. Private; small town. Awards B. Enrolls 883 T (33% women, 75% state res., 75% on fin. aid). Entrance difficulty: moderately difficult. Application deadline: rolling. Contact: Mr. H. Ray Sharpe, (803) 276-6974.

PRESBYTERIAN COLLEGE

Clinton 29325. Private; small town. Awards B. Enrolls 925 T (40% women, 67% state res., 72% on fin. aid). Entrance difficulty: moderately difficult. Application deadline: rolling. Contact: Mr. William K. Jackson, (803) 833-2820 Ext. 211.

SOUTH CAROLINA STATE COLLEGE

Orangeburg 29117. Public; small town. Awards B, M. Enrolls 3,201 T (57% women, 97% state res., 88% on fin. aid). Entrance difficulty: moderately difficult. Application deadline: 7/31. Contact: Miss Dorothy L. Brown, Director of Admissions and Records, (803) 536-7185.

UNIVERSITY OF SOUTH CAROLINA AT AIKEN

Aiken 29801. Public; small town. Awards A, B. Enrolls 1,693 T (53% women, 95% state res., 26% on fin. aid). Entrance difficulty: less difficult. Application deadline: 8/1. Contact: Mr. Robert Moldenhauer, (803) 648-6851.

UNIVERSITY OF SOUTH CAROLINA AT COLUMBIA

Columbia 29208. Public; urban. Awards A, B, M, D. Enrolls 26,006 T, 18,636 U (49% women, 84% state res., 35% on fin. aid). Entrance difficulty: moderately difficult. Application deadline: 8/1. Contact: Mr. John Bolin, (803) 777-7700.

UNIVERSITY OF SOUTH CAROLINA AT SPARTANBURG

Spartanburg 29303. Public; urban. Awards A, B. Enrolls 2,424 T (54% women, 99% state res., 35% on fin. aid). Entrance difficulty: noncompetitive. Application deadline: rolling. Contact: Mr. Eric S. Jolly, Acting Director of Admissions, (803) 578-1800.

UNIVERSITY OF SOUTH CAROLINA, COASTAL CAROLINA COLLEGE

Conway 29526. Public; rural. Awards A, B. Enrolls 1,888 T (47% women, 93% state res., 60% on fin. aid). Entrance difficulty: less difficult. Application deadline: 8/15.

University of South Carolina, Coastal Carolina College (continued)
Contact: Mr. Marsh H. Myers Jr, (803) 347-3161.

VOORHEES COLLEGE

Denmark 29042. Private; small town. Awards A, B. Enrolls 708 T (64% women, 81% state res., 98% on fin. aid). Entrance difficulty: noncompetitive. Application deadline: 8/23. Contact: Miss Iris D. Bomar, Director of Admissions and Records, (803) 793-3351.

WINTHROP COLLEGE

Rock Hill 29733. Public; urban. Awards A, B, M. Enrolls 4,979 T, 3,913 U (70% women, 89% state res., 36% on fin. aid). Entrance difficulty: less difficult. Contact: Dr. Edward N. Knight, (803) 323-2192.

WOFFORD COLLEGE

Spartanburg 29301. Private; urban. Awards B. Enrolls 1,078 T (22% women, 74% state res., 58% on fin. aid). Entrance difficulty: moderately difficult. Application deadline: rolling. Contact: Mr. Charles H. Gray Jr, (803) 585-4821 Ext. 275.

SOUTH DAKOTA

AUGUSTANA COLLEGE

Sioux Falls 57102. Private; urban. Awards A, B, M. Enrolls 2,146 T, 1,874 U (59% women, 55% state res., 78% on fin. aid). Entrance difficulty: moderately difficult. Application deadline: rolling. Contact: Mr. Harold K. Melemseter, (605) 336-5516.

BLACK HILLS STATE COLLEGE

Spearfish 57783. Public; small town. Awards C, A, B, M. Enrolls 2,056 T (55% women, 91% state res., 82% on fin. aid). Entrance difficulty: moderately difficult; noncompetitive for junior college program. Application deadline: rolling. Contact: Mr. Gene Bauer, Director of Admissions, (605) 642-6343.

DAKOTA STATE COLLEGE

Madison 57042. Public; small town. Awards C, A, B. Enrolls 895 T (54% women, 94% state res., 80% on fin. aid). Entrance difficulty: less difficult; noncompetitive for

2-year programs. Application deadline: rolling. Contact: Ms. Kathy Schneider, (605) 256-3551 Ext. 216.

DAKOTA WESLEYAN UNIVERSITY

Mitchell 57301. Private; small town. Awards C, A, B. Enrolls 521 T (60% women, 72% state res., 74% on fin. aid). Entrance difficulty: moderately difficult. Application deadline: 9/1. Contact: Mr. John Seveland, (605) 996-5510.

HURON COLLEGE

Huron 57350. Private; small town. Awards C, A, B. Enrolls 318 T (54% women, 79% state res., 90% on fin. aid). Entrance difficulty: less difficult. Application deadline: rolling. Contact: Mr. Douglas Almond, (605) 352-8721 Ext. 204.

MOUNT MARTY COLLEGE

Yankton 57078. Private; rural. Awards A, B. Enrolls 590 T (67% women, 46% state res., 73% on fin. aid). Entrance difficulty: moderately difficult. Application deadline: 8/15. Contact: Mr. Tom Streueler, (605) 668-1524.

NATIONAL COLLEGE OF BUSINESS

Rapid City 57701. Private; urban. Awards C, A, B. Enrolls 1,083 T (53% women, 62% state res., 70% on fin. aid). Entrance difficulty: noncompetitive. Application deadline: rolling. Contact: Mr. Earle G. Sutton, Vice President, (605) 394-4820.

NORTHERN STATE COLLEGE

Aberdeen 57401. Public; small town. Awards C, A, B, M. Enrolls 2,459 T, 2,320 U (57% women, 97% state res., 70% on fin. aid). Entrance difficulty: moderately difficult. Application deadline: 8/15. Contact: Dr. Richard W. Van Beek, Director of Admissions and Records, (605) 622-2544.

SINTE GLESKA COLLEGE

Rosebud 57570. Private; rural. Awards C, A, B. Enrolls 373 T (67% women, 97% state res., 71% on fin. aid). Entrance difficulty: noncompetitive. Application deadline: 8/20. Contact: Miss Sherry Red Owl, Registrar, (605) 747-2263.

SIOUX FALLS COLLEGE

Sioux Falls 57101. Private; urban. Awards A, B, M. Enrolls 770 T (55% women, 44% state res., 85% on fin. aid). Entrance difficulty: moderately difficult. Application deadline: rolling. Contact: Mr. Earl Craven, (605) 336-2850.

SOUTH DAKOTA SCHOOL OF MINES AND TECHNOLOGY

Rapid City 57701. Public; urban. Awards B, M, D. Enrolls 1,744 T, 1,552 U (23% women, 80% state res., 35% on fin. aid). Entrance difficulty: very difficult. Application deadline: 8/15. Contact: Mr. Robert H. Moore, Registrar, (605) 394-2414.

SOUTH DAKOTA STATE UNIVERSITY

Brookings 57007. Public; rural. Awards C, A, B, M, D. Enrolls 6,464 T, 5,992 U (71% women, 88% state res., 60% on fin. aid). Entrance difficulty: moderately difficult. Application deadline: 8/1. Contact: Mr. Vincent O. Heer, (605) 688-4121.

UNIVERSITY OF SOUTH DAKOTA

Vermillion 57069. Public; small town. Awards A, B, M, D. Enrolls 5,663 T, 4,419 U (50% women, 82% state res., 65% on fin. aid). Entrance difficulty: moderately difficult. Application deadline: 8/25. Contact: Mr. Gary Gullickson, (605) 677-5434.

UNIVERSITY OF SOUTH DAKOTA AT SPRINGFIELD

Springfield 57062. Public; small town. Awards C, A, B. Enrolls 828 T (22% women, 83% state res., 88% on fin. aid). Entrance difficulty: noncompetitive. Application deadline: rolling. Contact: Mr. David Lorenz, (605) 369-2289.

YANKTON COLLEGE

Yankton 57078. Private; small town. Awards A, B. Enrolls 289 T (97% women, 38% state res., 93% on fin. aid). Entrance difficulty: less difficult. Application deadline: 8/15. Contact: Miss Mary R. Johnson, Dean of Admissions, (605) 665-3661.

TENNESSEE

AMERICAN BAPTIST COLLEGE

Nashville 37207. Private; suburban. Awards B. Enrolls 125 T (15% women, 20% state res., 90% on fin. aid). Entrance difficulty: noncompetitive. Application deadline: 7/1. Contact: Mrs. Judy Banks, Registrar's Assistant, (615) 228-7877.

AUSTIN PEAY STATE UNIVERSITY

Clarksville 37040. Public; small town. Awards C, A, B, M. Enrolls 5,500 T, 4,407 U (51% women, 88% state res., 75% on fin. aid). Entrance difficulty: less difficult. Application deadline: 9/15. Contact: Mr. Dick Littleton, Director of Admissions, (615) 648-7661.

BELMONT COLLEGE

Nashville 37203. Private; urban. Awards A, B. Enrolls 1,483 T (50% women, 75% state res., 68% on fin. aid). Entrance difficulty: moderately difficult. Application deadline: 8/15. Contact: Mr. Ronald E. Underwood, Registrar, (615) 383-7001 Ext. 355.

BETHEL COLLEGE

McKenzie 38201. Private; small town. Awards C, B. Enrolls 360 T (49% women, 80% state res., 73% on fin. aid). Entrance difficulty: less difficult. Application deadline: 9/10. Contact: Jammie Foster, (901) 352-5321.

BRYAN COLLEGE

Dayton 37321. Private; rural. Awards B. Enrolls 645 T (55% women, 12% state res., 67% on fin. aid). Entrance difficulty: less difficult. Application deadline: rolling. Contact: Mr. Glen H. Liebig, Dean of Admissions and Records, (615) 775-2041.

CARSON-NEWMAN COLLEGE

Jefferson City 37760. Private; small town. Awards B. Enrolls 1,649 T (49% women, 52% state res., 75% on fin. aid). Entrance difficulty: moderately difficult. Application deadline: rolling. Contact: Mr. Jack W. Shannon, (615) 475-9061.

CHRISTIAN BROTHERS COLLEGE

Memphis 38104. Private; urban. Awards A, B. Enrolls 1,330 T (34% women, 79% state

Christian Brothers College (continued)
res., 60% on fin. aid). Entrance difficulty: moderately difficult. Application deadline: 5/1. Contact: Miss Dayna Caldwell, (901) 278-0100.

DAVID LIPSCOMB COLLEGE

Nashville 37203. Private; suburban. Awards B. Enrolls 2,293 T (52% women, 51% state res., 70% on fin. aid). Entrance difficulty: moderately difficult. Application deadline: rolling. Contact: Mr. Steve Flatt, (615) 385-3855.

EAST TENNESSEE STATE UNIVERSITY

Johnson City 37601. Public; urban. Awards C, A, B, M, D. Enrolls 9,947 T, 8,487 U (53% women, 86% state res., 45% on fin. aid). Entrance difficulty: noncompetitive. Application deadline: rolling. Contact: Dr. James W. Loyd, Dean of Admissions/Records, (615) 929-4213.

FISK UNIVERSITY

Nashville 37203. Private; urban. Awards B, M. Enrolls 1,101 T, 1,063 U (65% women, 10% state res., 60% on fin. aid). Entrance difficulty: moderately difficult. Application deadline: 6/15. Contact: Mrs. Aline Rivers, Director of Admissions and Registrar, (615) 329-8665.

FREED-HARDEMAN COLLEGE

Henderson 38340. Private; small town. Awards C, A, B. Enrolls 1,428 T (53% women, 39% state res., 80% on fin. aid). Entrance difficulty: less difficult. Application deadline: 9/1. Contact: Mr. Reeder Oldham, Vice President for Enrollment Development, (901) 989-4611.

FREE WILL BAPTIST BIBLE COLLEGE

Nashville 37205. Private; urban. Awards B. Enrolls 528 T (48% women, 16% state res., 34% on fin. aid). Entrance difficulty: noncompetitive. Application deadline: rolling. Contact: Mr. Charles Hampton, Registrar, (615) 297-4676.

JOHNSON BIBLE COLLEGE

Knoxville 37920. Private; rural. Awards C, B. Enrolls 396 T (46% women, 29% state res., 71% on fin. aid). Entrance difficulty: noncompetitive. Application deadline: 8/1.

Contact: Mr. Joel F. Rood, Registrar, (615) 573-4517.

KING COLLEGE

Bristol 37620. Private; suburban. Awards B. Enrolls 238 T (43% women, 36% state res., 70% on fin. aid). Entrance difficulty: moderately difficult. Application deadline: rolling. Contact: Mr. Edgar C. Torbert, (615) 968-1187.

KNOXVILLE COLLEGE

Knoxville 37921. Private; urban. Awards A, B. Enrolls 699 T (42% women, 21% state res., 84% on fin. aid). Entrance difficulty: moderately difficult. Application deadline: rolling. Contact: Mrs. Valencia Swaggerty, Coordinator of Recruitment, (615) 524-6524.

LAMBUTH COLLEGE

Jackson 38301. Private; urban. Awards B. Enrolls 807 T (63% women, 84% state res., 87% on fin. aid). Entrance difficulty: moderately difficult. Application deadline: 9/1. Contact: Mr. David Ogden, (901) 427-6743.

LANE COLLEGE

Jackson 38301. Private; urban. Awards B. Enrolls 673 T (51% women, 58% state res., 99% on fin. aid). Entrance difficulty: noncompetitive. Application deadline: rolling. Contact: Mrs. Ruth E. Maddox, Director of Admissions, (901) 424-4600 Ext. 265.

LEE COLLEGE

Cleveland 37311. Private; urban. Awards B. Enrolls 1,442 T (45% women, 30% state res., 80% on fin. aid). Entrance difficulty: noncompetitive. Application deadline: rolling. Contact: Dr. Stanley Butler, Dean of Admissions and Records, (615) 472-2111.

LEMOYNE-OWEN COLLEGE

Memphis 38126. Contact: Mr. Lynn Hardin, Director of Admissions.

LINCOLN MEMORIAL UNIVERSITY

Harrogate 37752. Private; rural. Awards A, B. Enrolls 1,067 T (52% women, 60% state res., 80% on fin. aid). Entrance difficulty: noncompetitive. Application deadline: rolling. Contact: Mr. Jim McCune, (615) 869-3611.

MARYVILLE COLLEGE

Maryville 37801. Private; small town. Awards B. Enrolls 634 T (45% women, 45% state res., 61% on fin. aid). Entrance difficulty: moderately difficult. Application deadline: rolling. Contact: Mr. Dana Paul, Admissions Coordinator, (615) 982-7191.

MEMPHIS ACADEMY OF ARTS

Memphis 38112. Private; urban. Awards B. Enrolls 217 T (53% women, 62% state res., 35% on fin. aid). Entrance difficulty: less difficult. Application deadline: 5/1. Contact: Mrs. Lucy Jones, (901) 726-4085.

MEMPHIS STATE UNIVERSITY

Memphis 38152. Public; urban. Awards B, M, D. Enrolls 21,248 T, 15,770 U (52% women, 93% state res., 24% on fin. aid). Entrance difficulty: moderately difficult. Application deadline: 8/1. Contact: Mr. David R. Wallace, (901) 454-2101.

MIDDLE TENNESSEE STATE UNIVERSITY

Murfreesboro 37132. Public; small town. Awards C, A, B, M, D. Enrolls 10,880 T, 9,144 U (59% women, 95% state res., 30% on fin. aid). Entrance difficulty: moderately difficult. Application deadline: rolling. Contact: Dr. W. Wes Williams, Dean of Admissions and Records, (615) 898-2111.

MILLIGAN COLLEGE

Milligan College 37682. Private; suburban. Awards C, A, B. Enrolls 772 T (53% women, 27% state res., 50% on fin. aid). Entrance difficulty: moderately difficult. Application deadline: rolling. Contact: Mr. Paul Bader, Student Enlistment Officer, (615) 929-0116.

SOUTHERN MISSIONARY COLLEGE

Collegedale 37315. Private; small town. Awards C, A, B. Enrolls 2,033 T (56% women, 24% state res., 65% on fin. aid). Entrance difficulty: less difficult. Application deadline: rolling. Contact: Mr. Ron Barrow, Director of Admissions, (615) 396-4312.

SOUTHWESTERN AT MEMPHIS

Memphis 38112. Private; urban. Awards B. Enrolls 1,024 T (49% women, 49% state res., 53% on fin. aid). Entrance difficulty: very difficult. Application deadlines: rolling, early decision 11/1. Contact: Mr. Ray M. Allen, Dean of Admissions and Financial Aid, (901) 274-1800.

STEED COLLEGE

Johnson City 37601. Private; suburban. Awards C, A, B. Enrolls 1,150 T (67% women, 85% state res., 72% on fin. aid). Entrance difficulty: noncompetitive. Application deadline: 9/10/1. Contact: Mr. Charles R. Murray, (615) 282-1391.

TENNESSEE STATE UNIVERSITY

Nashville 37203. Public; urban. Awards A, B, M. Enrolls 8,438 T, 8,438 U (40% women, 75% state res., 80% on fin. aid). Entrance difficulty: noncompetitive. Application deadline: 8/1. Contact: Mr. Cass Teague Sr, (615) 320-3420.

TENNESSEE TECHNOLOGICAL UNIVERSITY

Cookeville 38501. Public; small town. Awards C, A, B, M, D. Enrolls 6,652 T, 5,912 U (49% women, 94% state res., 31% on fin. aid). Entrance difficulty: moderately difficult. Application deadline: 9/1. Contact: Dr. James C. Perry, (615) 528-3317.

TENNESSEE WESLEYAN COLLEGE

Athens 37303. Private; small town. Awards B. Enrolls 453 T (50% women, 78% state res., 60% on fin. aid). Entrance difficulty: less difficult. Application deadline: rolling. Contact: Mr. Damon B. Mitchell, (615) 745-5872.

TREVECCA NAZARENE COLLEGE

Nashville 37210. Private; suburban. Awards A, B. Enrolls 1,225 T (49% women, 65% state res., 70% on fin. aid). Entrance difficulty: noncompetitive. Application deadline: rolling. Contact: Mr. Howard T. Wall, (615) 244-6000.

TUSCULUM COLLEGE

Greeneville 37743. Private; urban. Awards B. Enrolls 378 T (50% women, 36% state res., 82% on fin. aid). Entrance difficulty: moderately difficult. Application deadline:

Tusculum College (continued)
rolling. Contact: Mr. Robert Fleming, (615) 639-2931.

UNION UNIVERSITY

Jackson 38301. Private; small town. Awards A, B. Enrolls 1,217 T (63% women, 85% state res., 66% on fin. aid). Entrance difficulty: moderately difficult. Application deadline: rolling. Contact: Dr. Milburn W. Blanton, (901) 668-1818.

UNIVERSITY OF TENNESSEE AT CHATTANOOGA

Chattanooga 37403. Public; urban. Awards C, B, M. Enrolls 7,539 T, 6,050 U (52% women, 88% state res., 60% on fin. aid). Entrance difficulty: moderately difficult. Application deadline: rolling. Contact: Mr. Michael White, (615) 755-4157.

UNIVERSITY OF TENNESSEE AT KNOXVILLE

Knoxville 37916. Public; urban. Awards B, M, D. Enrolls 29,720 T, 22,592 U (46% women, 88% state res., 19% on fin. aid). Entrance difficulty: noncompetitive. Contact: Dr. Sandra R. Hughes, (615) 974-2184.

UNIVERSITY OF TENNESSEE AT MARTIN

Martin 38238. Public; small town. Awards A, B, M. Enrolls 5,125 T, 4,686 U (51% women, 92% state res., 55% on fin. aid). Entrance difficulty: less difficult. Application deadline: rolling. Contact: Mr. Jerry Lacy, (901) 587-7020.

UNIVERSITY OF THE SOUTH

Sewanee 37375. Private; rural. Awards B, M, D. Enrolls 1,075 T, 1,000 U (40% women, 22% state res., 46% on fin. aid). Entrance difficulty: very difficult. Application deadlines: 3/1, early decision 12/10. Contact: Mr. Albert S. Gooch Jr, (615) 598-5931.

VANDERBILT UNIVERSITY

Nashville 37212. Private; urban. Awards B, M, D. Enrolls 8,484 T, 5,860 U (50% women, 21% state res., 33% on fin. aid). Entrance difficulty: very difficult. Application deadlines: 2/15, early decision 11/1. Contact: Dr. William L. Campbell, (615) 322-2561.

TEXAS

ABILENE CHRISTIAN UNIVERSITY

Abilene 79699. Private; suburban. Awards A, B, M. Enrolls 4,372 T, 3,800 U (50% women, 65% state res., 70% on fin. aid). Entrance difficulty: moderately difficult. Application deadline: rolling. Contact: Mr. Clint Howeth, Director of Admissions, (915) 677-1911 Ext. 2650.

ABILENE CHRISTIAN UNIVERSITY AT DALLAS

Garland 75041. Private; suburban. Awards B, M. Enrolls 900 T, 600 U (35% women, 80% state res., 75% on fin. aid). Entrance difficulty: noncompetitive. Application deadline: 9/1. Contact: Mr. Lee Paul, Director of University Services and Research, (214) 279-6511.

ANGELO STATE UNIVERSITY

San Angelo 76909. Public; small town. Awards A, B, M. Enrolls 5,637 T, 5,292 U (49% women, 95% state res., 30% on fin. aid). Entrance difficulty: moderately difficult. Application deadline: 8/18. Contact: Dr. Steven Gamble, (915) 942-2041.

AUSTIN COLLEGE

Sherman 75090. Private; suburban. Awards B, M. Enrolls 1,110 T, 1,069 U (43% women, 90% state res., 60% on fin. aid). Entrance difficulty: moderately difficult. Application deadline: rolling. Contact: Ms. Beverly Barcus, Director of Admissions, (214) 892-9101 Ext. 233.

BAYLOR UNIVERSITY

Waco 76706. Private; urban. Awards B, M, D. Enrolls 9,933 T, 8,551 U (53% women, 60% state res., 85% on fin. aid). Entrance difficulty: moderately difficult. Application deadline: rolling. Contact: Mr. Herman D. Thomas, (817) 755-1811.

BISHOP COLLEGE

Dallas 75241. Private; suburban. Awards B. Enrolls 926 T (32% women, 38% state res., 91% on fin. aid). Entrance difficulty: moderately difficult. Application deadline: rolling. Contact: Mrs. Anne G. Lows, (214) 372-8056.

CONCORDIA LUTHERAN COLLEGE

Austin 78705. Private; urban. Awards A, B. Enrolls 334 T (48% women, 87% state res., 45% on fin. aid). Entrance difficulty: less difficult. Application deadline: rolling. Contact: Mr. James Koerschen, Director of Admissions Counseling, (512) 452-7661.

DALLAS BAPTIST COLLEGE

Dallas 75211. Private; urban. Awards B. Enrolls 1,008 T (48% women, 85% state res., 75% on fin. aid). Entrance difficulty: less difficult. Application deadline: rolling. Contact: Dr. Jeter Basden, Director of Admissions and Registrar, (214) 331-8311 Ext. 140.

DALLAS BIBLE COLLEGE

Dallas 75228. Private; urban. Awards C, A, B. Enrolls 225 T (34% women, 51% state res., 60% on fin. aid). Entrance difficulty: less difficult. Application deadline: rolling. Contact: Mr. James R. Crosby, (214) 328-7171.

DEVRY INSTITUTE OF TECHNOLOGY

Dallas 75235. Private; urban. Awards A, B. Enrolls 832 T (5% women, 61% state res., 63% on fin. aid). Entrance difficulty: noncompetitive. Application deadline: 10/1. Contact: Mr. Vijay Shah, (214) 638-0466.

EAST TEXAS BAPTIST COLLEGE

Marshall 75670. Private; suburban. Awards A, B. Enrolls 878 T (55% women, 87% state res., 80% on fin. aid). Entrance difficulty: noncompetitive. Application deadline: 8/1. Contact: Mr. Paul L. Saylors, (214) 938-3711.

EAST TEXAS STATE UNIVERSITY

Commerce 75428. Public; small town. Awards C, B, M, D. Enrolls 8,752 T, 5,402 U (52% women, 95% state res., 30% on fin. aid). Entrance difficulty: moderately difficult. Application deadline: rolling. Contact: Dr. James L. Vickery, Director of Admissions and Registrar, (214) 886-5074.

GULF COAST BIBLE COLLEGE

Houston 77008. Private; urban. Awards A, B. Enrolls 341 T (42% women, 98% state res., 85% on fin. aid). Entrance difficulty: less difficult. Application deadline: rolling.

Contact: Mr. W. Maurice Slater, (713) 862-3800.

HARDIN-SIMMONS UNIVERSITY

Abilene 79601. Private; urban. Awards C, B, M. Enrolls 1,839 T, 1,645 U (51% women, 93% state res., 85% on fin. aid). Entrance difficulty: moderately difficult. Application deadline: rolling. Contact: Mr. Edgar M. Jackson, Director of Admissions, (915) 677-7281 Ext. 205.

HOUSTON BAPTIST UNIVERSITY

Houston 77074. Private; suburban. Awards B, M. Enrolls 1,933 T, 1,757 U (58% women, 88% state res., 70% on fin. aid). Entrance difficulty: moderately difficult. Application deadline: rolling. Contact: Ms. Brenda Davis, Director of Community Relations and Student Development, (713) 774-7661.

HOWARD PAYNE UNIVERSITY

Brownwood 76801. Private; small town. Awards B. Enrolls 1,173 T (51% women, 95% state res., 75% on fin. aid). Entrance difficulty: moderately difficult. Application deadline: 8/15. Contact: Mr. W. Bennett Ragsdale, Director of Admissions and Registrar, (915) 646-2502 Ext. 241.

HUSTON-TILLOTSON COLLEGE

Austin 78702. Private; urban. Awards B. Enrolls 634 T (95% women, 56% state res., 70% on fin. aid). Entrance difficulty: less difficult. Application deadline: rolling. Contact: Mrs. Margaret McCracken, Dean of Students, (512) 476-7421.

INCARNATE WORD COLLEGE

San Antonio 78209. Private; urban. Awards B, M. Enrolls 1,468 T, 1,278 U (78% women, 87% state res., 85% on fin. aid). Entrance difficulty: moderately difficult. Application deadline: 8/24. Contact: Sr. Anne Dossmann, (512) 828-1261 Ext. 200.

JARVIS CHRISTIAN COLLEGE

Hawkins 75765. Private; rural. Awards A, B. Enrolls 622 T (49% women, 48% state res., 98% on fin. aid). Entrance difficulty: noncompetitive. Application deadline: rolling. Contact: Mr. Darnell Thomas, (214) 769-2174 Ext. 128.

LAMAR UNIVERSITY

Beaumont 77710. Public; urban. Awards C, A, B, M, D. Enrolls 12,781 T, 12,213 U (47% women, 91% state res., 31% on fin. aid). Entrance difficulty: noncompetitive. Application deadline: 9/1. Contact: Mr. Richard Neumann, Director of Admissions, (713) 838-7614.

LETOURNEAU COLLEGE

Longview 75601. Private; suburban. Awards A, B. Enrolls 962 T (10% women, 15% state res., 45% on fin. aid). Entrance difficulty: moderately difficult. Application deadline: 7/1. Contact: Mrs. Linda H. Fitzhugh, (214) 753-0231.

LUBBOCK CHRISTIAN COLLEGE

Lubbock 79407. Private; suburban. Awards C, A, B. Enrolls 1,128 T (51% women, 66% state res., 70% on fin. aid). Entrance difficulty: noncompetitive. Application deadline: rolling. Contact: Mr. John King, (806) 792-3221.

MCMURRY COLLEGE

Abilene 79605. Private; suburban. Awards A, B. Enrolls 1,450 T (49% women, 89% state res., 85% on fin. aid). Entrance difficulty: less difficult. Application deadline: rolling. Contact: Mr. Doug Wofford, (915) 692-4130.

MIDWESTERN STATE UNIVERSITY

Wichita Falls 76308. Public; suburban. Awards A, B, M. Enrolls 4,280 T, 3,884 U (49% women, 90% state res., 35% on fin. aid). Entrance difficulty: noncompetitive. Application deadline: 8/15. Contact: Mr. Hoyt Lovelace, (817) 692-6611 Ext. 333.

NORTH TEXAS STATE UNIVERSITY

Denton 76203. Public; small town. Awards B, M, D. Enrolls 17,228 T, 12,308 U (51% women, 83% state res., 29% on fin. aid). Entrance difficulty: moderately difficult. Application deadline: 8/1. Contact: Miss Billie Collins, Student Relations Coordinator.

OUR LADY OF THE LAKE UNIVERSITY OF SAN ANTONIO

San Antonio 78285. Private; suburban. Awards B, M. Enrolls 1,713 T, 1,150 U (80% women, 90% state res., 80% on fin. aid). Entrance difficulty: less difficult. Application deadline: rolling. Contact: Ms. Loretta Schlegel, (512) 434-6711.

PAN AMERICAN UNIVERSITY

Edinburg 78539. Public; rural. Awards A, B, M. Enrolls 9,603 T, 8,351 U (56% women, 95% state res., 74% on fin. aid). Entrance difficulty: noncompetitive. Application deadline: rolling. Contact: Mr. John Hook, Dean of Admissions, (512) 381-2206.

PAUL QUINN COLLEGE

Waco 76703. Private; urban. Awards B. Enrolls 421 T (53% women, 71% state res., 98% on fin. aid). Entrance difficulty: noncompetitive. Application deadline: rolling. Contact: Ms. Sarah J. Seldon, Director of Admissions, (817) 753-6565.

PRAIRIE VIEW A&M UNIVERSITY

Prairie View 77445. Public; small town. Awards C, B, M. Enrolls 4,991 T, 3,848 U (49% women, 83% state res., 97% on fin. aid). Entrance difficulty: moderately difficult. Application deadline: rolling. Contact: Mrs. Mary Clark, Associate Director of Admissions.

RICE UNIVERSITY

Houston 77001. Private; suburban. Awards B, M, D. Enrolls 3,450 T, 2,430 U (33% women, 60% state res., 65% on fin. aid). Entrance difficulty: most difficult. Application deadlines: 2/1, early decision 10/1. Contact: Mr. Richard N. Stabell, Assistant to the President for Admissions and Records, (713) 527-4036.

ST EDWARD'S UNIVERSITY

Austin 78704. Private; urban. Awards B, M. Enrolls 2,200 T, 1,893 U (40% women, 80% state res., 60% on fin. aid). Entrance difficulty: moderately difficult. Application deadline: rolling. Contact: Mr. John Lucas, (512) 444-2621.

ST MARY'S UNIVERSITY OF SAN ANTONIO

San Antonio 78284. Private; suburban. Awards B, M. Enrolls 3,374 T, 2,236 U (39% women, 77% state res., 75% on fin. aid). Entrance difficulty: moderately difficult. Application deadline: 8/15. Contact: Miss Candace J. Kuebker, Assistant Director of Admissions, (512) 436-3126.

SAM HOUSTON STATE UNIVERSITY

Huntsville 77340. Public; small town. Awards B, M, D. Enrolls 10,549 T, 9,326 U (51% women, 96% state res., 50% on fin. aid). Entrance difficulty: moderately difficult. Application deadline: 8/27. Contact: Mr. H. A. Bass, (713) 295-6211 Ext. 2971.

SOUTHERN METHODIST UNIVERSITY

Dallas 75275. Private; suburban. Awards B, M, D. Enrolls 8,973 T, 5,802 U (50% women, 45% state res., 37% on fin. aid). Entrance difficulty: moderately difficult. Application deadline: 4/1. Contact: Mr. Scott F. Healy, Director of Admissions, (214) 692-2058.

SOUTHWESTERN ASSEMBLIES OF GOD COLLEGE

Waxahachie 75165. Private; small town. Awards C, A, B. Enrolls 809 T (46% women, 44% state res., 92% on fin. aid). Entrance difficulty: noncompetitive. Application deadline: rolling. Contact: Rev. Robert D. Hogan, Director of Admissions and Records, (214) 937-4010 Ext. 50.

SOUTHWESTERN UNION COLLEGE

Keene 76059. Private; small town. Awards C, A, B. Enrolls 717 T (51% women, 59% state res., 95% on fin. aid). Entrance difficulty: noncompetitive. Application deadline: 8/30. Contact: Dr. Dallas Kindopp, (817) 645-3921 Ext. 222.

SOUTHWESTERN UNIVERSITY

Georgetown 78626. Private; small town. Awards B. Enrolls 1,001 T (56% women, 92% state res., 58% on fin. aid). Entrance difficulty: moderately difficult. Application deadline: rolling. Contact: Mr. William D. Swift, Vice President for Admissions, (512) 863-6511.

SOUTHWEST TEXAS STATE UNIVERSITY

San Marcos 78666. Public; small town. Awards C, A, B, M. Enrolls 15,924 T, 14,018 U (51% women, 98% state res., 40% on fin. aid). Entrance difficulty: moderately difficult. Application deadline: rolling. Contact: Mr. Robert E. Gaines, Director of Admissions and University Registrar, (512) 245-2364.

STEPHEN F AUSTIN STATE UNIVERSITY

Nacogdoches 75961. Public; small town. Awards B, M, D. Enrolls 10,400 T, 9,200 U (54% women, 97% state res., 20% on fin. aid). Entrance difficulty: moderately difficult. Application deadline: 7/15. Contact: Dr. Clyde Iglinsky, (713) 569-2504.

SUL ROSS STATE UNIVERSITY

Alpine 79830. Public; small town. Awards C, A, B, M. Enrolls 2,140 T, 1,574 U (46% women, 75% on fin. aid). Entrance difficulty: less difficult. Application deadline: rolling. Contact: Mrs. Dorothy M. Leavitt, Registrar, (915) 837-8050.

TARLETON STATE UNIVERSITY

Stephenville 76402. Public; small town. Awards A, B, M. Enrolls 3,423 T, 2,631 U (45% women, 74% state res., 52% on fin. aid). Entrance difficulty: noncompetitive. Application deadline: 8/15. Contact: Dr. Conley Jenkins, Director of Admissions, (817) 968-9125.

TEXAS A&I UNIVERSITY AT KINGSVILLE

Kingsville 78363. Public; small town. Awards B, M, D. Enrolls 6,060 T, 5,004 U (46% women, 90% state res., 65% on fin. aid). Entrance difficulty: moderately difficult. Application deadline: 8/15. Contact: Mr. Gustavo DeLeon, (512) 595-2811.

TEXAS A&M UNIVERSITY

College Station 77843. Public; small town. Awards C, B, M, D. Enrolls 31,331 T, 25,947 U (36% women, 89% state res., 35% on fin. aid). Entrance difficulty: moderately difficult. Application deadline: 7/31. Contact: Dr. Billy G. Lay, (713) 845-1031.

TEXAS CHRISTIAN UNIVERSITY

Fort Worth 76129. Private; suburban. Awards B, M, D. Enrolls 5,930 T, 4,493 U (57% women, 70% state res., 55% on fin. aid). Entrance difficulty: moderately difficult. Application deadline: rolling. Contact: Miss Janet George, Director of Freshman Admissions.

TEXAS COLLEGE

Tyler 75701. Private; urban. Awards B. Application deadline: 8/15. Contact: R.A.

Texas College (continued)
Moody, Admissions Counselor, (214) 593-8311 Ext. 36.

TEXAS LUTHERAN COLLEGE

Seguin 78155. Private; small town. Awards C, B. Enrolls 1,029 T (45% women, 81% state res., 85% on fin. aid). Entrance difficulty: moderately difficult. Application deadline: rolling. Contact: Mr. Robert A. Miller, (512) 379-0126.

TEXAS SOUTHERN UNIVERSITY

Houston 77004. Public; urban. Awards B, M, D. Enrolls 8,528 T, 7,010 U (45% women, 73% state res., 70% on fin. aid). Entrance difficulty: noncompetitive. Application deadline: 8/10. Contact: Mr. Collie Chambers, Director, Recruiting/Registration, (713) 527-7066.

TEXAS TECH UNIVERSITY

Lubbock 79409. Public; urban. Awards B, M, D. Enrolls 21,637 T, 19,444 U (43% women, 85% state res., 12% on fin. aid). Entrance difficulty: noncompetitive. Application deadline: rolling. Contact: Mr. Dale Grusing, (806) 742-3661.

TEXAS WESLEYAN COLLEGE

Fort Worth 76105. Private; urban. Awards B, M. Enrolls 1,555 T (53% women, 91% state res., 60% on fin. aid). Entrance difficulty: moderately difficult. Application deadline: 8/15. Contact: Mr. Kenneth J. Wallace, Dean of Admissions, (817) 534-0251.

TEXAS WOMAN'S UNIVERSITY

Denton 76204. Public; small town. Awards B, M, D. Enrolls 7,756 T, 4,146 U (97% women, 84% state res., 40% on fin. aid). Entrance difficulty: noncompetitive. Application deadline: rolling. Contact: Mr. John E. Tompkins Jr, Director of Admissions and Registrar, (817) 566-1451.

TRINITY UNIVERSITY

San Antonio 78284. Private; urban. Awards B, M. Enrolls 3,285 T, 2,554 U (52% women, 72% state res., 50% on fin. aid). Entrance difficulty: moderately difficult. Application deadlines: 7/24, early decision 11/1. Contact: Mr. Russell Gossage, (512) 736-7207.

UNIVERSITY OF DALLAS

Irving 75061. Private; suburban. Awards B, M, D. Enrolls 2,391 T, 1,111 U (46% women, 49% state res., 68% on fin. aid). Entrance difficulty: very difficult. Application deadlines: 8/15, early decision 10/15. Contact: Mr. Daniel J. Davis, (214) 438-1123.

UNIVERSITY OF HOUSTON

Houston 77004. Public; urban. Awards B, M, D. Enrolls 28,414 T, 21,665 U (45% women, 87% state res., 10% on fin. aid). Entrance difficulty: moderately difficult. Application deadline: 7/21. Contact: Ms. Lee Elliott Pacocon, (713) 749-1413.

UNIVERSITY OF HOUSTON, DOWNTOWN CAMPUS

Houston 77002. Public; urban. Awards B. Enrolls 4,612 T (46% women, 87% state res., 40% on fin. aid). Entrance difficulty: noncompetitive. Application deadline: rolling. Contact: Miss Molly Woods, (713) 749-2001.

UNIVERSITY OF MARY HARDIN-BAYLOR

Belton 76513. Private; suburban. Awards B. Enrolls 1,050 T (62% women, 81% state res., 64% on fin. aid). Entrance difficulty: moderately difficult. Application deadline: rolling. Contact: Mr. Bill W. Elliott, (817) 939-5811.

UNIVERSITY OF ST THOMAS

Houston 77006. Private; urban. Awards B, M. Enrolls 1,765 T, 1,637 U (65% women, 90% state res., 60% on fin. aid). Entrance difficulty: less difficult. Application deadline: 8/15. Contact: Dr. George K. Knaggs, Registrar, (713) 522-7911.

UNIVERSITY OF TEXAS AT ARLINGTON

Arlington 76019. Public; suburban. Awards B, M, D. Enrolls 19,138 T, 16,322 U (39% women, 87% state res., 30% on fin. aid). Entrance difficulty: moderately difficult; noncompetitive for students over 25 years of age. Application deadline: 8/1. Contact: Mr. R. Zack Prince, Registrar, (817) 273-3401.

UNIVERSITY OF TEXAS AT AUSTIN

Austin 78712. Public; suburban. Awards B, M, D. Enrolls 44,102 T, 34,617 U (46% women, 75% state res., 25% on fin. aid). Entrance difficulty: moderately difficult. Application deadline: 7/1. Contact: Dr. David E. Hershey, Director of Admissions, (512) 471-1711.

UNIVERSITY OF TEXAS AT EL PASO

El Paso 79968. Public; urban. Awards B, M, D. Enrolls 15,745 T, 13,907 U (53% women, 90% state res., 33% on fin. aid). Application deadline: rolling. Contact: Mr. William Nelsen, (915) 747-5550.

UNIVERSITY OF TEXAS AT SAN ANTONIO

San Antonio 78285. Public; urban. Awards B, M. Enrolls 9,453 T, 7,689 U (49% women, 98% state res., 30% on fin. aid). Entrance difficulty: less difficult. Application deadline: rolling. Contact: Dr. John H. Brown, Registrar and Director of Admissions, (512) 691-4535.

WAYLAND BAPTIST COLLEGE

Plainview 79072. Private; small town. Awards B. Enrolls 1,268 T (30% women, 87% state res., 85% on fin. aid). Application deadline: 8/31. Contact: Mrs. Audrey H. Boles, Registrar, (806) 296-5521 Ext. 23.

WEST TEXAS STATE UNIVERSITY

Canyon 79016. Public; small town. Awards C, B, M. Enrolls 6,600 T, 5,259 U (51% women, 93% state res., 25% on fin. aid). Entrance difficulty: noncompetitive. Application deadline: 8/15. Contact: Dr. Donald Cates, (806) 656-3331.

WILEY COLLEGE

Marshall 75670. Private; small town. Awards A, B. Enrolls 603 T (49% women, 52% state res., 84% on fin. aid). Entrance difficulty: noncompetitive. Application deadlines: 8/1, early decision 4/1. Contact: Mr. Edward Morgan, Director of Recruitment, (214) 938-8341.

UTAH

BRIGHAM YOUNG UNIVERSITY

Provo 84602. Private; small town. Awards A, B, M, D. Enrolls 26,373 T, 24,107 U (49% women, 31% state res., 15% on fin. aid). Entrance difficulty: moderately difficult. Application deadline: 4/30. Contact: Mr. Jeffrey M. Tanner, (801) 378-2507.

SOUTHERN UTAH STATE COLLEGE

Cedar City 84720. Public; small town. Awards C, B. Enrolls 2,048 T (46% women, 81% state res., 52% on fin. aid). Entrance difficulty: noncompetitive. Application deadline: 9/1. Contact: Mr. Galen Rose, (801) 586-4411 Ext. 311.

UNIVERSITY OF UTAH

Salt Lake City 84112. Public; urban. Awards C, B, M, D. Enrolls 21,996 T, 17,446 U (47% women, 86% state res., 40% on fin. aid). Entrance difficulty: noncompetitive. Application deadline: 8/1. Contact: Mr. John Boswell, Director of High School Services, (801) 581-8761.

UTAH STATE UNIVERSITY

Logan 84322. Public; small town. Awards C, B, M, D. Enrolls 9,266 T, 7,996 U (42% women, 65% state res., 30% on fin. aid). Entrance difficulty: moderately difficult. Application deadline: 9/1. Contact: Mr. G. Karl Lambert, Assistant Director of Admissions & Records, (801) 750-1108.

WEBER STATE COLLEGE

Ogden 84408. Public; urban. Awards C, A, B, M. Enrolls 9,674 T, 9,568 U (42% women, 93% state res., 29% on fin. aid). Entrance difficulty: noncompetitive except for nursing. Application deadline: rolling. Contact: Dr. Emil O. Hanson, (801) 626-6048.

WESTMINSTER COLLEGE

Salt Lake City 84105. Private; suburban. Awards B, M. Enrolls 1,159 T, 1,129 U (50% women, 65% state res., 46% on fin. aid). Entrance difficulty: less difficult. Application deadline: rolling. Contact: Shelia Herriott, Dean of Admissions, (801) 484-7651 Ext. 224.

VERMONT

BENNINGTON COLLEGE

Bennington 05201. Private; rural. Awards B, M. Enrolls 657 T, 655 U (70% women, 1% state res., 30% on fin. aid). Entrance difficulty: very difficult. Application deadlines: rolling, early decision 11/15. Contact: Mr. John Nissen, Director of Admissions, (802) 442-5401.

CASTLETON STATE COLLEGE

Castleton 05735. Public; rural. Awards A, B, M. Enrolls 2,082 T, 1,758 U (54% women, 65% state res., 75% on fin. aid). Entrance difficulty: noncompetitive; moderately difficult for nursing. Application deadline: rolling. Contact: Mr. Gary Fallis, (802) 468-5611.

COLLEGE OF ST JOSEPH THE PROVIDER

Rutland 05701. Private; suburban. Awards A, B, M. Enrolls 251 T, 212 U (80% women, 70% state res., 84% on fin. aid). Entrance difficulty: moderately difficult. Application deadline: rolling. Contact: Miss Amy M. Barna, Registrar, (802) 775-0806.

GODDARD COLLEGE

Plainfield 05667. Private; rural. Awards B, M. Enrolls 1,450 T, 1,050 U (50% women, 5% state res., 50% on fin. aid). Entrance difficulty: noncompetitive. Application deadline: rolling. Contact: Mr. Christopher Lovell, (802) 454-8311.

GREEN MOUNTAIN COLLEGE

Poultney 05764. Private; small town. Awards A, B. Enrolls 475 T (80% women, 10% state res., 38% on fin. aid). Entrance difficulty: moderately difficult. Application deadlines: 8/1, early decision 11/1. Contact: Mr. David T. Leach, Dean of Admissions, (802) 287-9313.

JOHNSON STATE COLLEGE

Johnson 05656. Public; rural. Awards B, M. Enrolls 972 T, 904 U (55% women, 72% state res., 73% on fin. aid). Entrance difficulty: noncompetitive. Application deadline: rolling. Contact: Mary Hoadley, Admissions Counselor, (802) 635-2356 Ext. 257.

LYNDON STATE COLLEGE

Lyndonville 05851. Public; rural. Awards A, B, M. Enrolls 1,072 T, 1,037 U (45% women, 48% state res., 75% on fin. aid). Entrance difficulty: moderately difficult; very difficult for meteorology majors. Application deadline: rolling. Contact: Mr. Russell S. Powden Jr, Director of Admissions and Financial Aid, (802) 626-9371.

MARLBORO COLLEGE

Marlboro 05344. Private; rural. Awards B. Enrolls 232 T (51% women, 10% state res., 40% on fin. aid). Entrance difficulty: moderately difficult. Application deadline: 8/15. Contact: Mr. Michael S. Newman, (802) 257-4333.

MIDDLEBURY COLLEGE

Middlebury 05753. Private; rural. Awards B, M, D. Enrolls 1,870 T (50% women, 7% state res., 23% on fin. aid). Entrance difficulty: very difficult. Application deadlines: 1/15, early decision 11/15. Contact: Mr. Fred F. Neuberger, (802) 388-4929.

NORWICH UNIVERSITY

Northfield 05663. Private; rural. Awards B, M. Enrolls 1,572 T, 1,448 U (10% women, 8% state res., 55% on fin. aid). Entrance difficulty: moderately difficult; very difficult for engineering, chemistry, mathematics, and physics. Application deadlines: 8/15, early decision 11/1. Contact: Dr. Melvin C. Somers, Dean of Admissions, (802) 485-5011.

SAINT MICHAEL'S COLLEGE

Winooski 05404. Private; suburban. Awards B, M. Enrolls 1,802 T, 1,575 U (42% women, 12% state res., 52% on fin. aid). Entrance difficulty: moderately difficult. Application deadline: rolling. Contact: Mr. Jerry E. Flanagan, (802) 655-2000.

SOUTHERN VERMONT COLLEGE

Bennington 05201. Private; small town. Awards A, B. Enrolls 364 T (54% women, 39% state res., 65% on fin. aid). Entrance difficulty: noncompetitive. Application deadline: rolling. Contact: Mr. Christopher Langlois, (802) 442-5427.

TRINITY COLLEGE

Burlington 05401. Private; small town. Awards A, B. Enrolls 648 T (86% women,

75% state res., 60% on fin. aid). Entrance difficulty: moderately difficult. Application deadline: rolling. Contact: Sr. Jessica Brugger Meserve, (802) 658-2471.

UNIVERSITY OF VERMONT

Burlington 05401. Public; suburban. Awards A, B, M, D. Enrolls 8,850 T, 7,670 U (55% women, 50% state res., 30% on fin. aid). Entrance difficulty: moderately difficult. Application deadline: 2/1. Contact: Mr. Jeff Kaplan, (802) 656-3370.

VERMONT COLLEGE

Montpelier 05602. Private; small town. Awards C, A, B, M. Enrolls 447 T (90% women, 50% state res., 60% on fin. aid). Entrance difficulty: moderately difficult; very difficult for nursing and medical technology programs. Application deadlines: 8/15, early decision 11/1. Contact: Dr. Melvin C. Somers, Dean of Admissions, (802) 229-0522.

VERMONT INSTITUTE OF COMMUNITY INVOLVEMENT

South Burlington 05401. Contact: Dr. Gunnar Urang, Director, Admissions.

VIRGINIA

AVERETT COLLEGE

Danville 24541. Private; suburban. Awards A, B, M. Enrolls 1,105 T, 1,077 U (66% women, 78% state res., 44% on fin. aid). Entrance difficulty: moderately difficult. Application deadline: 8/15. Contact: Mr. Walt Crutchfield, (804) 793-7811.

BLUEFIELD COLLEGE

Bluefield 24605. Private; suburban. Awards C, A, B. Enrolls 391 T (45% women, 68% state res., 75% on fin. aid). Entrance difficulty: moderately difficult. Application deadline: rolling. Contact: Mr. Charles R. Addington, Director of Admissions and Financial Aid, (304) 327-7137.

BRIDGEWATER COLLEGE

Bridgewater 22812. Private; small town. Awards B. Enrolls 914 T (50% women, 71% state res., 44% on fin. aid). Entrance difficulty: moderately difficult. Application

deadline: rolling. Contact: Mrs. Linda F. Glover, Director of Admissions, (703) 828-2501.

CHRISTOPHER NEWPORT COLLEGE

Newport News 23606. Public; urban. Awards B. Enrolls 3,918 T (52% women, 90% state res., 20% on fin. aid). Entrance difficulty: moderately difficult. Application deadline: 8/1. Contact: Mr. Keith F. McLoughland, Dean of Admissions, (804) 599-7015.

CLINCH VALLEY COLLEGE OF THE UNIVERSITY OF VIRGINIA

Wise 24293. Public; small town. Awards A, B. Enrolls 942 T (54% women, 91% state res., 55% on fin. aid). Entrance difficulty: less difficult. Application deadline: 8/15. Contact: Mr. Eric Wagner, Director of Admissions, (703) 328-2431 Ext. 200.

COLLEGE OF WILLIAM AND MARY

Williamsburg 23185. Public; small town. Awards B, M, D. Enrolls 6,387 T, 4,449 U (56% women, 70% state res., 13% on fin. aid). Entrance difficulty: very difficult. Application deadlines: 2/1, early decision 11/1. Contact: Mr. Robert P. Hunt, (804) 253-4224.

EASTERN MENNONITE COLLEGE

Harrisonburg 22801. Private; small town. Awards C, A, B. Enrolls 1,056 T (63% women, 29% state res., 80% on fin. aid). Entrance difficulty: moderately difficult. Application deadline: 8/15. Contact: Mr. J. David Yoder, (703) 433-2771.

EMORY AND HENRY COLLEGE

Emory 24327. Private; rural. Awards B. Enrolls 825 T (46% women, 78% state res., 70% on fin. aid). Entrance difficulty: moderately difficult. Application deadlines: rolling, early decision 10/15. Contact: Mr. Henry C. Dawson Jr, (703) 944-3121.

FERRUM COLLEGE

Ferrum 24088. Private; rural. Awards C, A, B. Enrolls 1,546 T (40% women, 85% state res., 50% on fin. aid). Entrance difficulty: less difficult. Application deadline: rolling. Contact: Mr. John C. Carter, (703) 365-2121.

GEORGE MASON UNIVERSITY

Fairfax 22030. Public; suburban. Awards B, M, D. Enrolls 12,249 T, 8,984 U (57% women, 89% state res., 16% on fin. aid). Entrance difficulty: moderately difficult. Application deadlines: 7/1, early decision 11/1. Contact: Mr. Clenton A. Blount Jr, (703) 323-2102.

HAMPDEN-SYDNEY COLLEGE

Hampden-Sydney 23943. Private; rural. Awards B. Enrolls 720 T (0% women, 70% state res., 34% on fin. aid). Entrance difficulty: moderately difficult. Application deadlines: 3/1, early decision 11/1. Contact: Mr. John H. Waters, (804) 223-4381.

HAMPTON INSTITUTE

Hampton 23668. Private; urban. Awards B, M. Enrolls 3,187 T, 2,700 U (67% women, 39% state res., 80% on fin. aid). Entrance difficulty: moderately difficult. Application deadlines: 6/30, early decision 12/15. Contact: Dr. Ollie M. Bowman, Dean of Admissions, (804) 727-5328.

HOLLINS COLLEGE

Roanoke 24020. Private; suburban. Awards B, M. Enrolls 935 T, 854 U (100% women, 32% state res., 63% on fin. aid). Entrance difficulty: moderately difficult. Application deadlines: 3/1, early decision 11/15. Contact: Mrs. Sandra J. Lovinguth, (703) 362-6401.

JAMES MADISON UNIVERSITY

Harrisonburg 22807. Public; small town. Awards B, M. Enrolls 8,387 T, 7,198 U (53% women, 81% state res., 50% on fin. aid). Entrance difficulty: moderately difficult. Application deadline: 2/1. Contact: Mr. Francis E. Turner, (703) 433-6147.

LIBERTY BAPTIST COLLEGE

Lynchburg 24505. Private; suburban. Awards A, B. Enrolls 2,537 T (46% women, 14% state res., 75% on fin. aid). Entrance difficulty: noncompetitive. Application deadline: 8/1. Contact: Mr. Tom Diggs, (804) 237-6294.

LONGWOOD COLLEGE

Farmville 23901. Public; small town. Awards B, M. Enrolls 2,385 T, 2,300 U (75% women, 92% state res., 65% on fin. aid). Entrance difficulty: moderately diffi-

cult. Application deadline: rolling. Contact: Mr. Gary Groneweg, (804) 392-9251.

LYNCHBURG COLLEGE

Lynchburg 24501. Private; suburban. Awards B, M. Enrolls 2,412 T, 1,852 U (58% women, 51% state res., 27% on fin. aid). Entrance difficulty: moderately difficult. Application deadline: rolling. Contact: Mr. Ernest R. Chadderton, (804) 845-9071.

MARY BALDWIN COLLEGE

Staunton 24401. Private; small town. Awards B. Enrolls 700 T (100% women, 48% state res., 38% on fin. aid). Entrance difficulty: moderately difficult. Application deadlines: 4/1, early decision 11/15. Contact: Mr. John A. Blackburn, (703) 885-0811.

MARYMOUNT COLLEGE OF VIRGINIA

Arlington 22207. Private; suburban. Awards A, B, M. Enrolls 900 T, 852 U (99% women, 34% state res., 50% on fin. aid). Entrance difficulty: moderately difficult. Application deadline: rolling. Contact: Mrs. Kathryn B. DelCampo, (703) 524-2500 Ext. 270.

MARY WASHINGTON COLLEGE

Fredericksburg 22401. Public; small town. Awards B. Enrolls 2,471 T (80% women, 78% state res., 25% on fin. aid). Entrance difficulty: moderately difficult. Application deadlines: 3/1, early decision 11/1. Contact: Dr. H. Conrad Warlick, Dean of Admissions, (703) 899-4681.

NORFOLK STATE UNIVERSITY

Norfolk 23504. Public; urban. Awards C, A, B, M. Enrolls 6,756 T, 6,550 U (56% women, 80% state res., 80% on fin. aid). Entrance difficulty: noncompetitive. Application deadline: 7/1. Contact: Mr. James S. Burton, (804) 623-8391.

OLD DOMINION UNIVERSITY

Norfolk 23508. Public; urban. Awards C, B, M, D. Enrolls 13,935 T, 10,768 U (49% women, 86% state res., 18% on fin. aid). Entrance difficulty: moderately difficult. Application deadline: 7/15. Contact: Mr. Thomas E. Powell Jr, (804) 489-6231.

RADFORD UNIVERSITY

Radford 24142. Public; rural. Awards B, M. Enrolls 5,623 T, 4,600 U (65% women, 90% state res., 45% on fin. aid). Entrance difficulty: moderately difficult. Application deadline: 6/1. Contact: Mr. Drumont I. Bowman, (703) 731-5371.

RANDOLPH-MACON COLLEGE

Ashland 23005. Private; small town. Awards B. Enrolls 959 T (41% women, 64% state res., 36% on fin. aid). Entrance difficulty: moderately difficult. Application deadlines: 3/1, early decision 12/1. Contact: Mr. C. Edwin Cox Jr, (804) 798-8372.

RANDOLPH-MACON WOMAN'S COLLEGE

Lynchburg 24503. Private; suburban. Awards B. Enrolls 760 T (100% women, 38% state res., 26% on fin. aid). Entrance difficulty: moderately difficult. Application deadlines: 3/1, early decision 11/1. Contact: Mr. Robert T. Merritt, (804) 846-7392.

ROANOKE COLLEGE

Salem 24153. Private; small town. Awards B. Enrolls 1,344 T (50% women, 50% state res., 60% on fin. aid). Entrance difficulty: moderately difficult. Application deadlines: rolling, early decision 11/1. Contact: Mr. William C. Schaaf, (703) 389-2351.

SAINT PAUL'S COLLEGE

Lawrenceville 23868. Private; small town. Awards B. Enrolls 615 T (50% women, 73% state res., 95% on fin. aid). Entrance difficulty: less difficult. Contact: Mr. Larnell R. Parker, Director of Admissions, (804) 848-4356.

SHENANDOAH COLLEGE AND CONSERVATORY OF MUSIC

Winchester 22601. Private; small town. Awards A, B, M. Enrolls 900 T, 875 U (54% women, 55% state res., 72% on fin. aid). Entrance difficulty: moderately difficult. Application deadlines: 8/15, early decision 12/1. Contact: Mr. Dwight D. Moore, (703) 667-8714.

SWEET BRIAR COLLEGE

Sweet Briar 24595. Private; rural. Awards B. Enrolls 685 T (100% women, 19% state res., 50% on fin. aid). Entrance difficulty: moderately difficult. Application deadlines: 3/1, early decision 11/15. Contact: Ms. Terry Scarborough, Acting Director of Admissions, (804) 381-5548.

UNIVERSITY OF RICHMOND

University of Richmond 23173. Private; suburban. Awards B, M. Enrolls 3,370 T, 2,583 U (43% women, 50% state res., 40% on fin. aid). Entrance difficulty: moderately difficult. Application deadlines: 2/15, early decision 12/1. Contact: Mr. Thomas N. Carter, Admissions Counselor, (804) 285-6262.

UNIVERSITY OF VIRGINIA

Charlottesville 22903. Public; suburban. Awards B, M, D. Enrolls 16,464 T, 10,838 U (47% women, 64% state res., 20% on fin. aid). Entrance difficulty: very difficult. Application deadline: 2/1. Contact: Dr. John T. Casteen III, Dean of Admissions, (804) 924-7751.

VIRGINIA COMMONWEALTH UNIVERSITY

Richmond 23284. Private; urban. Awards C, A, B, M, D. Enrolls 19,428 T, 10,407 U (60% women, 93% state res., 49% on fin. aid). Entrance difficulty: moderately difficult. Application deadline: 8/15. Contact: Dr. Jerrie J. Johnson, (804) 257-1222.

VIRGINIA INTERMONT COLLEGE

Bristol 24201. Private; urban. Awards A, B. Enrolls 631 T (87% women, 38% state res., 67% on fin. aid). Entrance difficulty: moderately difficult. Application deadline: rolling. Contact: Mrs. Margaret B. Crumley, (703) 669-6101 Ext. 14.

VIRGINIA MILITARY INSTITUTE

Lexington 24450. Public; small town. Awards B. Enrolls 1,310 T (0% women, 53% state res., 55% on fin. aid). Entrance difficulty: moderately difficult. Application deadline: rolling. Contact: Col. William J. Buchanan, (703) 463-6211.

VIRGINIA POLYTECHNIC INSTITUTE AND STATE UNIVERSITY

Blacksburg 24061. Public; small town. Awards B, M, D. Enrolls 20,780 T, 17,847 U (38% women, 80% state res., 20% on fin. aid). Entrance difficulty: mod-

Virginia Polytechnic Institute and State University (continued)
erately difficult; very difficult for architecture and engineering programs. Application deadlines: 1/1, early decision 11/1. Contact: Dr. M. P. Lacy, Dean of Admissions and Records, (703) 961-5460.

VIRGINIA STATE UNIVERSITY

Petersburg 23803. Public; suburban. Awards B, M. Enrolls 4,438 T, 3,998 U (55% women, 78% state res., 90% on fin. aid). Entrance difficulty: noncompetitive. Application deadline: 6/1. Contact: Mr. Edward L. Smith, (804) 520-6542.

VIRGINIA UNION UNIVERSITY

Richmond 23220. Private; suburban. Awards B, M. Enrolls 1,197 T, 1,112 U (51% women, 58% state res., 92% on fin. aid). Application deadline: 6/15. Contact: Mrs. Janice D. Bailey, Director of Admissions.

VIRGINIA WESLEYAN COLLEGE

Norfolk 23502. Private; suburban. Awards B. Enrolls 775 T (50% women, 70% state res., 60% on fin. aid). Entrance difficulty: less difficult. Application deadline: 5/1. Contact: Mr. Frank S. Badger, (804) 461-3232.

WASHINGTON AND LEE UNIVERSITY

Lexington 24450. Private; small town. Awards B. Enrolls 1,698 T, 1,364 U (0% women, 25% state res., 20% on fin. aid). Entrance difficulty: very difficult. Application deadlines: 2/15, early decision 11/1. Contact: Mr. William M. Hartog, (703) 463-9111 Ext. 203.

WASHINGTON

CENTRAL WASHINGTON UNIVERSITY

Ellensburg 98926. Public; small town. Awards C, B, M. Enrolls 7,909 T, 5,858 U (52% women, 97% state res., 25% on fin. aid). Entrance difficulty: moderately difficult. Application deadline: 9/1. Contact: Mr. James G. Pappas, Dean of Admissions and Records, (509) 963-1211.

CORNISH INSTITUTE

Seattle 98102. Private; urban. Awards B. Enrolls 422 T (61% women, 84% state res., 54% on fin. aid). Application deadline: 8/15. Contact: Miss Lois Pittenger, Admissions Officer, (206) 323-1400.

EASTERN WASHINGTON UNIVERSITY

Cheney 99004. Public; small town. Awards B, M. Enrolls 7,724 T, 6,069 U (50% women, 95% state res., 27% on fin. aid). Entrance difficulty: moderately difficult. Application deadline: rolling. Contact: Mr. Glenn E. Fehler, (509) 359-2397.

EVERGREEN STATE COLLEGE

Olympia 98505. Public; suburban. Awards B, M. Enrolls 2,554 T (52% women, 76% state res., 50% on fin. aid). Entrance difficulty: moderately difficult. Application deadline: 9/1. Contact: Mr. Arnaldo Rodriguez, (206) 866-6170.

FORT WRIGHT COLLEGE

Spokane 99204. Private; suburban. Awards B, M. Enrolls 405 T, 368 U (65% women, 78% state res., 75% on fin. aid). Entrance difficulty: noncompetitive. Application deadline: 9/1. Contact: Miss Mary Falkenreck, Dean of Admissions, (509) 328-2970 Ext. 30.

GONZAGA UNIVERSITY

Spokane 99258. Private; urban. Awards B, M, D. Enrolls 3,481 T, 1,937 U (49% women, 45% state res., 60% on fin. aid). Entrance difficulty: moderately difficult. Application deadline: 8/15. Contact: Mr. James T. Mansfield, (509) 328-4220.

LUTHERAN BIBLE INSTITUTE OF SEATTLE

Issaquah 98027. Private; rural. Awards C, B. Enrolls 260 T (55% women, 50% state res.). Application deadline: 8/15. Contact: Dr. Don Douglas, Director of Admissions, (206) 392-0400.

NORTHWEST COLLEGE OF THE ASSEMBLIES OF GOD

Kirkland 98033. Private; suburban. Awards A, B. Enrolls 787 T (45% women, 55% state res.). Entrance difficulty: moderately difficult. Application deadline: rolling. Contact: Mr. A. D. Millard, (206) 822-8266.

PACIFIC LUTHERAN UNIVERSITY

Tacoma 98447. Private; suburban. Awards B, M. Enrolls 3,376 T, 2,878 U (55% women, 72% state res., 60% on fin. aid). Entrance difficulty: moderately difficult. Application deadlines: rolling, early decision 11/15. Contact: Mr. James Van Beek, Dean of Admissions, (206) 531-6900 Ext. 227.

SAINT MARTIN'S COLLEGE

Olympia 98503. Private; suburban. Awards A, B. Enrolls 515 T (43% women, 77% state res., 68% on fin. aid). Entrance difficulty: less difficult. Application deadline: rolling. Contact: Miss Patricia A. Connors, Director of Admissions and Records, (206) 491-4700.

SEATTLE PACIFIC UNIVERSITY

Seattle 98119. Private; urban. Awards B, M. Enrolls 2,499 T, 2,185 U (63% women, 64% state res., 70% on fin. aid). Entrance difficulty: moderately difficult. Application deadline: 9/1. Contact: Mr. Joe Constance, Dean of Admissions, (206) 281-2021.

SEATTLE UNIVERSITY

Seattle 98122. Private; urban. Awards B, M, D. Enrolls 3,968 T, 2,705 U (50% women, 70% on fin. aid). Entrance difficulty: moderately difficult. Application deadlines: 9/15, early decision 12/1. Contact: Mr. Michael Fox, (206) 626-5720.

UNIVERSITY OF PUGET SOUND

Tacoma 98416. Private; urban. Awards B, M. Enrolls 2,971 T, 2,744 U (55% women, 52% state res., 65% on fin. aid). Entrance difficulty: moderately difficult. Application deadline: 9/1. Contact: Mr. George H. Mills, (206) 756-3211.

UNIVERSITY OF WASHINGTON

Seattle 98195. Public; urban. Awards B, M, D. Enrolls 37,037 T, 28,187 U (46% women, 92% state res., 33% on fin. aid). Entrance difficulty: moderately difficult. Application deadline: 5/1. Contact: Mr. James Furlan, Assistant Director of Admissions, (206) 543-9686.

WALLA WALLA COLLEGE

College Place 99324. Private; small town. Awards C, A, B, M. Enrolls 1,901 T, 1,813 U (46% women, 40% state res., 48%

on fin. aid). Application deadline: rolling. Contact: Miss Orpha Osborne, Director of Admissions and Records, (509) 527-2811.

WASHINGTON STATE UNIVERSITY

Pullman 99163. Public; rural. Awards B, M, D. Enrolls 16,692 T, 13,751 U (44% women, 84% state res., 20% on fin. aid). Entrance difficulty: moderately difficult. Application deadline: 6/1. Contact: Mr. Stan Berry, (509) 335-5586.

WESTERN WASHINGTON UNIVERSITY

Bellingham 98225. Public; small town. Awards B, M. Enrolls 10,104 T, 8,598 U (52% women, 87% state res., 37% on fin. aid). Entrance difficulty: moderately difficult. Application deadline: 9/1. Contact: Mr. Richard J. Riehl, (206) 676-3440.

WHITMAN COLLEGE

Walla Walla 99362. Private; small town. Awards B. Enrolls 1,110 T (49% women, 51% state res., 50% on fin. aid). Entrance difficulty: very difficult. Application deadlines: 3/1, early decision 12/20. Contact: Mr. William D. Tingley, (509) 527-5176.

WHITWORTH COLLEGE

Spokane 99251. Private; suburban. Awards B, M. Enrolls 1,653 T, 1,533 U (55% women, 65% on fin. aid). Entrance difficulty: moderately difficult. Application deadline: 9/1. Contact: Mr. Robert Hannigan, (509) 466-3212.

WEST VIRGINIA

ALDERSON-BROADDUS COLLEGE

Philippi 26416. Private; rural. Awards A, B. Enrolls 878 T (66% women, 43% state res., 92% on fin. aid). Entrance difficulty: moderately difficult; very difficult for nursing and physician's assistant programs. Application deadline: rolling. Contact: Mr. Kenneth H. Yount, Director of Admissions, (304) 457-1700 Ext. 255.

APPALACHIAN BIBLE COLLEGE

Bradley 25818. Private; small town. Awards C, B. Enrolls 230 T (40% women, 14% state res., 69% on fin. aid). Entrance diffi-

Appalachian Bible College (continued)
culty: moderately difficult. Application deadline: rolling. Contact: Dr. Joseph K. Pinter, Director of Admissions, (304) 877-6428.

BETHANY COLLEGE

Bethany 26032. Private; rural. Awards B. Enrolls 900 T (44% women, 16% state res., 65% on fin. aid). Entrance difficulty: moderately difficult. Application deadline: rolling. Contact: Mr. Robert F. Riley Jr, (304) 829-7611.

BLUEFIELD STATE COLLEGE

Bluefield 24701. Public; urban. Awards C, A, B. Enrolls 2,747 T (54% women, 8% state res., 45% on fin. aid). Entrance difficulty: noncompetitive; moderately difficult for nursing and respiratory therapy. Application deadline: rolling. Contact: Mr. James L. Branscome, Director of Admissions, (304) 325-7102.

CONCORD COLLEGE

Athens 24712. Public; small town. Awards B. Enrolls 2,081 T (55% women, 80% state res., 50% on fin. aid). Entrance difficulty: less difficult. Application deadline: rolling. Contact: Mr. Dale Dickens, (304) 384-3115.

DAVIS AND ELKINS COLLEGE

Elkins 26241. Private; small town. Awards C, A, B. Enrolls 1,098 T (45% women, 25% state res., 65% on fin. aid). Entrance difficulty: moderately difficult. Application deadline: rolling. Contact: Mr. David Wilkey, (304) 636-1900.

FAIRMONT STATE COLLEGE

Fairmont 26554. Public; small town. Awards C, A, B. Enrolls 4,848 T (55% women, 94% state res., 61% on fin. aid). Entrance difficulty: noncompetitive. Application deadline: 8/4. Contact: Mr. John G. Conaway, Director of Admissions and Assistant Registrar, (304) 367-4141.

GLENVILLE STATE COLLEGE

Glenville 26351. Public; small town. Awards A, B. Enrolls 1,845 T (12% women, 92% state res., 26% on fin. aid). Entrance difficulty: noncompetitive. Application deadline: 8/1. Contact: Mr. Mack K. Samples, Dean of Records and Admissions, (304) 462-7361.

MARSHALL UNIVERSITY

Huntington 25701. Public; urban. Awards C, A, B, M, D. Enrolls 11,530 T, 8,948 U (52% women, 88% state res., 34% on fin. aid). Entrance difficulty: noncompetitive. Application deadline: 8/1. Contact: Dr. James W. Harless, (304) 696-3160.

SALEM COLLEGE

Salem 26426. Private; rural. Awards C, A, B, M. Enrolls 1,496 T, 1,241 U (48% women, 25% state res., 63% on fin. aid). Entrance difficulty: less difficult. Application deadline: 8/15. Contact: Mr. W. Patrick Haun, (304) 782-5336.

SHEPHERD COLLEGE

Shepherdstown 25443. Public; small town. Awards A, B. Enrolls 2,862 T (54% women, 60% state res., 45% on fin. aid). Entrance difficulty: moderately difficult. Application deadlines: 8/1, early decision 11/1. Contact: Mr. Karl L. Wolf, (304) 876-2511.

UNIVERSITY OF CHARLESTON

Charleston 25304. Private; urban. Awards A, B. Enrolls 1,857 T (60% women, 78% state res., 65% on fin. aid). Entrance difficulty: moderately difficult. Application deadline: 8/15. Contact: Mrs. June D. Williams, Director of Admissions, (304) 346-1400.

WEST LIBERTY STATE COLLEGE

West Liberty 26074. Public; rural. Awards A, B. Enrolls 2,679 T (56% women, 65% state res., 40% on fin. aid). Entrance difficulty: less difficult. Application deadline: 8/1. Contact: Mr. Gray Williamson, Director of Recruitment, (304) 336-8077.

WEST VIRGINIA INSTITUTE OF TECHNOLOGY

Montgomery 25136. Public; small town. Awards C, A, B. Enrolls 3,005 T (33% women, 80% state res., 70% on fin. aid). Entrance difficulty: noncompetitive. Application deadline: rolling. Contact: Mr. Robert P. Scholl Jr, (304) 442-3167.

WEST VIRGINIA STATE COLLEGE

Institute 25112. Public; suburban. Awards C, A, B. Enrolls 3,905 T (53% women, 90% state res., 38% on fin. aid). Entrance difficulty: moderately difficult. Application deadline: 8/15. Contact: Mr. John L. Fuller, (304) 766-3144.

WEST VIRGINIA UNIVERSITY

Morgantown 26506. Public; small town. Awards B, M, D. Enrolls 21,289 T, 14,479 U (44% women, 59% state res., 42% on fin. aid). Entrance difficulty: less difficult. Application deadline: rolling. Contact: Mr. John D. Brisban, (304) 293-2121.

WEST VIRGINIA WESLEYAN COLLEGE

Buckhannon 26201. Private; small town. Awards A, B, M. Enrolls 1,850 T, 1,780 U (58% women, 32% state res., 64% on fin. aid). Entrance difficulty: moderately difficult. Application deadline: rolling. Contact: Mr. Wenrich H. Green, (304) 473-8510.

WHEELING COLLEGE

Wheeling 26003. Private; suburban. Awards B, M. Enrolls 1,197 T, 1,031 U (50% women, 40% state res., 70% on fin. aid). Entrance difficulty: moderately difficult. Application deadline: 9/2. Contact: Mr. Ken Rudzki, (304) 243-2359.

WISCONSIN

ALVERNO COLLEGE

Milwaukee 53215. Private; urban. Awards A, B. Enrolls 1,340 T (100% women, 95% state res., 75% on fin. aid). Entrance difficulty: moderately difficult. Application deadline: 8/15. Contact: Mr. Jeff Zahn, Acting Director of Admissions, (414) 671-5400.

BELOIT COLLEGE

Beloit 53511. Private; small town. Awards B. Enrolls 1,019 T (48% women, 17% state res., 60% on fin. aid). Entrance difficulty: very difficult. Application deadline: rolling. Contact: Mr. John W. Lind, Director of Admissions and Financial Aid, (608) 365-3391.

CARDINAL STRITCH COLLEGE

Milwaukee 53217. Private; suburban. Awards A, B, M. Enrolls 848 T, 597 U (80% women, 65% state res., 65% on fin. aid). Entrance difficulty: moderately difficult. Application deadline: rolling. Contact: Dr. William F. Stier Jr, (414) 352-5400 Ext. 307.

CARROLL COLLEGE

Waukesha 53186. Private; suburban. Awards B. Enrolls 1,168 T (52% women, 77% state res., 72% on fin. aid). Entrance difficulty: moderately difficult. Application deadline: 8/15. Contact: Miss Shirley Hilger, Dean of Admissions, (414) 547-1211.

CARTHAGE COLLEGE

Kenosha 53141. Private; suburban. Awards B, M. Enrolls 1,300 T, 1,134 U (50% women, 45% state res., 67% on fin. aid). Entrance difficulty: moderately difficult. Application deadline: rolling. Contact: Mr. Kent Duesing, (414) 551-8500.

EDGEWOOD COLLEGE

Madison 53711. Private; urban. Awards A, B. Enrolls 587 T (75% women, 75% state res., 60% on fin. aid). Entrance difficulty: less difficult. Application deadline: rolling. Contact: Sr. Barbara Hubeny, Director of Admissions, (608) 257-4861 Ext. 294.

HOLY REDEEMER COLLEGE

Waterford 53185. Private; rural. Awards B. Enrolls 55 T (7% women, 15% state res., 53% on fin. aid). Entrance difficulty: moderately difficult. Application deadline: 8/15. Contact: Fr. Robert P. Earl, (414) 534-3191.

LAKELAND COLLEGE

Sheboygan 53081. Private; rural. Awards B. Enrolls 609 T (45% women, 72% state res., 91% on fin. aid). Entrance difficulty: moderately difficult. Application deadline: rolling. Contact: Mr. Richard M. Leach, Dean of Admissions, (414) 565-1217.

LAWRENCE UNIVERSITY

Appleton 54911. Private; small town. Awards B. Enrolls 1,156 T (50% women, 45% state res., 51% on fin. aid). Entrance difficulty: very difficult. Application deadlines: rolling, early decision 11/1. Contact: Mr. David E. Busse, Director of Admission and Financial Aid, (414) 739-3681 Ext. 232.

MARIAN COLLEGE OF FOND DU LAC

Fond du Lac 54935. Private; small town. Awards B. Enrolls 499 T (89% women, 87% state res., 68% on fin. aid). Entrance difficulty: less difficult; moderately difficult for nursing. Application deadline: 8/15. Contact: Mr. Jerome Wiedmeyer, (414) 921-3900.

MARQUETTE UNIVERSITY

Milwaukee 53233. Private; urban. Awards A, B, M, D. Enrolls 11,195 T, 8,818 U (44% women, 54% state res., 65% on fin. aid). Entrance difficulty: moderately difficult. Application deadline: rolling. Contact: Mr. Leo B. Flynn, (414) 224-7302.

MILTON COLLEGE

Milton 53563. Private; rural. Awards B. Enrolls 320 T (30% women, 75% state res., 85% on fin. aid). Entrance difficulty: less difficult. Application deadline: 9/1. Contact: Mr. Charles Van Rens, Associate Director of Admissions, (608) 868-2906.

MILWAUKEE SCHOOL OF ENGINEERING

Milwaukee 53201. Private; urban. Awards A, B, M. Enrolls 1,450 T, 1,393 U (4% women, 70% state res., 70% on fin. aid). Entrance difficulty: moderately difficult. Application deadline: rolling. Contact: Mr. Robert Savatovic, (414) 272-8720.

MOUNT MARY COLLEGE

Milwaukee 53222. Private; suburban. Awards B. Enrolls 1,126 T (100% women, 91% state res., 68% on fin. aid). Entrance difficulty: moderately difficult. Application deadline: 8/15. Contact: Sr. Antony Mary Retinger, Co-Director of Admissions, (414) 258-4810.

MOUNT SENARIO COLLEGE

Ladysmith 54848. Private; small town. Awards A, B. Enrolls 474 T (54% women, 80% state res., 88% on fin. aid). Entrance difficulty: less difficult. Application deadline: 8/20. Contact: Mr. Max Waits, (715) 532-5235.

NORTHLAND COLLEGE

Ashland 54806. Private; small town. Awards B. Enrolls 622 T (40% women, 35% state res., 85% on fin. aid). Entrance difficulty: moderately difficult. Application deadlines: 8/15, early decision 11/22. Contact: Mr. James C. Miller, (715) 682-4531 Ext. 224.

RIPON COLLEGE

Ripon 54971. Private; small town. Awards B. Enrolls 928 T (41% women, 32% state res., 52% on fin. aid). Entrance difficulty: very difficult. Application deadline: rolling. Contact: Mr. Christopher M. Small, Dean of Admissions, (414) 748-8185.

SAINT FRANCIS DE SALES COLLEGE

Milwaukee 53207. Private; suburban. Awards B. Enrolls 55 T (2% women, 84% state res., 40% on fin. aid). Entrance difficulty: moderately difficult. Application deadline: rolling. Contact: Rev. Richard J. Molter, (414) 483-5807.

ST NORBERT COLLEGE

De Pere 54178. Private; suburban. Awards A, B. Enrolls 1,642 T (48% women, 45% state res., 75% on fin. aid). Entrance difficulty: moderately difficult. Application deadlines: 5/15, early decision 10/1. Contact: Mr. Matthew G. Flanigan, Director of Admissions and Financial Aid, (414) 337-3005.

SILVER LAKE COLLEGE

Manitowoc 54220. Private; small town. Awards A, B. Enrolls 320 T (88% women, 98% state res., 87% on fin. aid). Entrance difficulty: less difficult. Application deadline: rolling. Contact: Mr. Mark McLaughlin, (414) 684-5955.

UNIVERSITY OF WISCONSIN–EAU CLAIRE

Eau Claire 54701. Public; urban. Awards A, B, M. Enrolls 10,629 T, 10,111 U (57% women, 90% state res., 70% on fin. aid). Entrance difficulty: moderately difficult. Application deadline: 8/15. Contact: Mr. John L. Kearney, (715) 836-5415.

UNIVERSITY OF WISCONSIN–GREEN BAY

Green Bay 54302. Public; urban. Awards A, B, M. Enrolls 3,842 T, 3,541 U (51% women, 85% state res.). Entrance difficulty: moderately difficult. Application deadline: 8/10. Contact: Mr. Myron Van de Ven,

Director of Admission and Financial Aid, (414) 465-2111.

UNIVERSITY OF WISCONSIN–LA CROSSE

La Crosse 54601. Public; urban. Awards A, B, M. Enrolls 8,431 T, 7,926 U (55% women, 91% state res., 65% on fin. aid). Entrance difficulty: moderately difficult. Application deadline: rolling. Contact: Mr. Gale Grimslid, (608) 785-8068.

UNIVERSITY OF WISCONSIN– MADISON

Madison 53706. Public; urban. Awards C, B, M, D. Enrolls 40,233 T, 26,428 U (47% women, 82% state res., 50% on fin. aid). Entrance difficulty: moderately difficult. Application deadline: 3/1. Contact: Mr. David E. Vinson, (608) 262-3961.

UNIVERSITY OF WISCONSIN– MILWAUKEE

Milwaukee 53201. Public; urban. Awards B, M, D. Enrolls 25,078 T, 20,610 U (52% women, 96% state res., 30% on fin. aid). Entrance difficulty: moderately difficult. Application deadline: rolling. Contact: Mr. Benjamin J. Litwin, Acting Associate Director of Admissions, (414) 963-4876.

UNIVERSITY OF WISCONSIN– OSHKOSH

Oshkosh 54901. Public; suburban. Awards C, A, B, M. Enrolls 10,000 T, 8,500 U (50% women, 97% state res., 50% on fin. aid). Entrance difficulty: moderately difficult. Application deadline: rolling. Contact: Dr. R. Thomas Snider, (414) 424-0307.

UNIVERSITY OF WISCONSIN– PARKSIDE

Kenosha 53140. Public; suburban. Awards B, M. Enrolls 5,450 T, 5,292 U (47% women, 97% state res., 33% on fin. aid). Entrance difficulty: noncompetitive. Application deadline: 9/1. Contact: Mr. John Elmore, Director of Student Development, (414) 553-2339.

UNIVERSITY OF WISCONSIN– PLATTEVILLE

Platteville 53818. Public; small town. Awards A, B, M. Enrolls 4,713 T, 4,510 U (35% women, 89% state res., 63% on fin. aid). Entrance difficulty: moderately diffi-

cult. Application deadline: rolling. Contact: Mr. Edward Deneen, (608) 342-1125.

UNIVERSITY OF WISCONSIN–RIVER FALLS

River Falls 54022. Public; rural. Awards A, B, M. Enrolls 5,128 T, 4,733 U (48% women, 61% state res., 44% on fin. aid). Entrance difficulty: noncompetitive. Application deadline: rolling. Contact: Dr. Wilbur W. Sperling, (715) 425-3100.

UNIVERSITY OF WISCONSIN– STEVENS POINT

Stevens Point 54481. Public; small town. Awards A, B, M. Enrolls 8,942 T, 8,363 U (51% women, 91% state res., 60% on fin. aid). Entrance difficulty: moderately difficult. Application deadline: rolling. Contact: Dr. John A. Larsen, (715) 346-2441.

UNIVERSITY OF WISCONSIN– STOUT

Menomonie 54751. Public; small town. Awards B, M. Enrolls 7,096 T, 6,528 U (51% women, 70% state res., 61% on fin. aid). Entrance difficulty: noncompetitive. Application deadline: rolling. Contact: Mr. Donald Osegard, (715) 232-1233.

UNIVERSITY OF WISCONSIN– SUPERIOR

Superior 54880. Public; urban. Awards A, B, M. Enrolls 2,149 T, 1,706 U (45% women, 71% state res., 75% on fin. aid). Entrance difficulty: noncompetitive. Application deadline: rolling. Contact: Mr. Lowell W. Banks, (715) 392-8101 Ext. 230.

UNIVERSITY OF WISCONSIN– WHITEWATER

Whitewater 53190. Public; small town. Awards A, B, M. Enrolls 9,678 T, 7,793 U (51% women, 91% state res., 40% on fin. aid). Entrance difficulty: moderately difficult. Application deadline: rolling. Contact: Mr. I. A. Madsen, (414) 472-1440.

VITERBO COLLEGE

La Crosse 54601. Private; urban. Awards B. Enrolls 1,012 T (75% women, 80% state res.). Entrance difficulty: moderately difficult. Application deadline: rolling. Contact: Mr. M. Ray DuVall, (608) 784-0040.

WISCONSIN CONSERVATORY OF MUSIC

Milwaukee 53202. Private; urban. Awards B, M. Enrolls 180 T, 160 U (32% women, 90% state res., 85% on fin. aid). Entrance difficulty: moderately difficult. Application deadline: 8/15. Contact: Mr. Gregory P. Fish, (414) 276-4350.

WYOMING

UNIVERSITY OF WYOMING

Laramie 82071. Public; small town. Awards B, M, D. Enrolls 9,024 T, 7,332 U (45% women, 69% state res., 82% on fin. aid). Entrance difficulty: noncompetitive. Application deadline: 7/15. Contact: Dr. Arland L. Grover, Director of Admissions and Registrar, (307) 766-4272.

Nutshell 2:
Colleges and Universities Grouped by Minimum Costs

In this section, colleges are presented alphabetically within six yearly minimum cost ranges. In each case, the figure includes 1980 tuition, room, and board, *except* for those colleges that do not offer meals (indicated by *no B*) or do not offer either room or board (indicated by *no R&B*). Thus in those cases, you would have to add your estimates of your own living expenses to the given minimum figure in order to make realistic comparisons with other colleges. For public institutions, the tuition used is the rate for state residents.

LESS THAN $1000

Armstrong State College *no R&B*

Augusta College *no R&B*

Bluefield State College *no R&B*

Boston State College *no R&B*

California State University, Dominguez Hills *no R&B*

California State University, Fullerton *no R&B*

California State University, Hayward *no R&B*

California State University, Los Angeles *no R&B*

California State University, Northridge *no R&B*

Chicago State University *no R&B*

Christopher Newport College *no R&B*

City University of New York, Bernard M Baruch College *no R&B*

City University of New York, Brooklyn College *no R&B*

City University of New York, City College *no R&B*

City University of New York, College of Staten Island *no R&B*

City University of New York, Herbert H Lehman College *no R&B*

City University of New York, Hunter College *no R&B*

City University of New York, John Jay College of Criminal Justice *no R&B*

City University of New York, Queens College *no R&B*

City University of New York, York College *no R&B*

Cleveland College of Jewish Studies *no R&B*

Columbus College *no R&B*

Cooper Union for the Advancement of Science and Art *no R&B*

Coppin State College *no R&B*

Fisk University

Georgia State University *no R&B*

Gratz College *no R&B*

Harris-Stowe State College *no R&B*

Hebrew College *no R&B*

Indiana State University at Evansville *no R&B*

Indiana University at Kokomo *no R&B*

Indiana University at South Bend *no R&B*

Indiana University Northwest *no R&B*

Indiana University-Purdue University at Fort Wayne *no R&B*

Indiana University Southeast *no R&B*

Jones College, Jacksonville *no R&B*

Kennesaw College *no R&B*

Lincoln University, MO

Louisiana State University in Shreveport *no R&B*

Massachusetts College of Art *no R&B*

Metropolitan State College *no R&B*

Northeastern Illinois University *no R&B*

Northern Kentucky University *no R&B*

Ohio State University, Lima *no R&B*

Ohio State University, Mansfield *no R&B*

Ohio University, Lancaster *no R&B*

Portland State University *no R&B*

Purdue University–Calumet *no R&B*

Purdue University–North Central Campus *no R&B*

Rutgers University, Camden College of Arts and Sciences *no R&B*

Less than $1000 (cont.)

Rutgers University, Newark College of Arts and Sciences *no R&B*

Sinte Gleska College *no R&B*

Southern University in New Orleans *no R&B*

Troy State University at Fort Rucker/Dothan *no R&B*

Troy State University at Montgomery *no R&B*

United States Air Force Academy

United States Coast Guard Academy

United States Merchant Marine Academy

United States Military Academy

United States Naval Academy

University of Arkansas at Little Rock *no B*

University of Colorado at Colorado Springs *no R&B*

University of Colorado at Denver *no R&B*

University of Houston, Downtown Campus *no R&B*

University of Illinois at Chicago Circle *no R&B*

University of Massachusetts at Boston *no R&B*

University of Michigan—Flint *no R&B*

University of Missouri–St Louis *no R&B*

University of Nebraska at Omaha *no R&B*

University of South Carolina at Aiken *no R&B*

University of South Carolina at Spartanburg *no R&B*

University of South Carolina, Coastal Carolina College *no R&B*

University of Texas at San Antonio *no R&B*

University of the District of Columbia *no R&B*

University of Wisconsin–Parkside *no R&B*

Wright State University, Piqua Center *no R&B*

$1000-$2999

Abilene Christian University at Dallas *no R&B*

Academy of the New Church

Adams State College

Alabama Agricultural and Mechanical University

Alabama State University

Albany College of Pharmacy of Union University

Albany State College

Alcorn State University

American Baptist College

American Conservatory of Music *no R&B*

Angelo State University

Antioch University–Maryland at Baltimore *no R&B*

Appalachian State University

Arizona State University

Arkansas College

Arkansas State University

Arkansas Tech University

Armstrong College *no R&B*

Atlanta Christian College

Auburn University

Auburn University at Montgomery *no B*

Austin Peay State University

Ball State University

Baltimore Hebrew College *no R&B*

Beacon College *no R&B*

Bellevue College *no R&B*

Bemidji State University

Berea College

Blackburn College

Black Hills State College

Bloomsburg State College

Blue Mountain College

Boise State University

Bowie State College

Bowling Green State University

Bridgeport Engineering Institute *no R&B*

Bridgewater State College

Brigham Young University

California Polytechnic State University

California State College, PA

California State College, Bakersfield

California State College, San Bernardino

California State College, Stanislaus

California State Polytechnic University, Pomona

California State University, Chico

California State University, Fresno

California State University, Long Beach

California State University, Sacramento

Calumet College *no R&B*

Cameron University

Capitol Institute of Technology *no R&B*

Cardinal Glennon College

Castleton State College

Central Baptist College

Central Bible College

Central Connecticut State College

Central Missouri State University
Central State University, OK
Central Washington University
Chadron State College
Cheyney State College
Cincinnati Bible College
Circleville Bible College
Citadel
City University of New York, Medgar Evers College *no R&B*
Clarion State College
Cleary College *no R&B*
Clemson University
Cleveland State University *no B*
Clinch Valley College of the University of Virginia
Cogswell College *no R&B*
College of Charleston
College of Insurance *no R&B*
College of the Ozarks
College of the Southwest *no B*
Colorado State University
Colorado Technical College *no R&B*
Columbia College, IL *no R&B*
Concord College
Cornish Institute *no R&B*
Dakota State College
Delaware State College
Delta State University
Detroit Institute of Technology *no R&B*
DeVry Institute of Technology, AZ *no R&B*
DeVry Institute of Technology, GA *no R&B*
DeVry Institute of Technology, IL *no R&B*
DeVry Institute of Technology, TX *no R&B*
Dickinson State College
Dr Martin Luther College
Dominican College *no R&B*
Dyke College *no R&B*
East Carolina University
East Central Oklahoma State University
Eastern Connecticut State College
Eastern Illinois University
Eastern Kentucky University
Eastern Michigan University
Eastern Montana College
Eastern New Mexico University, Portales Campus
Eastern Oregon State College

Eastern Washington University
East Stroudsburg State College
East Tennessee State University *no B*
East Texas Baptist College
East Texas State University
Edinboro State College
Elizabeth City State University
Emporia State University
Evergreen State College
Fairmont State College
Fayetteville State University
Felician College, NJ *no R&B*
Ferris State College
Fitchburg State College
Florida A&M University
Florida State University
Fort Hays State University
Fort Lauderdale College *no R&B*
Fort Lewis College
Fort Valley State College
Framingham State College
Francis Marion College *no B*
Franklin University *no R&B*
Free Will Baptist Bible College
Frostburg State College
General Motors Institute
George Mason University
Georgia College
Georgia Institute of Technology
Georgia Southern College
Georgia Southwestern College
Glassboro State College
Glenville State College
Golden Gate University *no R&B*
Grambling State University
Grand Valley State Colleges
Henderson State University
Holy Family College, PA *no R&B*
Humboldt State University
Idaho State University
Illinois State University
Indiana State University, Terre Haute
Indiana University
Indiana University of Pennsylvania
Indiana University-Purdue University at Indianapolis *no B*
International College *no R&B*
Iowa State University
Jackson State University
Jacksonville State University
James Madison University

$1000-$2999 (cont.)

Jarvis Christian College
Jersey City State College
Jones College, Orlando *no R&B*
Johnson Bible College
Kansas State University
Kean College of New Jersey *no B*
Kearney State College
Keene State College
Kent State University
Kentucky Christian College
Kentucky State University
Kutztown State College
Lake Superior State College
Lamar University
Lander College
Langston University
Lewis-Clark State College
Lincoln University, CA *no R&B*
Livingston University
Lock Haven State College
Longwood College
Louisiana College
Louisiana State University and
  Agricultural and Mechanical College
Louisiana Tech University
Lyndon State College
Mankato State University
Mansfield State College
Marshall University
Marylhurst Education Center *no R&B*
Mary Washington College
Massachusetts Maritime Academy
Mayville State College
McNeese State University
Medaille College *no R&B*
Memphis Academy of Arts *no R&B*
Memphis State University *no B*
Mercer University in Atlanta *no R&B*
Mercy College *no R&B*
Mesa College
Michigan State University
Michigan Technological University
Middle Tennessee State University
Midwestern State University
Millersville State College
Minnesota Bible College
Minot State College
Mississippi State University
Mississippi University for Women
Mississippi Valley State University
Missouri Institute of Technology *no R&B*

Missouri Southern State College
Missouri Western State College
Montana College of Mineral Science and
  Technology
Montana State University
Montclair State College
Moody Bible Institute
Moorhead State University
Morgan State University
Murray State University
Museum Art School *no R&B*
Nazareth College
Neumann College *no R&B*
New College of California *no R&B*
New Jersey Institute of Technology *no B*
New Mexico Highlands University
New Mexico Institute of Mining and
  Technology
New Mexico State University, Las Cruces
New York Institute of Technology,
  Metropolitan Center *no R&B*
New York Institute of Technology, Old
  Westbury *no R&B*
Nicholls State University
Norfolk State University
North Adams State College
North Carolina Agricultural and
  Technical State University
North Carolina Central University
North Carolina School of the Arts
North Carolina State University at
  Raleigh
North Dakota State University
Northeastern Oklahoma State University
Northeast Louisiana University
Northeast Missouri State University
Northern Arizona University
Northern Illinois University
Northern Michigan University
Northern Montana College
Northern State College
North Texas State University
Northwest Bible College
Northwestern Oklahoma State
  University
Northwestern State University of
  Louisiana
Northwest Missouri State University
Nova University *no R&B*
Oakland University
Ohio Institute of Technology *no R&B*
Ohio State University, Columbus
Oklahoma Christian College

Oklahoma City Southwestern College
Oklahoma City University
Oklahoma Panhandle State University
Oklahoma State University
Old Dominion University
Oregon College of Education
Oregon Institute of Technology
Oregon State University
Otis Art Institute of Parsons School of Design *no R&B*
Our Lady of Holy Cross College *no R&B*
Pan American University
Pembroke State University
Peru State College
Piedmont Bible College
Pittsburg State University
Plymouth State College
Portland School of Art *no R&B*
Prairie View A&M University
Purdue University, West Lafayette
Radford University
Ramapo College of New Jersey *no B*
Rhode Island College
Rutgers University, College of Nursing *no B*
Sacred Heart University *no R&B*
St Cloud State University
Saint Francis de Sales College
St John's University, NY *no R&B*
St Joseph's College, NY *no R&B*
St Joseph's College, Suffolk Campus, NY *no R&B*
St Mary's College of Maryland
St Patrick's College
Salem State College
Salisbury State College
Sam Houston State University
San Diego State University
San Francisco State University
San Jose State University
Savannah State College
School of the Worcester Art Museum *no R&B*
Shaw College at Detroit *no R&B*
Shepherd College
Sherwood Music School *no R&B*
Shippensburg State College
Sierra Nevada College *no R&B*
Slippery Rock State College
Sonoma State University
South Carolina State College

South Dakota School of Mines and Technology
South Dakota State University
Southeastern Baptist College
Southeastern College of the Assemblies of God, FL
Southeastern Louisiana University *no B*
Southeastern Oklahoma State University
Southeast Missouri State University
Southern Arkansas University
Southern Connecticut State College
Southern Illinois University at Carbondale
Southern Illinois University at Edwardsville
Southern Technical Institute
Southern University and Agricultural and Mechanical College, Baton Rouge
Southern Utah State College
Southwestern Assemblies of God College
Southwestern Oklahoma State University
Southwest Missouri State University
Southwest State University
Southwest Texas State University
Spertus College of Judaica *no R&B*
State University of New York at Albany
State University of New York at Binghamton
State University of New York at Buffalo
State University of New York at Stony Brook
State University of New York College at Brockport
State University of New York College at Buffalo
State University of New York College at Cortland
State University of New York College at Fredonia
State University of New York College at Geneseo
State University of New York College at New Paltz
State University of New York College at Oneonta
State University of New York College at Oswego
State University of New York College at Plattsburgh
State University of New York College at Potsdam
State University of New York College at Purchase
Steed College *no R&B*
Stephen F Austin State University

$1000-$2999 (cont.)

Stockton State College *no B*
Strayer College *no R&B*
Suffolk University *no R&B*
Sul Ross State University
Tampa College *no R&B*
Tarleton State University
Tennessee State University
Tennessee Technological University
Texas A&I University at Kingsville
Texas A&M University
Texas Southern University
Texas Tech University
Texas Woman's University
Tiffin University *no B*
Towson State University
Trenton State College
Troy State University
Union for Experimenting Colleges and
  Universities *no R&B*
University of Akron
University of Alabama
University of Alabama in
  Birmingham *no B*
University of Alabama in Huntsville
University of Alaska, Fairbanks
University of Alaska, Juneau *no B*
University of Arizona
University of Arkansas
University of Arkansas at Monticello
University of Arkansas at Pine Bluff
University of California, Berkeley
University of California, Davis
University of California, Los Angeles
University of California, Riverside
University of Central Arkansas
University of Central Florida
University of Colorado at Boulder
University of Delaware
University of Florida
University of Georgia
University of Hawaii at Hilo
University of Hawaii at Manoa
University of Houston
University of Idaho
University of Iowa
University of Judaism *no R&B*
University of Kansas
University of Kentucky
University of Louisville
University of Lowell
University of Maine at Farmington

University of Maine at Fort Kent
University of Maine at Machias
University of Maine at Presque Isle
University of Maryland at College Park
University of Maryland Baltimore County
University of Maryland Eastern Shore
University of Michigan—Dearborn *no B*
University of Minnesota, Duluth
University of Minnesota, Morris
University of Mississippi *no B*
University of Missouri–Columbia
University of Missouri–Kansas City
University of Missouri–Rolla
University of Montana
University of Montevallo
University of Nebraska–Lincoln
University of Nevada, Las Vegas
University of Nevada, Reno
University of New Hampshire
University of New Mexico, Albuquerque
University of New Orleans
University of North Alabama
University of North Carolina at Asheville
University of North Carolina at Chapel
  Hill
University of North Carolina at Charlotte
University of North Carolina at
  Greensboro
University of North Carolina at
  Wilmington
University of North Dakota
University of Northern Colorado
University of Northern Iowa
University of Oklahoma
University of Oregon
University of Science and Arts of
  Oklahoma
University of South Alabama
University of South Carolina at Columbia
University of South Dakota, Vermillion
University of South Dakota at Springfield
University of Southern Colorado
University of Southern Mississippi
University of South Florida, St Petersburg
University of South Florida, Tampa
University of South Florida, New College
University of Southwestern Louisiana
University of Tennessee at
  Chattanooga *no B*
University of Tennessee at Knoxville
University of Tennessee at Martin
University of Texas at Arlington

University of Texas at Austin
University of Texas at El Paso
University of Toledo
University of Utah
University of Virginia
University of Washington
University of West Los Angeles *no R&B*
University of Wisconsin–Eau Claire
University of Wisconsin–Green Bay
University of Wisconsin–La Crosse
University of Wisconsin–Madison
University of Wisconsin–Oshkosh
University of Wisconsin–Platteville
University of Wisconsin–River Falls
University of Wisconsin–Stevens Point
University of Wisconsin–Stout
University of Wisconsin–Superior
University of Wisconsin–Whitewater
University of Wyoming
Utah State University
Valdosta State College
Valley City State College
Virginia Commonwealth University
Virginia Polytechnic Institute and State
    University
Virginia State University
Washburn University of Topeka
Washington State University
Wayne State College
Wayne State University *no B*
Webb Institute of Naval Architecture
Weber State College
West Chester State College
West Coast University *no R&B*
Western Carolina University
Western Connecticut State College
Western Illinois University
Western Kentucky University
Western Michigan University
Western Montana College
Western New Mexico University
Western State College of Colorado
Western Washington University
Westfield State College
West Georgia College
West Liberty State College
West Texas State University
West Virginia Institute of Technology
West Virginia State College
West Virginia University
Wichita State University

William Paterson College of New Jersey
Wilmington College, DE *no R&B*
Wingate College
Winona State University
Winston-Salem State University
Winthrop College
Wisconsin Conservatory of Music *no R&B*
Worcester State College
Wright State University
Youngstown State University

$3000-$4999

Abilene Christian University
Alabama Christian College
Alaska Pacific University
Alderson-Broaddus College
Alice Lloyd College
Allen University
Alliance College
Alvernia College
Alverno College
Ambassador College
Anderson College, IN
Anna Maria College
Appalachian Bible College
Art Center College of Design *no R&B*
Asbury College
Atlantic Christian College
Austin College
Averett College
Avila College
Baker University
Baptist Bible College of Pennsylvania
Baptist College at Charleston
Barber-Scotia College
Barry College
Bartlesville Wesleyan College
Baylor University
Belhaven College
Bellarmine College
Belmont Abbey College
Belmont College
Benedict College
Benedictine College
Bennett College
Berklee College of Music
Berkshire Christian College
Berry College
Bethany Bible College
Bethany College, KS

$3000-$4999 (cont.)
Bethany Nazarene College
Bethel College, IN
Bethel College, KS
Bethel College, MN
Bethel College, TN
Bethune-Cookman College
Birmingham-Southern College
Bishop College
Bluefield College
Bluffton College
Borromeo College of Ohio
Brenau College
Brescia College
Briar Cliff College
Bridgewater College
Brooks Institute *no R&B*
Bryan College
Bryant College
Butler University
Caldwell College
California Baptist College
California College of Arts and Crafts
California Maritime Academy
Calvary Bible College
Calvin College
Campbellsville College
Campbell University
Canisius College
Cardinal Stritch College
Carroll College of Montana
Carson-Newman College
Catawba College
Cathedral College of the Immaculate Conception
Cedarville College
Centenary College of Louisiana
Central Methodist College
Central Michigan University
Central New England College *no B*
Central Wesleyan College
Chaminade University of Honolulu
Chestnut Hill College
Christian Brothers College
Claflin College
Clark College, GA
Clarke College, IA
Coker College
College Misericordia
College of Great Falls
College of Mount St Joseph on-the-Ohio

College of Our Lady of the Elms
College of Saint Benedict
College of St Catherine
College of St Francis
College of St Joseph the Provider
College of Saint Mary
College of Saint Rose
College of Saint Thomas
College of Santa Fe
College of William and Mary
Colorado School of Mines
Columbia Bible College
Columbia Christian College
Columbia College, MO
Columbia College, SC
Columbia Union College
Conception Seminary College
Concordia College, IL
Concordia College, MI
Concordia College, St Paul, MN
Concordia College, NY
Concordia College, OR
Concordia Lutheran College
Concordia Teachers College, NE
Creighton University
Culver-Stockton College
Cumberland College
Dakota Wesleyan University
Dallas Baptist College
Dallas Bible College
Dana College
David Lipscomb College
Delaware Valley College of Science and Agriculture
Detroit Bible College
Dillard University
Divine Word College
Doane College
Don Bosco College
Dordt College
Dowling College *no B*
Drury College
Durham College
Eastern Mennonite College
Eastern Nazarene College
Edgecliff College
Edgewood College
Edward Waters College
Elon College
Embry-Riddle Aeronautical University
Emory and Henry College

Erskine College

Evangel College

Faith Baptist Bible College

Fashion Institute of Technology

Ferrum College

Flagler College

Florida Memorial College

Florida Southern College

Fontbonne College

Fordham University at Lincoln Center *no R&B*

Fort Wayne Bible College

Freed-Hardeman College

Fresno Pacific College

Friends Bible College

Friends University

Gannon University

Gardner-Webb College

Georgetown College

Georgian Court College

Goldey Beacom College *no B*

Goshen College

Grace Bible College

Grace College

Grace College of the Bible

Graceland College

Grand Canyon College

Grand Rapids Baptist College

Grand View College

Greensboro College

Gulf Coast Bible College

Gwynedd-Mercy College

Hampton Institute

Hannibal-LaGrange College

Hanover College

Harding University

Hardin-Simmons University

Hastings College

Hawaii Loa College

Hebrew Union College, Jewish Institute of Religion, NY *no R&B*

Hellenic College

Hendrix College

High Point College

Hillsdale Free Will Baptist College

Holy Apostles College

Holy Redeemer College

Houghton College

Houston Baptist University

Howard Payne University

Howard University

Huntingdon College

Huntington College

Huron College, SD

Huston-Tillotson College

Illinois College

Immaculata College

Incarnate Word College

Indiana Central University

Indiana Institute of Technology

Indiana University School of Optometry

Iowa Wesleyan College

Jamestown College

John Brown University

Johnson and Wales College

Johnson C Smith University

Johnson State College

Judson Baptist College

Judson College, AL

Judson College, IL

Juilliard School *no R&B*

Kansas Wesleyan

Kentucky Wesleyan College

King College

King's College, NY

Knoxville College

La Grange College

Lambuth College

Lancaster Bible College

Lane College

La Roche College

Lawrence Institute of Technology

Lee College, TN

Lenoir-Rhyne College

LeTourneau College

Liberty Baptist College

Limestone College

Lincoln Memorial University

Lincoln University, PA

Long Island University, Arnold and Marie Schwartz College of Pharmacy and Health Sciences

Loras College

Los Angeles Baptist College

Loyola College

Loyola University

Loyola University of Chicago

Lubbock Christian College

Lutheran Bible Institute of Seattle

Lynchburg College

Madonna College

Maharishi International University

$3000-$4999 (cont.)

Maine Maritime Academy
Malone College
Manchester College
Manhattan School of Music *no R&B*
Mannes College of Music *no R&B*
Marian College
Marian College of Fond du Lac
Marion College
Mars Hill College
Mary College
Marycrest College
Maryland Institute College of Art *no R&B*
Marymount College of Kansas
Maryville College, TN
Maryville College–Saint Louis, MO
Marywood College
McKendree College
McMurry College
McPherson College
Mercer University
Mercy College of Detroit
Mercyhurst College
Meredith College
Messiah College
Methodist College
Miami Christian College
Miami University, Oxford
Mid-America Nazarene College
Midland Lutheran College
Midwest College of Engineering *no R&B*
Miles College
Milligan College
Millsaps College
Mississippi College
Missouri Baptist College
Missouri Valley College
Mobile College
Molloy College *no R&B*
Morehouse College
Morningside College
Morris College
Mount Angel Seminary
Mount Marty College
Mount Mary College
Mount Mercy College
Mount Saint Mary College
Mount Saint Mary's College, MD
Mount Vernon Nazarene College
Multnomah School of the Bible
Nathaniel Hawthorne College

National College of Business
National College of Education, Urban Campus *no R&B*
National University *no R&B*
Nebraska Wesleyan University
Newberry College
New School of Music *no R&B*
North Carolina Wesleyan College
Northeastern Bible College
North Georgia College
Northrop University
Northwest Christian College
Northwest College of the Assemblies of God
Northwestern College, IA
Northwestern College, MN
Northwest Nazarene College
Northwood Institute–Midland Campus
Notre Dame College
Notre Dame College of Ohio
Nyack College
Oakland City College
Oglethorpe University
Ohio University, Athens
Oklahoma Baptist University
Olivet Nazarene College
Open Bible College
Oral Roberts University
Ottawa University
Ouachita Baptist University
Our Lady of the Lake University of San Antonio
Pacific Christian College
Paine College
Palm Beach Atlantic College
Park College
Parks College of Saint Louis University
Patten Bible College
Paul Quinn College
Pennsylvania State University–Behrend College
Pennsylvania State University–University Park Campus
Pfeiffer College
Philadelphia College of Bible
Philadelphia College of Pharmacy and Science *no B*
Philadelphia College of the Performing Arts *no R&B*
Philander Smith College
Phillips University
Piedmont College

Pikeville College

Point Loma College

Pontifical College Josephinum

Presbyterian College

Quincy College

Reformed Bible College

Ringling School of Art

Rio Grande College/Community College

Rivier College

Robert Morris College

Rockhurst College

Rockmont College

Rocky Mountain College

Rust College

Rutgers University, College of
    Engineering

Rutgers University, College of Pharmacy

Rutgers University, Cook College

Rutgers University, Douglass College

Rutgers University, Livingston College

Rutgers University, Mason Gross School
    of the Arts

Rutgers University, Rutgers College

Sacred Heart College

St Ambrose College

St Andrews Presbyterian College

Saint Augustine's College

St Edward's University

Saint Francis College, IN

St Hyacinth College and Seminary

St John Vianney College Seminary

Saint Joseph's College, IN

St Joseph's College, ME

Saint Joseph Seminary College

Saint Leo College

St Louis College of Pharmacy

Saint Louis Conservatory of
    Music *no R&B*

Saint Mary College

Saint Mary of the Plains College

Saint Mary-of-the-Woods College

Saint Mary's College, MI

St Mary's of the Barrens Seminary
    College

St Mary's University of San Antonio

Saint Meinrad College

St Paul Bible College

Saint Paul's College, VA

Saint Peter's College, Jersey City *no R&B*

St Thomas Aquinas College *no B*

Salem College, WV

Samford University

San Francisco Art Institute *no R&B*

San Francisco Conservatory of
    Music *no R&B*

San Jose Bible College

School of the Art Institute of
    Chicago *no R&B*

School of the Ozarks

Seton Hill College

Shaw University

Shenandoah College and Conservatory of
    Music

Shorter College, GA

Siena Heights College

Silver Lake College *no B*

Simpson College, CA

Sioux Falls College

Southeastern Bible College, AL

Southeastern Massachusetts University

Southeastern University

Southern California College

Southern Oregon State College

Southern Vermont College

Southwest Baptist College

Southwestern Baptist Bible College

Southwestern College, KS

Southwestern University

Spalding College

Spelman College

Spring Garden College *no R&B*

State University of New York College at
    Old Westbury

State University of New York Maritime
    College

Sterling College

Swain School of Design *no R&B*

Tabor College

Tarkio College

Temple University

Temple University, Ambler Campus

Tennessee Wesleyan College

Texas Christian University

Texas College

Texas Lutheran College

Texas Wesleyan College

Thomas More College

Tift College

Toccoa Falls College

Tougaloo College

Touro College *no B*

Trevecca Nazarene College

Trinity Christian College

Trinity University

$3000-$4999 (cont.)
Tri-State University
Tusculum College
Tuskegee Institute
Union College, KY
Union College, NE
Union University
United Wesleyan College
University of Albuquerque
University of California, Irvine
University of California, Santa Barbara
University of California, Santa Cruz
University of Charleston
University of Cincinnati
University of Connecticut, Storrs
University of Dallas
University of Dayton
University of Dubuque
University of Illinois at Urbana-
   Champaign
University of Maine at Orono
University of Massachusetts at Amherst
University of Michigan, Ann Arbor
University of Minnesota, Minneapolis-St
   Paul
University of Pittsburgh
University of Pittsburgh at Bradford
University of Pittsburgh at Johnstown
University of Rhode Island
University of St Thomas
University of San Francisco
University of Scranton
University of Southern Maine
University of Steubenville
University of Tulsa
University of Vermont
University of Wisconsin–Milwaukee
Upper Iowa University
Urbana College
Ursuline College
Vandercook College of Music
Vennard College
Villa Maria College
Virginia Intermont College
Virginia Military Institute
Virginia Wesleyan College
Viterbo College
Voorhees College
Walsh College
Warner Pacific College
Warner Southern College
Warren Wilson College

Washington Bible College
Wayland Baptist College
Wesleyan College
West Coast Bible College
Western Baptist College
Western Bible College
Westmar College
Westminster College, UT
Wilberforce University
Wiley College
William Carey College
William Jewell College
Woodbury University *no R&B*
Xavier University of Louisiana
Yankton College
York College of Pennsylvania

$5000-$6999

Adelphi University
Adrian College
Agnes Scott College
Albertus Magnus College
Albion College
Albright College
Alfred University
Allegheny College
Allentown College of St Francis de Sales
Alma College
American International College
Andrews University
Antioch College
Aquinas College
Ashland College
Assumption College
Atlanta College of Art
Atlantic Union College
Augsburg College
Augustana College, IL
Augustana College, SD
Aurora College
Azusa Pacific College
Babson College
Baldwin-Wallace College
Barat College
Barrington College
Beaver College
Beloit College
Bentley College
Bethany College, WV
Biola College

Biscayne College
Bloomfield College
Boston Conservatory of Music
Bradford College
Bradley University
Buena Vista College
Cabrini College
California Lutheran College
Capital University
Carleton College
Carlow College
Carroll College
Carthage College
Cedar Crest College
Centenary College
Center for Creative Studies–College of
    Art and Design
Central University of Iowa
Centre College of Kentucky
Chapman College
Chatham College
Clarkson College
Cleveland Institute of Art
Cleveland Institute of Music
Coe College
Colby-Sawyer College
College for Human Services *no R&B*
College of Idaho
College of Mount Saint Vincent
College of New Rochelle
College of Notre Dame
College of Notre Dame of Maryland
College of Saint Elizabeth
College of St Scholastica
College of Saint Teresa
College of the Atlantic
College of the Holy Cross
College of Wooster
Colorado College
Colorado Women's College
Combs College of Music
Concordia College, Moorhead, MN
Converse College
Cornell College
Covenant College
C W Post Center of Long Island
    University
Daemen College
Daniel Webster College
Davidson College
Davis and Elkins College

Defiance College
DePaul University
DePauw University
Dickinson College
Dominican College of San Rafael
Drake University
Drew University
Drexel University
Duke University
Duquesne University
D'Youville College
Earlham College
Eastern College
Eckerd College
Eisenhower College of Rochester
    Institute of Technology
Elizabethtown College
Elmhurst College
Elmira College
Emmanuel College, MA
Emory University
Eureka College
Fairfield University
Fairleigh Dickinson University, Florham-
    Madison Campus
Fairleigh Dickinson University,
    Rutherford Campus
Fairleigh Dickinson University, Teaneck-
    Hackensack Campus
Findlay College
Florida Institute of Technology
Fordham University
Fort Wright College
Franklin and Marshall College
Franklin College of Indiana
Franklin Pierce College
Friends World College
Furman University
Geneva College
George Fox College
George Williams College
Gettysburg College
Goddard College
Gonzaga University
Gordon College
Green Mountain College
Greenville College
Grinnell College
Guilford College
Gustavus Adolphus College
Hamline University
Hampden-Sydney College

$5000-$6999 (cont.)
Heidelberg College
Hillsdale College
Hiram College
Hofstra University
Holy Names College
Hood College
Hope College
Husson College
Illinois Benedictine College
Illinois Institute of Technology
Illinois Wesleyan University
Iona College
Ithaca College
Jacksonville University
John Carroll University
John Wesley College
Juniata College
Kalamazoo College
Kansas City Art Institute
Kansas Newman College
Kendall College
Keuka College
King's College, PA
Knox College, IL
Lake Erie College
Lakeland College
La Salle College
Lawrence University
Lebanon Valley College
Le Moyne College
Lesley College
Lewis and Clark College
Lewis University
Lindenwood Colleges
Linfield College
Loma Linda University
Loma Linda University, La Sierra Campus
Long Island University, Brooklyn Center
Long Island University, Southampton
    College
Loretto Heights College
Loyola Marymount University
Luther College
Lycoming College
Macalester College
MacMurray College
Manhattan College
Marietta College
Marist College
Marquette University

Mary Baldwin College
Marygrove College
Marymount College
Marymount College of Virginia
Marymount Manhattan College
Massachusetts College of Pharmacy and
    Allied Health Sciences
Merrimack College
Millikin University
Milton College
Milwaukee School of Engineering
Minneapolis College of Art and Design
Monmouth College, IL
Monmouth College, NJ
Moore College of Art
Moravian College
Mount St Mary's College, CA
Mount Senario College
Mount Union College
Mount Vernon College
Muhlenberg College
Mundelein College
Muskingum College
Nasson College
National College of Education
Nazareth College of Rochester
New England College
New Hampshire College
Newport College–Salve Regina
New School for Social Research
Niagara University
Nichols College
North Central College
Northeastern University
Northland College
North Park College
Norwich University
Oakwood College
Oberlin College
Ohio Dominican College
Ohio Northern University
Ohio Wesleyan University
Olivet College
Otterbein College
Pace University
Pace University, College of White Plains
Pace University—Pleasantville/Briarcliff
Pacific Lutheran University
Pacific Union College
Pacific University
Parsons School of Design

Philadelphia College of Textiles and
    Science
Point Park College
Post College
Pratt Institute *no B*
Principia College
Providence College
Queens College
Quinnipiac College
Randolph-Macon College
Randolph-Macon Woman's College
Regis College, CO
Regis College, MA
Rice University
Rider College
Ripon College
Roanoke College
Roberts Wesleyan College
Rochester Institute of Technology
Rockford College
Roger Williams College
Rollins College
Roosevelt University
Rosary College
Rose-Hulman Institute of Technology
Rosemont College
Russell Sage College
St Anselm's College
St Bonaventure University
Saint Francis College, PA
St John Fisher College
Saint John's University, NM
Saint Joseph College
Saint Joseph's University
St Lawrence University
Saint Louis University
Saint Martin's College
Saint Mary's College, IN
Saint Mary's College, MN
Saint Mary's College of California
St Mary's Dominican College
Saint Michael's College
St Norbert College
St Olaf College
Saint Vincent College
Saint Xavier College
Salem College, NC
Seattle Pacific University
Seattle University
Seton Hall University
Sheldon Jackson College

Shimer College
Siena College
Simpson College, IA
Southern Methodist University
Southern Missionary College
Southwestern at Memphis
Southwestern Union College
Spring Arbor College
Springfield College
Spring Hill College
Stephens College
Stern College for Women
Stetson University
Stevens Institute of Technology
Stonehill College
Susquehanna University
Sweet Briar College
Syracuse University, Utica College
Taylor University
Thiel College
Thomas College
Transylvania University
Trinity College, DC
Trinity College, IL
Trinity College, VT
Tulane University, Newcomb College
United States International University,
    San Diego Campus
Unity College
University of Bridgeport
University of Denver
University of Detroit
University of Evansville
University of Hartford
University of La Verne
University of Miami
University of New England, ME
University of New Haven
University of Notre Dame
University of Portland
University of Puget Sound
University of Richmond
University of San Diego
University of Santa Clara
University of Tampa
University of the South
Upsala College
Ursinus College
Valparaiso University
Vassar College
Vermont College

$5000-$6999 (cont.)

Villanova University
Virginia Union University
Wabash College
Wagner College
Wake Forest University
Walla Walla College
Wartburg College
Washington and Jefferson College
Washington and Lee University
Washington College
Waynesburg College
Webster College
Wentworth Institute of Technology
Wesley College, DE
Westbrook College
Western Maryland College
Western New England College
Westminster Choir College
Westminster College, MO
Westminster College, PA
Westmont College
West Virginia Wesleyan College
Wheaton College, IL
Wheeling College
Wheelock College
Whitman College
Whittier College
Whitworth College, WA
Wilkes College
Willamette University
William Penn College
William Woods College
Wilmington College, OH
Wilson College
Wittenberg University
Wofford College
World College West
Xavier University
Yeshiva College

$7000-$8999

American University
Amherst College
Bard College
Barnard College
Bates College
Bennington College
Boston College

Boston University
Bowdoin College
Brandeis University
Brown University
Bryn Mawr College
Bucknell University
California Institute of Technology
California Institute of the Arts
Carnegie-Mellon University
Case Western Reserve University
Catholic University of America
Claremont Men's College
Clark University
Colby College
Colgate University
Columbia College, NY
Connecticut College
Cornell University
Curry College
Dartmouth College
Denison University
Emerson College
Georgetown University
Goucher College
Hamilton College, NY
Hampshire College
Hartwick College
Harvard and Radcliffe Colleges
Harvey Mudd College
Haverford College
Hobart College
Hollins College
Johns Hopkins University
Johnston College of the University of
    Redlands
Kenyon College
Lafayette College
Lake Forest College
Lehigh University
Manhattanville College
Marlboro College
Massachusetts Institute of Technology
Menlo College
Middlebury College
Mills College
Mount Holyoke College
New England Conservatory of Music
New York University
Northwestern University
Occidental College

Peabody Conservatory of Johns Hopkins
  University
Pepperdine University, Malibu
Philadelphia College of Art
Pine Manor College
Pitzer College
Pomona College
Princeton University
Reed College
Rensselaer Polytechnic Institute
Rhode Island School of Design
St John's College, MD
St John's College, NM
Sarah Lawrence College
Scripps College
Simmons College
Simon's Rock of Bard College
Skidmore College
Smith College
Stanford University
Swarthmore College
Syracuse University
Trinity College, CT
Tufts University
Tulane University
Union College, NY
University of Chicago
University of Pennsylvania
University of Redlands
University of Rochester
University of Southern California
University of the Pacific
Vanderbilt University
Washington University
Wellesley College
Wells College
Wesleyan University
Wheaton College, MA
Williams College
William Smith College
Worcester Polytechnic Institute
Yale University

Glossary

Achievement Test   A test or measure of learned knowledge, usually offered in such subjects as English composition, biology, chemistry, history, math, etc. The ACT and the College Board Achievement Tests are examples of this type of test.

ACT   See American College Testing Student Assessment.

admissions counselor   Often recent graduates of an institution, these people do much of the traveling and interviewing for admissions committees. They may also have interviewing responsibilities for a specific region. They are the people you encounter most frequently in the admissions process.

advanced placement   Credit for college-level high school courses given on the basis of tests administered by the College Entrance Examination Board during the spring of the senior year of high school. They are scored from 1 to 5. Students who score from 3 to 5 on the tests may receive advanced placement and credit at the college level for the work they have done.

American College Testing Student Assessment (ACT)   Standardized admissions test consisting of four parts— English usage, mathematics usage, social studies reading, and natural sciences reading. Scores are reported in a range of 1 to 36. The current median composite score of college-bound seniors is 18.6.

AP   See advanced placement.

applicant pool   The total number of students who are applying to a given college or university in a particular year.

aptitude test   A test designed to measure a student's ability to learn. Such tests usually provide measures of verbal and quantitative ability. The SAT of the College Entrance Examination Board, which includes mathematical and verbal sections, is a familiar aptitude test.

AT   See Achievement Test.

ATP   Admissions Testing Program of the College Board; includes the SAT, Achievement Tests, Advanced Placement tests, and the reports that are sent to the students indicating their performance on the tests.

BEOG   Basic Educational Opportunity Grant, a federally funded aid program for undergraduates. (Discussed in the text.)

candidate notification date   The date by which an institution will announce its decision on a student's application.

candidate's reply date   The date by which students must notify each college that has accepted them whether they plan to attend that college in the fall.

CEEB   College Entrance Examination Board, a membership organization consisting of representatives from college admissions and financial aid officers and secondary school guidance personnel. Members of college and university faculty and staffs also serve on the Board. CEEB contracts with ETS to create and administer its Admissions Testing Program.

class rank

An indication of a student's approximate standing in his or her high school graduating class. Rank is based on grade point average and is expressed either in percentiles (e.g., top quarter, top 5%) or in rank order (e.g., 51st in a class of 240).

CLEP

See College-Level Examination Program.

college

An individual institution that offers undergraduate education only, or an educational division of a larger university, such as a College of Arts and Sciences. Colleges of the first kind tend to be small and emphasize teaching and undergraduate education over research, since no graduate programs are offered.

College-Level Examination Program (CLEP)

Tests offered by the College Entrance Examination Board that many colleges accept as credit toward a degree, even though the person taking the test may not have gained experience or knowledge in a formal educational setting.

college nights and fairs

Programs organized by high schools or local educational associations at which students and their parents have the opportunity to meet and talk with college representatives.

College Scholarship Service

The organization that computes the information submitted on the Financial Aid Form and estimates the amount students and their families can be asked to contribute toward college costs. The service also provides financial aid offices with guidelines on awarding funds to students.

college viewbook or prospectus

A pictorial brochure produced by colleges and universities to publicize themselves to prospective students. A viewbook usually provides succinct information on entrance requirements, campus life, courses of study, costs, etc., and is a good clue to an institution's image of itself.

College Work-Study Plan

A federally supported program that provides 80% of the money necessary for colleges to offer on-campus jobs to students with demonstrated need.

consortium

A group of colleges that have joined to offer certain advantages to themselves and their students. Often colleges in a consortium will share a common application and offer students the opportunity to take courses on each other's campuses.

cooperative education plan

A program offered by many colleges that enables a student to alternate periods of full-time study with full-time work. In most such programs, it takes five years to earn a bachelor's degree.

CSS

See College Scholarship Service.

dean/director of admissions

The person in charge of the admissions office. In some cases there will be a dean and a director in the same office. Usually the director will have responsibility for office procedures, and the dean will have broader policymaking responsibilities. Deans and directors will often have little

	to do with the actual processing of students' applications but will lead the committee that makes the final decisions.
deferred entrance	An admissions plan that allows accepted students to postpone their college entrance date for one to three years, with a guarantee of enrollment at the time they choose.
early action	An admissions option allowing students to learn of the decision on their application before the standard April notification date. Early action is distinguished from early decision in that students are not required to accept admission or withdraw other applications if accepted, and they have until the May 1 candidate's reply date to respond.
early admission	A program in which a college accepts high school students to begin college work before they graduate from high school. Admissions standards are more stringent for early admission candidates.
early decision	A plan in which students apply in November or December and learn of the decision on their application during December or January. This plan is suggested only for students who are academically superior. Accepted early decision students are often required to withdraw their applications to other colleges and to agree to matriculate at the college that accepts them.
early notification	Early notification programs are similar in purpose and process to the early action option. Under the early notification program, applicants must file their papers by December 1 in order to receive an admission decision by February 1. In contrast to the rule in early decision programs, an applicant is not morally obligated to attend if admitted.
enrollment deposit	A nonrefundable deposit required of accepted students at many colleges and universities to reserve a space in the incoming class.
ETS	Educational Testing Service, an organization that designs and administers tests for other groups, such as the College Board.
FAF	See Financial Aid Form.
family contribution estimate	The amount an outside agency estimates that you and your family should be able to contribute to the cost of your college education, as determined by such factors as your parents' income, assets, and debts; your earnings and savings; and the number of children in your family currently in college.
Family Financial Statement	The form for data on family assets and liabilities used by the American College Testing Program's financial aid service for evaluating student need.
FFS	See Family Financial Statement.
Financial Aid Form	The form on which parents or independent students list all income and net assets for the College Scholarship Service to estimate the amount students and their families will be expected to contribute toward college costs.

FISL

Federally Insured Student Loan. These loans are made by the college or university itself, not an outside lending agency. Students should apply directly to college financial aid offices for these loans. (Discussed in the text.)

FNAR

Financial Needs Analysis Report, a statement of the expected contribution the family can make to the student's educational expenses. This report is sent to the financial aid offices of the colleges that the student lists when the Financial Aid Form is filed.

grade point average

A system of scoring student achievement used by many colleges and universities. A student's GPA is computed by multiplying the numerical grade received in each course by the number of credits offered for each course, then dividing by the total number of credit hours studied. Most institutions use the following grade conversion scale: A = 4, B = 3, C = 2, D = 1, and E and F = 0 .

GSL

Guaranteed Student Loan (Discussed in the text.)

independent study

An option offered by many high schools and colleges which allows students to pursue independent research or undertake a creative project, usually with minimal faculty supervision.

information session

A program consisting of lectures, films, slide presentations, etc., offered by a college—usually in a hotel or club meeting room—for the purpose of presenting basic information about the college and answering students' questions.

matriculation

Enrollment at a college or university to begin work toward an academic degree.

midyear or January admission

An option some colleges are now offering to candidates who are placed on the waiting list for fall admission, allowing them to start classes in January or the second semester rather than in the fall.

NDSL

National Direct Student Loan, the loan component of most financial aid packages. (Discussed in the text.)

open admissions

A policy adopted by a number of institutions—mostly public—which allows virtually all applicants to be accepted, without regard to such traditional qualifying criteria as test scores, class rank, grades, etc.

pass/fail grading system

An alternative to traditional letter or numerical grading systems in which course credit is indicated simply by a pass or fail notation.

Preliminary Scholastic Aptitude Test (PSAT)

A shorter version of the SAT given during the sophomore or junior year of high school. It serves a dual purpose: (1) to give students a sample of what the Scholastic Aptitude Test will be like and to help them project their SAT scores, and (2) to serve as a basis for awarding the National Merit Scholarships.

quarter

A period in the academic calendar equivalent to approximately 10 or 11 weeks. Students enrolled at institutions operating on the quarter system usually attend for three quarters a year, unless they wish to accelerate their program by studying year round.

Reserve Officers' Training Corps (ROTC)	A scholarship and training program offered by the U.S. Army, Navy, and Air Force on many college campuses. ROTC students must fulfill a service obligation after graduating from college.
residential life	The term that has replaced "housing" in many colleges and universities. The office of residential life is responsible for housing assignments and maintenance, and for·student life in the dormitories and other campus residences.
rolling admissions	A program adopted by many colleges through which admissions applications are evaluated upon receipt and applicants are immediately notified of the decision.
Scholastic Aptitude Test (SAT)	Standardized test offered by the College Board Admissions Testing Program, composed of a verbal section, a math section, and a test of written English. Scores are reported on a 200-800 scale. The average scores for seniors in the class of 1979 college-bound students were 427 verbal and 467 math.
SDQ	Student Descriptive Questionnaire, part of the College Board's ATP in which students provide information on their high school record and their career and academic goals as well as other data. This material is provided to admissions offices in special reports.
semester	A calendar period equivalent to approximately half of the academic year (17-18 weeks).
SER	Student Eligibility Report, issued by the federal government to inform students of the amount of aid they may expect from the BEOG program.
standardized admissions tests	Tests such as the SAT and ACT designed to provide college admissions offices with a national comparative standard for rating a student's academic aptitude and thus predict likelihood of success in college.
student search	The ETS service that allows colleges and universities to purchase the names of students who have taken the PSAT in their junior year and have checked that they would not mind receiving unsolicited mail from colleges.
Test of Standard Written English	A 30-minute *placement* test that is administered with the SAT and consists of multiple-choice questions to evaluate a student's ability to recognize standard written English.
TOEFL	Test of English as a Foreign Language, for non-native speakers of English to determine their ability to deal with English in an American college or university program.
trimester	An academic calendar period equivalent to approximately 15 weeks. Students enrolled at colleges operating on the trimester system usually attend classes for two trimesters each year, unless they wish to accelerate their program by attending year round.
uniform methodology	Method by which the expected parental financial contribution is determined by the College Scholarship Service.
university	A large educational institution comprising a number of divisions, including graduate and professional schools.

Universities are geared toward research, and therefore less emphasis may be placed on undergraduate teaching. In fact, graduate student assistants may teach some undergraduate courses. Academic offerings are usually more comprehensive than at smaller colleges.

waiting list   A list of students who were not initially accepted by an institution but who will be accepted at a later date if space becomes available. In many cases, waiting list candidates are not notified of the final decision until late in the summer.

yield   The number of applicants who accept a college's offer of admission. The recent average yield rate at a particular college will determine how many students that college must accept to "yield" the final class size it desires for the fall term.

Index to Colleges in the Nutshells

WITHDRAWN